SECRETS OF THE GAME BUSINESS

SECOND EDITION

SECRETS OF THE GAME BUSINESS

SECOND EDITION

Edited by
François Dominic Laramée

CHARLES RIVER MEDIA, INC.

Hingham, Massachusetts

90469

Publisher: Jenifer Niles
Cover Design: The Printed Image

CHARLES RIVER MEDIA, INC.
10 Downer Avenue
Hingham, Massachusetts 02043
781-740-0400
781-740-8816 (FAX)
info@charlesriver.com
www.charlesriver.com

This book is printed on acid-free paper.

François Dominic Laramée. *Secrets of the Game Business, Second Edition.*
ISBN: 1-58450-399-8

All brand names and product names mentioned in this book are trademarks or service marks of their respective companies. Any omission or misuse (of any kind) of service marks or trademarks should not be regarded as intent to infringe on the property of others. The publisher recognizes and respects all marks used by companies, manufacturers, and developers as a means to distinguish their products.

Library of Congress Cataloging-in-Publication Data
Secrets of the game business / Francois Dominic Laramee, editor.-- 2nd ed.
    p. cm.
 Includes bibliographical references and index.
 ISBN 1-58450-399-8 (pbk. : alk. paper)
 1. Computer games--Programming. 2. Computer games--Marketing. I. Laramée, François Dominic. II. Title.

 QA76.76.C672S42 2005
 794.8'1526--dc22

                        2005001597

Printed in the United States of America
05 7 6 5 4 3 2 First Edition

CHARLES RIVER MEDIA titles are available for site license or bulk purchase by institutions, user groups, corporations, etc. For additional information, please contact the Special Sales Department at 781-740-0400.

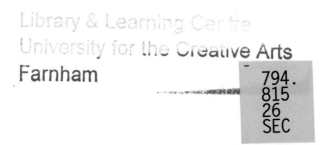

To game developers everywhere—onward!

Contents

Acknowledgments

As always, many thanks to all the wonderful people who contributed to the creation of this book: the authors who wrote such wonderful articles, the dozens of industry insiders who agreed to share their wisdom in interviews and case studies, and, of course, the entire crew at Charles River Media, starting with David Pallai (who actually came up with the idea for this book and offered me the editor's job) and Jenifer Niles. I am humbled by your talent and generosity.

Thanks to the readers who inspire me to continue writing these books and articles with their kind letters. You have my undying gratitude.

And, of course, thanks to Julie for pushing me to do something productive with my time!

Preface

François Dominic Laramée

fdl@francoisdominiclaramee.com

Welcome to the second edition of *Secrets of the Game Business*, a book that unveils the inner workings of the flashy but very serious game development and publishing industry. If you are thinking about creating a new game development company, want your existing studio to prosper for a long time, or just want to understand how and why the business evolved to its current dynamics, you have come to the right place!

This book gathers the wisdom of dozens of industry insiders, publishing executives, veteran producers, owners of independent studios, and writers. Readers of the first edition will notice that the book has undergone a not-insignificant reorganization, and that in addition to the expected updates and revisions, several new articles have been added to the book. Some of these additions are brand new, and some were originally published in my other book *Game Design Perspectives*. We wish to extend a warm welcome to the new contributing authors, and we hope that you will find their wisdom as enlightening as we did.

The book is split into five sections:

Section 1, "The Games Industry Then and Now," presents a snapshot of the state of the industry and discusses the challenges that developers will have to face in the future.

Section 2, "Publishers and Developers," examines the work of publishers and retailers, explains how games get from their developers to the players, and shows how the industry's economics influence the ways we work and live.

Section 3, "Startups," describes how to prepare for the creation of a new game development company and succeed in a difficult market.

Section 4, "Bringing Games to Market," teaches developers how to approach publishers, maximize the odds of their games reaching store shelves, and negotiate contracts that protect their long-term interests.

Section 5, "Managing Game Production," contains advice on ways to make the long, arduous production process as smooth and pleasant as possible for everyone involved.

This book can be read in many ways. Independent developers and people hoping to break into the industry and build a successful career should browse the entire book, more or less in sequence. Programmers, designers, and artists who want to learn more about the business side of the industry will turn to Sections 1 and 2 first. Current and aspiring producers will find Section 5 particularly worthwhile. Studio owners and managers will want to read Sections 2 and 4, and browse the others. Finally, seasoned developers who are thinking of launching their own game development companies should read Sections 1, 3, and 4 thoroughly.

Whether you bought *Secrets of the Game Business,* 2nd Edition to help orient your career, to improve your company's business, to plan the creation of your own studio, or simply as a desk reference, I sincerely hope that you will enjoy it and find the information contained within its pages useful.

Sincerely,

François Dominic Laramée

About the Authors

Sean Timarco Baggaley

Sean began his games industry career as an artist in the 1980s. He designed and programmed several games in the 1990s, ported a popular PC soccer management sim to the Amiga long after the platform had been pronounced dead, and was responsible for naming the comp.games.* newsgroup hierarchy. He also wrote the user guide for RenderWare Graphics, a popular middleware solution, and currently works as a freelance writer and game design consultant.

Ed Bartlett

Ed Bartlett has worked in a wide range of roles during his 10-year history in videogame development, from managing a team of 13 product analysts, through senior production and design roles, to his most recent position with famous UK developer The Bitmap Brothers as their business development director. In August 2003, Ed set up Hive Partners, an exciting new creative communications consultancy helping developers and publishers to commercially exploit their portfolios, and helping brands to use interactive digital entertainment to engage consumers more effectively. Recently noted as one of 30 key individuals in the game sector, Ed has already established Hive Partners as a market leader in the burgeoning interactive product placement market, with plans for global expansion currently underway.

Steven Bocska

Steve Bocska has worked in the videogame industry for over four years as a producer, lead designer, associate producer, and sound producer for Disney Interactive, Black Box (E.A.), and Radical Entertainment. He also has an additional three years of experience as an independent producer/writer of stage productions and short audio and video productions. Steve has 10 years of post-secondary education, including a B.A. (Honors), M.A. (Planning), and an M.B.A. (Entrepreneurship). He is an award-winning strategic planner and business planner. Steve is credited on game titles that have collectively sold over 6 million copies, including *Need For Speed: Hot Pursuit II*, *CSI: Crime Scene Investigation*, *CSI: Dark Motives*, *Simpsons: Hit & Run*, and *CSI: Miami*.

Tom Buscaglia

Tom is a principal in the law firm T.H. Buscaglia and Associates in Miami, Florida. He has been the chapter coordinator for the South Florida Chapter of the International Game Developers' Association since its inception several years ago, and is a moderator for the IGDA's Business and Legal Web forum. He is also the president of BallroomGames, Inc., which holds the exclusive license for the use of the Arthur Murray Dance Studio name and materials in conjunction with developing a series of games based on the exciting world of ballroom dance.

Beverly Cambron

Beverly Cambron is the founder of Rocco Media, LLC, a public relations and marketing firm. Before entering the world of games industry public relations, Beverly was a litigation attorney in both Texas and California. She received her degree in finance and international business from the University of Texas at Austin, and her law degree from Southern Methodist University in Dallas. Beverly has contributed to several games industry books, magazines, and online publications, and is a published writer on the subject of wine.

Melanie Cambron

Since 1997, Melanie Cambron has been recruiting for games industry leaders such as THQ, Midway, Turbine, and Sony. Featured in several books for her industry knowledge, she is a popular guest speaker at universities and high schools on the game development business. Melanie is frequently interviewed by major media such as the *Dallas Morning News* for her industry expertise. Having been a moderator and panelist at E[3] and GDC, she has also served as a consultant to the City of Austin's Interactive Industry Development Committee.

Chris Campbell

Chris has worked as quality assurance lead on the *Age of Empires* game series. He has also worked in the quality assurance field in several different sectors, including telecom, supply chain, and finance. For fun, he runs a videogame trivia mailing list, and has been an avid gamer for more than 20 years.

Heather Maxwell Chandler

Heather Maxwell Chandler is a multimedia producer with over eight years of videogame industry experience. She is currently a producer at Red Storm Entertainment. Prior to working at Red Storm, she worked in production at Activision, Electronic Arts, and New Line Cinema. Some of her credits include *Vigilante 8,*

Apocalypse, the *Shanghai* series, the *Heavy Gear* series, *Rainbow Six 3: Raven Shield*, and the *Ghost Recon* series. She holds a B.A. from Vanderbilt University and an M.A. from the USC School of Cinema-Television. For more information, go to *www.medi-asunshine.com*.

Sande Chen

Sande Chen has been active in the gaming industry for over five years, and has written for numerous mainstream and industry publications. Her past game credits include 1999 IGF winner *Terminus, Siege of Avalon, Scooby Doo*, and *JamDat Scrabble*. She graduated from the Massachusetts Institute of Technology with dual degrees in writing and in economics and received a full-tuition scholarship for postgraduate study at the London School of Economics and Political Science. Afterward, she continued her interest in screenwriting, earning an M.F.A. at the University of Southern California. While still a cinema student, she was nominated in 1996 for a Grammy in music video direction. As a freelance writer and consultant, she strives to combine her love of creative media with her analytical skills. She has received numerous honors in writing, music, and video.

Jason Della Rocca

As Executive Director for the International Game Developers Association, Jason oversees the day-to-day running of the IGDA, giving particular focus to outreach efforts and member programs, working to build the sense of a unified game development community, and providing a common voice for the development industry. Jason also oversees the running of the Game Developers Choice Awards, an annual industry event that recognizes and rewards outstanding achievement within the game development community. Jason has been a member of the game development community for many years, having spent time at Matrox Graphics, Quazal, and Silicon Graphics.

Shekhar Dhupelia

Shekhar Dhupelia's first foray into the games industry took the form of two years working with the SCE-RT group of Sony (SCEA) in San Diego, California, developing the online software and server infrastructure that power *SOCOM: US Navy Seals, Frequency, Twisted Metal Black Online, NFL Gameday*, and many other PlayStation 2 titles to this day. He then moved on to Microsoft's *NBA Inside Drive 2004* Xbox Live implementation, before spending some time at Midway Games, working on *NBA Ballers* for both PS2 and Xbox. Shekhar previously wrote for Charles River Media's *Game Programming Gems 4*, and is a contributor and section editor of *Game Programming Gems 5*. He has spoken at the Game Developer's Conference (GDC) and the Penny Arcade Expo (PAX) on various topics surrounding game design, and his most recent project was developing the Xbox Live implementation for Studio Gigante and THQ's *WWE Wrestlemania XXI*.

Thomas Djafari

Thomas has been working in the games industry for over 12 years. During this time, he has occupied various positions, has worked for major publishers, and has completed independent projects. He has been evaluating proposals made to publishers as well as seeking financial support for teams, earning knowledge from these two points of views.

François Dominic Laramée

A game development professional since 1991 and a full-time freelancer since 1998, François Dominic Laramée has designed, produced, and programmed more than 25 games for half a dozen platforms. In addition to this book, he edited Charles River Media's *Game Design Perspectives* and has published over 100 articles, most of them about game development, in a variety of print and online media. He holds graduate degrees in management and computer science, chairs the IGDA's Quality of Life committee, and moonlights as a stand-up comedy writer.

Mason McCuskey

Mason is the leader of Spin Studios (*www.spin-studios.com*), an independent game studio currently hard at work on a brand new game. Mason has been programming games since the days of the Apple II, and has run his own game development business for several years.

Mitzi McGilvray

Mitzi McGilvray has spent the last 15 years in the interactive entertainment business. She has worked with such premiere game publishers as Midway, Electronics Arts, Activision, Maxis, and Time Warner Interactive. Her production credits include *NCAA Football*, *Michelle Kwan Figure Skating*, *Figure Skating*, *March Madness*, *NHL 97*, *Wayne Gretzky Hockey*, and various ports of *SimCity* and *SimEarth*.

Prior to founding Slam Dunk Productions, Mitzi was most recently a senior producer at EA.COM, where she was responsible for building budgets and business plans for mass-market online games, project management, game integration, and leading production teams.

Max Meltzer

Max operates a management consultancy business and the ITM talent agency representing top music composers, both specifically for games. He has worked in the industry for several years and was a consultant or producer for a range of top titles such as *Earth 2150* and *XIII*. He is considered a leading expert in the management of games outsourcing, contracting, and team motivating. He also lectures at Hayes Media Arts, has written for Gamasutra and IGN, is well regarded as a speaker, sits on the IGDA London and Credits committee, and is a judge for the Independent Games Festival.

Javier Otaegui

Javier F. Otaegui is project leader of Sabarasa Entertainment, an Argentine game development outsourcing studio based in Buenos Aires. He has been creating games since 1996, when he started Malvinas 2032, a local success. Today, he is leading outsourced projects for American and European customers. Javier can be contacted via e-mail at *javier@sabarasa.com*.

Terri Perkins

Terri Perkins ventured into the online game world with Lambda Moo and a 1200-baud modem while completing a bachelor's degree in education in 1994. She has administered and worked with volunteer programs for the *Realms of Despair* MUD, *EverQuest*, and *DragonRealms* before finding her home as founder and director of Funcom Inc.'s *Anarchy-Online* volunteer program. She has assisted in public relations, customer service design, project coordination, and consulting for various game organizations and companies.

Terri presently works in IT for Information International Associates and devotes spare time to combating Internet illiteracy and studying cyberculture.

Borut Pfeifer

An avid gamer since the second grade, Borut Pfeifer co-founded White Knuckle Games with his partners Dedrick Duckett and Doug Hayes in May 2001. His responsibilities at White Knuckle Games include serving as lead designer and AI and gameplay programmer. They are currently working on a third-person cyberpunk noir action role-playing game entitled *Reality's Edge*. Borut can be reached at *borut@whiteknucklegames.com*.

Jay Powell

Jay Powell received his B.A. from the University of North Carolina at Chapel Hill. He has arranged numerous deals across the globe for PC, Game Cube, PlayStation 2, and Xbox games. Jay regularly provides advice for the development community through *GIGnews* and has lectured twice at the Game Developer Conference. Jay also contributed two articles to the Charles River Media book *Game Design Perspectives*. With almost two decades of gaming experience, Jay's industry insight has allowed Octagon to create and maintain a property evaluation and acceptance methodology that exceeds the standards and expectations of the interactive industry.

Jodi Regts

Jodi Regts has over 10 years' experience in business management and advisory services, with a focus on e-business consulting and strategic communications. She has led projects for Royal Roads University, Partnerships BC, Industry Canada, International Refugee Trust (UK), Citizens Bank of Canada, and several other companies, government agencies, and not-for-profit organizations. Jodi's educational background includes a B.A. in English literature from the University of Victoria, and an M.B.A. (International Business) from the University of Victoria/ENPC Paris. She currently resides in Vancouver, BC, Canada.

Kathy Schoback

As vice president, Content Strategy for Infinium Labs, Kathy Schoback oversees relationships with game publishers and developers worldwide, including title selection, prioritization, negotiations, and lifecycle management. She has spent previous lifetimes at Eidos and Sega, as well as at the Game Developers Conference as part of the show management team. In addition to serving as IGDA chair emeritus, Kathy is co-chair of the IGDA Business Committee.

Michael Sellers

Michael Sellers is the founder of Online Alchemy, a game development studio in Austin, Texas. He has co-founded two other companies, Archetype Interactive in 1994, where he led the design for *Meridian 59*, and The Big Network in 1997, where he led the development of several online games and the groundbreaking *MyPlace* community software. Following that, he spent three years as a senior designer for Electronic Arts, leading such efforts as *SimCity Online*, *The Sims 2*, and the next *Ultima Online*, and contributing to the *The Sims Online*. Sellers has a degree in cognitive science.

Tom Sloper

Tom's game business career began at Western Technologies, where he designed LCD games and the Vectrex games *Spike* and *Bedlam*. There followed stints at Sega Enterprises (game designer), Rudell Design (toy designer), Atari Corporation (director of product development), and Activision (producer, senior producer, executive producer, creative director). In his 12 years at Activision, he produced 36 unique game titles (plus innumerable ports and localizations), and won five awards. He worked for several months in Activision's Japan operation, in Tokyo, and is perhaps best known for designing, managing, and producing Activision's *Shanghai* line. Tom is currently consulting, writing, speaking, and developing original games. He can be contacted at *tomster@sloperama.com*.

Peter Smith

Peter is currently working with the Navy Education and Training Command (NETC) on the development of an open source game engine designed to meet the needs of the Modeling and Simulation and Serious Games industries. He received a degree in computer engineering from Rose-Hulman Institute of Technology in Terre Haute, Indiana. Now he is pursuing a Ph.D. in modeling and simulation at the University of Central Florida in Orlando, Florida.

Grant Stanton

Grant Stanton is executive vice president of TSC and a professional recruiter in the games industry. He has recruited development staff and executives in the games industry for over 12 years and has consulted with numerous game company startups offering strategies for staffing. He is a second-generation recruiter in the industry, his father having helped staff companies such as Midway, Taito, Atari, and Collecovision in the early 1970s. He can be reached via e-mail at *Grant@TSCsearch.com*.

THE GAMES INDUSTRY THEN AND NOW

1.0

Introduction

Game publishing is an enormous business. Global sales of game software are expected to top $20 billion per year by the time this book goes to print. In fact, games are just about the only high-technology industry that not only survived the stock market debacle of 2001 to 2002 unscathed, but actually experienced sustained growth in the process.

Furthermore, this industry is far more diverse than the consumer press would lead us to believe. In addition to the traditional publisher-developer-retailer model, we have online distribution, wireless gaming, browser gaming, and a host of "serious" areas of industry that are quickly adopting game technology for training and simulation.

The articles in this section present a snapshot of the state of the games industry, the various ways in which people earn a living making games, and the challenges that we must face in the future:

- In Article 1.1, "State of the Industry," François Dominic Laramée, freelance game writer/designer and consultant, presents an overview of the industry's economy, introduces the development communities that are active in several countries, and discusses some of the issues that game developers all over the world have to face on a daily basis.
- In Article 1.2, "The Shift to Middleware: Technological Forecast for Game Development," expert game programmer Shekhar Dhupelia discusses the middleware market and how it has changed the game development landscape.
- In Article 1.3, "How Developers Get Paid: The Retail Market for Games," François Dominic Laramée discusses the inner workings of the retail market for games and how developers can earn profits in this environment.
- In Article 1.4, "Invasion of the IP Snatchers: Exploring Licensed versus Original Games," IGDA Executive Director Jason Della Rocca discusses the roots of the "original intellectual property versus licenses" debate and outlines potential solutions.
- In Article 1.5, "Online Business Models: Using the Net for Profit," game writer and Grammy-nominated music video director Sande Chen describes the pros and cons of using the Internet as a distribution channel and a sales tool, based on the experiences of several companies.
- In Article 1.6, "Serious Games: Opportunities for Game Developers in Interactive Simulation and Training," simulation specialist Peter Smith describes the emerging serious games market and the opportunities that it holds for developers.

- Finally, in Article 1.7, "Creating a Successful Freelance Game Development Business," François Dominic Laramée explains how he has built and sustained a freelance game development career, and how other developers could do the same.

1.1

State of the Industry

François Dominic Laramée

fdl@francoisdominiclaramee.com

It is no secret that the videogame industry, barely three decades old, has grown into an entertainment powerhouse, and there is no end in sight for this expansion. This article provides a quick overview of the current state of the industry and of the lives of the people who make the games we love.

Market Overview

Sales figures for the games industry as a whole are staggering and getting more so every year. According to the Informa Media Group [IMG04], global interactive entertainment software sales reached $20 billion in 2004, more than twice the amount reported when this book's first edition was being written in 2002. Meanwhile, the industry's total revenues, combining sales of software and hardware, are expected to reach a historic peak of $52.1 billion at the height of the next generation of consoles, in 2007. The Entertainment Software Association, which represents the major game publishers, further reports that nine console games achieved sales of over 1,000,000 units in 2003, an all-time record, and that they were all rated "Everyone" or "Teen" [ESA04].

Demographic changes have also transformed interactive entertainment into a mass-market experience. [ESA04] reports that the average gamer is 29 years old, the average game *buyer* is 36, and women account for a healthy 39% of the industry's customer base. As players (and developers) keep growing older and more diverse, we can expect new genres and game topics to emerge to satisfy the increased demand.

The Flip Side

That being said, while the industry's revenues are impressive, they are still somewhat misleading as well. True, game software sales have exceeded Hollywood's box office receipts in North America since the late 1990s. However, one must remember that the unit price of a game is 5 to 10 times higher than that of a movie ticket—and box office revenues don't take into account the enormous home video market.

Furthermore, because of the very large number of games battling for a share of the players' attention, each title can only expect to receive a minute fraction of the industry's lofty revenues. While Hollywood releases approximately 100 movies to theaters every year—some of them in very limited distribution—the games industry launches thousands of titles on multiple incompatible platforms. Consequently, a game that sells a few hundred thousand units is considered a moderate hit, while a movie that fails to draw at least 10 million viewers to theaters is perceived as a commercial failure. Sure, movie production budgets dwarf ours—for the moment—and it takes many more $5 tickets to pay for a $100 million film than it takes $50 boxes to make a $3 million game profitable. However, in the end, while most movies end up being profitable, the vast majority of games lose money for their developers, their publishers, or both.

The games industry is still heavily hit-driven, with 5% of game titles accounting for roughly 95% of sales [William02], and a publisher who goes too long without releasing a hit will quickly find itself in trouble. Of course, the odds of publishing a hit increase when a company owns a viable franchise and has the wherewithal to bring many titles to retail; as a result, the market is more hospitable to publishing giants, such as Electronic Arts, which accounts for about 20% of the industry's total sales in the United States [Gamasutra03]. Meanwhile, many small- and medium-sized developers and publishers are having great difficulty surviving in this extremely competitive environment.

In this context, it is hardly surprising that industry consolidation should progress unimpeded. Once-prominent companies like Acclaim have fallen into bankruptcy, and with production budgets expected to reach an average of $20 million or more for an AAA title in the 2005–2008 console cycle, all but a handful of companies are going to experience mighty hardship. Since the first edition of this book was published, the number of publishers capable of handling the worldwide release of a top-tier game has shrunk roughly by half, and it seems likely that fewer than 20 global companies will survive the next console war, with the rest of the publishing landscape consisting of smaller players concentrating on specific nations and territories.

Game Hardware: Still a Loss Leader

While the major console manufacturers earn sizeable profits from first-party software and from the royalties paid by third-party publishers, they often lose money on the sale of their hardware. By keeping prices as low as possible (that is, below cost), they hope to establish a larger customer base for their platform's software, thus making up for the hardware's losses.

When a console manufacturer achieves market share dominance, this strategy can pay off handsomely. For example, in 2004, Sony's PlayStation 2 owned 75% of the worldwide current-generation console installed base [Gamasutra04]. However, if the strategy fails, the failure can be expensive: [GameScience04] quotes a report published in the Japanese newspaper *Kabushiki Shimbun* that claims that embattled Nintendo is losing 20 billion yen on hardware every year.

Growth Areas

While consoles (and, to a lesser extent, the PC) remain the dominant gaming platforms, several emergent segments are expanding the game development market in significant fashion:

Mobile gaming. [ScreenDigest04.1] predicts that the global wireless game download market will exceed 5 billion euros (about $6.5 billion US) by 2010. The year 2004 saw several American and British wireless game publishers secure venture capital funding totaling over $100 million.

Online gaming. Another *Screen Digest* report [ScreenDigest04.2] predicts that the online games market will double between 2004 and 2007 in the Western world, to reach more than $2 billion in revenues. Massively multiplayer games, pay-per-play browser gaming, and gaming on demand are expected to drive this growth. However, online console subscription services remained marginal as of late 2004, with Xbox Live and Sony's online services reaching fewer than 10% of console owners.

Downloadable games. According to research firm IDC, global sales of downloadable games should multiply by 10 between 2003 and 2007, to reach $760 million [Sharma03].

And Yet, Can Startups Still Thrive?

With fewer large publishers competing for their services, game developers will need to work harder to find a channel to market and to approach alternate sources of funding for their projects. Taking a game to market, which wasn't easy in the past, will become more difficult in the future.

However, this business is still built on talent. We must remember that many of the most successful games in history (e.g., *Half-Life, Zoo Tycoon, Asheron's Call,* and *Age of Empires*) were developed by startups or relatively young companies, not all of which were populated by industry veterans. Runaway hits can still, once in a while, be created by a small resourceful team working on a shoestring (*Deer Hunter*), or even by a single individual with very little help (e.g., *Roller Coaster Tycoon* and *Tetris*). Breaking into games can be difficult, especially if you dream of making a console blockbuster right out of college, but it is by no means impossible.

Players and Developers around the World

While *Secrets of the Game Business* focuses on the way things work in the Western world, the games industry is truly a global phenomenon, and the ways in which people work and play vary wildly from one part of the world to the next. Let's look at some of the interesting phenomena happening out of the North American public's eye.

Unknown Genres

The Japanese console game market is far more diverse than what we see in our stores. For example, small games sold for the equivalent of a few dollars and designed to be played through in a single sitting, possibly during a party, are, if not commonplace, at least relatively easy to find. And if you think some American games are edgy, you would be surprised to learn how far Asian games have pushed the envelope in terms of violent and sexy content.

Perhaps the most interesting game genre indigenous to Japan and all but unknown everywhere else is the dating simulator, where the player must flirt with and conquer the hearts of virtual characters with surprisingly well-rounded personalities. Sometimes campy, sometimes serious, the dating simulator subculture has given birth to a number of incredibly popular characters, whose appeal has outgrown the boundaries of their original platforms.

Serious Games

Every year, gaming's technology and design expertise is applied to a wider array of topics, many of which do not belong to the world of entertainment.

While military simulations and games share a long history of cross-fertilization, the "Serious Games" movement is fast expanding into very different domains, including hospital and university management, election campaign-related advergaming, and even learning to cope with deadly diseases. *Ben's Game* [Holmes04], written by LucasArts engineer Eric Johnston and nine-year-old Ben Duskin with help from the Make-a-Wish Foundation, is intended to help children understand how their bodies fight cancer. Other equally fascinating examples will undoubtedly have come to the public's attention by the time this book is released.

Fan Appropriation

[Carter02] reports on this growing phenomenon: Japanese players appropriate popular characters and storylines from videogames and create doujinshi, books that contain fan fiction, artwork, and similar materials. These *doujinshi* are then printed in small quantities and traded at fan conventions, by mail, and in specialty shops. In some cases, fans have even created completely new games featuring beloved characters; for example, there is an entire series of fan-produced fighting games starring the cast of a famous dating sim available in the gaming underground.

While legally dubious, the doujinshi movement has pushed the popularity of some game properties far beyond the wildest dreams of their creators, and has created a market for (legitimate) anime, manga, and novels based on them.

A Global Community

Finally, game development has truly gone global. Of course, the traditional demographic centers of the industry remain Japan, California, Texas, and Great Britain. However, large and/or highly successful game development communities have coalesced in Korea, Taiwan, British Columbia, Maryland, Germany, France, Québec, Florida, and Australia. Several companies located in Russia, Ukraine, the Czech Republic, and Poland entered the market over the past several years, often as subcontractors, and are becoming major players. And few are the areas of the world where no developers at all can be found.

As a result, the membership of the International Game Developers' Association (IGDA) has been growing by leaps and bounds (to over 6,400 as of this writing), and local chapters have been formed in over 30 countries.

CASE STUDY 1.1.1: EMERGING GAME DEVELOPMENT COMMUNITIES

The games industry is going global, with significant players emerging in countries located far from the centers of the business.

"Game development has been going on in Malaysia for more than 10 years," says Brett Bibby of GameBrains. "We have some large studios, small startups, amateur groups, and a few dozen hobbyists. In the last couple of years, more and more schools have added game-related courses to their curriculums, while the Malaysian government's Multimedia Super Corridor program has helped bootstrap the development of local companies. As a result, our industry has grown tremendously, but it is still fragile."

Malaysia's Multimedia Super Corridor is an area near Kuala Lumpur where companies can apply for a 10-year tax exemption. The program also relaxes restrictions on foreign ownership, and makes it easier for foreign knowledge workers to obtain visas.

Israel harbors another small but emerging game development community. "We have several companies, but only a few are 'mainstream' game developers," says Ohad Barzilay, coordinator of the Israeli chapter of the IGDA. "We have several mobile game studios, probably because mobile publisher Eurofun is based here. The most high-profile company in the country is Majorem, which develops online 3D technology and games; their chief scientist invested the seed money, and now they have brought investors from the Far East on board."

Developers based in distant areas of the world often suffer from a lack of contact with the centers of the industry. "Distance is clearly a challenge for Israeli companies," says Ohad Barzilay. "Travel isn't cheap, and we lack the ability to make contacts with people and companies who can provide money, trained manpower, and projects. Thankfully, the studios that are in business are doing fine nonetheless. But if we had a local publisher that could finance console and PC projects and

$\rightarrow$

offer a little guidance, like Eurofun does for the mobile developers, we would probably see some major studios emerge very fast."

A recipe combining government assistance and the presence of a local publisher certainly worked in Montreal, Québec. A government grant program attracted UbiSoft to the city in 1996, at a time when the local game development community was limited to a handful of independent companies. Eight years later, there are over 2,000 professional game developers in the Province of Québec, and with its 1,000 employees, UbiSoft Montreal is one of the largest studios in the world—and also one of the most successful, with commercial and critical hits like *Splinter Cell* and *Prince of Persia: The Sands of Time* to its credit.

And sometimes, going far away has its advantages. "Malaysia has a very active and supportive investment community, willing to work with game companies," says Brett Bibby. "This helps overcome the experience problem because there are funds available for training. Besides, Malaysia rocks! The cost of living is low, the country is near the equator so the weather is tropical year-round, it has many resorts and beaches nearby, it is extremely modern, has excellent healthcare and education, and the people are very nice."

CASE STUDY 1.1.2: GAME DEVELOPMENT IN BRAZIL

Jeferson Valadares, co-founder of Jynx Playware and coordinator of Brazil's IGDA chapter, says that his country now hosts 43 companies in various stages of development, twice as many as when we talked to him before publishing the first edition of this book. "Projects include PC work-for-hire contracts with European and American companies," he says, "as well as mobile games, Web games, and even massively multiplayer online worlds. We also have a few developers tinkering with consoles, but nothing that has reached retail yet."

SouthLogic Studios, one of the country's most successful developers, has completed three titles for Atari: *Trophy Hunter 2003, Deer Hunter 2004,* and *Deer Hunter 2005.* Furthermore, at least two Brazilian massively multiplayer games, including Jynx Playware's own soccer management title, will hit the European market in 2005.

Indeed, the Brazilian industry has greatly increased its profile both in its home nation and abroad in recent years. "Studios are hitting the media, universities are opening programs, more and more of our games are published abroad, and we now have our own game-related national conferences and expositions."

While only a handful of Brazilian studios employ staffs of more than 20 people, independent developer André Kishimoto notes that several of the country's post-secondary institutions have created industry-specific programs, and that the availability of college graduates with game development degrees should fuel the

→

industry's future expansion. "The pioneers were Centro Universitário Positivo (UnicenP), which created a postgraduate course in game development in 2002, and Anhembi-Morumbi University (UAM), which started a bachelor's degree in game design and development in 2003. Others institutions are also involved, like the Rio de Janeiro Pontifical Catholic University, where the Lua scripting language was invented."

Kishimoto says that the importance of the Brazilian national market to local developers should not be understated. "Many companies from various fields have helped our studios get off the ground by commissioning games based on Brazilian properties. Recent examples include games based on the reality television show *Big Brother Brasil*, as well as *Vampiromania*, which is derived from the vampire-themed soap opera *Beijo do Vampiro*."

However, the range of games being developed in Brazil is very wide, says Kishimoto. "Outlive, by Continuum Entertainment, is a major retail game. The first Brazilian MMO, Ignis Games' *Erinia* (also known as Erynis), will be released in Europe and North America. Several mobile developers have published games in America, Europe, and Asia. Green Land Studios' *Acquaria* and Perceptum Informática's *Scooter Challenge* fall into the family/mass-market category. We even have cultural games, like Itaulab's *Paulista 1919*. And the resources for game developers keep expanding. A TV network started a program called *G4 Brasil*, dedicated to games and the industry, in 2003. Even game development books and portals written in Portuguese are also beginning to appear."

The Major Issues Facing the Industry

It is no secret that the games industry receives copious amounts of bad press. Interactive entertainment has been blamed for everything, including school violence, exploitation of women, childhood and teenage obesity [Warner04], dysfunctional development of children's social skills, degradation of society's moral fiber, and even permanent damage to the areas of the brain controlling creativity and emotion [Gamasutra02].

Some of the issues facing our community, however, are more serious than others.

Developer Quality of Life

It is no secret that game developers work hard, but exactly *how* hard? The IDGA's white paper on developer quality of life [IGDA04], written by a committee chaired by this author, was the first widely distributed effort to document working conditions in the industry. Among its findings:

- Nearly three out of five developers who responded to the IGDA's survey reported working 46 hours or more every week, including 20% who said they had to work more than 55 hours a week on a regular basis.
- "Crunch time" (i.e., periods of mandatory overtime above and beyond the norm), is omnipresent, with nearly 50% of respondents saying they have to work 65 hours a week or more before certain milestone deliveries.
- A majority of developers think that their managers consider crunch time a normal part of doing business or a necessary evil, while only 2.3% of respondents said that their companies implemented active no-crunch policies.
- The principal cause of crunch time is the industry's poor project management practices, which are probably related to lack of management training and experience; according to the survey, only 18.4% of developers are at least 35 years old, and less than 1 lead developer in 10 has over 10 years of experience.

The long hours take their toll not only on the employees themselves, but also on their families. While the IGDA's white paper documents the pressures that game development careers put on relationships, nothing demonstrates this sad state of affairs better than the more than 3,000 messages of support and confirmation that were posted within a matter of weeks, in November 2004, in response to an anonymous *LiveJournal* entry written by the spouse of a game developer [Anonymous04] decrying their loved one's working conditions.

As of this writing, the industry's problematic practices are being challenged in the courts. Neil Aitken, a programmer and former employee of Vivendi Universal Games, is suing his former employer for unpaid overtime, claiming that management ordered him and others to falsify time sheets [Feldman04.1]. A San Francisco law firm has also filed a class-action lawsuit on behalf of Electronic Arts employees seeking overtime pay [Feldman04.2]. Regardless of the outcomes of these lawsuits, developer quality of life should remain a prominent issue for the industry in the coming years.

Violence and Censorship

Violent games and their supposed impact on the mental health of children have been a major political issue for over a decade. Commentators, both on the right and on the left, have blamed games for driving the Columbine murderers and the perpetrators of other school shootings to action. *Grand Theft Auto*'s content, especially the part where the player can hire, rob, and kill a prostitute, has been the stuff of headlines all over the world. In addition, in the days following the Washington D.C. sniper shootings of October 2002, [Levine02] stated that the suspected killers were avid chess players, as if a love of the noble game were somehow relevant to the affair.

There is no doubt that a sizable share of the industry's production is made up of violent games. Among the reasons for this phenomenon is the fact that violence is much easier to implement into nonplayer characters than other human behaviors and emotions, like compassion and self-sacrifice. In addition, some of these games' content is, indeed, very edgy. However, anyone who is susceptible to be driven to murder by a game obviously suffers from serious mental health issues and could just as easily be "motivated" by acquaintances or by a completely imaginary source.

Stereotypes

Tangentially related to censorship is the issue of stereotypical game characters. While some of the industry's mainstays, like the *Rambo*-like walking arsenal and the wise-cracking sidekick, are relatively harmless, others may actually cost the industry some customers.

Chief among these potentially harmful stereotypes is the heroine with unrealistic proportions. A bizarre situation occurred in July 2004, when actress Kirsten Dunst demanded that the developers of the *Spider-Man 2* videogame redraw her character and tone down its "gigantic" breasts [MND04]. While some may find this incident humorous, the relative paucity of strong, physically realistic female characters in games may be one of the reasons why the industry and its products haven't yet reached the levels of popularity among females that they enjoy among males.

CASE STUDY 1.1.3: FREEDOM OF EXPRESSION

Jason Della Rocca, executive director for the IGDA, comments on the issues of violent games and freedom of expression:

"Public concern over violence in games, the addictiveness of games, and sexual stereotyping are just a few of the ongoing issues affecting the games industry and its perception in the media. And, with some courts stating that games are a medium incapable of expressing ideas, it is tough not to become overwhelmed by the battering of our creative endeavors.

"The various ratings systems around the world, and their associated marketing guidelines, have been a significant initiative in dealing with these negative perceptions. Yet, what is the true impact—creatively and financially—of a game's rating? What influences does the looming threat of government regulations have? How does all this play into the retail side, which seemingly wields the most power to censor content?

"Simply put, many developers do not take into account the full ramifications that game ratings, the threat of government regulation, and retail sensitivities have on the ultimate success (or failure) of their game. It is not uncommon for large retailers to reject your game because of questionable content—never mind an entire country banning it, which has happened in Australia and Germany, for example.

"Yes, but what about our creative freedom? True, this is a nascent art form, but we still have to sell our games. While we are pushing boundaries on many fronts, it is still important that we play by the rules. The last thing we need is for our games to be sold from the back room wrapped in brown paper..."

Links to help you stay in the loop:

www.igda.org, www.theesa.com, www.esrb.org

Hate Games

While playing the role of a drug dealer bent on revenge, as in *Grand Theft Auto: Vice City*, is bound to raise some controversy, there is much worse. Religious fundamentalists and racist fringe groups have taken to using games as vehicles for their repulsive political statements—and even as recruitment tools. [Blenkinsop02] reports that, among the hate games available for download on the Internet, are titles in which the player:

• Takes on the role of a suicide bomber trying to kill as many innocent civilians as possible.
• Manages a concentration camp.
• As a member of the Ku Klux Klan or of a skinhead gang, scores points by shooting at members of racial minorities.

While the industry can do little to prevent this sort of thing, it is our duty to denounce it at every occasion.

Piracy

Hackers and other software pirates are costing us a huge share of the income that is rightfully ours. The Entertainment Software Association, which regroups the world's major publishers and organizes the Electronic Entertainment Expo, estimates that worldwide piracy has cost the U.S. games industry alone over $3 billion in 2001 [ESA04]. The problem isn't limited to games: the Business Software Alliance [BSA04] estimates that 36% of all software installed on the world's computers is pirated, and that the worldwide trade in pirated software of all kinds amounted to $29 billion in 2003—whereas the entire legal software market is only worth $51 billion!

Piracy is changing the face of game development in many parts of the world. In Case Study 1.1.4, Erik Bethke explains that virtually all of Korea's industry is devoted to online gaming, because the extreme levels of piracy in Asia would make it just about impossible to earn a profit on a PC or console game that can be copied. Indeed, the BSA study identifies Vietnam and China as the worst offenders, with astounding 92% piracy rates. Several of the most widely anticipated games of 2004, including *Grand Theft Auto: San Andreas, Half-Life 2,* and *Doom 3*, were even available illegally on the Internet before their official release dates; [Jenkins04] reports that developers at id Software were expected to lose between $15 and $20 million in *Doom 3* sales because of piracy, and that over 50,000 illegal copies of the game were being downloaded simultaneously at one point during the week prior to the game's official launch.

Pirates always come up with new types of fallacies to justify their actions: games cost too much, all of the money goes to greedy publishers instead of developers anyway, and so forth. The bottom line is that the game developers are always the ones who end up paying for piracy. Publishers have to account for probable losses by paying lower advances and royalties. Independent developers selling their games online lose sales to "warez" sites and illicit peer-to-peer file sharing systems. Countless developers have to waste time that would be better spent making new games on anti-hacking routines. Therefore, we make less money for our work. We don't have any sympathy for robbers who break into our homes, and we shouldn't have any for those who break into our computers.

CASE STUDY 1.1.4: GAME DEVELOPMENT IN KOREA

The most successful persistent online game of all time isn't *EverQuest* or *Quake III Arena*: it is *Lineage*, a product of Korean developer NCSoft. *Lineage* was already the most lucrative game of its kind, with over 4 million subscribers, by the time it was first marketed in the United States—a feat that is even more impressive when considering that the overwhelming majority of its players don't even own home computers.

Indeed, Korean players gather to play online games in "PC rooms," where they rent computers and online access by the hour. A given game room can host dozens or hundreds of people at the same time, many of whom never use a computer for any other purpose. Jake Song, one of *Lineage*'s creators, told an amazed audience at the 2002 Game Developer's Conference that the game's extremely simple gameplay was made necessary by the fact that many of its players weren't very comfortable with a mouse, and that his company's customer support had to rely on the telephone because the players did not know to send e-mail to ask for help!

Online games are so popular in Korea that a number of first-rate players have moved there to play professionally on a full-time basis—and the best of them can't get out of their homes without being mobbed by autograph chasers. That isn't necessarily the case for developers, however. "Developers are not treated like rock stars, but they do indeed get good respect from society in general," says GoPets' Erik Bethke. "As an American in Seoul, Koreans first assume I am either a GI or an English teacher; when I tell them I work in games they are universally surprised and appreciative!"

GoPets, based in Seoul, is one of an enormous number of development houses in Korea: it is estimated that there are between 500 and 1,000 companies making games in the country, maybe more. "Every year, about 400 new massively multiplayer online games apply for a rating from the government," says Bethke, "and the Korean game market is expected to generate $3.7 billion in revenue in 2004. However, shops are closing and we have been seeing a general trend towards consolidation, higher quality, and better-financed companies having more success."

Like virtually all of its competitors, GoPets develops and publishes online games exclusively. "Koreans make full-scale MMOs, casual games, avatar experiences, and mobile games, but no console or PC games, except for a handful of projects being quietly produced here to benefit from lower labor costs. Because of the extremely high piracy in Asia, Koreans will never produce a game that can be

→

copied." Korean online games dominate the entire Asian market, from Japan to China and Taiwan to South East Asia. "This is an area that Japanese, European, and American developers and publishers have ceded to the Koreans without much of a fight."

Life in a Korean game development house is fairly different from the experience in its American counterparts. "The official workweek is 44 hours a week; however, there are far, far more holidays here in Korea than back in the U.S. I urge my fellow Americans to grab a foreign calculator and demand more holidays! Time with the family is a must. And the Korean government's medical insurance program is awesome!"

The Korean games industry benefits from a strong national association and from extensive government support. "The Ministry of Culture and the Ministry of Information Technology compete with each other to benefit the games industry in amazing ways. This is great, because we must prepare for strong competition that will be coming in the near future from the emergent Chinese industry."

Conclusion

The games industry is a fascinating, exhausting, fun, stimulating, stressful, blissful, and sometimes cruel place to be. However, above all, it is a business, and its economics have a significant impact on the way we live and work. We hope that this book will help shed some light on the way the industry works, and give you one more tool on the way to success.

References

[Anonymous04] Anonymous posting by 'EA_Spouse,' available online at *www.livejournal.com/users/ea_spouse/274.html*, November 10, 2004.

[Blenkinsop02] Blenkinsop, P., "Hate Games Spread on Web, Group Says," Reuters, July 8, 2002.

[BSA04] Business Software Association, "Global Software Piracy Study," available online at *www.bsa.org/globalstudy/*.

[Carter02] Carter, B., "Character Interaction Outside the Game World," *Game Design Perspectives*, Charles River Media, 2002.

[ESA04] Entertainment Software Association anti-piracy program; outline available online at *www.theesa.com/pressroom.html*.

[Feldman04.1] Feldman, C., "VU Games Slapped with Lawsuit," available online at *www.gamespot.com/all/news/news_6101709.html*, June 30, 2004.

[Feldman04.2] Feldman, C. and Thorsen, T., "Employees Readying Class-Action Lawsuit Against EA," *www.gamespot.com/news/2004/11/11/news_6112998.html*, November 11, 2004.

[Gamasutra02] Gamasutra news report, July 9, 2002.

[Gamasutra03] Gamasutra news wire, "Top 15 US Game Publishers Revealed," November 20, 2003.

[Gamasutra04] Gamasutra news wire, "PS2 Sales Pass 25 Million in US," March 3, 2004.

[GameScience04] GameScience.com report available online at *http://game-science.com/news/000671.html*.

[Holmes04] Holmes, S., "Ben's Game," available online at *www.gamerarchive.com/site/articles/bensgame.php*, June 28, 2004.

[IMG04] Informa Media Group, "Dynamics of Games–Fourth Edition," August 2004.

[IGDA04] International Game Developers Association, "Quality of Life in the Game Industry: Challenges and Best Practices," available online at *www.igda.org/qol/whitepaper.php*, March 2004.

[Jenkins04] Jenkins, D., "Doom 3 Falls Prey to Pirates," available online at *www.gamasutra.com/php-bin/news_index.php?story=4104*, August 2, 2004.

[Levine02] Levine, D., "Muhammad et Malvo aimaient jouer aux échecs," *La Presse*, October 26, 2002.

[MND04] Men's News Daily newswire, "Spider-Man's Kirsten Dunst demands videogame boob job," available online at *www.mensnewsdaily.com/ archive/newswire/news2004/0704/newswire071804-dunst.htm*, July 18, 2004.

[ScreenDigest04.1] Screen Digest, "Wireless Gaming: Operator Strategies, Global Market Outlook and Opportunities for the Games Industry," available online at www.screendigest.com/publications/reports/games/wireless_gaming/readmore/view, October 2004.

[ScreenDigest04.2] Screen Digest, "Online Gaming Markets to 2007: The New Growth Opportunities," available online at *www.screendigest.com/publications/reports/games/online_gaming_markets_to_2007/readmore/view*, June 2004.

[Sharma03] Dinesh, S., "Study: Game Growth to Spur For-Fee Downloads," C-NET News, October 1, 2003.

[Warner04] Warner, J., "Video Games, TV Double Childhood Obesity Risk," WebMD Health, available online at *http://my.webmd.com/content/Article/90/100540.htm*, June 2, 2004.

[William02] William, J. F., *William's Almanac: Everything You Ever Wanted to Know about Video Games*, IQ Guides, May 2002.

1.2

The Shift to Middleware: Technological Forecast for Game Development

Shekhar V. Dhupelia

sdhupelia@gmail.com

There is a new wave of middleware technology, improving upon itself every few months, that aims to take the engineering hurdles out of game development, reduce its cost, and leave the studios with the core responsibilities of game design and artistic design. But is this truly the case? While many studios, both large and small, are integrating middleware for everything from networking to rendering to physics, team sizes continue to grow unabated.

This article looks at the expectations and promises of middleware, the areas in which middleware technologies are growing, and the realities of integration, maintenance, expectations, and scope. These additional aspects, often overlooked in the quest to "make development easier," may leave schedules and budgets growing at the usual pace while providing better technology and features for the player.

Definition

The term "middleware" is a broad, catchall term in this context. While a programmer might think of the GameBryo or RenderWare software development kits (SDKs), an artist might think of SpeedTreeRT. An online developer might think of the GameSpy SDK suite, while a physics developer would concentrate on Havok Physics.

In reality, all of these can be considered middleware. The term essentially refers to software, often with some attached services or maintenance, which is either integrated into the game engine itself, or used to optimize the development pipeline. In short, any tool that eliminates the need to "do it yourself" constitutes middleware. In the game console or mobile game space, software or tools that are provided directly by the platform licensor usually aren't considered middleware per se, but they provide similar kinds of functionality and are therefore included in the middleware definition we use for the purposes of this article.

A Look Back

This new, modern, process of game development is just that: new. For many years, the games industry followed a much more primitive model, especially in game programming, which lagged far behind the world of business application development. A quick look at the growth of the game development process will help put the promises of middleware into historical context.

The Dark Ages

The earliest games were far simpler, both in technology and in design, than most modern games. Development was almost completely done in assembly or other low-level languages. Each game was essentially written from scratch by one or two people who shared the roles of designers, writers, programmers, and artists. The resources of consoles and PCs were so scarce that programmers spent a great deal of time optimizing every last byte and CPU cycle out of their code. Porting a game from one system to the next usually resulted in a complete rewrite.

Games, the Industry

As console and PC gaming really hit its stride in the 1980s, "professional" development practices began to emerge. Larger companies, such as Nintendo and Sega, started developing higher level programming tools that could be shared across teams.

However, specialization of roles within game teams really came to the forefront with the transition to 3D. On the engineering side, most 3D titles require advanced math and engineering, physics, artificial intelligence, online connectivity, and more. On the artistic side, 2D and 3D art, character and object animation, motion capture, and sometimes other disciplines became distinct specialties within game development teams. As the industry became a major part of popular cultural after 1990 (arguably reaching the same importance attributed to movies, music, and television), higher level tools and engineering methodology became a requirement. Advanced art tools such as 3D Studio and Maya became standard, while high-level 3D programming SDKs, such as DirectX and OpenGL, have been an integral part of just about every game released since the days of Windows 95 and the 32-bit consoles. As the roles and requirements of game development have become more complex, and further refined, many more middleware technologies have come to the forefront. Companies such as Criterion, Havok, Logitech, and GameSpy began to focus on their particular niche of expertise within the game development process. Companies such as Garage Games and TrueVision3D have released their own game "engines," to serve the smaller development teams and budgets of independent developers. As the expertise of these companies grows, along with the sophistication of their tools, more and more work has been delegated to these dedicated, specialized technologies.

The Value Proposition

An important business concept that is now making its way into the games industry's vocabulary is that of "Total Cost of Ownership" or TCO. The concept of TCO basically comes down to the fact that making a decision according to the upfront costs of a particular technology (or employee) may not be the best possible strategy, and that all of the ancillary costs, including maintenance, need to be taken into consideration as well.

TCO is actually only one item out of a range of benefits that a vendor might list as reasons to license their technology. This overall list of advantages can be referred to as "The Value Proposition." This term simply asks, "What are the overall gains to be had by using this product?" These gains might be material, such as gaining access to proprietary technology, or abstract, such as saving time or money on development.

If you ask a technology company to explain their value proposition, they will likely cite the TCO near the top of the list of benefits. The reason is this: Let's say that a team is planning on hiring three programmers, each to work on one particular aspect of the game for the duration of the project. If, as an example, they earned $50,000 (US) annually apiece, that's a cost of $150,000. However, looking at the total cost of employing these engineers requires consideration of benefits, office space, equipment, proportional costs for support staff, and so forth. The cost for these three employees may now hover between $250,000 and $300,000 annually.

However, using this same project, if the three aspects of the technology were covered by three different middleware application programming interfaces (APIs), the cost of the additional software might be $100,000. The process of integrating these three APIs might well be simple enough to require the services of a single programmer, instead of three building technology "from scratch," which might bring the TCO for these portions of the game to $200,000 for the first year. Further, if the development schedule is longer than one year, the cost ratio gets better, as only the employee gets paid throughout the project, while technology is often licensed "per project," rather than "per year." In addition, of course, one must also factor in the risk that in-house technology development may fail to match the results of the middleware—or that it might exceed them, for that matter.

Some companies operate with a different perspective. Logitech, for example, is in business primarily to sell various accessories and devices related to the gaming experience, directly to the end user. As Logitech's Fred Swan [Swan04] told us, "We provide functionality that is typically not otherwise available. For example, we have enabled devices such as force feedback steering wheels, USB headsets, Webcams, and corded and cordless mice and keyboards to function on PlayStation 2 and were the first peripheral company or middleware provider to do so." However, certain technology is required to enable some of these accessories.

Logitech has taken the successful route of doing what it takes to make their accessories playable in more games, by keeping prices low. [Swan04] explains, "The price of our services is right for any organization. At this time, all of our tools and support are provided free of charge. We make money through retail and OEM sale of our hardware. And of course developers are not required to buy this hardware in order to use our software."

Most technology vendors would also point to decreased development time as a direct impact on TCO. The Online Technology group of Sony Computer Entertainment America prides itself on the ease of their API. Sony's Glen VanDatta [VanDatta04] describes their middleware, the SCE-RT SDK: "The SCE-RT SDK is a networking SDK allowing PlayStation games to support community-based dynamic content, player lobby functions, and gameplay functions. Any online feature a game would like is included in the SCE-RT SDK. The SDK also provides connectivity and security for the Internet, paramount to protecting the online community." When discussing the efficiency of the toolkit, [VanDatta04] responds, "The SCE-RT SDK provides an easy API that is object oriented and can be used directly by the developer studios. The studios can then concentrate on the gameplay issues. Getting connected and passing game messages occurs in about one day's worth of programming."

Realities

As the middleware market for many types of game development tools and systems grows, more choices and more competitive pricing are available to the developer. Using the massively multiplayer architecture as an example, the market has grown enough to support new solutions and the development of these games is too risky for much innovation, so new systems like TeraZona and Butterfly.net have arisen to handle the low-level issues [Ferguson03]. The point of a system such as this is to allow more time to be spent on game design, rather than software implementation. The functionality of the TeraZona system is briefly outlined in Case Study 1.2.1.

CASE STUDY 1.2.1: THE TERAZONA MIDDLEWARE SYSTEM

Zona, Inc. offers a complete network solution for massive multiplayer online games (MMOGs) [Zona04]. An MMOG is much more difficult to develop than a standard game, largely because of the additional server and client engineering and support required to function over the Internet. Zona's TeraZona product is an end-to-end network solution that provides both client and server software, as well as hosting facilities and support.

The game developer can use the client libraries for leading platforms such as PlayStation 2, Xbox, or PC and not worry about the low-level requirements of establishing connections, security, or sending and receiving data. Further, they are provided a framework to develop the world logic, for the servers, again without having to worry about much of the normally tedious, low-level networking code. The servers use automatic server fail-over and redundancy, for maximum reliability. Further, they provide a "Game Master" system to access user accounts and

→

problems, and configure various game resources, which is of considerable help for deployment and customer support staff [Zona04].

TeraZone additionally offers many of the standard expected features, such as chat services, user profiles, and offers a thorough billing system, something with which many game developers have little experience.

However, does the middleware developer's promised value proposition come to fruition? It seems that the majority opinion is that selecting middleware technologies indeed saves time and money. One developer found that middleware was the only option for them, as they were required to develop new technology late in the cycle. They found that developing a new technology in-house, which might not carry forward into a future title, would require hiring programming specialists of all different disciplines, with experience across multiple platforms. This would have presented an unacceptable amount of risk [Keith03].

The Future

The industry was rocked by a surprise announcement on July 28, 2004, when publisher Electronic Arts announced the purchase of Criterion Software, a company best known as the developer of the ubiquitous RenderWare middleware solution. In one article published on the day of the acquisition, the author clearly explained how well the technology would suit Electronic Arts, while putting a scare into the rest of the industry. Having the industry's biggest competitor also in control of one of the biggest game engine solutions implied a dire future for RenderWare licensees [Fahey04].

Indeed, lack of control is one of middleware's largest drawbacks—and the reason most often cited to resist its adoption. Not developing the technology in-house, and not having complete control over the source code, could end up making an entire product (or even an entire company) dependent on the whims of an external entity.

Meanwhile, console platform developers, particularly Microsoft, have announced big plans to provide even more low-level technology to developers on future systems, and thus reduce the burden on game studios. The XNA suite is an attempt to bridge many of the software interfaces between various versions of the Xbox, as well as Windows-based gaming PCs [Becker04].

ATI is another company leading the charge toward easier and better game development, but from a hardware standpoint, as much as from a software perspective. ATI has been expanding their reach from PCs to console platforms in recent years; [Chou04] describes an ATI chipset that is expected to power the next generation of the Xbox. As graphics hardware continues to grow in complexity, and offers more and more programmability and customization, so must ATI's software suite. Andrew Thompson, director of Advanced Technologies Marketing for ATI, says that ATI will continue to refine their development kits to be as developer-friendly as possible [Wilson04].

While some developers and artists may balk at relying more heavily on outside companies, the typical game's production schedule and cost may grow beyond the typical game's studio's ability to develop everything on its own. Eighty percent of the time spent producing a game traditionally has gone into programming, and only 20% into design [Morgenstern04], and this trend is only getting worse.

Conclusion

While the gain from middleware technologies varies between teams and companies, middleware certainly is here to stay. The complexities of future game consoles and PCs, coupled with the vast scope of big-budget gameplay, make these products virtually indispensable. Moreover, as the games industry continues to mature in terms of business acumen, team management, and production, it is likely that more and more studios will want to slow the growth of budgets, team sizes, and schedules by using more "off-the-shelf" components.

That being said, large companies are not the only ones whose developers are turning to middleware. Independent studios, and even homebrew enthusiasts, are increasingly going to alternative products such as the Torque Game Engine, TrueVision3D, and others, in an attempt to flatten the ever-growing learning curve associated with OpenGL, Direct3D, pixel and vertex shaders, physics, and so on. Middleware will continue acting as an alternative for studios that cannot afford the research and development costs of modern game engines and other game technologies [Wong04]. Middleware could also very well flatten the learning curve necessary to transition to a future console era, as the outside vendors handle much of the work.

It is a sign of the industry's maturation that projects of all scopes and sizes can now turn to middleware providers for assistance; there are now offerings to match any level of difficulty and expertise. Engineering and research are most effective when the fundamental building blocks become cheap commodities, available to all. This provides teams the opportunity to build upon previous gains, without reinventing the wheel, and lets them focus more time on new ideas and breakthroughs. In the end, this can only result in positives, not only for the developer, but also more importantly for the player.

References

[Becker04] Becker, D., "Game Publishers Sweat Console Change," available online at *http://news.com.com/Game+publishers+sweat+console+change/2100-1043_3-5377871.html?part=rss&tag=5377871&subj=news.1043.20.*

[Chou04] Chou, C., "ATI to Roll Out R500 GPU for Xbox 2 in 1Q 2005," available online at *www.digitimes.com/news/a20040930A7056.html.*

[Fahey04] Fahey, R., "Focus: EA Sets the Criterion," available online at *www.gamesindustry.biz/content_page.php?aid=3883*, July 28, 2004.

[Ferguson03] Ferguson, M., "Product Review: Massively Multiplayer Online Game Middleware," available online at *www.gamasutra.com/features/20030115/ferguson_01.htm*, January 15, 2003.

[Keith03] Keith, C., "From the Ground Up: Creating a Core Technology Group," available online at *www.gamasutra.com/features/20030801/keith_01.shtml*, August 1, 2003.

[Morgenstern04] Morgenstern, S., "Developers Embrace the Piece Process," available online at *www.popsci.com/popsci/computers/article/0,20967,708930,00.html*.

[Swan04] Swan, Fred, Logitech, Inc., Personal Interview, 2004.

[VanDatta04] VanDatta, G., Sony Computer Entertainment America, Inc., Personal Interview, 2004.

[Wilson04] Wilson, D., "Next-Gen Technology: What's Under the Hood," available online at *www.gamespot.com/news/2004/05/17/printable_6098654.html*.

[Wong04] Wong, K., "Postcard from GDC 2004: Entering the Console Age," available online at *www.gamasutra.com/gdc2004/features/20040324/postcard-wong_02.shtml*, March 24, 2004.

[Zona04] Zona, Inc., available online at *www.zona.com/*.

How Developers Get Paid: The Retail Market for Games

François Dominic Laramée

fdl@francoisdominiclaramee.com

While online distribution and subscriptions have become viable revenue models for specific segments of the game development community, the industry as a whole remains bound to the retail market, and will stay bound to it for the foreseeable future. However, the way the retail market for games is organized doesn't make it easy for developers and publishers to make money—at least not in a reliable and predictable fashion.

This article explains the inner mechanics of the retail game market, how publishers cope with its limitations, and how its dynamics impact the financial well being of developers.

Monetary Aspects of Development Contracts

Before we look at the retail market itself, let's examine the contracts that developers sign with publishers, specifically the clauses that specify how (and when) the developers get paid. For the purposes of this discussion, the enormous variability of development contracts will be reduced to two broad categories: cost-based deals and royalty-based partnerships.

Cost + Margin Deals

This model, commonplace in subcontracting but also becoming more prevalent in the context of full development deals, minimizes risk for the developer, but at the cost of lower potential profits. In short, cost + margin deals involve four steps:

1. **Call for proposals.** The publisher asks the developer for a proposal based on broad parameters; for example, a racing game featuring the publisher's licensed property, for console X, to be delivered in the third quarter of 2006.
2. **Evaluation.** The developer evaluates the cost of making the game.

3. **Negotiation.** The parties agree on an acceptable profit margin for the developer. Sometimes this is done explicitly: the developer discloses their cost evaluation and the price is set at 20% or 40% above this figure. More often, the publisher asks several teams for competing bids, and the developers include their own (secret) profit margins in their proposals.

4. **Development.** If the developer is able to deliver the product for less than the expected cost, they pocket the difference. Conversely, if costs run out of control, their profits diminish. In extreme cases, the developer might end up completing the project at a loss; while publishers will occasionally agree to pay more than expected rather than seeing a high-payoff game be cancelled, they will only do so if they are convinced that it is the only way to save the game—and they won't forget the incident.

For developers, cost-based contracts might be attractive because risk is confined to the developer's own operations: accurate evaluations and smooth projects guarantee profitability, no matter what happens in the marketplace. However, if the game turns out to be a hit, the developer might regret trading away a share of royalties in exchange for safety.

Advance + Royalty Deals

The royalty model, borrowed from book publishing, is the traditional framework in the game business. It involves three major steps:

1. **Advance.** The publisher agrees to pay the developer a fixed amount, which might or might not cover development costs, before the game is published.

2. **Earning back the advance (or "recouping").** The advance is tied to the game's initial sales. For example, if an advance of $1,500,000 is paid based on $10 per copy, the developer will receive no additional money until the game has sold over 150,000 units. (If the game never reaches this sales target, the developer will never see another dollar, but at least they get to keep the advance. Deals that require reimbursement of unrecouped advances are all but unheard of, and should be avoided at all costs.)

3. **Royalties.** Once the game's sales have earned back the advance, the developer receives additional money for each copy of the game sold. This amount might be defined in dollars (e.g., $5 per copy) or as a percentage of the publisher's gross sale price, which can vary a great deal during the game's life cycle.

For developers, the royalty model might involve greater risk if the advances do not cover the cost of production. However, if the game becomes a best seller, the developer stands to earn much more money than in a cost-based arrangement.

Retail Statistics

Unfortunately, while the royalty model worked reasonably well in the old days of $100,000 development budgets, the associated risks are far less manageable in today's market.

A Hit-Driven Business

The overwhelming majority of PC games sell fewer than 100,000 units before going out of print; for most professionally developed and published titles, sales will begin to taper off at 15,000 to 40,000 copies, with any remaining inventory being liquidated by the publisher for little more than the cost of printing the box and CD-ROM. On the console side, the average title stands a much better chance of breaking even, but few teams can break into the console market without proving their worth elsewhere first. The bottom line: the vast majority of game projects lose money for the developer, the publisher, or both.

Therefore, the industry must rely on a small number of best-selling titles to earn enough profits to offset the losses suffered on the bulk of the projects.

Hedging Your Bets

Since all but the largest independent development companies release at most one or two PC or console games a year, the low probability of a hit makes it very difficult for developers to finance their own work. Therefore, most developers seek to shift the risk toward their publishers by negotiating advances that cover production costs and a reasonable profit margin.

The publishers, however, have no one else on whom to offload their risks. Thus, their strategy becomes one of cost reduction (limiting the losses on any individual title by reducing advances to a minimum) and risk balancing (by publishing as many different games as possible to increase the odds of a hit).

Selling to Retailers

As explained by [Schoback05], gaining wide and deep access to the retailers' shelves is the determining factor in a game's commercial success. Securing good shelf space is therefore the game publisher's most important job.

A Concentrated Business

In North America, a small number of major national retail chains accounts for the overwhelming majority of the games industry's total sales. For publishers, this makes relationships with these retailers especially crucial: if Wal-Mart refuses to stock a game, many potential buyers will not see it on the shelves—and if another major retailer notices the refusal, there is a chance it might reconsider its own decision to buy the game.

The largest brand-name publishers, like Electronic Arts and Sony, can usually assume that anything they publish will be stocked in every retail store. For smaller companies that can't supply stores with a steady stream of sure-fire novelties every month, the situation is much more difficult: store buyers will decide on a case-by-case basis, and they have very limited shelf space to allocate. Even then, an effective strategy can yield success: Case Study 1.3.1 describes how a small development house has achieved success self-publishing its first original intellectual property in its national market.

CASE STUDY 1.3.1: SELF-PUBLISHING

Kutoka Interactive, a small developer of children's edutainment titles starring a mouse named Mia, chose an unusual approach: they publish their games themselves in their home country (Canada) and sell licenses to publishers elsewhere on a country-by-country basis.

"We felt that establishing partnerships with multiple companies was less risky than to rely on a single, big company to market our game everywhere," explains Tanya Claessens, Kutoka's vice president. The strategy has paid off: today, the Mia series is distributed in 42 countries and in 14 languages. Moreover, finding the partners was easier than most people would expect: "When we first introduced Mia at MILIA, we received 43 proposals before the show was even over!"

Like many other companies in the field, Kutoka started out as a contract development house and used the income generated by this work to fund development of its own intellectual property. Mia's success on the trade show floor led to great press coverage, which in turn helped Kutoka secure precious shelf space for the games in Canada. "Thanks to the media's enthusiasm, we were able to get our first title into stores in December, which is almost unheard of." Since distributors could not handle the game at this late date, Kutoka's employees had to assemble the boxes in the office at night and ship the games directly to retailers themselves. And despite the positive press, even the retailers who ordered the game remained skeptical: "All we got at first were trial periods of two to four weeks. The game had to sell by then, or it would have been taken off the shelves."

Fortunately, Mia did sell, and the company has grown into a comfortable niche. "For the 2004 Christmas season, our lineup will include seven in-house productions and six third-party titles," Tanya Claessens concludes. "We're glad we're not starting out today, though. With fewer and fewer major retailers in the market, it is becoming more difficult to win 'mindshare' and to sell original properties. Major retailers such as Costco have scaled back their software offerings from 250 to 40 SKUs in recent years—that's utilities, console games, and edutainment combined—so we have to fight and scrap for every inch of shelf space. But I hope that we've hit the bottom of the barrel and that demand will pick up; after all, parents want edutainment for their kids, and retailers will have to follow suit."

The Publisher's Headaches

Convincing retailers to put a game on their shelves is unfortunately not nearly enough to ensure a game's financial success. This is because games are sold as consignment items: the retailer will only pay the publisher for copies of the game that consumers actually buy—the rest will be returned, often at the publisher's expense.

Therefore, not only must publishers convince retailers to order the game, they must also entice them to put it on the best shelf space, at the right time, and for as long as possible. Retailers will therefore study the publisher's marketing plan, sell the right to advertise the game in their store fliers, demand preferential pricing to convince consumers to buy the game in their stores instead of the competitors', and so on.

And sometimes, a relationship with a retailer will be so important that the publisher will be forced to accept the retailer's demand for a temporary exclusivity, or even to change the game's content to satisfy the retailer's standards.

The Channel-to-Market Throttle

Compared to other popular forms of entertainment such as music CDs and movies on DVD, games suffer from three serious disadvantages in the retail market:

Retailers don't stock many titles. The major specialty music stores routinely offer tens of thousands of different recordings. Game shops rarely if ever have more than a few hundred games in stock. In addition, the large surface discounters often propose 10 to 100 times more movies and music CDs than games.

Games are perishable. A weak-selling game will be taken off the shelves in six to eight weeks—there is no second chance. A success story like that of the Austin Powers movie franchise, which was revitalized in home video after the first film drew poorly at the box office, would be impossible in our medium. Even moderate hits rarely last more than a year in the marketplace.

Platforms are perishable. When music lovers were forced to switch from vinyl to cassette tapes and then to CDs—two platform changes in 50 years—the public rose into an uproar. Game players have been through six generations of consoles, from the Pong machines to the Atari VCS to the 8-bit Nintendo to the 16-bit Sega Genesis to the 32-bit PlayStation to the Xbox, in half that time, with the first representatives of the next generation likely to reach market shortly after this book goes to print. Moreover, unlike the music of the Beatles, the overwhelming majority of the classic games of the DOS and 8-bit era have never been re-released commercially. While players can still enjoy many of these games (despite publishers' best legal efforts to the contrary) thanks to emulators and the so-called salvage community, this sort of noncommercial effort generates no income for the developers who created the games in the first place.

The Developer's Headaches

Suppose that a developer sells a game to a publisher for an advance of $2,000,000 that matches its development cost exactly, plus a royalty of $10 per copy. The developer will earn royalty checks and turn a profit only if the game sells more than 200,000 units.

Now, if the publisher invests $400,000 in the game's manufacturing and marketing and sells it to retailers at a gross price of $30, it will have earned back its own investment as soon as the game sells (2,400,000 / 30) = 80,000 units. Therefore, if the game's sales begin to decline after 100,000 units, the project has already achieved profitability from the publisher's point of view. Consequently, the publisher might not be highly motivated to stimulate sales any more, because such an effort will quickly run into diminishing returns. Meanwhile, the developer hasn't received one dollar in royalties.

Of course, if the advance paid to the developer didn't even cover the cost of developing the game, this phenomenon can lead to profits for the publisher and disaster for the developer. For this reason, smart developers will negotiate the largest possible advance, even at the expense of a modest royalty rate.

On the Shelves

Different outlets might sell the same game at different prices for reasons of strategy: for example, some retailers will choose to sell a high-profile game at a discount for a short time to draw customers. However, publishers will also change their suggested retail prices with time [Laramée05], lowering them when demand decreases. What happens to developer royalties at that time?

If the royalty rate has been set as a fixed percentage of the publisher's sale price—for example, 20%—the royalty amount decreases proportionally with the price. One consequence of this fact is that, if the game has not yet earned back its advance at the time of a price drop, the developer might have to wait until unit sales reach much higher levels than expected before he receives a check.

The other royalty model, in which the developer receives a fixed dollar amount per copy of the game sold no matter what the publisher's sale price might be, would therefore seem more attractive. Unfortunately, this model has a serious flaw of its own: as the publisher's price drops, the fixed royalty accounts for an ever-increasing share of the publisher's revenue, until it becomes economically preferable for the publisher to stop marketing the game even if there is still a demand for it.

From the developer's point of view, the optimal agreement ought to generate royalty income as soon as possible and keep the game on the shelves as long as possible. One way to build this strategy into a contractual clause would be to:

Set a ceiling to the unit sales that can be used to recoup the advance. For example, an advance of $1,800,000 at a royalty rate of $9 per unit corresponds to 200,000 units sold at full price. The contract might therefore specify that the developer is entitled to receive royalties as soon as unit sales reach 250,000 copies, even if the advance has not yet been recouped due to price cuts.

Set an escalating royalty percentage once the advance has been earned back. For example, the royalty on the first 100,000 units might be 20% of the publisher's price, the rate on the next 100,000 might be 25%, and so on. This way, the developer shares in the success of a hit, but since the royalty remains bound to the publisher's price as a reasonable percentage, there will never be any incentive for the publisher to drop the game as long as demand stays strong, since both parties earn money on each unit sold. After all, by the time the higher royalty rate comes into effect, the game is already profitable for both parties.

When Do Royalty Checks Arrive?

Finally, most publishers pay royalties on a quarterly basis, and only on copies that retailers have paid them for (because they have been sold to consumers). This means that it takes some time for money to flow back into developers' pockets: if a game reaches the target sales numbers required to generate royalties on October 21, the fact will be reflected on the publisher's fourth-quarter report, which might only be completed in February—and accounting might not print the developer's check until March.

CASE STUDY 1.3.2: ROYALTIES VERSUS GUARANTEES

Sarbakan, a developer of online games based in Quebec City, is most notorious for its mystery serial *Arcane* and its action series *SteppenWolf*, both published by Warner Bros. Online. Sarbakan's business model relies on a balance between original intellectual property (whether sold outright, work-for-hire style, or licensed to distributors according to nonexclusive agreements) and service deals.

"We want to maintain a 50–50 split between creating our own projects and providing our services to other intellectual property owners," says Richard Vallerand, Sarbakan's vice president for creative affairs and production. "These are very different businesses, but they complement each other very well."

In *SteppenWolf*'s case, Sarbakan sold all rights to the property to Warner Bros. The publisher provided a budget sufficient to insure profitability, and Sarbakan retained a share of future earnings tied to the property. "This way, we gained access to Warner's tremendous marketing machine. This allowed us to gain more players faster than we could have on our own. And since they own the rights, our partners will be more interested in migrating the property toward other media; television, for example. Obviously, they are in a much better position to do so than we are."

By selling the rights to *SteppenWolf* to Warner Bros., Sarbakan accepted a smaller share of the property's revenue. However, with the power of the conglomer-

→

ate behind *SteppenWolf*, this small share might actually amount to more, in the long run, than what Sarbakan might have been able to generate on its own.

"Plus, Warner has allowed us to retain a great deal of creative control over the characters and storylines. This is not the case when we work on someone else's intellectual property: when we do so, the decision process always involves a lot of back and forth."

Conclusion

Not very many games ever earn anything beyond the initial advance for their developers. Even in the best case, it will take months for the game to start earning royalties, and a few more months for the money to reach the developer. As a result, smart companies now base their budgets on the advances alone—and they try to build a healthy profit margin into them. Thus, the "cost and margin" pricing model becomes more prevalent, in fact if not in intention.

The retail market for games is difficult for developers, and not much easier for most publishers. Retailers wield enormous power over our livelihoods: they stock few products, don't keep them on the shelves for very long, and reap much of the income the games generate. Yet, alternative distribution schemes (e.g., online sales) have not yet supplanted retail, because of download sizes, consumer habits, and publishers' fears over channel conflicts. Learning how the retail market for games works will help developers thrive in this competitive environment.

References

[Laramée05] Laramée, F. D., "A Publishing Project: From Concept to Launch and Beyond," in *Secrets of the Game Business*, 2nd Edition, Charles River Media, 2005.

[Schoback05] Schoback, K., "The Role of Each Entity in Game Publishing," in *Secrets of the Game Business*, 2nd Edition, Charles River Media, 2005.

1.4

Invasion of the IP Snatchers: Exploring Licensed versus Original Games

Jason Della Rocca

jason@igda.org

These days, it would seem that everyone has an idea they think would make for a great game. That, or, they at least intuitively "know" how to make a current game better. So why, then, is it that the computer and videogame industry, known for its boundless creativity, must so often turn to ideas from other industries (e.g., movies, books, sports, comics, toys, TV, etc.) to serve as the basis for a game?

This article explores the issue of licensed content intruding on territory that may be better served by the games industry's original creativity. Is the trend of increased reliance on licenses valid, and sustainable? What are the pros and cons? Can the industry achieve a healthy balance between original concepts and licensed properties?

Some Definitions

Before we get started, let's lay out some basic definitions:

Intellectual property (IP): IP is a complex set of legal constructs to protect creators' ideas (as opposed to physical property). For purposes of this discussion, IP mainly refers to copyrights and trademarks.

Original IP: Original IP is just that, original. This means that a game is based on ideas (i.e., story, characters, concept, setting, world, etc.) first imagined in the minds of those working within the games industry and used for the first time in a game. Some examples of games based on original IP include *The Sims*, *Doom*, *Tomb Raider*, *Halo*, and *Myst*.

Licensed IP: Games based on licensed IP leverage ideas that come from outside the games industry. While game licenses are most commonly derived from Hollywood movies, professional sports, and literature, a game is based on a license any time it is set on ideas that are "brought in" from outside the games industry. Some examples of games based on licensed IP include *Enter the Matrix*, *Madden NFL*, *Lord of the Rings: Battle for Middle-Earth*, and *CSI: Dark Motives*. Game publishers pay a licensing fee in order to use others' IP within games (hence the term "licensed" IP).

Franchise IP: A long-standing and successful series of game sequels is often referred to as a franchise, and can be based on either original or licensed IP. Some examples include the *Mario* series of games from Nintendo, the *SimCity* franchise from Maxis, the prolific *Final Fantasy* franchise of Square, and the successful series of *Tony Hawk* skateboarding games from Activision.

The topic of franchises invariably comes up in a discussion of licensed IP, as many view a long-standing game franchise based on original IP to be a form of license. While important to note, exploring the industry's overt reliance and dependence on game sequels/franchises (regardless if they are based on original or licensed IP) is beyond the scope of this article.

The License Curse

Despite its short history, the games industry is full of its own myths and legends. One such legend is the story of the game based on the film *E.T.*, published in the early 1980s. Given the film's tremendous success, the game was expected to become a major hit. However, it was so poorly received by critics and players alike that Atari had no recourse but to bury millions of unsold cartridges in a landfill in the desert outside Alamogordo, New Mexico.

Someone, Please Phone Home!

Indeed, all of the early classics—like *Space Invaders*, *Pac Man*, *Frogger*, and *Defender*—were based on original intellectual property. The prevalence of licensed games came much later, and is tied to the notion of risk.

As the games industry has matured and grown into a serious business, the financial risks associated with a game development project are astronomical. Much like other media and entertainment industries, games are a hit-driven business. As game budgets continue to grow, publishers need to do whatever they can to ensure that a game is indeed a hit—or at least breaks even.

Exacerbating the challenge of operating within a hit-driven business, publishers have no real tools to predict what will be a hit! Overall, the games industry has a problem figuring out what consumers would really enjoy. To minimize the risk of a catastrophic failure, publishers will favor products they assume will sell well, often based on spreadsheet calculations of past performances, or that developers themselves want to create and play. While the industry works to improve in this regard (partially due to increased involvement from the academic world), the marketplace's unpredictability hinders its ability to expand appeal and broaden markets—witness the ever-elusive female market.

Consistency Is King

Furthermore, most publishers are publicly traded corporations, and Wall Street demands predictability in corporate financials. Stock market success is largely based on setting predictable expectations for profits and then meeting or exceeding those expectations, hence the need for publishers to reliably forecast sales and expenses.

Many in the industry believe that by relying on licenses (and sequels), a publisher can minimize their risk and/or increase their chances of success. We'll look into this thinking shortly.

Designing for Risk Aversion

While the industry faces countless business challenges, many of these issues are derived from the design of the games themselves. Most people can come up with an idea for a fun game. The real challenge is in executing that idea—actually creating the game. As such, a lot of power rests in the hands of those with the ability to execute on ideas (game developers and designers), and those who have the money to fund them (the publishers).

An inherent risk with any expressive medium is that the creator will express ideas or thoughts that are relevant and meaningful (or even comprehensible) to themselves and those like them, but not necessarily to anyone else. In the games industry, this is manifested by the notion that young white tech-savvy male game developers create games that other young white tech-savvy males would enjoy. This approach to design carries the great risk of content and audience homogeneity.

The Hardcore

Focusing on a homogeneous market was probably a wise strategy for the early games industry to establish itself with its core audience: hardcore gamers. However, as the business continues to expand, the industry can no longer survive on the core alone. Publishers needed to diversify content and create games that were more accessible and approachable by consumers who were not hardcore gamers. Enter licensed IP.

Once again, licensed IP is viewed as a cure to the long-standing challenge of creating games to appeal to a broader mainstream audience. The theory goes that if someone is a Tolkien fan, has read *The Lord of the Rings*, has watched the movies, owns the DVD set, and so forth, then it is very likely that this person will be hungry to also consume videogames based on the same world, characters, story, and so on. Games are rightly viewed as an excellent means to further immerse oneself into a world you already know and love.

Unjust Justification

So, it seems like publishers are justified in turning to licenses to increase the appeal and profitability of the games they release. However, is this really the case? Once again, taking a historical perspective, games based on original IP are the top selling games, and the games that are most critically acclaimed. See Table 1.4.1 for a list of some top games, and game franchises. Arguably, it is original IP (or at least franchises based on original IP) that has generated much of the economic value, notoriety, and fun for the games industry.

TABLE 1.4.1.   Some Highly Successful Games and Franchises.

Doom	Myst
Final Fantasy	Pokemon
GoldenEye	Quake
Gran Turismo	SimCity
Grand Theft Auto	Soul Calibur
Half-Life	Star Wars
Halo	Tetris
Madden NFL	The Sims
Mario	WarCraft
Metal Gear	Zelda

Given that there are not many games based on licensed IP in Table 1.4.1, why is it that the industry seems to be overrun by licenses? Once again, it is a question of risk.

Hitting Hard

As it turns out, it is quite rare for a game based on original IP to be a big hit. Figure 1.4.1 is a theoretical bell curve of how many games sit in various sales ranges. As the figure demonstrates, few games based on original IP make sales at the right end of the curve (i.e., BIG sales)—but there are some. Rather, the curve is "bottom heavy," with many more games falling below the middle of the chart, or what is figuratively labeled as the "break-even point." The curve shows us that many original games barely make their money back, with just as many selling next to nothing.

Turning to games based on licensed IP, we can see a much different-looking curve in Figure 1.4.2. This curve has most of the games huddled around the break-even point. That is to say, even fewer licensed games sell toward the right end of the chart. However, few of them fail miserably. Rather, roughly as many licensed games will make their money back (and make some decent profit) as will lose a bit of money.

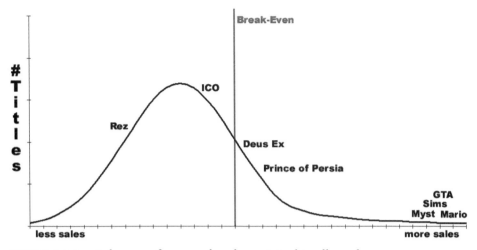

FIGURE 1.4.1   *Sales curve for games based on original intellectual property.*

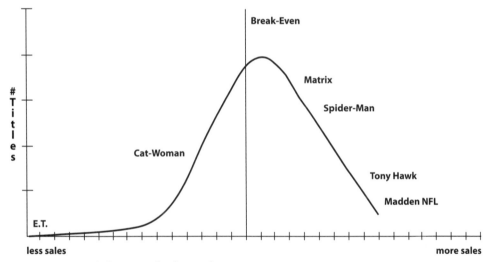

FIGURE 1.4.2   *Sales curve for licensed games.*

The Decision

Presented with the theoretical sales probabilities demonstrated in Figures 1.4.1 and 1.4.2, what is a publisher to do? While it is hard to reduce the extremely complex nature of deciding which projects/games to approve, fund, sell, and so forth, we can deduce several factors in the decision process. For starters, most of us have an innate human instinct for self-preservation: people aren't going to consciously make a decision that will get them fired. That is to say, there is a strong do-not-take-unnecessary-risk motive when publishing execs are making decisions on multimillion-dollar game projects.

Another factor is the inability to predict which games will be successful, as we explored earlier. Couple that with the corporate pressure to meet and beat stock market expectations (i.e., the need for consistent profits), and the odds are really stacked against green-lighting games based on original IP.

To summarize the decision, risk-averse publishing execs looking to keep their jobs and not lose their company money will more than likely go with projects that leverage licensed IP, providing a much better chance of at least breaking even.

To be fair to publishers, not all of them are so risk-averse. Some publishers rely on their ability to gamble on original IP and hit it big. As noted, this is an attempt to generalize and simplify a massively complex decision-making process. Moreover, developers are certainly part of the issue, as they often create what they think publishers' conservative mindset will approve.

Making Money Is Good

All of these decisions lead us to a situation where licensed games dominate the retail shelves and sales charts. Looking at weekly sales charts, we invariably see a dearth of new games based on original IP. In 2003, the world's largest game company, Electronic Arts, generated nearly $3 billion in sales, with only 3% of their production based on original IP! Yet, no one can deny that making money is a good thing. Strong sales fuel the industry, allowing more projects to be funded and ensuring that development studios stay in business.

Licenses are not an inherently bad thing for the games industry. And, like most other forms of art and entertainment, there is always a certain amount of crossover and exploitation borrowed from other industries. But…

Where's the Problem?

The challenge lies in finding the right balance between using licensed IP versus fostering original ideas. Given the current proliferation of licenses, the games industry is at risk of losing its identity as a unique and emerging art form. Rather, games will simply be viewed as tools to help market and extend IP from other industries.

This trend also leads to a lopsided generation and accumulation of wealth. To begin with, for every game based on licensed IP, the publisher must pay a licensing fee. This fee is money that flows out of the games industry and cuts into the profitability of publishers and developers. Further, the truly big selling games (e.g., *The Sims*, *Myst*, *GTA*, etc.) are more often than not based on original IP. Therefore, here too, by taking a safe bet on licenses, a publisher has a much smaller probability of really hitting it big and generating vast wealth for the industry. In addition, when a publisher invests in original IP, it controls that IP and can choose to license it to other industries (e.g., Eidos selling the *Tomb Raider* movie rights to Paramount)—another lost opportunity with licensed IP, since the publisher is not in a position to sell rights in what they do not own or control.

At a more fundamental level, many licenses are not "tuned" to interactivity. That is to say, content from linear media (i.e., movies, books, etc.) are not well suited to replay in a nonlinear and interactive context. Converting from one form to another is a great design challenge that not everyone is able to solve. While developers have been getting better, with several current licensed games receiving strong reviews (e.g., *The Chronicles of Riddick: Escape from Butcher Bay*), the linear nature of the content will always be an obstacle.

At a more selfish level, most game developers and designers would simply state that they prefer to work on their own ideas and bring their dreams to fruition—rather than toil on the ideas of others. The increased productivity from such passion and enthusiasm is immeasurable.

A Balanced Approach

Many of the preceding criticisms could be overcome if a more balanced approach were taken. As noted throughout this article, games based on licensed IP do have benefits to bring the industry:

- Access to a broader and/or more diverse audience
- Leverages excitement/marketing generated by other industries
- More consistent at generating positive revenue

Conversely, we see that games based on original IP bring us:

- Greater probability of becoming a huge hit and generating wealth for the industry
- Best demonstrate games as a distinct form of art and entertainment
- More fun to work on

Further still, games based on licenses could be helped if many developers (and publishers) didn't use the license as an excuse to do poor work. As alluded to earlier, this attitude could be due to a lack of interest in working on others' ideas, a notion that the game won't be a big hit anyway, or that it is impossible to create fun gameplay from linear content. As the esteemed Warren Spector has noted, licenses are not an excuse to do bad work:

> *"I really, truly, don't see how setting/character/context—a license or previous game, in other words—significantly limits a game developer's ability to introduce original GAMEPLAY elements into his or her work." —Game Developers Conference 2003*

If there were fewer bad games based on licensed IP, there could be an overall more positive contribution to the games industry by bringing in these external ideas.

Conclusion

In many ways, the industry's current dependence on licensed IP is just a symptom of the greater issue of risk. As such, the industry needs to find ways to minimize risk—or at least the perception of it—in order to cultivate a healthier mix of IP generation and usage. Part of the solution is in creating tools that will allow for greater insight into gamer (and nongamer) playing and buying behavior.

Greater insight into consumers will likely lead to the realization that the marketplace can support a greater diversity of content, beyond what the industry is currently supplying. In part, this demands that those creating games need to be made up of a more diverse set of people (i.e., gender, age, race, culture, etc.) in order to deliver content and ideas that truly reflect a diversity of interests and biases.

This diversity of content and broadening audience will require that the industry build up alternate business models and means of distribution. Reliance on limited retail shelf space and/or the blockbuster-only approach to publishing games will simply not support this diversity of content—much of which will not likely be created by the mainstream industry (think Web games, mods, shareware, art house, etc.).

The games industry needs a thriving "ecosystem" to succeed. Licensed IP and original games can happily coexist in that ecosystem, along with an overall greater diversity of creators and content. Ignoring our responsibility to maintain a healthy environment may mean that the fundamental values of the games industry will be snatched away from us.

Additional References

[Costikyan04] Costikyan, G., *Games * Design * Art * Culture* blog, available online at *www.costik.com/weblog/*.

[Donovan04] Donovan, T., "Top 20 Publishers," *Game Developer* magazine, October 2004, pp. 10–15.

[Graner04] Graner Ray, S., *Gender Inclusive Game Design*, Charles River Media, 2004.

[IGDA03] IGDA IP Rights Committee, "Intellectual Property Rights and the Video Game Industry," available online at *www.igda.org/biz/ipr_paper.php*, October 10, 2003.

[IGDA04] IGDA Business Committee, "Developer Business Summit Report and Proceedings," available online at *www.igda.org/biz/summit.php*, March 2004.

[Kent00] Kent, Steven L., *The First Quarter*, BWD Press, 2000.

[Miller04] Miller, S., *Game Matters* blog, available online at *http://dukenukem.typepad.com/game_matters/*.

Additional Resources

The *Hollywood Reporter*'s Tech Reporter column available online at *www.thehollywoodreporter.com/thr/columns/tech_reporter.jsp*.

Game Developers Conference archives, available online at *www.gdconf.com/archives/*.
Gamasutra business and legal feature articles, available online at
www.gamasutra.com/php-bin/article_display.php?category=2.
DFC Intelligence Game Articles, available online at *www.dfcint.com/gamearticles.html*.

1.5

Online Business Models: Using the Net for Profit

Sande Chen

Sande.Chen@alumni.usc.edu

With estimated revenues of $9.8 billion to be earned in 2009 [DFC04], online gaming has emerged as a likely powerhouse in the industry's future. Consulting firm DFC Intelligence further reports that 2001's top multiplayer online games each cashed in over $100 million in revenue, and predicts that by 2009, 376 million people worldwide will be playing games online.

In addition, casual gaming has proven to be an extremely profitable segment over the past few years. An IDC report [Sharma03] states that in 2003, sales from downloadable games topped $52.7 million, and forecasts that revenue could reach over $760 million in 2007. Game companies, from Microsoft to small independents, are eager to develop online business models capable of capturing this lucrative market.

Web-savvy companies intent on capitalizing on the Internet's potential can sell directly to customers, serve as intermediaries, or employ a combination of online strategies. This article by no means intends to discuss the myriad possibilities. Instead, relevant examples will be examined using the structure of atomic business models explained in [Weill and Vitale01].

Bypassing the Traditional Retail Model

Since the Web's inception, e-tailers have learned to harness the power of the Internet to reach thousands of would-be customers. The direct-to-customer business model bypasses intermediaries and ideally offers consumers a better value, better customer service, and increased convenience. The e-tailers, in exchange, might gain higher profit margins through cost reduction, product placement fees, and the sale of advertising space or customer data. The direct-to-customer business model can be extremely profitable, but its success depends on several key factors.

As [Weill and Vitale01] details, a successful direct-to-customer business must first capture customer awareness and then maintain interest through marketing or good press. The business must woo repeat customers by understanding their needs and by ensuring that transaction processing, fulfillment, and payment are conducted in a secure and efficient way. In addition, the product must be unique enough to deter price competition.

To the independent game developer, self-publishing and self-distribution via the Internet might be an appealing proposition because the game developer retains control over the product. However, the experiences of independent developers CogniToy and Digital Tome indicate that both retail and direct-to-customer markets can be difficult for small independent self-publishers.

Traditional Retail Model

The traditional retail model, which is discussed extensively elsewhere in this book, is a proven method to generate revenues. As shown in Figure 1.5.1, the publisher, the distributor, and the retailer all act as intermediaries between the developer and the customer.

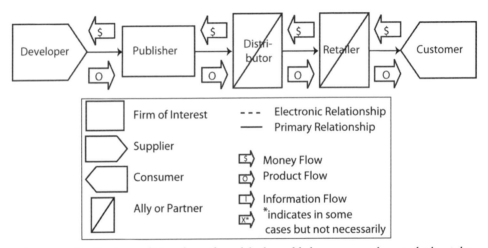

FIGURE 1.5.1   *In the traditional retail model, the publisher owns and controls the rights to the game. The developer supplies the game to the publisher, who then negotiates with distributors and retailers to reach the customer.*

Each of these middlemen decreases profits for the developer. Even though the consumer might pay $50 at the store, the developer tends to receive little or none of that purchase price. Moreover, since the advance payment by the publisher is recoupable, the developer will not receive any royalties until the game's development costs have been fully repaid. From the standpoint of the game developer, this model tends to be more favorable to publishers.

CogniToy: Web and Retail Sales

Independent developer CogniToy chose to use the direct-to-customer approach and later expanded to traditional retail channels. Located in Acton, Massachusetts, Cogni-Toy was founded in March 1997 to make "intelligent toys for intelligent minds." Its award-winning robot simulation game, *Mind Rover: The Europa Project*, was released in November 1999 and at that time, only available through CogniToy's Web site. Like other small companies on the Web, CogniToy used a third-party credit card validation service to facilitate sales.

Despite scanty advertising, *Mind Rover* sold pretty well via the Web site. Reviewers raved about CogniToy's first product. Within months, *Mind Rover* was available for purchase on Amazon, EBWorld, The Robot Store, and several other online sites. It sold so well at EBWorld, Electronics Boutique's online home, that the retail giant asked CogniToy to consider selling the game at its regular stores.

However, CogniToy soon found traditional retailing quite difficult. It lacked the marketing resources and the clout of the big software publishers to get in-house advertising or retail shelf placement. The company needed to package *Mind Rover* in a glossy four-color box for the retail version. Originally, *Mind Rover* had sold as a CD and manual only. To keep its cost per unit constant, CogniToy cut the 250-page manual down to 64 pages.

Moreover, since game retailers sell on consignment, a company only gets paid if the product sells. If it doesn't sell, the company pays to ship the unsold merchandise back. CogniToy found itself waiting months to get paid, if at all. While traditional retailing might have increased CogniToy's exposure, it yielded significantly less profit per copy than the Web site sale.

CogniToy's CTO Kent Quirk advises, "I would not recommend that small companies attempt to crack the retail market without knowing exactly what they're doing."

CogniToy's retail experience resembles that of Figure 1.5.1, while its online business model corresponds to Figure 1.5.2. Like other companies that sell direct-to-customer and also use intermediaries, there are potential channel conflicts. For example, the Web site sales might destabilize a relationship with the retailers. Instead, CogniToy could have pursued another revenue stream through the licensing of its technology. Indeed, it now sells a downloadable development kit to owners of the Lego RCX robot. In hindsight, Quirk admits that retailing might have been a bad decision for CogniToy. If there's a next time, CogniToy intends to leave retailing to a publisher.

Digital Tome: Episodic Digital Distribution

Like CogniToy, Houston-based Digital Tome opted for a direct-to-customer model but with episodic downloads. Co-founders Van Collins and Jim Shiflett planned to digitally distribute what would be equivalent to a traditional retail CD. In 2000, *Siege of Avalon*, a single-player RPG in six chapters, was released over the course of several months. Three chapters were central to the story's plot while the other three were

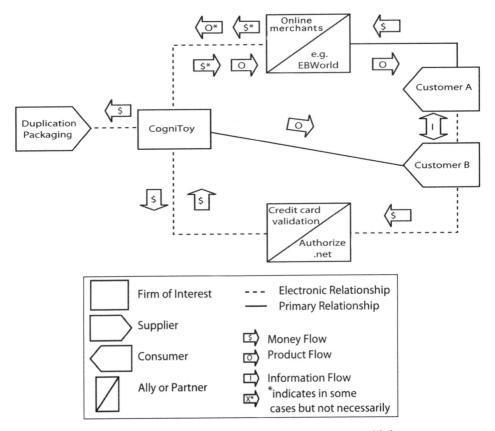

FIGURE 1.5.2   *CogniToy's self-published game,* Mind Rover, *was sold direct-to-customer via its Web site and through intermediaries. EBWorld, like its parent company, sells on consignment.*

expansion chapters designed to give further opportunities to explore the fictional world. Players could purchase each chapter separately or all six in a bundle. This business model, depicted in Figure 1.5.3, had never been tested before.

Digital Tome soon ran into problems with customer expectations. Even in a downloadable format, gamers expected premium quality cinematics, voice actors, music files, and sound effects, all of which would necessitate huge file downloads. Without widespread access to broadband Internet access, such a huge download led to long and often costly download times.

Digital Tome also ran into high fixed costs for distribution. Digital River, a third-party transaction company, handled transactions and hosted the downloads. Since each chapter was larger than the download limit, penalties were assessed for each downloaded purchase.

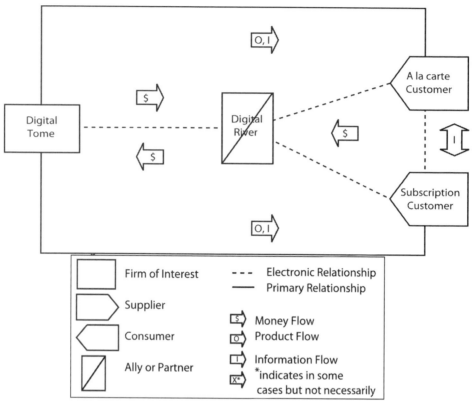

FIGURE 1.5.3   *Digital Tome's game,* Siege of Avalon, *was sold to consumers through a subscription or a la carte. Digital Tome paid Digital River, a third-party transaction company, a percentage of the sales.*

Other potential customers resisted paying online for a downloadable product. They wanted a physical object in a box. In September 2001, Digital Tome released an anthology CD with a manual and additional content. This immediately caused a channel conflict, which led to the suspension of online subscriptions. Earlier U.S. customers had paid $35 for the 500 MB download, while the retail product was selling in stores for $20. Consumers outside the United States complained that the cost of the subscription after exchange rates and download charges were about three times more expensive than the box.

In 2002, Digital Tome ceased new product development, and the co-founders launched *Expedition Games.* Despite the difficulties, Shiflett still believes in the future viability of digital distribution. At the time of *Siege of Avalon*'s launch, broadband penetration rates in the United States were lower than expected and Digital Tome did not have its own capability to handle high-volume downloads. Certainly, digital distribution, if it's convenient, secure, and profitable, has the potential to overtake the traditional retail market.

Online Gaming and Virtual Communities

A vibrant virtual community is critical to the success of online gaming businesses. Unlike Digital Tome and CogniToy's games, which do not require an active Internet connection to play, online games are usually played with friends. Because of the tight-knit communities that develop online, gaming sites are known to be among the "stickiest" sites on the Web. Portal sites, like Lycos and Yahoo, routinely use their gaming zones to place interstitial advertising and to cross-promote other offerings.

Generally, online games are geared toward two target customers: hardcore or casual gamers. Of the approximately 50 million online players, hardcore gamers are a small minority but they are the least price-sensitive. Hardcore gamers, predominately young males, are attracted to massively multiplayer or multiplayer games, often spending over 20 hours per month online. Casual gamers are more interested in little "coffee break" browser-based or downloadable games that last 10 to 15 minutes per session. Casual gamers, older and predominately female, are the fastest growing audience for online games.

Opportunities exist for the independent developer, as the experiences of Samu Games and Tams11 Software indicate, but the high costs of developing and maintaining massively multiplayer online games will need the support of publishers.

Massively Multiplayer Online Role-Playing Worlds

Currently, the top massively multiplayer online role-playing games, or MMORPGs, each have about 200,000 to 400,000 paying subscribers. Games are sold at retail stores and after the free month of play, the purchaser can opt to continue the subscription for a monthly fee. Thus, the retail model follows that of Figure 1.5.1.

The development costs for an MMORPG can range well over $10 million, but because the games reach so many people, there can be economies of scale. The sheer volume of ongoing subscriptions, combined with the sale of the retail box, adds up to a significant sum. However, with new entrants competing for the same hardcore players, there might be market saturation, or a limit to future revenues.

Samu Games: Multiplayer Arena

A dedicated fan base has proven to be invaluable to independent developers like Samu Games of Tulsa, Oklahoma. Formed in 1999 by brothers David and Douglas Michael, Samu Games released the multiplayer war game *Artifact* in October 1999 and its sequel in November 2000. The real-time strategy game is freely available to anyone to download, but there are benefits to paying for Citizenship, as Samu Games terms it.

At any given time, there might be about 33 war games running simultaneously. Each active game runs continuously until one side emerges as the victor, and the game might last anywhere from two days to a couple of weeks.

Samu Games offers a mixture of payment options based on access. The Freeman level, designated for free accounts, is limited to four hours of gameplay per day. For a one-time payment, players are allowed to play a greater number of hours daily in more games according to a five-tier structure. The premium level, Full Access, which allows the player to play all day, every day, in as many as 12 games, is offered as a monthly subscription.

Approximately 3,000 players download the game each month. Typically, 1.5% of the newbie players become Citizens. Samu Games' sole revenue comes directly from subscriptions and a good percentage is from repeat customers, who continually upgrade their access level. One third of the new players come from player referrals. The company refuses to have advertising because it would annoy players.

The active community on *Artifact* generates most of the content for the monthly newsletter, and fan volunteers serve as in-game administrators. The game itself was designed to support a virtual community, and players use the chatrooms and note systems extensively. The team-oriented nature of the game promotes community building since teamwork is essential to playing the game well.

Samu Games releases periodic bug fixes to *Artifact*, but other than that, there are no changes made to the game. However, to the player, each active game is different given the variables of players and skills. Samu Games hasn't given up the idea of a publisher or possibly licensing *Artifact*, but for the time being, it is committed to providing hardcore players with quality entertainment.

Samu Games successfully combines the direct-to-customer model with a virtual community, as shown in Figure 1.5.4. For a two-person company with volunteer staff, this is quite an accomplishment. It proves that when a company caters to its audience, fans are more than willing to devote time to improving and contributing to the community.

Tams11 Gaming Community

The Tams11 Gaming Community, which started up in January 2002, is maintained and run by Tamera Shaw-McGuire. A one-woman workforce, she programs the majority of the card, word, or puzzle games. The games appeal mostly to women, who appreciate Shaw-McGuire's personal commitment. The community started to take off in March 2002, mostly through word of mouth, and the site received the Gaming Friends Multiplayer Excellence Award for the 3rd Quarter 2002.

Shaw-McGuire envisioned a gaming community that would be different from the larger, well-known sites. A casual gamer since 1999, she found that she disliked having to deal with the advertising on sites like Pogo and Yahoo. Her biggest complaint was that those sites were cold and commercialized. She didn't want a "play to win" site, but a place where players could feel more involved with a community. Therefore, she says, "I wanted to make the players feel more at home at my site, knowing that I will try and be there to help whenever I can."

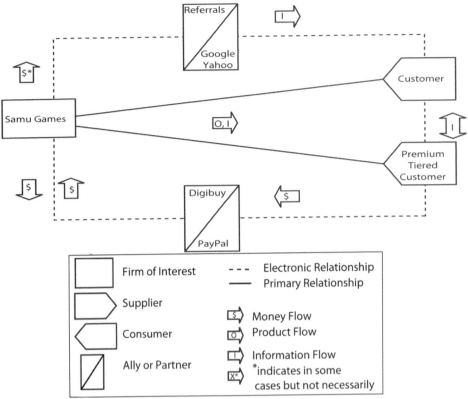

FIGURE 1.5.4   *Samu Games' self-published game,* Artifact, *is free to play, but access time is sold direct-to-customer via the Web site. The company relies on referrals and low-cost word-of-mouth advertising from its virtual community to increase its subscription rate.*

Tams11 members often converse with Shaw-McGuire, pointing out bugs and suggesting new games. Aware of her own penchant to chat online, she created a central lobby where any member can chat with another even if the other person isn't playing the same game. She also put up a tournament lobby that allows members to set up their own tournaments. The games offered are her unique creations but are similar to deleted games from other sites.

Shaw-McGuire's direct-to-customer business model resembles that of Figure 1.5.4. All of the games are free to play offline, but a subscription is required to continue playing online with friends after 30 days. Offline, the games are not very challenging and not much fun. The computer opponent usually loses.

So far, the hobby turned business has enough subscription revenue to cover costs, and Shaw-McGuire is pleasantly surprised that her startup is doing so well. Now in its third year, Tams11 has about 500 active subscribers, many of whom are loyal repeat customers. As the community grows, she hopes that her level of personal service can stay constant.

Intermediaries and Combined Models

While the direct-to-customer model trumpets disintermediation, other companies have found success as intermediaries. Sites like Real's RealArcade, MSN Games, and GameSpy attract a large audience of gamers by offering content, matchmaking services, and access to a large number of games. These larger sites employ a combination of online models and can provide valuable insights to independent developers.

Combined models can cause potential conflicts or synergies. Almost all gaming sites have forums or chatrooms because a loyal virtual community generally leads to repeat business and a good direct-to-customer relationship. However, a game reviewer site that also sells games has a clear conflict of interest: it might be tempted to give glowing reviews to its own products.

RealArcade

In the fall of 2001, Real launched its games division called RealArcade. As shown in Figure 1.5.5, RealArcade is essentially an aggregator that collects comparable products for display in one site. For customers, it concentrates information about offered products, which lowers search and decision costs. For developers and publishers, it profiles their products with editorial content and user reviews. Registered users have access to forums and lobbies for multiplayer matchmaking. Thus, RealArcade serves as a content provider, a virtual community, a direct-to-customer business, and an intermediary.

As the first mover in the downloadable casual games market, RealArcade occupies a dominant position. The service has grown from an initial offering of 70 to 80 games to an excess of 250 games. In 2003, RealArcade's revenue topped $22.2 million, with over 300,000 games downloaded daily. According to comScore Media Metrix, in May 2004, 82.4 million unduplicated users visited the Web site, representing 52.7% of the total U.S. Internet audience. In January 2004, Real purchased leading casual game developer GameHouse, and as a result can be considered a developer, publisher, and distributor. Still, RealArcade continues to work with over 150 developers. It is expanding rapidly into the international arena with sites in Japanese, German, Spanish, and other languages.

For the independent developer, RealArcade performs many of the duties of a publisher, such as quality assurance, marketing, localization, distribution, and transaction processing. Both publishers and developers use RealArcade as a value-added distribution channel. Just like a regular retailer or distributor, RealArcade receives a cut of the profits. All the parties benefit from these arrangements. Indie developers are eager to showcase their work on such a high-volume site. For RealArcade, the presence of diverse games helps to spur its virtual community, which in turn justifies its advertising rates.

Of the games on RealArcade, many are free Web-based games supported by advertising. The higher quality, downloadable games are available at different price levels. Consumers can buy games a la carte or through a subscription service called GamePass. Real's proprietary anti-piracy software ensures that the distribution is secure.

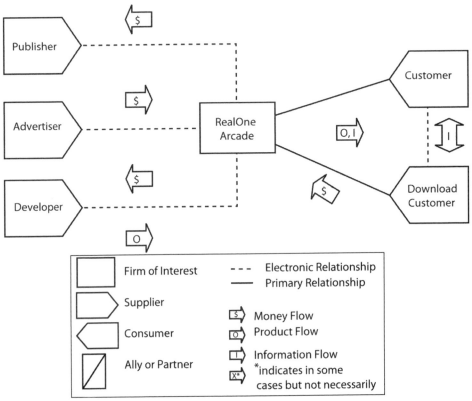

FIGURE 1.5.5 *RealArcade aggregates games from publishers and independent developers. The bulk of its revenue comes from the downloadable games segment.*

Unlike Digital Tome's *Siege of Avalon*, all of RealArcade's games are small "coffee break" games intended for casual gamers. Most are single-player and can even be downloaded to PDAs. The download sizes range from 5K to 10K. According to Andrew Wright, vice president of games of Real Networks, traditional retail distribution remains the best channel to reach hardcore gamers but the situation is completely different for casual gamers. He says, "For the casual audience, they can't walk into retail to find games that are relevant. They need ease of use. Digital delivery provides a level of convenience that the retail brick-and-mortar crew can't compete with."

MSN Games

MSN's gaming channel MSN Games, as depicted in Figure 1.5.6, also uses a combination of the content provider, virtual community, direct-to-customer, and intermediary models. A few years ago, its goal as an aggregator was not to sell games but to provide multiplayer support for a variety of games, but since then, it has switched strategies in order to respond to a changing demographic. From its onset, MSN

Games has catered to both hardcore and casual players, but now its audience of 30 million registered users is two-thirds female due to an increase in casual gaming interest and a concerted effort on MSN Games' part. Although retail matchmaking is still supported on MSN Games, its emphasis has been largely replaced by a focus on downloadable games.

In the past, MSN Games had over 100 games available for retail matchmaking. Hardcore gamers rely on matchmaking services to find teammates and challengers. Microsoft does have its own games up on MSN Games, but other game publishers are represented as well. This would appear to be a direct conflict, but MSN Games has no incentive to drive players toward one game or the other. The retail games supported on the Web site have been sold already, and publishers tend to view multiplayer play as a value-added service. The other publishers do not pay MSN Games to host their games. However, the service proved very labor intensive compared to its payoff and MSN Games no longer actively seeks partnerships to create custom lobbies for games.

These AAA titles tended to have outside-in matchmaking, whereby a player would join a community and launch into a game from within that community. As a result, the virtual community for a game like the subscription-based MMORPG *Asheron's Call* was unlikely to spill over to other parts of MSN Games. The more mainstream casual games, however, supported inside-out matchmaking, whereby a player with an interest in a game naturally becomes a part of the community. For instance, a bridge player may initially come on MSN Games for the free advertising-sponsored bridge hub and then end up subscribing to the subscription-based bridge club to have enhanced support. To generate interest in its games, MSN Games regularly holds tournaments and allows players to organize their own tournaments.

Advertising and sponsorship constitutes about 60% of revenues. MSN Games pioneered what it calls "advergaming." Advergaming would include the 3D racing game *Toyota Adrenaline,* which featured a Toyota Tundra truck in the gameplay and coincided with a six-month Toyota sales promotion. Other sponsorship opportunities exist with the trivia game *OutSmart.* Launched in 2001, *OutSmart* pits a celebrity against players to answer questions about the celebrity's work. Players compete for prizes donated by the sponsor. Various TV shows, music publishers, and movie studios have paid MSN Games to host a celebrity on *OutSmart* in order to reach MSN's large Internet audience.

Games like *OutSmart* appeal to casual gamers, and for Don Ryan, studio manager for MSN Games, casual gaming has seen an explosion in growth. Downloadable games sales for MSN Games are now its second primary source of revenue. Like RealArcade, MSN Games offers higher quality downloadable games. It works with developers as a distributor and retailer. The site averages about 9 million users monthly and has emerged as a serious contender in the casual gaming market.

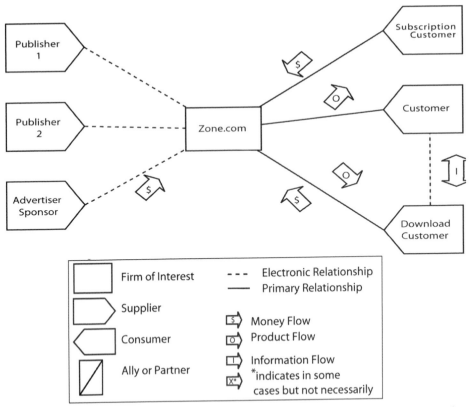

FIGURE 1.5.6 *Advertisers promote products to consumers through sponsored games. The bulk of MSN Games' revenue comes from advertising, followed closely by downloadable sales and subscriptions.*

GameSpy

In a way, GameSpy encompasses all of the business models discussed previously. As indicated in Figure 1.5.7, GameSpy has many revenue streams. The site has grown considerably from its humble beginnings as a *Quake* fan site to become one of the Web's most popular and successful gaming sites. Even today, GameSpy continues to expand its service offerings. In March 2004, GameSpy became a subsidiary of IGN Entertainment, which owns a suite of gaming-related Internet properties. Combined, IGN's Web sites reached 20.2 million users in July 2004 according to comScore Media Metrix.

GameSpy is a vortal, meant to be "Gaming's Homepage" and the #1 destination for people to read, try, buy, and play games. GameSpy is a content provider, the largest creator of editorial content with GameSpy Daily and over 55 player-run Web sites. Each hosted Web site aims to be the information source for a specific game with forums, content, chat, and an active community. In addition, GameSpy runs its own forums and aggregates all available forums on ForumPlanet. Capitalizing on its virtual community, GameSpy sells advertising, which generates the majority of its revenue.

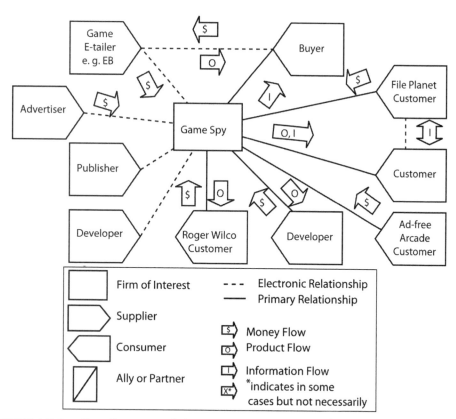

FIGURE 1.5.7 *GameSpy, a vortal, is a one-stop service station for gamers. Users can read articles, download files, subscribe to services, play online games, and/or make purchases.*

Like RealArcade, GameSpy Arcade has a large number of free and pay-to-play casual games. Like MSN Games, GameSpy Arcade supports retail matchmaking for hardcore gamers. It contains the largest catalog of multiplayer games on the Web. Unlike the casual gaming sites, GameSpy's audience has a strong male concentration, nearly 97%.

Besides advertising, GameSpy has other noteworthy revenue streams. GameSpy licenses technology for anti-piracy systems, in-game matchmaking, in-game voice chat, and other software tools for PC and console development. It has worked with almost every large publisher in the industry. In fact, RealArcade is a customer of GameSpy in this way.

For consumers, GameSpy offers a variety of services and subscriptions. In File-Planet, gamers can pay to have high priority to GameSpy's extensive library of cheats, files, and guides. On GameSpy Arcade, players can pay a fee to turn off the ads that would run on the free service. HitPoints, its customer loyalty program, encourages repeat business.

Other user services, such as free Web hosting and game ladders, are supported by advertising or sponsorship. GameSpy also acts as an intelligent price-comparing agent for buyers. GameSpy receives a commission for sending leads to online retailers. All of these services add value to the more than 20 million consumers who make up Game-Spy's vibrant virtual community. Almost every day, new content, even mods of existing games, are submitted to GameSpy by users. In doing so, GameSpy is assured of fresh and relevant updates.

GameSpy owns the relationship with the users. Since the company understands its demographic so well, its customers trust the brand and loyally return to GameSpy for their gaming needs. In September 2004, IGN Entertainment launched Direct2Drive to digitally distribute products from leading publishers. The titles include recent and past top-tier hits. To avoid alienating the physical channel, Direct2Drive games are priced to match the prevailing marketplace price. Despite Digital Tome's experience, GameSpy is poised to test the concept of a digital retail store.

IGN CEO Mark Jung says, "At the end of the day, a videogame is a digital file. It may come on a CD and be stored in jewel cases inside a box and sit on a shelf at GameSpot or at Wal-Mart, but it's really on that CD. It's bits and bytes in digital form." While he does not believe that digital distribution will ever replace the traditional retail market, Jung is betting that the digital download of games will become as commonplace as downloading music off the Internet.

GameSpy has certain core competencies that erase many of the obstacles Digital Tome faced. GameSpy is the world's largest downloader of game-related digital files. Already, on FilePlanet, more than 4 million files are downloaded monthly. Files could be patches, demos, trailers, screenshots, FAQs, mods, or other assorted files. In one case, over 120,000 copies of a 2 GB game's beta version were downloaded in a 48-hour time span. GameSpy has proven expertise on handling high-volume downloads and its FilePlanet users are familiar with its download and transaction procedures. In addition, GameSpy has no need to spend marketing dollars to drive potential customers to its site, a cost that can be prohibitive for a small indie. Furthermore, a significant chunk of its user base, more than 80%, uses broadband connections. Nowadays, broadband penetration rates in the United States are such that over 40% of U.S. households are on broadband.

In the future, GameSpy may consider becoming a digital distribution channel for large independent games, but it will need to be careful not to disintermediate game publishers. With a digital retail store that never runs out of stock and has no physical inventory, it would be quite easy to add more products.

Conclusion

The continued trend of online gaming has the potential to transform the economics of the industry. Whether it's due to streamlined digital distribution, licensing opportunities, or a shift from banner advertising to subscriptions, online business models will continue to evolve accordingly. Undoubtedly, informed independent developers will play an important role in this future.

References and Additional Resources

[DFC04] DFC Intelligence, "The Online Game Market 2004," available online at *www.dfcint.com/game_report/Online_Game_toc.html,* August 2004.

[IGDA02] IGDA Online Games Committee, "2002 Online Games White Paper," available online at *www.igda.org/content/reports.php*, March 2002.

[IGDA04] IGDA Online Games Committee, "2004 Web and Downloadable Games White Paper," available online at *www.igda.org/content/reports.php*, March 2004.

[Kary02] Kary, T., "Study: Sixfold Growth for Online Games," available online at *http://news.com.com/2100-1040-933295.html,* June 6, 2002.

[Sharma03] Sharma, D. C., "Study: Game Growth to Spur For-Fee Downloads," available online at *http://news.com.com/2100-1043-5084898.html,* October 1, 2003.

[Weill and Vitale01] Weill, P. and Vitale, M. R., *Place to Space: Migrating to e-Business Models,* Harvard Business School Press, 2001.

Serious Games: Opportunities for Game Developers in Interactive Simulation and Training

Peter A. Smith

peter@smithpa.com

The interactive simulation and videogame industries are undeniably linked, and are often described as cousins. However, this is not a proper analogy. They are more like the left and right brains of a person, so explicitly connected that they cannot be separated; however, completely different in their approaches to the same problem, creating believable and compelling virtual worlds. The simulation industry is the left brain; everything it does is taken seriously. The employees show up on time, usually leave on time, and create interactive simulations used for training tasks with similar results as real-world training counterparts; proper attire required. The games industry is the right brain: creative, fun loving, and exciting, the games industry challenges the way the world perceives machines. The employees work long hours for less pay for what must be a deep and devoted love for what they do.

Why the Simulation Industry Is Interested in Game Developers

The simulation industry is interested in working with game designers because game designers possess the unique skills that the simulation industry lacks, among them creativity and design sense. A game designer interested in Serious Games is the missing link that will bring both industries together.

The Economics

The simulation industry is accustomed to developing a simulation over a period of years. This development could take hundreds of millions of dollars and result in a very accurate portrayal of whatever event is being simulated. In the case of the *Close Combat Tactical Trainer*, which was fielded in the 1990s, an amazingly accurate simulation of vehicle training was produced. This top of the line, multimillion-dollar installation using Evans & Sutherland Image Generators supported impressive graphics for the time, and soldiers are still being trained on the same simulators today.

CASE STUDY 1.6.1: MILITARY SIMULATIONS

Curtis Conkey, lead developer at NETC PC Simulation Beta Lab, describes the opportunities for game developers in the military simulation market like this:

"Low-cost gaming technology brings the opportunity for three-tier training to the war fighter. Hands-on or live training with end-user equipment is the first tier of training with traditional high-fidelity, high-cost simulators offering excellent second-tier training. However, even with the tremendous cost savings second-tier trainers offer over actual equipment, simulation equipment cost can lead to accessibility issues. Time in these trainers is valuable and not to be wasted. Third-tier, low-cost, PC trainers offer introductory training that enables high-quality use of upper tier trainers. Third-tier gaming offers the opportunity for extended, personalized training time where the student has access to repeated training/gaming exercises."

Sadly, to upgrade the *Close Combat Tactical Trainer*, the military would have to redevelop both the system hardware and the training environments that use this system as well. With each installation costing millions of dollars, the idea of using standard PCs and gaming technology looks very appealing. Of course, some special equipment associated with the CCTT, such as actual tank interiors, cannot be reproduced on the PC, but many other aspects of the simulation could be. Conventional simulation saves the military money by not having to use live vehicles, ammunition rounds, and training ranges. Similarly, PC simulation can save them money by not needing as large or as many full-sized simulators.

Engineers Are Not Artists

The people developing simulations, for the most part, are engineers. More importantly, they are not artists, creative geniuses, or interface designers. When tasked to develop a user interface for a simulation, they may deliver something that requires as much training as the military system they are simulating. Game designers collaborating with a simulation company will be considered experts in design aesthetics and will make things not just easy to use but obvious, thus optimizing the soldiers' time. The simulation company will be bringing knowledge of how a particular system works, such as a tank, airplane, or boat, what it looks like, and how realistic the simulation has to be.

A Brief History of Using Games for Training

Although this article is not meant to present an all-inclusive history, it is important for anyone planning to work in the serious games industry to have some understanding of its roots. Videogames have been finding their way into the training domain for many years although the concept has only recently gained widespread acceptance by the mainstream. There are three basic ways in which games have been used in training: commercial off-the-shelf games (COTS), game mods, and custom games.

COTS Games—The Beginning of Serious Games

Developers and publishers of commercial off-the shelf games inadvertently started the Serious Games field. COTS games do not require any modification, but teach and train while being fun at the same time. Examples include *Sim City*, *Harpoon*, *Microsoft Flight Simulator*, and any game that takes a serious look at its subject matter while maintaining the fun aspects that make them games.

Harpoon is one of the most successful COTS trainers, because it was fun and extremely realistic. It is still being used by the Navy to train today. It may seem unlikely that new COTS games, not funded by the military, would be used for training with the rise in the number of custom-built games. However, even in the last year, independent game developer 2by3 games' *Uncommon Valor: Campaign for the South Pacific* and Battlefront's *Combat Mission: Afrika Korps* were licensed by the Australian Navy to train their soldiers in historical tactics. [Proctor02] says that the results of the study performed with *Combat Mission: Beyond Overlord* resulted in the United States Military Academy contracting a modern version of the game. [Prensky00] provides a list of other such endeavors.

Game Mods—The Evolution of Serious Games

A mod is a game modification to add new features, levels, or modes of play to the game. In 1996, project officer Scott Barnett, of the Marine Corps Modeling and Simulation Management Office, created *Marine Doom*, the first Serious Game mod. This mod set the player character's life points to 20% and required the players to use real-life team-based military strategy to make it through the levels alive. Although id Software did not take the modification too seriously, the military did.

The military is used to paying millions of dollars for the development of a simulator, and hundreds of thousands of dollars for each simulator fielded. However, a mod can be fielded for much less. As a result, mods of countless games have been made that repurpose the game engines for constructive training exercises. *Quake 3* mods have been used to teach the use of chemical detection equipment, and to train crews on how to safely lead people away from hazardous waste. A group at the University of Central Florida is attempting to create a game mod for training their campus police. They have looked into modifying both *Neverwinter Nights* and *Grand Theft Auto III*, a game criticized for its violence.

Custom Games—The Present State of Serious Games

Several branches of the military have sponsored development of their own games for training purposes—and released them to the general public as well. *America's Army*, developed by the MOVES Institute, the Naval Post Graduate School, is the official game of the United States Army. (Yes, the Naval Post Graduate School developed it; it is still the Army's game.) It runs on the Unreal 2 Engine, has been extremely successful, and UbiSoft has licensed it for future iterations. This success has led the MOVES Institute to begin looking into even cheaper ways to accomplish the same goals, such as open source engines, and technology.

Full Spectrum Warrior, however, was developed by a commercial game company, Pandemic Studios, in conjunction with the Institute of Creative Technologies (ICT). ICT is a part of the University of Southern California; it brings together experts from the entertainment and scientific communities to help foster collaborations between the two, and is at the forefront of research for the Serious Games industry. *Full Spectrum Warrior* took Serious Games to a new level of cost and convenience, by running on the Xbox game console. This raised the bar for economic efficiency, with the consumer version further cutting production costs.

The Future of Serious Games

Many projects are underway that will change the way people train. The most high-profile Serious Game project in development is There.com's military training massively multiplayer game. It will include a whole world database and is already under development with an Iraq database. The game will be used to train soldiers how to properly deal with people in other countries. They will learn to communicate and read the communications of other people who may not have the same culture. In current times, improved communications between cultures has become a matter of life and death, and games are coming to save the day.

Types of Games Used for Training and Simulation

What platforms are used for simulation and training? The short answer is all types, including PC-based, console-based, and mobile-based games.

PC Games

The obvious platform for Serious Games is the PC. After all, the PC is a serious piece of equipment on which people are used to learning. More importantly, the PC is easily accessible to all developers. Even the games already developed for the PC make it an attractive platform: PC games are generally modifiable, a rarity in the console world. In addition, games like *America's Army* are first-person-shooters (FPSs), a genre that holds a greater market share in the PC universe, due to the mouse and keyboard control scheme preferred by most FPS players.

Console Games

Full Spectrum Warrior has brought about a new revolution of training on consoles, which are roughly 10 times cheaper than PCs. However, there is a huge barrier to entry in the console market. Console manufacturers typically require a minimum run of any console title, and charge an upfront royalty for each game printed. Therefore, if the minimum run is 100,000, while the royalty per title is $10 and the manufacturing costs another $5 per unit, a minimum run could cost $1.5 million.

This extra royalty cost is why Pandemic is selling *Full Spectrum Warrior* commercially—with a code used to activate the training mode. Without the commercial sales that cover most of the printing run, each training copy would be far too expensive. The training version is much more difficult than the commercial version of the game, and would not be much fun for the average consumer.

Of course, development costs remain the same whether the game is sold commercially or not. It's the unit cost to the user that is dramatically changed by using console-based games, not the cost of development.

Mobile Games

Mobile games may be the most exciting medium for games for training. These games run on Palms, Pocket PCs, portable game machines, cell phones, or countless other devices. As of late 2004, the mobile game training market is a virtually untapped venue for training, but that situation may change in the very near future. NDL, the company behind the GameBryo game engine used in *Elder Scrolls III: Morrowind* and *Freedom Force vs. the Third Reich* has launched GameBryo S|T, targeted at the simulation and training industry, which includes a mobile component that allows training on the Pocket PC.

However, the Pocket PC is just the beginning, with new technologies like embedded graphics processors and OpenGL ES. Portable devices are gaining in capability to support simulation and training applications. This is remarkable because the simulator can literally be carried onto the battlefield. Imagine a soldier is sent on a mission in a city and receives training with an environmental database of the city. When the soldier is deployed, the mobile simulator (say, a Palm Pilot with a GPS component) can be taken along, used to check proposed paths, and receive database updates in real time. As the soldier examines the environment, his reports can be correlated with those of other soldiers using similar devices. The mobile device could even contain preplanned exit routes for each building, secondary paths, and locations of real-world snipers and other enemy combatants.

Moreover, of course, the fact that mobile games can be developed much faster and cheaper than PC or console applications makes them very attractive training options as well.

How to Get Involved

For a game developer, the concept of using a game not just to entertain but also to educate may be an interesting proposition. However, few if any know where to begin.

Create a Serious Game

The most obvious, and yet hardest, way to get involved in the Serious Games industry is to build a Serious Game: hire a subject matter expert, or happen to be one on some topic that requires training, and build a game that teaches this in a fun way. Many games in the Serious Games industry were created this way; for example, Atomic Games developed *Close Combat: Marines*, for the U.S. Marine Corps. Ben Sawyer developed *Virtual U*, won acclaim at the Independent Games Festival, and then started the Serious Games Initiative and the Serious Games Summit. The list continues to grow, and so do the opportunities.

Get on a team and make a game that trains. Build the next version of *Typing of the Dead*, a Sega shooter modified to teach typing, or maybe a piano tutor that is fun to play. Take any topic and create a game to train on it. Just make something, anything, and then build a game around it, even a mod. Then use this to woo prospective Serious Game employers, or contractors.

CASE STUDY 1.6.2: NONMILITARY TRAINING

"Designing a game for a non-entertainment purpose is not a trivial undertaking," says Ben Sawyer, co-founder of Digital Mill and the leader of the Serious Games Initiative. "Sure, we've all seen those trivia games people design to help learn something. These types of games as learning devices have existed for years. We've even see lots of board games, paper war games, and paper role-playing used by organizations for a long time now. However, just as computer and console videogames took over from their board game cousins, so too are computer-based training games.

"Besides the military, many other fields are applying the techniques and talents of game developers to training and learning. Thanks to efforts like the Serious Games Initiative (*www.seriousgames.org*) and The Education Arcade (*www.educationarcade.org*), there is a much broader and pervasive effort to build a market for next-generation game-based training and learning software.

"These groups, and others, are working to build the necessary acceptance of games as problem-solving tools, be it for training, learning, analytics, or advertising. If the successes reach the level of the military's early efforts, it may define a whole new class of games that let us game our way to a better future."

Some Great Examples of Current Nonmilitary Efforts

Virtual U (*www.virtual-u.org*): A game-based simulation of running a university. →

> ***Incident Commander*** (*www.breakawaygames.com*): A game that puts you in charge of a local accident, natural, or man-made catastrophe.
> ***Advanced Cardiac Life Support*** (*www.reallifetraining.com*): Where you are in charge of diagnosing and treating cardiac arrest patients.
> ***Infinite Teams*** (*www.infiniteams.com*): A game that teaches people how to work better in teams.
> ***Revolution*** (*www.educationarcade.com*): A game that recreates Colonial Williamsburg to teach students about the American Revolution.

Get Involved in an Open Source Serious Game Project

There is a growing trend toward using open source engines to develop Serious Games. With the financial clout of the simulation industry backing the open source projects, the odds of success are higher than many other open source projects. There are multiple open source engines being targeted by the Serious Games industry; the two most popular are Delta3D, which is in development by the Navy, and PANDA3D, which was developed by Disney. As they become more mature, these engines could also become a viable solution for mainstream game companies as well.

Dealing with the Culture Clash

The members of the gaming community and the simulation and training community are substantially different. When these people start working together there is bound to be a culture clash. Some problems are more obvious, like clothing, behavior, and language. Other problems are subtler, like business structures, and security clearances. [Zyda96] and [Zyda04] explain many more challenges to collaborations between the communities, and are an invaluable source for more information on this topic.

Language

The language barrier between simulation and gaming industries is subtler than the difference between English and French, or between hip and stuffy. The actual vocabulary in the simulation and training industry is completely different from the vocabulary of the gaming industry. When a gamer uses the acronym NPC in front of someone in simulation, he will draw a blank stare. Gamers recognize NPC as "Non Player Character," a game character controlled by the computer, but the simulation industry uses the term "entity" instead. Gamers say "player character," the simulation industry says "avatar." Indeed, it is possible to have a perfectly intelligent conversation about a specific topic with neither party having any idea what the other is saying.

Make sure that both parties work at understanding the vocabulary of the other, and that neither assumes incompetence when the other doesn't recognize something that "should be obvious."

Social Structure

The games industry is casual, with people who work at any odd hours as long as they get the job done. The simulation industry has fixed schedules, dress codes, and the occasional casual Friday. Imagine trying to manage a team with members from both communities:

1. An engineer in the simulation group will show up at eight and begin to work.
2. At noon the first gamer comes in, and starts to play a game.
3. The engineer goes to lunch, comes back, and now there are two gamers playing together.
4. The engineer leaves at five with most of the gamers in the team only being there for an hour at most.
5. The engineer then goes home and complains to his wife about the lazy gamers.
6. The gamers leave at five in the morning wondering where all the simulation engineers have gone.

This seems like a problem for management, but it causes trouble for everyone. The gamers may need to get information from the simulation engineers and not be able to get it. The engineers may want to add a feature to the engine and not be able to contact the gamers. Everyone gets mad, disengages from the group, then quits, and the project fails.

Being aware of the fact that this situation can happen will help prevent some of the problems, but finding the perfect solution is difficult because neither party is wrong: they are just different. When working in a multidisciplinary group this diverse, working through the problems will always be a challenge, but the outcome is usually worth the effort.

Economics Again

Many Serious Games customers, including the government, recognize that game developers do not always operate with the same business structure as conventional government contractors do. Therefore, they are experimenting with new contract structures. For example, *Full Spectrum Warrior* was co-developed by Pandemic and ICT, with the Army using the game for training and Pandemic getting the consumer publishing rights. This appears to have been a successful model, so expect to see more of it in the future. In addition, the government awards grants. Small Business Innovative Research Grants, or SBIRs, allow small businesses to create innovative technologies. Many Serious Games companies are using grants to fund development.

Secret Clearance

A major difference between the games industry and the simulation industry is security clearance. Security clearance is a must for almost every employee of a simulation company. Those who do not qualify are limited in the types of projects on which they can work. Employing people who do not qualify for secret or top-secret clearance will make it more difficult to pursue some Serious Games opportunities. In fact, everyone involved in the development and testing of a Serious Game, which uses information deemed secret, needs to have clearance. This includes beta testers and end users as well.

Now, obviously, *America's Army* has been released to the public, but the sensitivity of the information provided is not a matter of national security. However, if the cockpit of certain vehicles were accurately reproduced, this would cause the game to be considered secret. In that case, fictional cockpit displays would be used for public release, and realistic versions reserved for training purposes.

Coming into this situation unprepared will cause the loss of valuable time and money. When pursuing Serious Games in the military domain, start adding the question: "Do you now possess or do you believe you would qualify for secret or top-secret clearance?" to the interview process. It will be worth it.

Conclusion

Being part of the Serious Games industry requires constant learning. Understanding how the industry works, what file formats educators are interested in, and what makes an effective Serious Game is not easy.

Go to next year's Serious Games Summit if you can. Try to attend I/ITSEC as well; it is the largest simulation conference in the world and is held in Orlando, Florida every fall. NDL, Anark, Bionatics, and many other conventional games industry middleware providers had booths there recently. The potential for future growth for these companies in Serious Games is staggering. Take advantage of this same trend.

References

[Prensky00] Prensky, M., *Digital Game-based Learning*, McGraw-Hill, 2000.

[Proctor02] Proctor, M. D., Williams, Wilburn C. Jr., "Interoperable Training through a Simulation Game," SISO Conference (2002).

[Zyda96] National Research Council, *Modeling and Simulation: Linking Entertainment and Defense*, National Academy Press, 1996.

[Zyda04] Zyda, M., and Mayberry, A., "From Viz-Sim to VR to Games: How We Built a Hit Game-based Simulation," available online at *www.npsnet.org*, September 6, 2004.

Also see *www.smithpa.com* for a frequently updated "further reading" section.

1.7

Creating a Successful Freelance Game Development Business

François Dominic Laramée

fdl@francoisdominiclaramee.com

Long hours, interminable projects, bad bosses, and layoffs are but a handful of the reasons why some game developers forego the relative security of regular paychecks and create their own freelance businesses. The rewards of self-employment are such that most of them never go back to regular jobs, except under extreme financial duress. However, going into business is a risky proposition, and one not suited to everyone.

This article summarizes the techniques developed by the author, over a period of seven years, to minimize the risks associated with a freelance business. Valuable insight gathered when the author hosted the Freelancer's Roundtables at the GDC from 2001 to 2003 [Laramée01, Laramée02] and while he prepared his GDC 2004 lecture "The Well-Fed Freelancer: A Survival Guide in 24 Easy Lessons," [Laramée04] is also presented.

Should You Make the Switch?

Before you invest in a home office, ask yourself whether freelancing would be good for you:

- Will you develop an ulcer if you go three months without receiving a check?
- Will insecurity cause friction between you and your spouse?
- Do you love chatting with co-workers over lunch or coffee every day?
- Do you have nightmares before important meetings and presentations?
- Do you have trouble organizing your own life?
- Do you enjoy being able to delegate responsibility?
- Do you have trouble handling rejection?
- Are you afraid you'll procrastinate and spend all day watching soap operas?
- Are you too timid to call a client, repeatedly, until he pays what he owes you?

If you have answered "yes" to most of these questions, freelancing might not be your best choice. Perhaps you should consider going into business with partners, or merely changing jobs.

What Kind of Business Do You Want?

Some choose freelancing as their main career path, while others do it part-time while holding a regular job, or on an intermittent basis to fulfill specific goals, like saving for a vacation or a down payment on a house. Whatever your situation, you must know the skills you can sell, and the companies likely to buy them.

Generalists

Generalist freelancers take on a variety of roles, often at a moment's notice, and routinely handle multiple projects of wildly different durations in parallel.

For example, in 2004, this author received assignments in game design, translation, artificial intelligence, business consulting, book and magazine writing, editing, live event organization, teaching, and comedy writing. Some lasted 30 minutes and had to be completed within 24 hours; the longest required about three months of full-time effort.

Generalists fare well in most environments. They can often rely on a small stable of regular clients to provide most of their income, particularly in geographical areas where few experienced developers live.

Content Specialists

3D artists, audio specialists, some programmers, scriptwriters, and other professionals who provide well-defined, isolated game components fall into this category. They can literally set up shop anywhere; well-designed character models, for example, can be plugged into an engine with a minimum of back and forth between freelancer and client, so it doesn't matter if the two are next-door neighbors or if they live on different continents.

The amount of repeat business that a content specialist will receive varies a lot; an artist can work on a project for years, while a piece of code might be paid for once and used in several products. If your perspectives are weak in this regard, do not hesitate to take advantage of geographic freedom and market yourself far and wide.

Process Specialists

Producers, lead designers, and project salvage specialists are intricately involved in the corporate process. That makes it difficult for them to become freelancers; the few who succeed tend to be *very* senior people whose tremendous credentials overwhelm clients' natural reluctance to risk so much of their projects on external resources. Even then, process specialists must spend significant amounts of time in their clients' offices, interacting with the rest of the team. Thus, many of them live in high-density game development areas, like California or Texas, while the others travel extensively.

Setting Your Priorities

Before you start your freelance business, you must define the criteria by which you will judge its success. Do you want to work fewer hours, and have more time to spend with your family? Choose your projects? Make more money? Work from home, and move to the mountains? Acquire prestige within the game development community? Make games that the usual studio structure can't develop profitably?

Be honest with yourself. You can't be satisfied unless you aim for goals you really care about. And once you set your priorities, stick to them: judging your own success by someone else's standards will get you nowhere. If you want to work three days a week and use the rest to take care of your children, to write a novel, or to volunteer at the Red Cross, who cares if you earn less than you could as a studio executive?

Business Priorities

However, within the boundaries of your work, your priorities must be:

- Completing projects on deadline
- Generating new and repeat business
- Maintaining your skills
- Managing your money

Nothing else matters. If your office is a little messy, clean it up—but only after you return that new client's telephone call.

The Freelancer's Finances

In any business, the ultimate key to success lies in making sensible financial decisions. For freelancers, this means selling services at optimal prices, and managing cash flow effectively.

Your Target Income

First, you must determine how much revenue you have to generate every year to meet your goals and obligations. Again, depending on why you want to freelance, this might be significantly more *or significantly less* than what you earn right now. Don't lose sight of your goals, even when money is involved.

At the very least, the amounts you invoice to customers must cover the following:

Living expenses. How much must you contribute to your household every month? What do you need to be happy? Make a reasonable budget, and include everything you need and want: rent/mortgage payments, transportation, insurance, clothing, vacation, petty cash, groceries, cable TV, savings, and so forth.

Income tax. Fill out a tax return in reverse, starting with the after-tax income you need for your household budget, and determine the required pre-tax, after-expenses income.

Business expenses. You will need a new computer every two to three years, software, office furniture, books, Internet access (don't forget anti-virus and firewall software), postage, trips to trade shows, training, transportation, professional services, and various supplies. Talk to a tax specialist to see what you can write off, what you must amortize over several years, and how you can use your home office as a deduction. Typical expenses amount to about 20% of sales every year, give or take 5%. Yours might be higher, especially if you need to lease office space or hire an assistant, but tax authorities frown upon anything in excess of 50%.

Case Study 1.7.1 includes a simple target income calculation.

CASE STUDY 1.7.1: FINANCIAL PLANNING

Here is a sample grid to help you plan your business' finances:

Sales Objectives	Value	Formula	Result
Monthly household needs	$2,500	× 12	$30,000
Average tax rate	30%	$30,000 / 70%	$42,800
Expenses	$10,000	$42,000 + $10,000	$52,800

Working Hours	Value	Result
52 weeks × 5 days	260 days	260
Minus: Vacation	20 days	240
Minus: Holidays	10 days	230
Minus: Sick days	5 days	225
Minus: Trade shows	15 days	210
Total, at 7 hours per working day:		1,470 hours

Billable Hours	Value	Result
Working Hours	1,470 hours	1,470
Minus: Training	200 hours	1,270
Minus: Banking and invoicing	30 hours	1,240
Minus: Shopping for supplies	20 hours	1,220
Minus: Marketing and promotion	150 hours	1,070
Minus: Office maintenance	25 hours	1,025
Minus: Various contingencies	25 hours	1,000

Hourly Rate

Basic average rate:	$52,800 / 1,000 hrs = $52.80 per hour
"Rule of 800" target rate:	$52,800 / (80% × 1,000 hrs) = $66 per hour

→

The Rule of 800: Calculating Your Billable Hours

Next, you must determine how many of your working hours you will be able to bill to clients. Again, refer to Case Study 1.7.1 for an example.

First, find out how many hours a year you will spend working. Take into account the length of your normal workweek, vacation, holidays, sick days, and travel time going back and forth from your home to trade shows and clients' premises.

Then, subtract time spent on tasks not directly related to client assignments, like marketing your services, banking, shopping for supplies, invoicing, training, cleaning up the office, installing software upgrades, and handling of all the other chores someone else would be taking care of in an ordinary company.

For most full-time freelancers, this computation will result in about 1,000 billable hours a year. However, you may want to cut that number by 20%, to about 800, to account for slow periods (which you can't always spend training) and for bad payers.

Your Target Hourly Rate

To determine your hourly rate, divide target income by billable hours. This is an average; on occasion, you will have to accept a lower rate because a client has limited resources or a project is just too interesting to pass up. This is another reason to apply the Rule of 800: having a higher base rate will give you a margin with which to work.

In most cases, the calculations in Case Study 1.7.1 will yield a rate that is about twice an employee's hourly salary for similar work. This is perfectly normal; the client expects a higher fee because he does not have to pay office space, benefits, vacation time, and so forth. That, plus the fact that clients only pay you when they actually assign work to you, is what makes your higher hourly rate more economical in real terms.

Financial Safety Margins

[Laurance88] suggests setting aside the equivalent of three months' living expenses and three months' business expenses before you launch your business. This is enough to bridge the gap between your last paycheck and the first payments you will receive from clients, 30 to 60 days after you have delivered the work.

Then, to assure your business' long-term viability, gather an emergency fund twice as large—and restore it as fast as possible after drawing funds from it. Otherwise, a few months without assignments or a big client going out of business while he owes you money will leave you in financial difficulty.

Other Considerations

The pricing method outlined previously will work in most cases, but be wary of the extremes:

- Even if you need little money, do not undersell your services. Clients often assume that "cheap" equals "shoddy."

- If you determine that you need $100 an hour for work that full-time employees do for $30,000 a year, your business is unsustainable. Change your assumptions.
- If you constantly find yourself turning down business because you're too busy, you might be able to raise your prices at no risk.
- If you're in a bind, you might have to take assignments at discount prices. The shorter the better in this case, because you don't want to tie up time that you could sell at premium rates later on.

Marketing Freelance Services

Now comes the most delicate part of the operation: securing enough assignments to make your business self-sufficient. This requires excellent knowledge of your market and a significant promotional effort.

Who Will Retain You?

Companies hire when they have needs, and only if the service fulfilling the need can be acquired at an economically sensible price. Of course, "economically sensible" is a relative term:

- In some jurisdictions, game companies receive government subsidies when they create full-time jobs, but not when they subcontract. Thus, it becomes almost impossible to convince them to hire freelancers for anything that could be done by employees.
- The greater and more urgent the need, the higher the fees that the company will be willing to pay.
- An artist who lives in Montana will be able to charge more for the same work if she sells it to a California company than to one based in Kentucky, because the price of an employee is higher on the West Coast.
- Freelancers living in countries where the cost of living is low will have an easier time underselling their foreign competition.

In general, you will have to prove that giving you a freelance assignment will result in better, cheaper, and/or more convenient work for the company. This is not as difficult as it might seem, because the cost of a regular employee is much higher than his or her salary: hiring costs, office space, computer equipment, benefits, social charges, management overhead, vacation, paid holidays, and layoff costs all have to be taken into account. Examples of situations in which hiring an employee at $30 an hour might end up costlier and less practical than hiring a freelancer at two to three times the rate include:

Frequent but small assignments. Ex: Sound effect design, translation, press releases, and second opinion on management decisions.
Very specialized knowledge. Ex.: Music composition, screenwriting.
Seasonal overflows. Ex.: Beta testing, trade shows.

Unusual tasks. Ex.: Business plan writing, staffing, employee training.

Disaster recovery. Ex.: Project salvage, critical bug fixes, filling the gap between an employee's departure and a new hire.

Shortage of experienced people in a specialty. Ex.: Senior programmers, game design.

A volatile job market. Why go to the expense of a formal hiring process when the employee is likely to quit within three to six months?

Your Marketing Targets

That being said, it is always easier to secure freelance assignments from people who already know and trust you. Talk to former co-workers and employers first, and once you complete an assignment with a company, keep asking them for more (unless the first project went horribly wrong). You can expect repeat business to account for 80% or more of your income after a couple of years.

That's the good news. The bad news is that existing relationships are the *only* reliable source of assignments. Finding work in any other way will require time, effort, and the stoic handling of many rejections.

Thus, you should spend your promotion effort on the following, in decreasing order of importance:

Repeat business. Call your current clients a month after completing a project, and every three months thereafter.

Former clients/co-workers who change companies. Producers, in particular, know when a project team needs assistance, and they often recommend the freelancers to hire.

Referrals. Make contacts at local institutions where people with limited knowledge of the industry are likely to call for information. Good relationships with schools and chambers of commerce might be especially helpful.

Visibility. Build a Web site advertising your credentials and current projects. Write for magazines and books like this one. Teach at a local college. Get involved in the IGDA. People who have seen your name before are likely to think of you when they have a project to assign.

Companies you can meet in person. If you can visit a client's offices during off-peak periods or set up a meeting at an IGDA chapter event, do so. Face time is valuable.

Trade shows. You can meet many people at E3 or the GDC, but they will have limited time for you. Make sure to book key meetings at least four to six weeks in advance.

Direct marketing. When you call, write, or e-mail potential clients, concentrate on those not actively looking for full-time staff; they will have more time to look at your proposals.

One final word: never stop marketing yourself. Companies go out of business all the time. A regular client might grow until it becomes cheaper for him to hire a full-time employee to take over your duties. Or a new manager with her own stable of freelancers might replace your key contact. As a rule of thumb, you shouldn't let one client account for more than a third of your income on a consistent basis, because if this client ever disappears, you will be in trouble. On the other hand, marketing takes time, and time is what you sell, so marketing costs you money; be relentless in your promotion efforts, but not foolish.

Handling Bad Debts

Speaking of trouble, what should you do if a client refuses to pay you?

Unfortunately, your options are limited. [Laurance88] says that law firms won't get involved unless a debt of $10,000 to $25,000 has been outstanding for at least six months. Collection agencies might present an alternative, but they will cost you 20% to 50% of the amount they recover, and in case of failure, you are still going to have to get a court order and have it executed by bailiffs—at your own expense.

Indeed, the best way to deal with bad debts is to not let them happen in the first place. Protect your interests:

Keep the first assignment small. This way, if the client shows bad faith, you have limited your losses.

Initiation of service fee. When dealing with a new client, or starting any large project, ask for 20% to 50% of the assignment's value up front. This establishes good faith on both parts.

Split large assignments into several milestones. [Onder02] also recommends making payments part of the project schedule: inscribe payment due dates in the contract, and put in a clause stating that any delay will push back all further milestone deliveries accordingly.

Avoid making the final payment too large. Once you have delivered all of the work, a bad client has no further incentive to pay you.

Apply these rules to everyone, even people you know and like. A former co-worker and friend still owes this author thousands of dollars, four years after a project's completion.

Be careful if you spread the word about the bad client. It is all too easy to acquire a reputation as a troublemaker—and a libel lawsuit can ruin your life, whether you win or lose in court.

Mark Barrett went directly from college to being a freelance screenwriter, and he wouldn't have it any other way.

"Freelancing affords me two main benefits: I get to move from project to project, which keeps my interest high, and whenever I'm not employed I get blocks of time to pursue my own initiatives, some of which also generate income. Plus, since most of my freelancing is done via telecommute, I'm able to live where I want."

Since Mark's family has never seen him work any other way, obtaining their support for his freelance venture was not an issue. "While a steady paycheck might provide us greater liquidity—primarily because we wouldn't have to keep reserves on hand for the lean months—I think that would be the only direct benefit of being an employee. Having said that, if the lean months ever turned into lean years, the level of support I am currently receiving would probably drop precipitously."

Mark receives most of his assignments through word of mouth. "I am almost always contacted by people who know my work and my reputation from a trusted third party, rather than because of claims I have made about myself. Since it can be difficult for a company to get over the fear associated with hiring outside workers, particularly offsite ones, first contacts usually happen when the prospective client is in trouble: the original writer or designer failed, and there is little time in which to correct the damage and finish the job."

For Mark, the most important quality freelancers must possess is discipline. "If you are not comfortable working alone and being alone, and if you do not have a history of initiating and completing your own projects, freelancing is not for you."

Managing Your Schedule

Freelancers sell time. It is imperative that you learn to assess workloads accurately, and that you always know how much of your time is already sold.

Figure 1.7.1 is a fictionalized version of the author's schedule as of January 17, 2005. Only the first quarter of the year is represented in the figure to fit the page, but using a spreadsheet containing a full year's schedule is recommended. Darkened lines indicate weeks in the past and weeks with immovable constraints: vacation time (January 31) and the GDC (March 3).

Several columns indicate the number of days allocated to assignments already received, and the income that these assignments are expected to generate. "Regular" income can be predicted with relative certainty, as it is based on hourly or daily contracts; "royalty" income is an estimate that will have to be adjusted as the checks flow in.

The "safety margin" section indicates that cash flow variations will not become a problem during the quarter, since the freelancer's bank account will never dip below the equivalent of a 3.5-month cushion; indeed, the quarter will end with a sizeable surplus, even if the four days that remain unallocated are never sold to a client.

The "days left" section is the one that helps plan for new assignments. If a client calls on January 17 to offer a three-day assignment, it is possible to promise delivery by the end of the week of February 25 without changing anything to the schedule for existing projects. If the client is in a hurry, some shuffling will become necessary; for example, by postponing the next two weeks' comedy writing to February, deadlines permitting.

Finally, the "statistics" section indicates whether the freelancer's goals in terms of daily and quarterly income are being met. In this case, everything is fine.

Q1 2005 Work and Income Calendar

Dates	Days		Work Assignments							Days Left		Income			Safety Margin ($12,300)		$/day	Statistics	
	Week	Off	Writing	Teach	Consult	Design	Comedy	A.I.	Total	Week	Cumul	Regular	Royalties	Total	Months	Dollars		% goal	% time
Jan.3	5						1	4	5	0	0	$1,600		$1,600	6.8	$12,936	$320	12.6%	7.7%
Jan.10	5		1					3	5	0	0	$1,200	$100	$1,300	7.1	$13,277	$280	23.2%	15.4%
Jan.17	5		1				1	3	5	0	0	$1,200		$1,200	7.3	$13,515	$267	32.8%	23.1%
Jan.24	5		2		1		2		5	0	0	$450	$150	$600	7.0	$13,154	$223	37.6%	30.8%
Jan.31	5	5							0	0	0			$0	6.0	$12,192	$223	37.6%	38.5%
Feb.7	5		1		2		2		5	0	0	$900		$900	6.0	$12,131	$214	44.8%	46.2%
Feb.14	5		2				2		4	1	1			$0	5.1	$11,169	$184	44.8%	53.8%
Feb.21	5		1				2		3	2	3			$0	4.1	$10,208	$167	44.8%	61.5%
Feb.28	5				2		2		4	1	4	$1,000	$250	$1,250	4.4	$10,496	$176	54.8%	69.2%
Mar.7	5	5							0	0	4			$0	3.5	$9,535	$176	54.8%	76.9%
Mar.14	5					5			5	0	4	$2,500		$2,500	5.0	$11,073	$216	74.8%	84.6%
Mar.21	5					5			5	0	4	$2,500		$2,500	6.4	$12,612	$247	94.8%	92.3%
Mar.28	5					5			5	0	4	$2,500	$100	$2,600	8.0	$14,250	$272	115.6%	100.0%
Total	65	10	8	2	3	15	13	10	51			$13,850	$600	$14,450					
Goals	65	10							55			$12,000	$500	$12,500					

FIGURE 1.7.1   *Sample schedule.*

Scheduling Flexibility

In addition, you should maintain a detailed two-week schedule in electronic form on your computer. (Paper won't do, because you will have to update it frequently.) The reason for this is that when a client calls, odds are he'll want to schedule a meeting or hand you a short assignment immediately; the two-week schedule lets you determine if and when that will be possible.

Vacation

Don't be afraid to go away if you want to. Most jobs can wait: in seven years, this author has lost only about 20 hours' worth of assignments because of vacation-related unavailability. The period between December 15 and January 15 is always a good choice, as many game development companies shut down for the holidays and won't require any urgent work in the preceding and following weeks. Summertime might be a different matter: companies that must ship titles for Christmas might need a lot of help.

Downtime

At some point in your freelance career, you will probably experience a period of several months without assignments. (In seven years, this author has gone through this experience twice, roughly for three months each time.) If you have accumulated a comfortable financial cushion, this downtime need not be a source of stress, and it may even give you the perfect opportunity to learn new skills and initiate projects that you might not have attempted otherwise.

Conclusion

With each passing year, more opportunities for freelancers arise in the games industry. With proper marketing and financial management, a freelance business can be extremely rewarding. The tricks and techniques explained in this article will help the self-employed maximize their odds of success.

References

[Laramée01] Laramée, F. D., "Tales from the Loneliest Frontier: GDC 2001 Freelancers' Roundtable Moderator's Report," available online at *www.gamedev.net/reference/business/features/freelancer/*.

[Laramée02] Laramée, F. D., "GDC 2002 Moderator's Report: The Freelancers' Roundtable," available online at *www.gamedev.net/reference/articles/article1816.asp*.

[Laramée04] Laramée, F. D., "The Well-Fed Freelancer: A Survival Guide in 24 Easy Lessons," GDC lecture, slides available at *www.gdconf.com/archives/2004/index.htm*.

[Laurance88] Laurance, R., *Going Freelance: A Guide for Professionals*, John Wiley & Sons, 1988.

[Onder02] Onder, B., "Negotiating a Freelance Game Design Contract," in *Game Design Perspectives*, Charles River Media, 2002.

2

PUBLISHERS AND DEVELOPERS

2.0

Introduction

The games industry's canonical business model remains the developer-publisher-retailer continuum. This second section of the book explores the inner workings of each of its components and discusses such issues as the consequences of the ever-increasing cost of game development; concentration of the publishing world as a result of the high risks of game marketing; how developers can make the most of their relationships with publishers; the power wielded by retailers; who makes money from games, how, and when; and how a publishing company takes a game to market.

The articles in this section explore these issues from the (at times contradictory) points of view of developers and publishers:

- In Article 2.1, "The Top Ten Misconceptions New Game Developers Have about Publishers," Mason McCuskey, president of independent development company Spin Studios, explains the mistaken assumptions that mine the relationships between some developers and their publishers.
- In Article 2.2, "The Role of Each Entity in Game Publishing," Kathy Schoback, chair emeritus of the International Game Developers Association and a long-time publishing executive, discusses the roles of all of the entities involved in game publishing, including lesser-known contributors such as testing studios and regional distributors.
- In Article 2.3, "The Many Faces of Game Development," François Dominic Laramée presents a taxonomy of the game development world and profiles a number of representative companies.
- In Article 2.4, "A Publishing Project: From Concept to Launch and Beyond," François Dominic Laramée explains the process through which publishers bring games to the retail market.
- In Article 2.5, "Diagnosing Immaturity in Development Studios: Symptoms and Treatment," designer and producer Steve Bocska and management specialist Jodi Regts describe the maturing process that game development studios must go through in order to achieve perenniality.
- Finally, in Article 2.6, "The Producer, Friend or Foe?," senior producer and IGDA director Mitzi McGilvray explains how developers can establish harmonious relationships with the producers assigned to their projects by the publisher.

2.1

The Top Ten Misconceptions New Game Developers Have about Publishers

Mason McCuskey

mason@spin-studios.com

For most game developers, the most difficult problem isn't 3D math or complicated AI systems. In fact, it isn't even how to make a game, but rather how to get that game out to the gamers. To many aspiring game developers, the definition of success is getting one of their games on the shelf at a major retailer—it brings profit, as well as the prestige of being able to walk in to a retailer anywhere in the country and show your creation to the masses.

Unfortunately, the path toward that goal is shrouded in mystery. Publishers seem to be magical beasts, capable of granting wishes or destroying fortunes, often for no better reason than their own whims or desires. Some games they publish, other games they don't, and most developers don't know why one game, seemingly inferior to another, gets a spot on the shelf at the local videogame store.

This article attempts to shed some light on that, by enumerating the top 10 misconceptions of new game development teams regarding publishers. We'll spare you the suspense and start with the most prominent misconception, then progress downward to number 10, showing you at each stage what the misconception is and why it's detrimental, as well as some things you can do to increase the chances of landing a publishing deal.

#1: You Can Get a Publishing Deal on a Design Doc Alone

This is easily the most common misconception of all. Most amateur developers elaborate master plans that go something like this:

1. Create a 400-page design document outlining the entire game in excruciating detail.

2. Send this tome to a publisher, who will carefully read it and realize the greatness contained within.

3. Achieve fame and retire on the royalty checks the publisher sends you.

Unfortunately, that's not how it usually works. If you're Sid Meier, Will Wright, or Bruce Shelley, you might have a chance of getting a game funded this way, but otherwise, this method is not going to work.

Obviously, to land a publishing contract you're going to need a good design. However, the general rule of thumb is that once you have that design, you have about 10% of what you need to approach a publisher. The other 90% includes:

- A solid playable demo
- A good team with strong skills and a proven track record
- A whole slew of other budgeting, marketing, treatment, and scheduling documents ([Powell05] and [Bartlett05] describe the contents of the submission package—and how to approach publishers once you have assembled one—in some detail.)

So, how big should your design doc be? You should strive to create enough documentation to adequately describe your game, but no more. Einstein once said, "Things should be made as simple as possible, but no simpler." Take this advice to heart when writing your design doc. If you're developing a highly complex war game, you might need a few hundred pages explaining how the simulation works. If you're designing a simple puzzle game, you might be able to get by with a dozen pages, maybe less.

In fact, disregard the page count entirely. Have your design doc address all of the major variables in your game: enemies, levels, player actions, back story, and so forth. You need to think about all of these matters, and more. If it turns out that you can adequately describe a topic in half a page of bullet points, then keep those bullet points and move on. If it turns out that you need dozens of pages, then you need dozens of pages.

An important point: write your design doc with your development team as your audience, not the publisher. The primary purpose of a design doc is to explain your game to the people who will be developing it. Rely on other documents (such as treatments or key feature lists) to convey your game to potential publishers.

#2: Publishers Are Your Biggest Fans

This misconception probably accounts for more broken development deals than any other. Realize that publishers are not game players. Specifically, this means that:

- Not all publishers like playing games.
- Not all publishers know gamer lingo.
- Not all publishers know how your real-time strategy game is different from its competitors.
- Not all publishers have your interests at heart.

Publishers Are Not Game Players

Sure, most publishers have game players working for them, but just because they publish games doesn't mean that everyone there loves videogames. Moreover, even the people there who do like to play games won't want to (or won't have the time to) play through yours entirely, getting stuck on the hard puzzles and trying for days to beat the tough bosses.

This means that any demo you send to a publisher should also contain walk-through documentation, and preferably a way to quickly jump to the game's most exciting parts. A guided tour is also a good idea, as is anything that will let the publisher see why they would want to publish your game, without having to actually play it. You want to make it very easy for them to see why your game is better than the other submissions they have received—you need to hook them as quickly as possible.

Don't Assume That Publishers Know the Lingo

They know some of it—for example, genres—but they don't usually know the meaning of words such as *llama* or *camper* or *LPB*. In addition, even if you're pretty sure they do understand these terms, you should leave them out of your documentation, because they're a form of slang and make you appear unprofessional.

Publishers Don't Know What Makes Your Game Unique

Taking this to heart is essential to developing the proper demo and pitch. Although it might appear on the surface that publishers are only interested in me-too titles, underneath, most publishers want something that's new—just not *too* new. By explicitly presenting what makes your title unique, you do yourself a big favor.

Publishers Pursue Their Own Interests

Finally, realize that publishers do not always have your own financial, creative, or artistic interests at heart. Both parties are in it to make as much money as possible, which naturally puts them at odds with each other. For example, what you see as an awesome design idea, the publisher might see as a financial risk, while the licensed property the publisher wants you to use in the game to drive its sales might seem unnecessarily stifling to you. Contract negotiations are a difficult and sometimes distressing process for this reason.

You can spend all day debating whether this is good, but at the end of the day, it is reality. Just remember this fact, and you'll go a long way toward establishing empathy toward your publisher. Knowing what the other side is after is often your most valuable tool when negotiating.

#3: The Game Stands On Its Own

Another thing some aspiring developers assume is that quality is everything: the game stands alone, the good games will naturally get publishing deals, and it doesn't matter who you are, just as long as your game is "cool enough."

This is referred to as the *inventor mindset*. Inventors live and die by the strength of their ideas, and they tend to think (incorrectly) that the rest of the world does too. We game developers, being inventors of a sort, also live in the idea plane, so even though we routinely see horrible excuses for interactive entertainment littering the shelves, we have a habit of thinking that the strength of our games will single-handedly carry us to greatness.

The reality is that having a strong game idea and a strong demo still isn't enough. Even if your game is almost entirely finished, potential publishers will still look at the people behind the game, and they'll still rely on demographic and marketing data to determine if a game gets the green light. In addition, there's a whole bunch of other variables in the equation too, including how well you pitch your game, how good your company's financial picture is, how responsive you are to change, how well you connect with people, and even how prompt you are about returning telephone calls.

One big variable developers forget to account for is the track record of the team making a game. Publishers look at this very carefully—they want to know for certain that the team is going to be able to deliver the final product, on time and on budget.

On a related note, publishers also look at how mature the team is. Even if your team consists of proven professionals, if this is their first game together, a publisher will be a little concerned. It takes a professional development team some time to find a groove, and there's no guarantee that even an all-star team will be able to click and deliver a solid product right away. Of course, every team will have new members—but to have the best chances of getting a publishing deal, the core of the team will need to have a few successes under their collective belt.

So, what do you do if this doesn't describe your company? The best thing you can do to help yourself is get the game as close to done as you can. If your game is at beta and looking solid, publishers are going to be less concerned about your team's dynamics. Not completely unconcerned, but less concerned.

#4: Any Deal Is a Good Deal

Getting a publishing deal is a great reason to throw a party, especially if it's the first for your new game development shop. However, your goals extend much farther than that important milestone. Ultimately, you must be concerned with distribution (e.g., how many stores your game gets into), the advance money you will receive to pay for development, the royalty you will get for each copy sold, and how the relationship with this publisher works after the game is released. All of these things are important—they play a part in determining whether you'll still be in business long enough to finish your title and see it succeed.

It's hard to get a publishing deal. It's even harder to get one you can live with. Be careful about selling yourself short, about capitulating to any terms for the sake of getting a deal. Sometimes, no deal is better than a bad deal.

Think long and hard about the terms you need in a deal in order to survive. For example, it hurts you (and it hurts the publisher) to sign a deal with an advance so low that you go bankrupt before you complete the game. You can also doom yourself by setting your schedule too short, your scope too large, or by giving the publisher too much control over your company's future. You need to recognize your goals and your situation and bring those to the negotiating table to craft out a contract that won't kill you.

A basic negotiating skill is to identify your BATNA: Best Alternative To Negotiated Agreement. In other words, it's the alternative you have if you can't come to an agreement during the negotiation. For example, depending on your situation and how many publishers you've talked to, your BATNA might be to self-publish your game, or to go with another publisher's less-appealing (but still profitable) terms.

You should also know at what point a publisher's terms become worse than your BATNA. This is the point at which you abandon negotiations—you thank the publisher for their time, get up, and leave the room.

If you don't know your BATNA before you enter negotiations, you might very well come out of negotiations with a contract that's so horrible that it's worse than having no contract at all. Be careful.

#5: Publishers Negotiate through E-Mail

We "nerds" rely on e-mail much more than "normal" people do. We type at each other in IRC, we debate on ICQ, and sometimes we e-mail each other when we're within speaking distance. This works fine for us, but it's often detrimental when it comes to talking to, and especially negotiating with, a publisher.

The simple rule is, "never negotiate through e-mail." Pick up the telephone or arrange to speak face to face. E-mail is an impersonal way of communicating, good for conveying technical facts but embarrassingly bad for conveying the nuances of personality. When negotiating, these nuances matter as much as (and possibly more than) the words being spoken.

When you communicate with a publisher, use your voice as your primary communication device, backed up by e-mail. However, do not assume that publishers always return telephone calls. Most of the time they do, but everyone gets busy, forgets, or accidentally deletes someone's contact information, so err on the side of safety and don't be afraid to pick up the telephone just to ask "how's it going?"

Don't overdo it, however. Use good judgment, as if you were looking for a job. When in doubt, just ask the persons on the other end of the line when you should contact them next, and then don't call them back until then.

#6: Your Publisher Will Create a Schedule for Your Game

This one is partly true—usually, once you and your publisher agree to work together, you'll negotiate the dates of the milestones and what will be expected at each. However, this doesn't mean that you shouldn't develop a schedule on your own. If you approach a publisher without a definite finish date (backed up by a comprehensive project plan), you'll either look like someone who doesn't know what he's doing, or someone who is way too egotistical to be bothered with things such as due dates. Either way, it's a strike against you.

Of course, this shouldn't be the main reason why you write up a schedule. Like design docs, schedules are just as beneficial for you as they are for your publisher. Take the time to draft a schedule, and review it periodically to make sure it's accurate and that you're on track.

This is a big enough job that most game companies now have full-time producers and/or project managers, responsible for wrangling the dependencies of a project and making sure that everyone is working on the right thing at the right time.

#7: Make a Good Pitch to the Right Person and You're Good to Go

Most publishers have teams or bureaus of people who evaluate incoming submissions and decide which ones to publish. You might be able to isolate and pitch your game to one of these team members, but you usually won't be able to pitch to all of them at once. Therefore, even though your initial pitch to a publisher is important, it's not the only thing that matters.

When you pitch to a publisher, you should play your best cards, but you should also be truthful. Pitching the features that set your game apart from the competition is a smart move; saying you're in beta when you're not is asking for trouble.

Your pitch should be supported by paper materials that reiterate what you've just talked about. Your materials should project the best (accurate) image of your company and your product, as concisely as possible. Be professional—don't hard sell, and don't get too technical. Whet their appetite, show them the greatness of your ideas, and make sure they know whom to contact if they'd like to know more. Don't just give a sales@somewhere.com e-mail address—give complete contact information for a specific individual.

#8: All Publishers Are the Same

You owe it to yourself to pitch your game to as many different publishers as possible. However, you should also realize that not all publishers are the same. Some work with definite genres, platforms, or budgets, while others seem to be scattered all over the shelves.

Before you approach a publisher, make sure that your title would fit with their repertoire. Research titles they've already published, and ask them where they'd like to concentrate their efforts in the future.

In addition, play some of their games. This not only gives you a clever excuse to play more games, but also could give you a good sense of whether the publisher is right for you. Also, even though this should go without saying, buy the games or have the publisher give you some evaluation copies.

#9: Platform Doesn't Matter

Another facet of the "not all publishers are the same" misconception is the sister misconception that the platform you develop your game on doesn't matter. This is incorrect—don't develop your game for the easiest platform (the PC) thinking that you'll get a publishing deal and port it later. A much better approach is to choose the prominent platform for your particular genre (e.g., PC for real-time strategy, PS2 for sports), develop for that platform, and be ready to port to the other platforms if you and your publisher decide that it would be worth your time.

Sometimes this is easier said than done; some console manufacturers require large amounts of cash, an approval process, or even a signed deal with a prominent publisher before they'll give you access to the development kits. Try very hard to get a development kit, but don't give up if you can't. Just make sure the publisher knows that the demo they're seeing isn't running on the proper hardware, and that they know why.

#10: Publishers Are the Enemy

This last item is key. After the last nine misconceptions, you might find yourself thinking that a publisher is an enemy, an evil entity one must deal with in order to accomplish a greater good. It can't be stressed enough that this is not the case. Virtually all publishers are moral, ethical entities comprised of people trying to earn an honest living by providing entertainment to large audiences. You and the publisher might have different priorities and different approaches, but ultimately you are working toward the same end—you both want to release a good game.

Don't forget that a developer/publisher relationship is a win/win situation—the end result benefits both parties. Both you and the publisher make money when things go well, and lose money when they don't, so remember that publishers are your allies, not your enemies. With the right publisher, a developer can go farther than other developers, and with the right developer, a publisher can go farther than other publishers. Approach publishers in the spirit of cooperation and respect, and if everything works, you'll end up with a game on the shelves.

Conclusion

One could fill an entire book on the topic of how to get a publishing deal. This article has given you a start; you now know the 10 misconceptions that can sabotage your own efforts. However, you are far from knowing everything you need to secure a successful deal.

If you are seriously pursuing a deal, you need to do much more research. You also need to find a good lawyer, someone you trust who can look over contracts and show you where the gaping holes are. You might think that you can identify these holes on your own, but you can't—get a lawyer.

In addition, talk with other developers who have been there. All of them have opinions and things they wish they had done, or hadn't done. Find a developer with a situation similar to your own and talk to the deal-maker for that company—learning from the experience of others is always a good idea.

In addition, keep up with the times. The games industry changes very quickly, and people have been predicting the death of retail for a long time. Again, it all goes back to your own situation. Make sure you're doing things not because of some superficial reason ("I want to walk into the store and show my mom/spouse/arch-nemesis my game sitting there on the shelf!"), but because it's really the best move.

Finally, don't stop trying. The road to the store shelf is long, but many companies have walked it, and some have achieved tremendous success. You might be next. Good luck!

References

[Bartlett05] Bartlett, E., "Securing a Development Contract: The Art of Pitching," *Secrets of the Game Business*, 2nd Edition, Charles River Media, 2005.

[Powell05] Powell, J., "Showing Publishers What They Want to See," *Secrets of the Game Business*, 2nd Edition, Charles River Media, 2005.

2.2

The Role of Each Entity in Game Publishing

Kathy Schoback

kathy@igda.org

Delivering a game into a consumer's hands has become an increasingly complex, lengthy, and costly process. Members of the interactive entertainment industry constantly debate the relative importance of game developers as creative auteurs versus publishers as soulless businesspeople, or retailers as channel arbiters versus media as opinion mongers. However, financial and logistical market forces have created a system in which each "driver" entity on the highway to the consumer—developer, publisher, platform owner, retailer—is essential to the transaction, and profits accordingly. "Adjunct" entities that feed into the channel offer a plethora of service alternatives that reduce cost, save time, or improve quality along the channel and, ultimately, for consumers.

In this article, we examine the roles of 14 entities that collaborate to bring a game to market.

Game Developers

Without game developers, entertainment would no doubt be a duller and more complacent activity. Whether independent companies of 15 to 200 people or subsidiaries of larger publishers, developers create the immersive experiences that inspire millions to forego reality for fantasy. Game development involves the very technical disciplines of programming, including code optimization for target hardware, physics and artificial intelligence simulations, camera and interface development, and creation of tools to improve development efficiency. The art of game development lies with designers who envision everything from game balance to placement of doors in a level, artists who realize previously unimagined characters and worlds with an eye toward technical efficiency, and animators who marry a character's appearance and personality through motion. Producers keep the train on the track, identifying roadblocks before (or as) they occur and negotiating solutions among all stakeholders (see Figure 2.2.1).

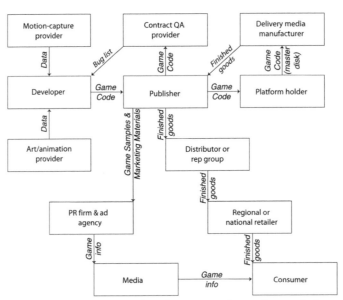

FIGURE 2.2.1   *Position of each entity in the product path for a console game.*

Full-Service Game Developers

Game developers in this category incorporate all the disciplines necessary to create millions of lines of game code from a single idea. Projects range from six-month, tightly focused opportunistic releases to three years of complex asset integration into a whole that is vast in scope. More than one recent project has exceeded five years and US$50 million to complete, although the cost for a current-generation console release on a single platform now ranges 12 to 36 months and US$3 to $8 million.

The proverbial brainstorm-turned-million-seller is rarer than industry aspirants care to believe. Of games actually published, the majority are based on intellectual property owned or controlled by the publisher, initiated by the publisher with a team whose qualifications (not the least of which is cost) complement that IP. Publishers can initiate "surefire" projects based on a blockbuster movie or book license, or "questionable" pet projects of a particular executive. Larger publishers can mine the seam of past releases for remakes, due to the hotly debated publisher practice of acquiring intellectual property rights to a promising developer's original game idea. Two truisms unite all these methods: a "no-brainer" concept does not guarantee a great game, and an offbeat idea, regardless of the source, sometimes sells spectacularly.

Developers interact primarily with their publisher and, on occasion, with the platform provider, who provides them with direct technical assistance for the target platform. Developers also promote themselves and their titles to the media, frequently in conjunction with their publisher.

Independent development companies work with publishers on a contract basis. The publisher pays the developer "advances" against a schedule of development milestones. Frequently, the publisher also grants a royalty per unit sold to the developer; however, the royalty is only paid once the publisher's advance payments have been recouped against sales volume. In one recent example, a developer was granted $4/unit royalty, but recoupment against significant development advances ensured the developer would only receive royalties after the 900,000th unit sold. Scenarios like this feed ongoing industry debates about more equitable revenue sharing for developers. Many developers have quietly resorted to building their target profit margin into their advance payment schedule.

Development groups also exist as wholly or partially owned subsidiaries of publishers. As employees of either the parent company or the subsidiary, internal team members draw corporate salary and benefits. Stock options, bonuses for achieving sales targets, and profit-sharing programs vary widely by publisher; the development community generally acknowledges that the relative stability of working for a major publisher goes hand in hand with a smaller piece of the profit pie on momentous successes.

Other funding alternatives such as venture capital, completion bond funding, and angel financing play a small but growing part in game development, and are addressed elsewhere in this book.

Historically, many development groups have gotten their technological start creating PC games. Wide availability of technical information and a small but active engineering community supported many of today's marquee developers as they created early hits such as *Doom*. Today, developers such as Bioware, id Software, Valve, and 3D Realms include user-creation modules in their games, with which their player communities can modify parts of their games. Many entry-level designers or programmers in the industry today earned their position through a compelling "mod" presented as part of their portfolio.

Development for today's consoles—Sony's PlayStation 2 computer entertainment system, the Nintendo Game Cube, and the Xbox videogame system from Microsoft—is harder to break into. The expense of proprietary development kits—up to US$10,000—and the requirement of a preexisting relationship with a publisher closes the door to all but the most innately talented startup groups with previous platform experience. Consequently, many developers earn their credentials in PC gaming, and then make the leap to console on the strength of proven technology, design, and relationships.

Motion-Capture Service Providers

As hardware platforms follow Moore's law of increasing computing power, consumers and publishers have demanded increasing realism in certain types of games. In particular, developers can now replicate the uniquely identifiable characteristics of human motion with great accuracy for the first time in gaming. Mechanical leg movements on a football player gliding as if on ice have been replaced by true running steps with the inherent force, momentum, and style of the original human player. To be sure, we cannot ignore the stunning contributions of painstaking manual animation to this advancement. However, for the speed and efficiency of achieving realism in human movement, we have motion-capture technology to thank.

Motion capture is the technological process by which scripted movements of human actors are "captured" by magnetic or optical sensors, yielding data that is then inserted into the game engine. "Mocap" is usually used when lifelike human movement is essential to the game concept. For example, a perfectly replicated signature move in a football videogame is a selling point to consumers playing as their favorite wide receiver, while a cartoon character might benefit from manual exaggeration of certain animations to emphasize its unreality. A mocap session is similar to a movie shoot, usually involving a director, a script or "moves list," an engineer manipulating the software that processes captured data, and actors selected for their ability to repeat the desired action sequence accurately. Once the session is complete, the animation team works through the raw data, tweaking an elbow position or sword arc until the model behaves exactly as desired in-game.

Developers access motion-capture facilities in two ways: the publisher makes its onsite studio available, with costs allocated internally to the project, or the publisher directly subcontracts an external mocap service provider. Only rarely does a developer possess its own mocap studio, as costs involve much more than purchasing the hardware. As with any marriage of the subjective with technology, mocap works best with trained specialists at every level. Publishers with key franchises requiring mocap (such as football games) can recoup on the investment and training for an in-house studio; for most others, mocap is contracted out at costs exceeding US $150,000 for a full-service session.

As demand has increased for motion-capture services, the competition among independent mocap studios has led to price pressure. Some leading providers have honed their service-side offering as a result, providing not only shoot management but also data processing, animation tuning, assistance with engine integration, and post-shoot troubleshooting. One provider has productized their data processing software, offering it for license independently of its services. All providers continue to refine the accessibility of data throughout their processes, so developers can benefit from the efficiency of mocap without sacrificing the artistry of key-framed animation.

Art and Animation Service Providers

The increase in computer processing capability in game hardware has provoked an exponential increase in the quantity of art assets required. Onscreen processing limits of several characters comprising a few hundred textured polygons have exploded to millions of polygons making up a main character, several AI characters, a 3D deformable environment with actionable objects, extensive special effects, and realistic environmental lighting. The resulting productivity demands sometimes require outsourcing of the art production process.

Generally, the publisher and developer agree upon the outsourcing of art at contract. A full-service developer might bring an art group to the table based on a previous working relationship, or a publisher might specify a group on its vendor list. In either case, the cost of outsourcing is factored into the project cost and paid during the advance period. Developers generally list contracted art as a separate line item in their proposal.

Art production is one way for fledgling developers to build their reputation on a console platform, particularly if the group's members have a PC background. The developer not only gains access to the proprietary development systems, but also learns the constraints of art production for the target platform and game engine—from simpler matters such as per-character polygon count to the currently bedeviling issue of limited texture memory. Art production teams who master these issues, build impeccable working relationships with their partner publishers, and carefully hire top-flight programmers have the best chance at breaking through to full-service independent development.

The cost of art production varies wildly with desired quality level, quantity of assets requested, duration of project, and extent of process/logistical integration with the full-service development team. In addition, art production houses run the gamut from long-established, full-time art houses charging top dollar for experience, to startup groups and offshore companies looking to break in at any price. Billing can be per man-month, per minute of cut-scene animation, or flat-fee, and can occasionally include royalties if the artwork is integral to the project's brand identity. For the pressured development team who receives a perfectly executed art asset delivery in time to hit a key milestone, and for the publisher whose high expectations for graphic quality were met in that milestone, every dollar is worth it.

Publishers

If developers are the artistic brain behind videogames, publishers are the muscle and nerve that coordinate all aspects of bringing a game to a consumer. The publisher's role is so extensive and influential that publishers have taken on the aura of medieval fiefdoms, where money flows in mysterious directions and decisions are cloaked in secrecy. Acting as the "suits" to developer "geeks," publishers make up the second half of the classic "art versus commerce" conflict that inspires hyperbolic excesses on games industry message boards. If we step back from the rhetoric, we see wide variation within the category: global conglomerates with multiple regional divisions covering internal and external development, marketing and sales, quality assurance, finance, and licensing for any viable delivery platform; smaller companies specializing in marketing and sales of certain genres for certain territories; groups specializing in specific platforms such as PC or mobile phones; entities focusing on discovering gems in one territory for distribution in another; and Web sites offering pay-per-play downloads.

To choose the best partner, developers must extensively research prospective publishers' strategic priorities, business model, and execution strengths and weaknesses—much of which can be inferred from publicly available information. Mismatched expectations on any of these fronts can doom the best-executed game to the bargain bin before its time.

Console and PC Publishers

For brevity, and because the vast majority of packaged games wind up in consumers' hands through this model, we will focus on "traditional" console/PC publishers such as Electronic Arts, Activision, THQ, Infogrames, and Sega. We examine the role of publishers who also control a hardware platform (such as Sony or Nintendo) in a later section. Finally, since we reviewed game development previously, for this overview we will set aside that function of a publisher's role.

Traditional publishers sit in the conceptual center of the videogame industry, primarily because they bear the executional and financial burden of every process between code creation and game purchase. Responsibilities and accountabilities include:

Management of the game development process. Publishers are involved in everything from time-to-market scheduling to creative input. The foundation of a publisher's relationship with retail partners is a good product shipped on time in the right quantities.

Debugging, playtesting, and other quality assurance. Publishers are legally liable for the game's quality to both consumers and the platform holder.

Securing all necessary licenses. These include in-game music; creative properties, trademarks, or technologies controlled by other companies; athletic leagues and players; and the right to publish on controlled platforms (consoles). Experienced developers obtain an indemnity from the publisher against any licensing omissions the publisher might make.

Manufacturing and shipping the finished game. This responsibility includes writing and printing the manual, designing the cover, buying the case, placing orders with media manufacturers, assembling all the elements into a game package, and shipping it to the channel. Aside from the QA implications of an unstable assembly process, lackluster packaging encourages consumers to look elsewhere on the store shelf.

Maintaining good relationships with retailers via cooperative channel inventory management. More than just the "schmooze" of golf and expensive dinners, publishers' sales efforts must include in-store merchandising programs, funding for product placement in retail circulars ("white space"), joint assessment of a title's sales potential, and markdowns or returns at publisher cost if the title does not perform as expected.

Communicating title features and availability to the consumer. Whether via "meta-channels" such as press events for games industry media, or direct communication with gamers via television, print, demo opportunities, Web site, or Internet/direct mail, publishers are responsible for letting the public know what's out there.

Housekeeping. This responsibility includes all the human resource, tax and finance, investor relations, and legal services issues involved in running the company.

Industry voices frequently criticize publishers for "unfairly" sharing revenue with their developer, without whose creativity there would be nothing to sell. Since revenue sharing is established at contract, a knowledgeable and firm negotiating stance goes far in ensuring fairness for the developer; the many factors that can strengthen a developer's negotiating position are covered elsewhere in this book. In pure financial terms, however, the market law of risk versus reward explains why publishers keep the lion's share of revenue, if not of profit. Table 2.2.1 answers the gamer's frequent question: "Where does my $50 go?"

Table 2.2.1 Generalized Breakdown of Revenue from a $50 Console Game

Amount	Purpose	Paid By	Paid To
$3	Cost of goods	Publisher	Media manufacturer
$7	Publishing license royalty	Publisher	Platform holder
$13	Retailer profit	Consumer	Retailer
$3	Markdown reserve	Publisher	Retailer
$8	Development cost	Publisher	Developer
$10	**Operating cost**	Publisher	Internal (overhead, freight, co-op, bad debt)
$6	**Marketing**	Publisher	Ad agencies and media

Items in **bold** can be converted to profit through careful publisher cost management.

Quality Assurance Service Provider

Occasionally, a publisher will decide not to maintain quality assurance as an internal core competency. Companies such as Absolute Quality or Beta Breakers provide complete debugging and gameplay evaluation to such publishers on a contract basis. The clear advantage is peace of mind about product quality without the necessity of managing the significant human-resource issues and financial overhead of an in-house test team.

Contracted QA has a long history of success with PC publishers, who bear the unique burden of ensuring that their latest release works within a range of hardware specifications. Depending on the publisher's defined compatibility set, the contract QA house can be asked to test hundreds of variants on PC game software + operating system software + hardware + peripherals, as well as projecting results for configurations not tested. Such companies can recoup the significant investment in equipment representing the current gaming market (the "test bed") over multiple projects.

Console publishers are gradually warming up to the idea of contract testing. One obstacle to date has been the expense and proprietary nature of development and debugging systems for controlled platforms. If the publisher provides such equipment to its external QA partner, the platform holder holds the publisher responsible for proper security and authorized use. Another more emotional than factual objection is the perceived risk of code leaks from sources beyond the publisher's own walls; if a game is to be pirated, better to control the leak internally than pursue legal remedies against a partner. During the most recent console transition, contract QA houses made great strides in accommodating these issues, and have since worked closely with both publishers and platform holders to ensure that the figurative firewall includes rather than excludes their services.

Public-Relations Firms, Advertising Agencies, and Merchandising Teams

Although marketing departments at some publishers look as populated as E3 on opening day, few heads of marketing deny the efficiencies of contracting external firms for public relations, advertising generation, and in-store merchandising assistance. Much more than additional heads and hands, such companies combine effectiveness through relationships, the creativity that comes from time to brainstorm, and a reach that falls just short of handing a game directly to the consumer.

Publishers occasionally learn to their dismay that some brand-name PR firms specializing in national media such as *USA Today* and *Newsweek* can fail miserably at communicating their message to videogame industry media such as *Electronic Game Monthly* and *Edge*. The best games industry communications managers successfully pitch the latest role-playing game to a sophisticated news outlet while, on the other phone line, explaining this year's business plan to the local game journalist. The publisher gives the PR firm complete access to its game's development, while the PR firm coaches the publisher on speaking skillfully and consistently to all of its constituencies.

Similarly, a lack of alignment between publisher and ad agency on the creative vision for the marketing plan directly impacts sales. Many top-shelf ad agencies approach the videogame industry as a creative soul mate, believing that innovative interactive entertainment requires bleeding-edge advertising. Experienced games industry marketing executives, however, know that their audience wants to see in-game footage. (Such creative tension results in either a memorable commercial or a new ad agency.) Agency partnerships range from a fully retained relationship covering all software releases, to different agencies retained for distinct product lines, to per-title arrangements.

In-store merchandising assistance is a luxury best afforded by platform holders. With anywhere from 4 to 24 linear feet devoted to its hardware and software in key retailers, for example, Nintendo is legendary for its merchandising team's deep relationships with store managers, enabling them to update signage, straighten displays, restock empty shelf slots, and chat up the electronics section manager on upcoming releases. Publishers whose key releases are integral to a platform holder's lineup can obtain preferential placement and subsequent coddling of their titles by the platform holder's in-store team. Publishers have been known to maintain merchandising teams for shorter or longer periods, but the justification for such cost begins with shelf space; sending staff to straighten up just a few facings is desirable in principle but questionable in financial practice.

Platform Holders

"Platform holders" are companies that manufacture the hardware (and in some cases, the software) on which game software runs. As with publishers, a wide variety of companies comprise game platform holders: cell phone providers, personal digital assistant (PDA) and other handheld device manufacturers, PC makers (both the boxes and the chips inside them), videogame console manufacturers, development software/tools providers such as Microsoft and Silicon Graphics, and Web-based development and delivery services such as WildTangent. Such companies share the characteristic of owning, controlling, or influencing the software that appears on their platform, whether by providing application programming interfaces (APIs) to help developers access the features of their hardware, or by outright permission-based control of anything that involves the platform. Frequently, platform holders also create software for their own hardware; in this section, we review the platform holder's role exclusive of publishing functions.

Platform holders derive their revenue from any of the following sources:

- Sales of the hardware itself
- Sales of (or licensing fees from) any peripherals compatible with the hardware
- Sales of their own games compatible with the hardware ("first-party games")
- Licensing fees from compatible games made by other companies ("third-party games")
- Licensing of development tools or APIs necessary to create games for the hardware
- Manufacturing proprietary delivery media for the hardware (such as game cartridges)

Consoles and PCs differ fundamentally in that console makers strictly regulate access to their platform via various licensing permissions, while PC makers provide their APIs for free to any interested developer. For this reason, we categorize the PC platform as "open" and consoles as "closed." Handhelds such as PDAs and to a certain extent cell phones follow the "open" PC model, while proprietary handhelds such as Nintendo's Game Boy® Advance™ are just as "closed" as Nintendo's Game Cube®.

PCs as a Platform

The "PC platform" is in fact a conglomeration of intersecting partnerships among CPU manufacturers, development software/tools providers, graphics chip manufacturers, and box assemblers. Look in the manual for your new PC and you might see:

- AMD primary processor (CPU)
- NVIDIA GeForce graphics processor
- Microsoft Direct X application software layer
- Assembled and sold by Dell

Each of these categories provides support to game developers, mostly for free, with the intent of making money from compatible software or hardware sales.

As the most visible example of successful "ingredient marketing," Intel has spent years courting game developers in order to maintain its image as provider of the fastest CPUs available. It provides sample boards and technical assistance to game developers, and will even work closely with leading game developers on R&D for its future generations of chips. The objective, of course, is for gamers to specify "Intel Inside" when they purchase their next gaming PC.

Graphics chip companies such as NVIDIA and ATI have built a healthy complementary market to CPUs by creating graphics chips customized for multimedia and, of course, games. In addition to the developer benefits already listed, graphics chip companies will secure cutting-edge games under development on an exclusive basis, paying the developer to incorporate the technological bells and whistles that set their chip aside from the rest. Graphics chipmakers also create APIs that allow developers to take advantage of their chip's unique features. Once "hardcore" gamers realize that their longed-after new releases look best when run on a particular graphics chip, they gladly upgrade.

Two well-known technology companies have made names for themselves in the development software/tools space. Microsoft, with its Direct X API, has succeeded over the years in stabilizing the technological risk of game development on PCs, much as it has standardized its operating system for the user. Silicon Graphics has created a less widespread, but popular among game developers, API called Open GL. Both companies give their APIs away to qualified engineers for free, encouraging information sharing among their developer communities and placing as few limits as possible on use. The advantage for developers is learning a software platform that is invisibly compatible with the multiple hardware combinations available in the market.

PC "box-makers" such as Dell and HP play a less active part in promoting game development on their PCs, since the tough work is done by their "ingredient" companies. However, to the extent they target gamers as potential customers, they might secure an exclusive set of games to pre-load on the PC before it's sold to consumers.

One important factor in PC publishing for developers and publishers is the lack of royalty paid to the hardware company for the privilege of platform compatibility. The beneficial effects are lower cost-of-goods and higher profit margins for publishers, and easier access to both development and self-publishing for developers. However, since nearly any competent and inspired PC development group can complete and ship a PC game at relatively low cost, many groups do so. The resulting competition among thousands of titles for shelf space at retail has created a cutthroat sales channel for PC games, where retailers return units unsold after eight weeks to publishers, and only the top 30 games sell more than 300,000 units.

Consoles as a Platform

In direct contrast to the open and loosely affiliated PC game development scenario, development for game consoles such as Sony's PlayStation 2, Nintendo's Game Cube, and Microsoft's Xbox is tightly controlled at all levels by the respective companies. To create and sell games on these platforms, a developer/publisher requires the following licenses and permissions:

License to use development software and hardware. Only provided after the console platform holder's favorable evaluation of the applicant's potential for bringing quality games to market. For developers, a publisher's recommendation carries great weight in obtaining development systems.

License to conduct general marketing and sales activities. Again, granted only if the platform holder believes the company has the structure and resources to succeed. Smaller publishers without a direct sales force or consistent product flow struggle to establish credibility on a console platform, sometimes signing its products over to a licensed publisher for distribution.

License to use the platform holder's trademarks and logos in-game, on packaging, and in advertising. Platform holders provide templates for all logo and trademark use, and review all materials for correct use before the product can be assembled.

Permission to create a game. Granted after platform holder review of the game concept early in the development process. Instances in which platform holders reject a concept, although rare, cause great vexation, as usually the publisher has already sunk funding into the project.

License to release the game to the channel. Given after extensive testing by developer, publisher, and platform holder. Platform holder certification is a tense part of the process, as the game can be rejected any number of times for bug fixes or standards violations.

According to industry logic, the company that creates the console, engineers the APIs that developers use to build games for the hardware, and incurs the cost for marketing and selling the hardware to consumers is entitled to royalties from game sales—generally around $7/unit—to cover those costs. At launch, the retail price of the console rarely covers its actual component cost, and that cost doesn't include R&D amortization. Many millions of units later, after multiple reengineering efforts to reduce actual cost of goods, successful console platforms can generate vast software-side profits while the platform holder breaks even on the hardware. Over a successful console's lifespan of five to seven years, the platform holder recoups the current console's R&D costs over the first few years, and invests in R&D for the next-generation console during the last few years. An imbalance of software revenues against hardware costs has driven more than one console platform holder out of the hardware business entirely.

Delivery Media Manufacturers

An often-overlooked cog in the publishing machine is the actual game manufacturing and assembly company. With the exception of Nintendo's Game Boy Advance, today's platforms are disk-based; this welcome change reduced cost of goods for publishers and cut manufacturing time dramatically, enabling (almost) just-in-time inventory management. Manufacturers obtain a license from console platform holders to work with the proprietary disk medium and/or other anti-piracy technology on the disk, and generally pay a nominal per-unit royalty for that technology to the platform holder.

Historically, console platform holders have always controlled manufacturing directly, with Sony and Nintendo continuing this model. Publishers submit their orders directly to the platform holder, or simultaneously to the platform holder and the manufacturer. The publisher pays both manufacturing cost and royalty directly to the platform holder, sometimes on a cash-in-advance basis. During busy seasons when manufacturing capacity is strained, the platform holder has final say over which products receive priority. However, in general the manufacturer adheres to a certain turnaround time as part of its terms of service. All the same, for an AAA title release date when every day in the schedule counts, even one day over "the standard turnaround time" can cause headaches and urgent telephone calls up and down the publishing chain.

With its Dreamcast, Sega was the first to offer complete publisher control of the manufacturing process. Microsoft has continued this trend with its Xbox. In this scenario, once the platform holder releases tested game code to the manufacturer, the publisher is free to negotiate turnaround times and pricing based on the strength of its relationship with the manufacturer. In practice, the cost of goods does not vary widely, but the licensing of three or four manufacturing companies ensures that the terms remain competitive.

To save additional time or cost, publishers often receive their goods from the licensed manufacturer as unpackaged disks on spindles, and ship them to a separate facility to assemble. Since such "pack-out houses" are not licensed or controlled by the console platform holder, the publisher is free to pursue the most advantageous partnership based on cost, turnaround time, proximity to the publisher's distribution center, or expertise with different kinds of packaging. Such processes must be managed carefully to prevent Murphy's law from afflicting the extra shipping and handling steps.

Retail

As the most visible part of the videogame publishing trail to the consumer, retail is rewarded handsomely with as much as 30% margin on a game sale. Many routes a game takes to a consumer's hands are not visible to the consumer, but certainly influence the game choices with which he's presented. For the purposes of this discussion, we examine primarily brick-and-mortar stores; online sales of packaged goods have steadily increased but are largely controlled by brick-and-mortar establishments. Long download times and insufficient storage on the client device continue to hamper commercial downloading of games over the Internet, excluding casual games with smaller file sizes. In practice, mass-market online distribution of games awaits greater penetration of broadband connections and further reduction of memory cost.

Distributors

Although it might seem odd to begin a discussion of retail with the middleman, it's useful to know that distributors enable smaller regional store chains, individual "mom and pop" stores, and other niche retail outlets to service their customer base uniquely in the face of stiff competition from national discount chains. Distributors buy nearly every game a publisher releases; their strengths are breadth of selection, close cost management, and the ability to sell to stores whose size or business practices preclude dealing directly with the publisher. In short, the distributor brings the publisher incremental sales more efficiently than if the publisher were to service those accounts directly.

Distributors might specialize in differing product lineups. Some distributors located closer to major population centers claim the advantage of quickest delivery of the latest releases. Although the service is frowned upon by publishers, distributors also try to boost their allocation of high-demand titles to supplement national retailers' supply in the critical days between sellout of the first shipment and arrival of the next. Others might focus on "closeouts"—marked-down or discontinued games that make their way from the publisher or retailer's warehouse to the bargain bin at a loss for the publisher but profit for the distributor and retailer. Some distributors focus on making games "rental-ready," repackaging games in sturdy cases for small rental chains. Some distributors act as publishers on import or other low-visibility titles, taking the financial risk on the hope that one might turn out a gem.

In its role of making the market for games more efficient, the distributor itself must be extremely efficient in order to secure its roughly 3% margin on sales. Generally, distributors secure massive warehouse space in low-rent areas, depend on the publisher for sales materials rather than creating their own, and pay their salespeople with heavy emphasis on commission. The cliché of "making it up on volume" is possible for a distributor that works every angle to its benefit.

Manufacturers' Representatives

Manufacturer's representatives, or "rep groups," are a testament to the lasting power of relationships in a high-tech world. Usually small companies of just a few people, rep groups secure agreements allowing them to act as contracted salespeople on the publisher's behalf. They're responsible for knowing the product line, the target retailer's operation, publisher practices, and when to sell more versus mark down (although they must recommend the latter to their publisher first). For these services, the publisher pays them a percentage of net sales (all sales minus any returns).

Rep groups are usually of most value in situations where the rep group's relationship and credibility with a retailer is stronger than the publisher's is. This includes launches of new product lines, a new publisher's entry into the market, or reaching out to a retailer not yet included in the publisher's existing retailer base. The rep group acts as go-between, advising both publisher and retailer on how to work through new processes on each side. Despite hard work and sincere commitment by leading rep groups, publisher sales executives constantly reexamine the wisdom of contracting external companies for such a vital task. Perhaps it's disappointing sales on a key product that prompts the initial questioning, or cost watchers eyeing the rep group's commission percentage. The result in either case, and the bane of every rep group, is the publisher's call informing them "we've decided to go direct."

Regional Retailers

Despite the increasing standardization of the retail experience nationwide, successful regional retailers have learned the keys to survival: know your customer, provide exactly what he wants, give great service, and offer occasional surprises. These precepts apply perfectly to the game market, where smaller videogame-only retailers and mom-and-pop stores can't compete on price or speedy availability of new releases. The smaller retailer can provide detailed knowledge on the latest game or on an obscure release from years back—and if the store manager or buyer is very good, he will know where to lay his hands on both.

The key to regional retailers' success is good relationships with both their distributor and, ideally, with each publisher as well. Although economies of scale prevent a publisher from servicing regional retailers directly, solid chains with several stores can attract the publisher's notice, either through the grapevine or via distributor's advocacy with the publisher on their behalf for things such as in-store merchandising items and, rarely, markdowns. Since regional chains are frequently staffed by hardcore gamers, publishers can use such chains to create word-of-mouth recommendations from "experts" for their latest releases.

Rental Retailers

Rental retailers such as Blockbuster Video and Hollywood Video have emerged from relative obscurity as a retail category to major drivers in the channel. Until recently, publishers treated rental retail with respect but not much attention; although the sell-in quantity "per door" was less than at traditional retailers, those units were never returned or marked down. Recently, however, industry market research from many sources has shown that the primary driver behind consumer purchase intent is hands-on experience with the game. As rentals can encourage sales of a good game, so also can they stop a bad game's sales dead at launch. As a result, publishers now work their lineup out carefully with rental retailers, evaluating rental retailers' value in advance promotion side by side with actual units sold.

Rental retailers, in turn, have identified the game market as a potential growth segment of their business. Some chains are experimenting with revenue-sharing models. Other rental retailers are moving into sales as well; having created a potential buyer for a game through rental, such retailers have stopped sending the buyer to a competitor for the purchase. In short, rental retailing is transforming into a new service model for gaming consumers.

National Retailers

Finally, we come to the names that consumers know: Wal-Mart, Target, Best Buy, Toys-R-Us, and Electronics Boutique. The lineup varies slightly from publisher to publisher, but this group of national retailers makes up the core of the industry's sales efforts, and represents the most cost-efficient way for publishers to get a game into a consumer's hands.

National retailers have direct relationships with the publisher, which means that that publisher provides them with:

- Games shipped directly to the retailer's warehouse, or direct to store if the retailer can accommodate.
- In-store merchandising materials, such as standees, posters, shelf talkers, and box fronts for display.
- Extensive sales materials on each title, usually including a direct pitch by the publisher's marketing and sales staff to the buyer.
- Generous terms on sales (average net 60, although retailers with clout stretch this as desired).
- Hands-on inventory management, including publisher sales staff poring over store-by-store inventory to increase sales efficiency.
- Various relationship-building perks, such as tickets to a local sports event or an expensive dinner after the sales call. (Wal-Mart is notably strict in its policy of "no freebies" to its buyers.)
- Credits against existing invoices or free goods to help the retailer mark down and move through stagnant inventory.
- Unique sales programs customized by retailers, whether a gift-with-purchase, in-store event or celebrity appearance, or sales contest for in-store staff.

The retail buyer has tremendous influence in the process of getting a game to consumers. The buyer is usually responsible for the entire videogame category, but depending on the relative importance of videogames to the retailer's revenue, videogame buyers might also be responsible for related categories such as video, electronics, or toys. The best buyers listen to the salespeople but also conduct their own research, accept the publisher's stance but listen to the needs of their own customers. The worst buyers pay little attention to videogames, failing to keep abreast of trends or failing to pass information along to store-level employees. Frequently, the difference between a coherent, well-stocked videogame department at one retailer and a disorganized jumble of last year's games at a different chain is directly attributable to the buyer.

For publishers, the buyer controls several elements that can mean sales success or failure: whether to stock a game at all, how deeply to stock it, "white space" or co-op advertising in retail circulars, and in-store pricing. The decision to pass on a game can mean forecast deficits of thousands of units if that retailer is responsible for 40% of a game's launch volume. Smaller publishers suffer from buyers "cherry picking" the best titles only, while larger publishers and platform holders can benefit from the buyer's courtesy in taking the entire product line. A buyer's decision to stock a game in "gamer-heavy" stores in key locations, but not in minor secondary locations, is a strong sign to a publisher to redouble its in-store efforts, in order to achieve chain-wide distribution. A buyer's decision to show a title in the retailer's "white space" circulars (usually bundled with the daily newspaper) creates a measurable sales spike the week the ad is viewed by millions of avid gamers watching for the next release. Finally, buyers have the authority to designate a key title as a loss-leader, pricing it below the usual $49 at launch to drive store traffic to higher-margin purchases. For hot releases, publishers designate a manufacturer's advertised price ("MAP") program, in which any retailer who reduces their advertised price below a certain level is denied co-op funding for the offending ad. However, this relatively weak penalty is only effective when combined with a strong buyer-salesperson relationship that neither party wishes to damage.

Much as "going direct" are two words rep groups dread, "no open to buy" are four words that bedevil publishers. "Open to buy" is the amount of money the buyer can spend buying games within a certain period, usually quarterly or 30 days. Essentially a budget, it's calculated from a combination of cost of inventory on hand, sales rate or "turnover" of that inventory, and revenue expected against that inventory for the period. Open to buy is very restricted around the Thanksgiving–Christmas holiday interval, when large numbers of games are expected to sell huge quantities. A publisher salesperson pitching an excellent game who receives the response "no open to buy" is chastised by his or her management for not pitching the buyer earlier on the game's quality. A salesperson hearing the phrase in response to a poor-quality game should understand this message: Your game isn't good enough to compete with the other releases during this time period. In short, if the publisher manages its retail relationships well, open-to-buy issues should be no surprise.

To manage such relationships to this degree, publishers require voluminous data quickly and frequently. Publishers can derive sales of their own games from internal sales information, of course, but sales data on competitive games or titles released during the same period puts an important context around one's own sales. For example, poor sales of a publisher's franchise platform title can mean anything; poor sales of the next platform to appear might mean that that console's audience doesn't look for the platform genre; and poor sales of all games during that period might indicate overall industry softness, or poor supply of the hardware platform at retail. Fortunately, major retailers report their sales, which then get aggregated and sent back to the publisher on a monthly basis.

Conclusion

With luck, hard work, and good knowledge about who touches your game after you're done with it, the next game consumers buy will be yours.

The Many Faces of Game Development

François Dominic Laramée

fdl@francoisdominiclaramee.com

Game development companies come in all shapes and sizes. From the "lone wolf" doing everything on his or her own, to the thousand-person studios operated by major publishers and console manufacturers, through the small independent self-publishers and third-party companies, each has dynamics all its own—not to mention the fact that life as a developer of "serious games" or coin-operated arcade machines can be significantly different from the experience of the industry's mainstream.

This article presents a taxonomy of the game development world, as well as profiles of several representative companies.

First, Second, and Third Parties

The classic relationship between developer and publisher can present many faces, depending on the exact nature of the link between the two companies. Roughly speaking, the industry recognizes three categories of developers: first, second, and third parties.

- A *first-party* developer is an integral, and often indivisible and indistinguishable, part of a console manufacturer's operations. Nintendo is notorious for the high proportion of its catalog produced by internal teams, including Shigeru Miyamoto's.
- A *second-party* developer is tied to a single console manufacturer but remains a separate corporate entity. In some cases, like Rare's, the console manufacturer owns the second-party developer; in other cases, the two companies are tied together by exclusive, often long-term publishing contracts.
- A *third-party* developer is completely independent from all hardware manufacturers and is free to publish each of its games on its own terms, on whichever platform(s) it chooses.

According to [NumériQC03], there are approximately 100 large third-party developers capable of producing two or more PC and console games a year in the world today, as well as about 1,250 smaller companies that release one title a year or less. All publishers except Microsoft, Nintendo, and Sony are third-party entities. Blue Fang Games, the creators of the *Zoo Tycoon* series, is a typical third-party developer; they are profiled in Case Study 2.3.1.

CASE STUDY 2.3.1: AN INDEPENDENT STUDIO PROFILE: BLUE FANG GAMES

Blue Fang Games is the award-winning development house behind *Zoo Tycoon*, the 12th highest-selling PC game of all time in North America with over 4.5 million copies sold. The company was founded in 1998 by Adam Levesque, who had designed *NASCAR 1* and *NASCAR 2* at Papyrus, and John Wheeler. Hank Howie, president of the 32-person studio, joined soon thereafter. "Adam and I had been friends for many years," says Howie. "Given that I wasn't doing anything particularly productive at that point, other than proving that golf was never going to be a revenue generating endeavor, I jumped on board!"

But the early days were difficult for the startup.

"The game idea that the company was formed around was called *Dragon Hoard*. It was a strategic, role-playing flight simulator—yes, we had issues—in which you played a dragon and did all of the wonderful, powerful and terrible things that dragons of legend and fantasy can do: fly, breathe fire, amass treasure, terrorize villages, and so on. We knew we needed a demo to get publishers interested, so we hired a staff with our own money to make it happen. But while we got some very positive initial feedback from publishers, they always wanted to see more before committing, and we were running out of resources."

In the spring of 1999, Blue Fang abandoned *Dragon Hoard* and decided to do contract work for Hasbro Interactive on their *NASCAR Heat* franchise. "We'll always be grateful to the folks at HI at the time, and especially Rich Garcia at Monster Games for getting us the work that enabled us to stay in business."

The *Dragon Hoard* experience taught Blue Fang's team an important lesson: "We would be much better off creating a game with a more realistic scope, given our small team size. We genuinely liked *Roller Coaster Tycoon*, considered and shot down several ideas in that genre, until one of our engineers said 'What about zoos?' and the idea immediately clicked. We drafted a 10-page game concept proposal based on the *Zoo Tycoon* idea and sent it out to a select few game publishers just prior to the 2000 GDC. Microsoft in particular showed great interest, and about six months later we signed a publishing deal."

Meanwhile, the team had to wrestle with publishers' discomfort with their lack of "relevant genre experience." "I can't tell you how many times that issue came up: that our folks had produced million unit sellers, yes, but those games were racing sims, and the team's experience might not translate to a game about dragons or, to

→

only a slightly lesser extent, to a game about zoos. In the end, we were able to convince Microsoft that we were the right team for *Zoo Tycoon*. It probably helped that we made it clear to everyone that we were going to make *Zoo Tycoon* with someone—and that they might as well be the beneficiaries."

When evaluating new projects, Blue Fang's team balances their personal and business interests. "While nothing is guaranteed in this business, we will only pursue projects that we believe to have strong commercial potential. While that sounds greedy, it also reflects the fact that it's depressing to make games that nobody plays. Having nearly 5 million *Zoo Tycoon* players is exciting to us, as well as financially rewarding. And of course, we want to work on projects that we'll enjoy developing for two years and more."

While Blue Fang has a strong relationship with its publisher, the company remains independent. "We're in an enviable position: we work with one of the top publishers in the world on a game we enjoy making and which millions of players enjoy playing (and buying). Our relationship with Microsoft is terrific, it works well for everyone, so why change it? Besides, it's just so great to run your own company. You can create the work environment that suits your employees best—you can even correct all of the things that you saw were wrong when you were working elsewhere. My greatest satisfaction comes when an employee tells me that this is the best company he or she has ever worked for."

The key to Blue Fang's success? "We work with the belief that publishers want what we all want: great, high-quality games, preferably shipped on time. In addition, most publishers want to build longer term relationships with top developers. In working with a publisher, it's important to maintain completely open and honest communication throughout the development process. We just came through our most difficult development challenge yet in shipping *Zoo Tycoon 2* for the 2004 Christmas season. If we hadn't had a strong, open, and honest relationship with Microsoft, it would have been very difficult to get through."

Careful scheduling (and sticking to the schedule) is one of the best ways to strengthen a relationship with a publisher. "The publisher must believe that the developer knows what they are doing and will deliver what was promised on time and on budget. When that happens, the publisher will more readily trust the developer when the latter makes recommendations regarding the game, even if that entails cutting features to add others, or adjusting the scope of the game to maintain the schedule."

Hank also says that attracting employees to Blue Fang is easier than in most other organizations, big or small. "Potential employee concerns usually revolve around stability, culture, and the games we work on. It helps us tremendously from a stability standpoint that we work on the *Zoo Tycoon* franchise for Microsoft, and that our bank account is healthy. Thanks to the franchise's success, we are very profitable, and we share those profits pretty generously with our employees. The
→

prospect of considerable financial upside is a powerful tool when talking to prospective new employees. Besides, we still have just about all of the folks who worked on the original *Zoo Tycoon*—and even the first five who worked on *Dragon Hoard*."

As for the future, Blue Fang's success record is a boon when discussing new projects with publishers, but "genre experience" or lack thereof is still an issue. "Due to the tremendous—and hopefully continued—success of the *Zoo Tycoon* franchise, Blue Fang is currently in a strong financial position that allows us to be very selective in the projects we pursue. Within the management simulation genre, we have developed a reputation as a leading developer and a great deal of credibility with publishers. This credibility, however, does not necessarily enable us to create any type of game. We could finance a completely different project prototype and development pretty readily if we chose to, but we are not especially inclined to do so. Games have become so expensive to develop that we're not very interested in taking the risk. That's why I'm always very sympathetic to the publishers' plight."

Still, Blue Fang may yet surprise the industry again. "For the right project, would we, in effect, bet on ourselves? We risked the company on *Zoo Tycoon* and the gamble paid off. If we come up with another equally promising idea, would we do it again? We'll see…"

Advantages and Disadvantages

From a development team's perspective, first- or second-party status usually provides preferential access to the console manufacturer's new hardware, tools, and support, especially in the early stages of a console's life cycle. First and second parties also get to devote all of their research and development effort to a single platform, which allows them to exploit the platform to the fullest. As a result, it is not uncommon for the most successful amongst a console's launch titles to come from first-party teams.

Furthermore, console manufacturers (with the possible exception of Sega in the days of the Dreamcast) tend to wield exceptional resources in their roles as publishers. First- and second-party titles get high exposure, high marketing budgets, and great launch dates. Only a handful of third-party publishers can afford to do as much.

However, an independent second-party company tied to a failing console can quickly find itself in trouble, while third-party developers get to hedge their bets by being able to publish for multiple platforms—at the cost of dispersing their research effort over multiple platforms.

Finally, a successful third-party developer can leverage its talents by selling its next title(s) to the highest bidder, thus increasing its profitability. Second-party developers tied to a console manufacturer through a long-term contract don't have as much freedom, while the question is meaningless for first-party teams.

A Fluid Continuum

Of course, the boundaries between first, second, and third parties are somewhat fuzzy. The distinction between first-party and second-party developers is often tenuous, especially in cases where the console manufacturer owns the developer. A small third-party developer that signs a two-game publishing contract with Sony and agrees not to publish the games on other consoles can be considered a second-party developer for the purpose of these titles. A second-party developer may be allowed to port its games to the PC (especially if it is associated with Microsoft's Xbox) or wireless platforms, thus behaving like a third-party company with somewhat limited options. Giants like Electronic Arts, while technically third parties, wield enough clout that console manufacturers often give them the same level of attention and support that they would otherwise reserve for their own teams. And major publishers' branded studios (like EA Tiburon, featured in Case Study 2.3.2) are third-party developers relative to console publishers, but first- or second-party developers relative to the publisher's main corporate entity.

CASE STUDY 2.3.2: A MAJOR THIRD-PARTY STUDIO: ELECTRONIC ARTS—TIBURON

EA—Tiburon, currently located in Maitland, Florida, has about 375 employees working on EA SPORTS and EA SPORTS BIG branded titles and evaluating new intellectual properties for future development. We asked general manager Steven Chiang and corporate communications specialist Trudy Muller to describe life at one of the industry's premier studios.

Question: Please give us a quick historical account of EA—Tiburon and its signature franchises.
Answer: Tiburon Entertainment was founded in 1994 by John Schappert, Steven Chiang, and Jason Andersen. Electronic Arts acquired the company in 1998. *Madden NFL Football* is in its 15th year as an EA franchise and has sold close to 40 million copies to date; our first version was *Madden NFL 97*. The NCAA franchise is in its 11th year, and our first version was *NCAA Football 98*. EA has been building NASCAR games since 1997 and now holds exclusive interactive entertainment rights to the property; our first version was *NASCAR Thunder 2002* and our most recent is *NASCAR 2005: Chase for the Cup*. We're also in our second iteration of the EA SPORTS BIG branded *NFL Street*.
Question: How does Electronic Arts decide which studio will handle a new franchise?
Answer: If it's a homegrown idea, the studio that came up with the idea will build the product. That's what happened with *NFL Street*. When EA signs a licensing deal for a property, like *Harry Potter* a few years ago, the EA →

Worldwide Studio organization assigns the franchise based on which studio has capacity and expertise in the genre.

Question: Can you describe the internal acceptance process for new games? Is the ultimate sign-off handled at the studio level or at corporate headquarters? How are responsibilities split between the local and global organizations?

Answer: EA—Tiburon is a complete studio that handles all aspects of product development, design, programming, art, sound, and marketing. We're the ones who handle the ultimate sign-off on new versions. We also have many support functions that keep the studio running, like human resources, a facilities team, finance, and technical services. We work with the publishing and Worldwide Studio teams to define what titles we will be building for the year. We also work closely with headquarters on legal matters, graphic services, business affairs, public relations, and Worldwide Studio management.

Question: What are the specific challenges related to handling yearly franchises with such high profile, beyond the obvious no-delay rules?

Answer: As you note, with yearly franchises, hitting your release date is very important, since the game's release is usually timed with a real-world event like the beginning of a season. That means that our development cycle is less than a year long, which makes it a challenge to ensure that each iteration of a franchise is a significant improvement over the previous one. Our goal has always been to make any title we work on the best $50 a consumer spends each year.

Question: How do you minimize turnover? One would think that successful franchises would attract a lot of applicants but that people might burn out after a couple of years of working on the same type of game.

Answer: Tiburon turnover has been under 9% the last few years. It's not easy to work on the same game year after year, but we have passionate sports gamers who love what they do. We also work hard to challenge our staff, we rotate people amongst product lines and give them opportunities to lead teams, refine their skills, and obtain training through EA University. Most importantly, we try to have fun: whether it's seeing a new *Harry Potter* movie before its theatrical release or attending launch parties, we make sure that our people have fun as they work hard.

Question: What are the main advantages of belonging to a large third-party organization like Electronic Arts?

Answer: In my nine years with the company, I have had new challenges every year and I continue to learn more and more about making games. EA has an incredible number of talented people and shares tools, libraries, and best practices, so that each studio can push the others to innovate and make the best games.

Self-Publishers and Independents

While we often associate "independent" or "indie" game development to limited-scale projects developed on tiny budgets, often by a single individual or a small amateur or semi-professional team working for a share of future royalties, the independent game development landscape is vast and diverse. Indeed, the Independent Games Festival accepts any project that isn't funded by a publisher—which means that a multiyear, massively multi-player, capital-funded project like Netamin's *Ultimate Baseball Online* (profiled in Case Study 2.3.3) would qualify just as easily as a student team's graduation project.

Self-publishing is a risky venture, but one that may yield excellent returns. Since there is no separate publishing entity involved, the developer gets to keep a higher share of the retail price—sometimes paying as little as 3% to 10% to a credit card company, payment service, or online sales site. As a result, games developed under moderate budgets can become profitable at very modest sales levels, the kind of which major publishers could never afford, which means that indie self-publishers can (at least in theory) take on a variety of oddball projects that are totally unfeasible as far as the industry's mainstream is concerned.

A number of companies also provide a middle ground between the traditional retail market and self-publishing. Entities like GarageGames, RealArcade, and Pogo.com allow developers to sell their games online and keep a relatively high share of royalties without having to handle all of the effort and expense associated with marketing the games on their own.

A number of other articles in this book discuss various aspects of independent development and self-publishing. [Michael03] delves into much greater depth and is recommended to readers with a specific interest in this market.

CASE STUDY 2.3.3: SELF-PUBLISHING A MASSIVELY MULTIPLAYER GAME

After several years of development and testing, Netamin Communications decided to self-publish *Ultimate Baseball Online*, its flagship massively multiplayer online base-ball game. "UBO belongs to a new genre," says Gabriel Law, the game's producer. "We feel that we have a unique understanding of the issues involved in running a game that is both massively multiplayer and sports-based. No other publisher in the market can match our years of experience catering to this type of community."

Andy Wang, the company's founding president, started Netamin in 1999 to take advantage of the explosion in MMO subscriptions in Asia. "However, to make a splash in this market, we believed that a new company needed to provide something unique. This is why we decided to build a sports-based online world, something that had never been done before."

Funding was undoubtedly the most difficult challenge for the startup. "Many standalone games can be developed in 12 to 15 months, and there is a lot of middle-ware available in the marketplace to cut costs. For a massively multiplayer game, 48

→

months is a bare minimum, which means an enormous investment. This is definitely not a market for garage hackers." Fortunately, Netamin was able to attract experienced developers to ensure the project's success. "Our experience indicates that the industry's talent pool is large enough to sustain new companies. We hired a project lead who had already developed MMOs before, so networking technology isn't too big of an issue. We were also able to find a quality assurance manager with over 10 years of experience."

As of late 2004, Netamin is gearing up for the commercial release of the *9-on-9* real-time game in Taiwan and North America, with Korea and Japan to follow. "The Taiwanese market has been exceptionally receptive," notes Gabriel Law. The company is also in the early stages of planning two more sports-based massively multiplayer games.

Netamin's workforce includes over 30 people in the United States and Korea. "Managing offices across the globe is always a big challenge. Aside from time zone and language issues, we must also pay attention to the local gaming cultures, because expectations will vary between offices."

And despite the long years of development, Gabriel Law has no regrets. "There are not many professions that allow you to create a new reality. We have received so many encouraging posts and e-mails from the player community that I can't imagine doing anything else." (See Figure 2.3.1.)

FIGURE 2.3.1   *This Ultimate Baseball Online third baseman is watching the action at home plate.*

Other Ways to Play: Arcade Development and Serious Games

Until the mid-1980s, coin-operated machines dominated the games industry. Such icons as *Pong, Pac-Man, Space Invaders,* and *Defender* were developed for the arcades first and ported to home systems only after they had already established their legendary status. Today, arcade game development remains a niche that can be exploited profitably by companies with specialized knowledge and technology, like the one presented in Case Study 2.3.4, Incredible Technologies.

While the influence of the arcades over the games industry has diminished, another channel has emerged and may grow in importance in the coming years: the so-called "serious games." While the application of gaming technology to simulation and training is hardly a new phenomenon—the U.S. armed forces used a version of *BattleZone* to train tank crews two decades ago—the high-profile releases of dual-market titles like *America's Army* and *Full Spectrum Warrior* have confirmed the validity of the concept, and a considerable amount of work is being done to extend serious games to various other domains, including health care and management. BreakAway Games, featured in Case Study 2.3.5, is among the leaders in this field.

CASE STUDY 2.3.4: ARCADE GAME DEVELOPMENT

Founded in 1985, Incredible Technologies is best known for *Golden Tee Golf*, the most successful coin-operated video game in history, with over 100,000 units sold since 1995—in a market where a title is considered a hit when it achieves sales of 3,000. "The proof is in the cashbox," says Gary Colabuono, the company's director of marketing. "If amusement operators, the companies that actually buy and service the games, are confident that the game will earn back its cost and generate a profit, then the word will spread and sales will rise."

Many other differences between the coin-op and home markets exist, especially at the design level. "For an arcade developer, the biggest challenge is getting the first play. Then, it is getting the second play, then the third and fourth. This is a fundamental difference from the publishers of consumer games, who want you to buy the game but don't really care how long you play it. Therefore, gameplay for coin-op is much more focused and immediate, with short-term goals and big rewards for achieving them. Competition and social interaction also play a big part in the experience, especially in today's street-location market."

The coin-op development cycle also presents unique challenges. Indeed, when they have developed a new game, coin-op manufacturers test a few prototypes in select arcades and only push the game into mass production if these prototypes earn enough money during the trials. "Incredible Technologies believes in testing as thoroughly as possible. We now test for longer periods, in more locations spread out across the country, than ever before. And since we focus on short, intense experiences, we tend to have smaller development teams that put a concerted emphasis on immediate playability. As a result, while a typical consumer game may require 60 to 100 man-years of development or more, a coin-op game usually requires no more than 15 or 20."

Incredible Technologies is the first coin-op manufacturer to sell its games directly to amusement operators; other manufacturers sell to distributors instead.

→

The coin-op industry's counterpart to E³ is the Amusement and Music Operators Association Expo, held each year in Las Vegas, Nevada where operators can see and try out the newest games first-hand. "Early spring and mid fall are the busiest buying seasons, but not by as much as they used to be. The development cycle of a coin-op machine is tough to predict, and the machine needs to come out when it is ready and earning well in trials."

CASE STUDY 2.3.5: SERIOUS GAME DEVELOPMENT AT BREAKAWAY GAMES

BreakAway Games was founded in 1998, after Doug Whatley and Deborah Tillett closed down a joint venture they were running in conjunction with The Walt Disney Company and the ABC television network. "Doug took his severance pay and kept a small group of developers together to continue to create games," says Tillett, the company's president.

Today, BreakAway is equally active in the interactive entertainment and simulation markets. Its best-known consumer games include *Waterloo: Napoleon's Last Battle* and *Emperor: Rise of the Middle Kingdom*, while its proprietary software model is in use at the U.S. Army War College, the Naval War College, and the Joint Chiefs Office of Net Assessment. As of late 2004, BreakAway is also developing a game to train nurses and doctors in coping with emergency room situations. "We expect to stay equally active in both fields in the future. It is our strength and distinct advantage to remain so."

BreakAway got involved in military war-game contracting as early as 1998. By 2002, the market's size had grown to $4 billion annually, with excellent growth potential, so the company hired dedicated personnel and invested in a sustained business development effort. "We penetrated the market with good, old-fashioned cold calls, networking with contacts, and a real dogged determination."

Tillett warns that there are organizational issues to handle before making the transition from consumer entertainment to "serious" games. "The back office structure to support government contracting is essential. In other words, the lawyers, separate sales staff, accountants, and so forth are all nonbillable overhead that needs to be supported." As for the terms of military contracts, BreakAway charges what it expects its costs to be—just like it would for a work-for-hire game development deal.

That being said, one of the keys to BreakAway's success is to remember that games should remain games no matter what the subject matter. "Our philosophy is to keep everyone focused on the fact that even our military projects must still be games at the core. We also try to rotate talent on projects to maximize skills and to keep everyone fresh—after all, our customers are quite clear that they don't want us to become as institutional as they are!"　　　　　　　　　　→

Still, the culture clash between typical game developers and giant health corporations or military departments can be daunting. "It is part of life, but we have a couple of adult types like me to run interference!"

As of late 2004, BreakAway had studios in Hunt Valley, Maryland, and Austin, Texas, with 13 projects of various sizes in the works, 70 people on staff, and plans to grow to 100 or 125 by the end of 2005.

Conclusion

There are a number of other ways for companies to earn a profit making games, besides the ones discussed in this article: outsourcing, producing middleware, free-lancing, Web-based advergaming, and so forth. Some of them are discussed elsewhere in this book, but all of them are viable options you should consider if you decide to launch your own company.

References

[Michael03] Michael, David, *The Indie Game Development Survival Guide,* Charles River Media, August 2003.

[NumériQC03] Alliance NumériQC, "Analyse de positionnement de l'industrie du jeu interactif au Québec," February 2003.

2.4

A Publishing Project: From Concept to Launch and Beyond

François Dominic Laramée

fdl@francoisdominiclaramee.com

Unfortunately treated by many game developers as a necessary evil, publishers are in fact the developer's greatest allies. Not only can publishers open the door to the retail market (and to profitability), but their resources can also shield the developers from many sources of conflicts and mistakes, and thus help them make better games.

This article outlines the work that the publishing company performs at various stages of the production and marketing process.

Selecting a Project

Even the largest publishing house only has the wherewithal to market a tiny fraction of the games submitted to it. Therefore, the process through which publishers select the projects they will invest their precious resources in is extremely crucial.

Publishers evaluate projects with a "profits and losses statement" like the one presented in Case Study 2.4.1; let us examine the factors that influence this calculation.

The Two Risks

Sadly, game development studios are inherently unstable. For every company that achieves long-term success, many close their doors after releasing only one or two games, and even more never manage to ship a single title. Furthermore, the game market is highly hit-driven; according to numbers quoted by [Laramée00], only 3% of PC games and 15% of console games sell more than 100,000 units in any given year—and 100,000 copies is rarely enough to make a high-budget game profitable. For a publisher investing time and money in a project, these facts translate into a pair of major risk factors:

> **The risk of cancellation.** That the project will never yield a product, because it will be cancelled along the way.

The risk of commercial failure. That the finished product won't find success in the marketplace.

The publisher's decision process must balance these risks against the product's inherent appeal, to determine whether its potential payoff warrants the investment.

Reducing the Risk of Cancellation

Most game project cancellations derive from excessive delays and/or poor quality. Thus, well-established teams with proven track records of success stand the best chance of securing publishing deals. When Sid Meier created Firaxis, the press reported contract signings involving the new company within weeks.

For the typical startup, the situation is more complicated. Some publishers will demand to see an almost complete version of the game as a proof of the developers' credibility before they invest. Others will sign a contract based on a fully functional demo, but for a modest advance only. In both cases, the new team will have to find alternative sources of funding (debt, capital, or sweat equity) for part of the development process.

Reducing the Risk of Commercial Failure

With thousands of games released every year, and room for but a fraction of those on retailers' shelves, publishers will favor projects with built-in target audiences. For example:

A sequel to a current best-seller. If *Zombie Rodent Disco Kings* sold 3 million copies, retailers and consumers will clamor for *Zombie Rodent Disco Kings II.*
A game that fits the general parameters of a popular genre. It is easy to assess the potential sales figures for a war game, a shooter, or a golf simulator.
A game based on a popular license. When deciding between two games to buy, the typical consumer will tend to choose the one featuring *Star Trek* or *Sesame Street* characters.

While these "franchise games" by no means guarantee success, they are perceived as more likely to make an impact in the retail market than their wholly original or offbeat competitors are.

Making the Decision

A variety of strategies is available to publishers seeking further risk reduction:

Cross-collateralization: This is an accounting process that ties together the earnings of several games (or of the same game on multiple platforms) so that the profits made by one have to recoup the losses of the others before royalties are paid to the developer.
Budget games: If a game can turn a profit on sales of 5,000 units, the risk is minimal.

Hedging the bets: Larger publishers might play the odds by acquiring the rights to many high-profile games and hoping that one of them will turn into such a hit that it will more than make up for any losses on the others.

Affiliate label status: Some small and mid-sized publishers will delegate the massive sales and distribution effort to a larger company to reduce their costs. Strategy First, a PC game publisher profiled in Case Study 2.4.4, is an affiliate of Atari in North America.

However, the most important factor in the decision remains the individual game's odds of making it to market and being successful there.

CASE STUDY 2.4.1: ESTIMATING A PROJECT'S PROFITABILITY

Here are examples of profits and losses spreadsheets for a mid-range PC game and a franchise console title.

PC Game

	Early Adopter	Peak	Budget	Total
Gross unit price	$40	$30	$15	
Expected units	0	80,000	40,000	120,000
Gross revenue	**$0**	**$2,400,000**	**$600,000**	**$3,000,000**
Cost of goods	$0	$120,000	$60,000	
Advance/R&D	$1,500,000			
Marketing	$200,000	6.7%	of sales	
Direct expenses	**$1,880,000**			
Breakeven	**62,667**			
Profitability ratio	**1.6**			

Franchise Console Game

	Early Adopter	Peak	Budget	Total
Gross unit price	$40	$30	$10	
Expected units	350,000	500,000	150,000	1,000,000
Gross revenue	**$14,000,000**	**$15,000,000**	**$1,500,000**	**$30,500,000**
Cost of goods	$2,450,000	$3,500,000	$600,000	
Advance/R&D	$3,500,000			
Marketing	$2,500,000	8.2%	of sales	
Direct expenses	**$12,550,000**			
Breakeven	**313,750**			
Profitability ratio	**2.4**			

Let's define the line items in this spreadsheet:

Gross unit price: The price at which the publisher sells to retailers. This is usually 50% to 60% of the retail price paid by consumers.

Expected units: Target sales numbers.

Gross revenue: Gross unit price multiplied by expected number of units sold.

Cost of goods: The cost of printing game media, manuals, packaging, and shipping and handling. For console games, this includes the unit royalty paid to the platform owner; for example, $3 to $8 depending on the retail price and the platform.

Advance/R&D: The nonrefundable sums paid to a third-party developer, or the money invested in developing the game internally.

Marketing: The sums devoted to advertising the game in print, online, and on TV, plus in-store marketing and promotion. For most projects, this is roughly 8% to 10% of gross revenue, but some publishers will invest much more.

Direct expenses: Advance/R&D plus marketing.

Breakeven: Number of units that must be sold to cover the game's direct expenses.

Profitability ratio: Gross revenue divided by total direct expenses.

Note that indirect costs, including trade show expenses and publisher staff salaries, are not accounted for in the profitability ratio calculation. Neither are profit margins. The actual ratio that the project must generate to justify investment depends on publisher overhead and profit objectives; for a small publisher with limited staff, a ratio of 1.5 might be sufficient, while giant companies traded on the stock market might need a ratio of 3.0 or more.

Guiding Development

Funding is not the only benefit that a good publisher provides during development. Others include help fine-tuning the game design for maximum market impact, securing approved developer status from console manufacturers, equipment loans (those console development kits are expensive), better exposure in the press, and any number of morale-boosting fringe benefits such as free games and invitations to exclusive parties at industry trade shows.

Perhaps most important of all, the publisher will assign an internal producer to your project [McGilvray05]. This person's job is to make it as easy as possible for you to complete the project on time. The producer might provide services such as getting the publisher to pay for an external testing studio, obtaining extra equipment, organizing special training, or applying a little pressure to get your game certified by a console manufacturer in time for a November release. The best internal producers will even shield you from sources of stress emanating from their own companies!

CASE STUDY 2.4.2: HOW A PUBLISHER SELECTS A TEAM FOR CONTRACT DEVELOPMENT

Veteran producer Seth W. Rosenfeld, who directed the development of a number of NewKidCo International Inc.'s *Tom and Jerry* games among others, says that choosing a development partner involves considerations of technology, expertise, and cost.

"Small publishers have limited financial resources," says Seth. "We also try to match games to developers based on their capabilities. For example, if we want a platform game based on a cartoon license, we will approach a company with strong animation skills and an appropriate 2D or 3D engine."

It is also crucial that developers deliver products carefully tailored to the specific development cycles. "Often, developers make promises that they are unable to fulfill due to schedule or budget restrictions. Tight schedule management, including bi-weekly or even weekly build reviews, will insure that any slippage will be noticed immediately. Developers should be candid with their publishers with regard to risk, so that potential problems can be dealt with at the earliest opportunity."

Preparing for Launch

Some games catch the public eye years before release—sometimes on purpose, sometimes because of schedule slips. However, in most cases, publishers begin to work on a launch campaign approximately six months before release. In the United States, much of this activity happens at the Electronic Entertainment Expo (E^3), which takes place almost six months to the day before the most important shopping weekend of the year, Thanksgiving.

Selling to Retailers

At E^3, publishers meet buyers from all of the retail chains and show them the games of the Christmas season in almost-finished form. (Demos of the next year's releases are also shown, often behind closed doors.) The publishers' goal is to guarantee that their games will be available in as many outlets as possible, in sufficient quantities, and on the best shelf space. Therefore, they spare no expense; the high-tech booths and hundreds of thousands of square feet of floor space that publishing giants buy at E^3 cost them millions of dollars for the three-day event.

[Laramée05] discusses the retail market in more detail.

Selling to the Press

At the same time, game magazine reporters receive previews and interview the games' developers.

Most print magazines have lead times (e.g., delays between writing and publishing of articles) of about two to three months. Therefore, E^3 previews appear in print in August or September—just in time to condition consumers for Christmas shopping. Full reviews follow a few months later, to coordinate their appearance in print with the game's release.

Marketing Campaigns

It is no secret that magazines tend to give better and more favorable coverage to publishers who fund their business through advertising purchases. Retailers also want to know how much advertising a publisher will buy to support a game, when it will appear, and in which publications.

A print advertising campaign for a typical game will cost about $150,000 to $350,000. That amount will buy full-page and two-page ads in several major magazines for three to six months. Television ad support is usually reserved for flagship titles and brands (e.g., *Tomb Raider* or *EA Sports)* and can easily cost 10 to 20 times as much.

Other major marketing expenses include:

Store promotions. These include preferential pricing and rebates granted to a specific retail chain, in-store displays, and advertising in a store's fliers.

Online marketing. Publisher staff members discuss upcoming games with consumers in chat rooms, on Web sites, and so forth. Once marginal, this labor-intensive practice now sometimes accounts for half of a game's marketing budget.

The Final Countdown

Once the game is complete, the publisher runs final testing, manufactures copies of the game and packaging (sometimes in-house, usually through subcontractors), stores the boxes in its warehouse, and ships orders to retailers.

For a PC game, this sequence takes approximately one month. For console games, it often takes three times as long, for two reasons:

- Since it is impossible (for now) to release a patch for a console game, the platform owner must certify that the game is bug free. This makes the final testing and approval period much longer.
- Platform owners usually retain the exclusive right to print copies of game media, using special formats and processes to minimize the risk of piracy. If the platform owner has limited manufacturing capacity, which is typical during a console's first year on the market, it might take a while for them to fulfill orders.

CASE STUDY 2.4.3: SELF-PUBLISHING

Kutoka Interactive, the publisher of children's games profiled in Case Study 1.3.1, relies on effective press relations to offset their competitors' larger advertising budgets. "When a magazine like *MacHome* writes that our animation is as good as Pixar's and better than Disney's, consumers notice," says Kutoka vice president Tanya Claessens.
                                                                                →

Aggressive brand promotion also helps ensure market penetration. "We have bundled the games with plush dolls, created a complete line of ancillary products such as backpacks, puzzles, and action figures, and we are going to expand the license into children's books and television as well."

But ultimately, it all comes down to sales. "Stores only stock best-sellers, so we have to move more units than the competing product that could replace us on the shelves."

CASE STUDY 2.4.4: A PUBLISHER PROFILE

One of the world's leading publishers of strategy games for the PC, Strategy First has marketed such titles as the *Disciples* and *Europa Universalis* series. When evaluating a game proposal, the company adopts an iterative approach.

"Anyone in the company can submit a design treatment," says Chuck Kroegel, Strategy First's vice president for product development. "If it is approved by our executives, the project advances to the proof of concept phase, during which a brief design document and a playable demo are created. After another review, a promising project is assigned to a team of six or seven people who develop a prototype, a technical design, and better gameplay specifications. Only if there is a strong hook in the prototype will the game progress to full-scale development."

As a result of this iterative review, about 50% of the projects that pass the proof of concept stage eventually reach store shelves. "I have seen hundreds of games in my career," says Kroegel, "and many get waylaid because they lose their core vision. We work hard in the early stages of our projects to avoid the mistakes that lead to cancellations."

Third-party developers seeking a publishing agreement with Strategy First go through the same process, but they have to create the proof of concept on their own. "We usually act as a publishing partner, paying more in royalties than in advances, although we plan on funding more development in the future."

As an affiliate of Atari in North America, Strategy First handles advertising and online marketing for its games, while Atari takes care of sales, distribution, manufacturing, and store promotions. The company begins a game's pre-launch campaign three to six months before the planned release date. "War games are one of our specialties, and they don't require much advance warning. We know who and where the consumers are, so reaching them is straightforward." For this type of niche product, online promotion is key, and accounts for 50% of the marketing budget and 70% of the labor.

Thanks to its low overhead, Strategy First can turn a profit on games that bigger publishers must decline. Kroegel concludes: "We can often break even on sales of 50,000 units and earn significant profits if we reach 100,000. That makes us an attractive outlet for developers whose games target smaller but well-established niches."

Beyond the Launch Campaign

The publisher's job isn't finished when the game ships [Sloper02]. To maximize earnings, the publisher must extend the title's life cycle.

Support

First, the buying public must receive the support they need to enjoy their purchase. For classic retail games, support involves little more than a Web site, an e-mail address, a telephone number, and possibly a few patches to correct the bugs that have slipped through the quality assurance process. However, massively multiplayer online game customer support [Perkins05] requires dozens or even hundreds of people monitoring the happenings in the game world around the clock to foil hackers, stifle aberrant player behavior, and solve transient bugs.

Price Reductions

Highly anticipated games are released at premium prices ($60 or $70), so that the publisher will generate as much income as possible from early adopters. This is standard marketing strategy: DVD players, microwave ovens, and a host of other devices cost much more when they were introduced than they do now that they have reached mass-market acceptance.

Unfortunately for publishers, early adopters account for only 20% of the population. Therefore, premium sales drop off within a few weeks or months of release. At that point, the publisher will stimulate demand by lowering the price to $50. (Games that do not justify premium release prices start at that level, or even lower.)

The price reduction process will be repeated periodically, as long as reports show that the drop causes an increase in sales. A highly successful game's retail price can go from $60 to $50 to $40 to $30 to $20 over a period of 12 to 18 months, before remaining stock is liquidated at $5 to $10 once demand has all but vanished. If the game fails to find an audience, retailer pressure might drive the price down to budget or liquidation levels within 6 to 12 weeks.

Add-Ons

For many types of games, an expansion pack containing new quests, new levels, or new units is a quick and relatively inexpensive way to generate additional income from the existing user base.

In the future, some games might be sold with minimal content included, and additional "episodes" be distributed online by weekly or monthly subscription. This way, publishers will be able to exploit a successful franchise for several years, much like the creators of a hit television series do now. (A potentially even more appealing benefit is that they will be able to cancel unpopular games before millions of dollars are sunk into development.)

Bundles

Once a game reaches the end of its retail life cycle, the publisher can entice additional consumers by bundling the game and several add-on packages into a single budget-priced bundle. By adding special features to the bundle (e.g., a metal box, cloth map, action figure, music CD, etc.), the publisher might even turn it into a "lifestyle purchase" that consumers who already own the game might want to buy or receive as a present, much in the style of "greatest hits" music compilations.

Finally, once a game is completely out of the retail channel, the publisher might want to bundle it with hardware, books, or even include it in cereal boxes. Revenue generated from such bundling agreements is minimal (often less than $0.25 per unit), but volume and/or visibility might be sufficient to justify the deal.

Sequels

And of course, a successful game creates a built-in audience for a sequel, which might be easier to sell to retailers and consumers than a brand new product. In fact, it might be easier to make money on a sequel, even at lower sales volumes, because the sequel costs less to market—and possibly to develop as well, if assets can be reused, although the rapid evolution of game technology has made this unusual to say the least.

Conclusion

Game publishing is a high-risk, high-yield business. Most games lose money. The hits are expected to compensate; therefore, small publishers (who can't afford to release many titles) struggle, and big ones hedge their bets through mergers and acquisitions.

For developers, concentration of the publishing business is unwelcome: fewer outlets for games means less favorable deals. However, until online self-publishing becomes a viable option for high-budget games, the trend is likely to continue unabated.

References

[Laramée00] Laramée, F. D., "How I Spent My Spring Break: A Report on the 2000 Game Developers Conference," available online at *www.gamedev.net/reference/articles/article959.asp*, March 15, 2000.

[Laramée05] Laramée, F. D., "How Developers Get Paid: The Retail Market for Games," in *Secrets of the Game Business*, 2nd Edition, Charles River Media, 2005.

[McGilvray05] McGilvray, M., "The Producer, Friend or Foe?" in *Secrets of the Game Business*, 2nd Edition, Charles River Media, 2005.

[Perkins05] Perkins, T., "Customer Support in Massively Multiplayer Online Games," in *Secrets of the Game Business*, 2nd Edition, Charles River Media, 2005.

[Sloper02] Sloper, T., "Following Up after the Game Is Released: It's Not Over When It's Over," in *Game Design Perspectives*, Charles River Media, 2002.

2.5

Diagnosing Immaturity in Development Studios: Symptoms and Treatment

Steve Bocska and Jodi Regts

strategus@shaw.ca

Pop psychology author Dan Kiley coined the term "Peter Pan syndrome" [Kiley83] to describe men who never grow up and, ultimately, refuse to accept responsibility. Some video game development studios could be diagnosed with a similar affliction. Child-like imagination and an appreciation for play are obviously desirable traits in an industry that creates imaginary worlds. However, rapid growth without a corresponding maturation has created significant problems that negatively impact studios from both a creative and a business perspective. For some studios, there may be an erroneous assumption that this kind of stunted growth or immaturity enhances creativity.

Many developers use the youthfulness of the industry as an excuse for their lack of sound business practices and frequent ad-hoc behavior—a clear symptom of "stunted" professional growth. To be clear, this immaturity complex is not limited to companies that choose to focus on small revenue streams, or those that plan to never exceed a small number of employees. In fact, those developers are demonstrating a maturity in planning and focus.

Looking at the industry as a whole, there may be a pandemic of studios that are aging without growing up—while struggling to survive as businesses and effectively bring their creative ideas to life. In reality, the symptoms of this "aversion to growing up" are easy to spot. If left untreated, its effects can be fatal for a business, and severely damaging to the industry as a whole.

The Symptoms

Small, successful companies often have no lack of enthusiasm and dedication early on. It's easy to see everything in a positive light, but this perspective isn't always realistic. It is no wonder, then, that one of the big mistakes made by video game development studios is to allow themselves to become overly optimistic. Early success with expansion can also fuel the growing optimism, making it difficult to recognize when things are going wrong—or even the possibility of poor decisions being made.

Unfortunately, this emotional bias is likely to remain endemic throughout the industry for years to come due in large part to the cyclical nature of the software development cycle. The evidence of rapid growth in any form often fosters a misguided belief that somehow, because of some *current* growth situation or development contract, *future* success is guaranteed. As projects ramp up to their production limit, there is often a dizzying euphoria throughout the team space as they experience an overnight expansion of team members, equipment, facilities, and resources. However, this euphoria is fleeting and temporary in an industry with finite production cycles, potentially leading to large "crashes" of emotion that can ripple through even larger companies as projects wind down and team members are reorganized, or in worst-case scenarios, laid off.

Optimism should not be regarded as a bad thing, however. In healthy doses, it does wonders for the opportunism and flexibility of a company. The real danger lies in allowing raging optimism to affect the objectivity of those in positions of making critical decisions.

Feelings of Invincibility

Success-inspired optimism can also foster a belief that the company is capable beyond its knowledge base, resources, or cash flow. For example, Radical Entertainment—a Vancouver-based studio—is by all accounts a very successful developer today. However, years ago, Radical made the decision to expand their influence and foray into software publishing. The transition from a developer to a publisher was more difficult than they had imagined, and one that nearly caused the company's demise. The company had banked much of its future on a massive and complex deal that would have critical funds arriving just in time to fund the company's foray into publishing. The funds never arrived, and the results were devastating. However, this particular story happens to have a happy ending, for Radical's recovery from this fiasco has been dramatic, with the company currently standing as one of the most successful independent developers in the industry. Nevertheless, the lessons learned were nonetheless painful at the time.

Small developers sometimes find themselves second guessing their intuition and signing contracts out of sheer desperation to survive. The terms in these contracts force the company to rely on elusive and oft-delayed milestone approvals to fill the coffers and pay their staff. This is unfortunate, but not uncommon, as it is much easier to expect that everything will work out favorably than to picture utter failure. In general, this "invincibility" symptom can lead to mistakes in strategic decision making, and an over-commitment of resources in an excessively risky venture. Add to this the possibility that the studio is lacking a highly developed core business, and a company can be left in a very vulnerable state.

Another result of this feeling of invincibility can be a focus on new, unproven business lines, while not leaving enough effort focused on renewing "cash cow" development contracts. Simply put, premature risks are taken by companies possessing unrefined core competencies. In hindsight, the focus of companies in similar situations to Radical's at the time should not be on aggressive growth and spending at this point in its development, but instead on building gradually upon existing competencies and nurturing ongoing publisher relationships.

Naivety and Misplaced Trust

Wisdom is best gained from experience. In the early years of a development studio, there are often too few people who possess the business "wisdom" necessary to strategically lead the small company. Typically consisting of gaming enthusiasts who have joined forces and rallied around a vision, these small studios struggle to effectively negotiate with publishing giants.

What may seem like a fortune to invest for one company is a trifling pittance to another. Unfortunately, many small developers learn this the hard way. They might come to the table committing what they consider a "large" investment in time, money, and resources to a deal. However, the same investment is little more than a curious experiment for a publishing company at least 100 times larger. For the small developer, it seems inconceivable that another company would be able to walk away with barely a flinch. Yet that is exactly what can happen.

Like many powerless developers disadvantaged by their, "small numbers bargaining position" [Williamson85], these smaller companies find themselves negotiating unfavorable contracts with inconvenient payment schedules, one-sided intellectual property consideration, and poor royalty deals. Too often, promises that favor the developer are not committed to paper. Agreements made on a handshake display an honorable measure of trust. However, good intentions are sometimes victimized by the reality of circumstance—people leave companies, taking verbal commitments with them. Many early struggles of small developers can be averted with extra effort to formalize publisher arrangements and deals.

"Over-Promising"/"Under-Planning" Compulsion

Sometimes, it is not simply naivety that creates lopsided agreements. Without a clear plan or project evaluation in place, many developers find themselves unwittingly over-promising outcomes to publishers, without even realizing that resources will be unavailable or simply stretched too thin. Shawn Storc, a producer with publisher UbiSoft, sums up his feelings about this trait in some development studios:

"I get wary of new developers when they feel that they've got 'one shot' to make a reputation for themselves. This is when they start making bad decisions based on fear. Over-promises abound, but once the contract is secured, they're unable to keep up with the workload. Lacking experience and skill sets, they desperately need a plan for development and growth."

Although a bad development or project plan is often better than no plan at all, what may be even worse is a good plan that is not properly communicated to the key stakeholders—a common symptom of introverted management who are unaware of the benefits of open communication. For other owners or managers, the development plan or strategic vision is firmly articulated; unfortunately, it exists almost exclusively in their minds as opposed to being formalized on paper. And while this leadership may be enthusiastic, that enthusiasm does not necessarily presume solid communication of vital information.

By failing to properly formalize and distribute these plans to those who could help make it happen, companies risk creating a rudderless ship unable to sail in the direction the leaders desire. The final step in project or strategic planning should always be aggressive communication and monitoring to ensure that there are frequent reminders of the direction in which the company intends to travel. If there is a broad understanding of the company's desires—no matter how ambitious—employees at all levels are better able to behave and perform in ways that would help fulfill the company's vision. Instead, many employees are essentially working "head down" to simply get immediate project-specific tasks completed. Communicating the long-term strategic vision is vital for companies hoping to self-fulfill their own prophecies.

Severe Growing Pains

One of the most significant symptoms of this specific immaturity syndrome is an inability to maintain a high-quality production facility throughout a period of rapid growth. Most business analysts agree that corporate growth is healthy and desirable. However, much like an individual's personal growth, a company's basic needs change from infancy through adolescence and into maturity. Some developers are simply not prepared for the challenges and "growing pains" that an organization faces as it develops from a startup into a large company with 100 employees or more.

Staffing is always an issue in a company experiencing rapid growth. The promote-from-within strategy that works so well for a small company tends to have unexpected consequences as highly skilled and long-standing coders, artists, and designers are expected to suddenly demonstrate expert levels of strategic, financial, managerial, and leadership qualities. Realizing this, many studios do the obvious and set out to hire highly qualified specialists to fill key positions. However, searching for a "silver bullet" solution also has its challenges, especially in a young industry that lacks an abundance of truly seasoned veteran managers and specialists. What reads well on paper as relevant experience in the film or record publishing industry doesn't always translate perfectly into video game production.

Information Blockages

When a company grows, the flow of information also tends to increase, and consequently, difficulties arise in managing that flow. New reporting structures and larger development teams mean that the simple "everybody knows everything" approach that worked perfectly fine in smaller organizations is no longer realistic or even desirable. This poorly structured management of information can lead to a general state of confusion, and more specifically, reduced accountability and availability of the facts. Unfortunately, this symptom often manifests itself during critical times when the company most needs to be honestly apprised of things that are going wrong.

Even worse, once the situation surrounding a company's financial woes worsens, management often becomes even more hesitant to share bad news with creative teams, fearing that it will be too distracting and an impediment to production. Thus, employees are only selectively informed of the difficulties being faced by the company, sometimes leading to rumors, confusion, conflicts, and low morale.

Sometimes, even good news can be poorly managed. Many developers are caught off guard when presented with an exit strategy from bigger companies that are offering to buy them out once a studio has reached a certain size or number of employees. Recently, in the case of Vancouver developer Black Box, the owners had been presented with a favorable buy-out offer from a large publisher, which would ensure all 100+ employees were retained; yet rumors abounded. Senior management wisely recognized that productivity would be negatively impacted if this news were not properly communicated, so they sat down with the entire staff and openly outlined the possibilities and options, encouraging employees to ask questions and generate dialogue. Ironically, this frank and open informal communication philosophy was one of many traits of Black Box that made the eventual acquisition of the company the owners' best alternative—the company had a "small studio" personality, but had unfortunately outgrown itself. Management lacked the experience, and likely even the desire, to institute the kinds of reporting structures and information systems that are necessary once a company grows beyond 100 employees.

The Treatment

Fortunately, there is a treatment for the "Peter Pan Syndrome." The following five tactics are a prescription for development studios that recognize some of the symptoms, are afraid of losing their creativity if they impose formal methods, yet feel that they can truly benefit from growing up.

Use Positive Visualization

The ability of a company to succeed depends on people who commit themselves and persevere through the lean times. Many organizations founded on a "small company" philosophy experience great stress and hardship when adding new teams, formalizing reporting structure, and adopting organizational structures to accommodate rapid growth. However, with enough of the right people who "believe in the dream," a company can continue to pursue the values on which it was founded. These people bring within them enough of the enthusiasm and spirit necessary to maintain the core company—even if rebuilding is necessary. According to UbiSoft content manager Laurentiu Rusu, "To make truly great games, producers and team leads need to have the ideal mix of charisma, leadership, and vision. Otherwise, the team will end up in a hopelessly chaotic state."

It is also important to translate this clear corporate vision to the individual project or game team. It is often up to the experienced team leaders who instill employees with the unwritten core values. These leaders—producers, directors, and "character" employees—must be extremely well versed in core culture and attuned to the impact of rapid growth and other related symptoms. According to Kirsten Forbes, a producer at Radical Entertainment, "Good developers know the importance of project planning. They have the fundamental knowledge of how to make games—and more importantly—the diversity of experience to know how to deal with a crisis when it arises."

Communication of the corporate vision is a powerful unifying tool, even able to overcome distance and international boundaries. Until recently, Disney Interactive owned a small game development studio in Victoria, British Columbia. Despite its small size, distance from California, and relatively remote location—Victoria is on an island only accessible by ferry or airplane—they were still able to sustain the studio and keep it an integral part of their product development plans for several years. They placed strong emphasis on solid communication with upper management and the marketing departments in the California head office. In effect, the studio was an outpost maintaining a small, flexible, independent culture, while still benefiting from the considerable expertise of the large, corporate parent body protecting its interests, setting its strategic vision, and formulating its guiding principles.

Practice Role Reversal

Most developers pride themselves on a solid commitment to building good games and earning a strong reputation for quality. In addition, most companies in this industry are not founded as "get-rich-quick" ventures. Yet, one of the simplest business tenets—keep your customer happy—is often forgotten or seen as too difficult a commitment when the customer is a big publisher.

However, keeping publishers happy isn't as difficult as some people believe. A simple role reversal gives a good insight into this. Imagine you (the publisher) are commissioning an artist (the developer) to paint a painting that you intend to sell on the open market. You've done your research and know that most people like paintings of snow-capped mountain scenes. You hand your money to the artist and tell him to get started. In your position, how would you like the artist to manage the relationship? Would you like it if the artist told you that your research was bogus and that snow-capped mountains were a ridiculous subject? Would you like to find out at the last minute that the artist decided to paint a fruit basket instead? Would you be happy if the artist tried to nickel-and-dime you for every little change you asked for in the painting? If you were like most people, you'd want the artist to frequently give progress updates, support your understanding of the marketplace, consult with you when he is contemplating taking "creative liberties," and deliver the painting on time and for the amount originally quoted.

Shawn Storc of UbiSoft recently summarized another frustration for publishers: an ever-changing design: "Games that gradually change their design or fundamental vision throughout production show an inherent immaturity in the teams' knowledge of the production process—and ultimately show a lack of respect for the client." Mature developers always remember that the publisher is their customer. To put it bluntly, publishers pay developers so they don't have to put up with the perceived grief of developing games. Most importantly, publishers should be happy with the final product that is delivered—even if it requires multiple revisions to get to that point.

Put Pride Aside and Pick a Plan

There is very little room for stubborn, misguided pride in a company when things are going seriously astray. Of course, knowing—or even strongly suspecting—that there is a problem is an important first step, but it alone won't ensure survival. Actually asking for help during a difficult time when the road ahead is likely to be increasingly treacherous is often one of the hardest things for an "I've-done-it-all-myself" entrepreneur to do. If a company assembles a loyal following of employees, suppliers, and publishers, it is much easier to ask stakeholders and employees for assistance when really needed.

Even more importantly, employees and stakeholders should be given full disclosure and an opportunity to decide what role they should play in the company's future. Key personnel and producers should also be given the authority to communicate honestly with their reports to prepare them for the difficult times ahead. This can be a classic "gut check" moment in a company's development—with some key personnel choosing other paths with other companies. However, without honest communication about the company's state of affairs, the employees and managers would be at a tremendous disadvantage in trying to chart a path to recovery.

CASE STUDY 2.5.1: BOUNDED RATIONALITY AT RADICAL GAMES

In 1978, Herbert Simon won a Nobel Prize for his work on an area of economics known as "bounded rationality." Simply put, bounded rationality deals with the fact that decision makers can't always behave in a completely "rational" manner because of their uncertainty about the future and the high costs in gaining information about things that haven't happened yet. Even more simply put: if you don't have a crystal ball, you can't make perfect decisions. According to Simon, overcoming
→

bounded rationality is perhaps the greatest challenge in running a successful, competitive company. Fortunately, there is a way that decision makers can break down the barriers that keep companies from making rational decisions and be granted a glimpse into the future—the practice of planning.

Radical Games recently took the teachings of Simon to heart and undertook a massive strategic planning initiative. The exercise was lengthy and extensive, involving all levels of the company, countless meetings, external advisors, homework assignments, and hours of healthy and meaningful debate. Formalized planning exercises were enacted to first identify—then align—the company's core values with its strategic and operational practices. From that, they were able clearly define and enact a blueprint that would help guide the company into a state of excellent corporate health. The result was a set of documents that remains one of the most frequently referenced and consulted set of internal guidelines for the company today, and one that has already led to great improvements in both the quality of games—as evidenced by increasing favorable review scores—and profitability.

This commitment to planning is important not just at the corporate level, but also at the project level. Yannis Mallat, senior producer at UbiSoft Montreal, credits formalized planning as a critical success factor when designing games. When describing the intense planning process for the very successful *Prince of Persia: Sands of Time* title, Mallat states: "Planning early on involved getting eights guys in a room for three weeks to thrash out the game's ingredients." This up-front planning ensured that time was spent proving concepts and mechanics before diving into the production process.

Optimized Leadership

There is a body of business research called "stakeholder theory" that proposes that every category of stakeholder possesses varying degrees of Power, Legitimacy, and Urgency. An individual who possesses all three of these characteristics is a "definitive" stakeholder, and worthy of your utmost and immediate attention. A successful leader recognizes this instinctively and is able to funnel his efforts to please that individual. What a *charismatic* leader possesses is an ability to take this one step further and instill the feeling of being needed and important in all stakeholders—even those who are not "definitive."

Charismatic and persuasive leadership is about more than just being enthusiastic. It requires empathy, conviction, attentiveness, vision, and often, an ability to speak in meaningful generalities that permit the listener to translate and customize the message into something personal that speaks directly to him. Even at the height of turmoil and uncertainty, when leaders demonstrate these qualities, they create an environment that is confident and reassuring.

Although it may seem obvious, even with a competent CEO in charge, it is essential to have a strong CFO. Unless there is already somebody in the company who has a dozen years of experience successfully managing the cash flow of a large company, be prepared to bring an expert in to help guide the financial activities. Find an assertive "bean counter" who will challenge assumptions, question decisions that aren't based on responsible fiscal management, and who has a passion for following generally accepted accounting principles. You don't want somebody to just "keep the books." You want someone who will give you frequent and honest appraisals of the financial health of the company.

Experience dictates that only fully functioning teams create great products; people feel more valued when they are empowered. People want to do great things. One of the biggest leadership challenges is to give workers an environment that allows them to succeed and achieve new heights. If you do, great things will happen. At Radical, for example, the company has created development teams that are independent business units—essentially, small businesses unto themselves—under direct control of the producers. These teams cooperate and compete with one another for contracts, support, and resources. Reporting structures are kept simple, and corporate bureaucracy is minimized. Administration is separate from the production floor, both conceptually and physically, to encourage teams to keep their focus on their unique skills and talents. In addition, employees are encouraged to innovate and experiment in the pursuit of discovery, even at the cost of occasional failure. The result has been great synergies and an overall positive work environment.

Master the Expert Level

Getting good at something is not difficult. In most cases, it simply takes a reasonable degree of dedication and practice. However, becoming an "expert" is considerably more challenging. One statistical definition of an "expert" is a person who operates at a level of skill at least two standard deviation units above the norm—in other words, the top 2.5% of performers in a field. Research shows that we typically need to practice a skill regularly for 10 years or 20,000 hours to reach this level of competence. For an entire company, these minima are most certainly even higher still. The bottom line? If you want to get really good at something, you have to do it over and over and over.

For a company, maintaining a perpetually high level of competitive expertise is an extraordinary achievement. It requires a commitment to excellence as well as a willingness to accept the realization that a critical prerequisite to staying on top is continuous ongoing learning—and often "relearning" what you thought you already knew. In a constantly changing universe, it is only possible to "know everything" for a fleeting instant. Then, it's back to the drawing board to try to learn how the new universe is different from the way it was just a moment ago.

When striving to master the expert level, hiring and retention strategies are key. While matching skills and experience with job roles is important, strong consideration should also be given to ensure candidates "fit" within the culture of the company. Although there is great value in continuity and promoting from within, it is a delicate balance. Looking outside the industry, people in traditional business environments aren't always used to the creative, flexible, and demanding work environments. Nor are they always immediately skilled at the unique approaches required in the making of video games, which unlike other products, is not about the management of ongoing production. Furthermore, production teams cannot simply grow unchecked and be expected to instantly demonstrate the synergies necessary to create blockbuster video games.

Ongoing Therapies

To ensure a healthy future, organizations should undergo ongoing therapies, while remaining vigilant for warnings signs of regression. For those developers who feel as though they have successfully grown up, there are some additional strategies to ensure that they do not slip back into immature ways.

Don't Be Afraid to Cut Expenses

No company can hope to survive for the long haul when expenses are exceeding revenues. Remember: you won't lose employees if you're making decisions that keep the company financially healthy—but you'll definitely lose them if you don't. Recurring red ink on the financials may mean that it is time to move to a smaller studio, sell some unused equipment, scale back on some perquisites, or temporarily hold back bonuses or raises to stop the hemorrhaging. You have to stop the bleeding before you can focus on the long-term health of the company.

Continually Assess Risks

There was a time not long ago when the videogame industry was small and the expectations of gamers relatively unsophisticated. During this "Wild West" phase, game studios of varying backgrounds could more easily convince publishers that they were capable of making a game in a genre even if they had no previous experience. After all, how difficult would it be to build upon your knowledge of side-scrolling shooters and make an isometric platform game?

Today, it is a much different story. If a studio with only real-time strategy experience were to pitch a console flight simulator to a publisher, they would rightfully raise a suspicious eyebrow. (As Case Study 2.3.1 in [Laramée05] shows, even highly successful studios like Blue Fang Games, developers of the *Zoo Tycoon* franchise, have to contend with this bias toward "genre experience.") Mature studios will be successful by focusing on their core competencies and reinvesting in the core technologies and skills, with only small investments being made in areas of uncertainty.

Conclusion

In an industry that creates worlds of fantasy and entertaining escapes from the boredom of the day-to-day world, perhaps it's not surprising that video game developers might develop something of a Peter Pan Complex. However, the important thing to remember is that this affliction is not a positive trait for a developer. Immaturity is not a way to guarantee creativity. In fact, some of this immature behavior can hinder creative teams—and put the future of the company in jeopardy.

Kirsten Forbes of Radical puts it this way: "Bad developers are easy to spot in this young industry—they don't know how to treat people like adults." The good news is that the prescription for treatment is not difficult. Companies are more than capable of putting the customer first, properly assessing risk by focusing on their core competencies, and creating strong strategic plans and clear visions for employees and other stakeholders.

Indeed, developers should welcome this maturation as a kind of security to be able to do what they love to do: create games. Taking the Peter Pan analogy further: developers should focus on growing up—but never growing old.

References

[Kiley83] Kiley, D., *The Peter Pan Syndrome: Men Who Have Never Grown Up*, Dodd Mead, 1983.

[Laramée05] Laramée, F. D., "The Many Faces of Game Development," in *Secrets of the Game Business*, 2nd Edition, Charles River Media, 2005.

[Williamson85] Williamson, O. E., *The Economic Institutions of Capitalism*, The Free Press: New York, 1985.

2.6

The Producer, Friend or Foe?

Mitzi McGilvray

mitzi@slamdunkproductions.com

The role of the producer varies depending on whether the producer works for a publisher or a developer. This article deals specifically with those producers who are employed by publishers.

Step 1: Establish a Relationship with Your Producer

By establishing a positive relationship with a producer, you are taking the first important step toward a successful relationship with a game publisher. Prior to having a deal with a publisher, a producer can:

Recommend you for a project he has. When a producer has an upcoming project, he will be on the lookout for a good development team. He will typically have two to three developers in mind whom he will contact to get proposals.

Recommend you to other producers within his company. The producer will know which projects are getting funded and are in need of a developer. If you are on good terms with him, he might recommend you to other producers.

Help you prepare for a successful pitch to the publisher. The producer can provide you with document templates and sample information to help you prepare the most effective pitch possible.

Help you with key introductions within his company. By introducing you to key decision makers within his organization, the producer can help you extend your network throughout that company. Those relationships might even outlive the producer's employment with that publisher.

Alert you to opportunities for contracts or product proposals. The proper timing can significantly increase your odds of obtaining a contract with a publisher. Knowing when a publisher is looking for developers and what types of titles they are looking to publish will help you focus your presentation or pitch.

Once you have inked a deal with a publisher, the producer assigned to you can help you with the following:

Put together the perfect project plan. Most publishers have approved examples of technical designs, game designs, schedules, and budgets. Having these available prior to starting your work on these deliverables will help ensure a quick approval and a happy publisher. If a producer does not offer these documents, ask for them.

Proactively keep you on good terms with the publisher. If you succeed, he succeeds. He will review your progress, alerting you to any potential issues in terms of milestone approvals, direction, or impending changes with the publisher.

Get you a quick sign-off and prompt payment for your milestones. Assuming you meet your milestone, most producers can expedite approvals and check deliveries. Remember, however, that getting you an expedited payment is extra work for a producer.

Gain support for your product from other divisions. A good producer knows how to get the most from the various other organizations within his company. This can translate to increased marketing, public relations, and sales support.

Recommend you for future work. Do a good job and maintain a positive working relationship, and he will recommend you for additional work.

Unfortunately, not developing a positive working relationship with a producer will affect both your short- and long-term business goals. A negative relationship with a producer might:

Make it difficult or impossible for you to ever work for that publisher or even perhaps other publishers as long as he is employed there. This situation can cost you additional work with that publisher and any future publisher for whom he might work.

Critique every milestone approval to the point that it is impossible for you to successfully complete your project. A producer can make a developer's life miserable if he so chooses. Having very well-defined milestones and a solid, approved project plan can help prevent this.

Get your project canceled. A disenchanted producer can get your contract cancelled in the hope that a different developer can do a better job.

Speak poorly of your company to his peers. The producer network is very tight. Most producers have worked for several publishers and have a solid network of peers. Obviously, it is important to always maintain a positive relationship with your producer. This is especially important when things go wrong, as the producer can help you stay in good graces with the publisher. This might enable you to work with that company again in the future.

Step 2: Plan for Checks and Balances

It is important to note that the producer is probably not the final decision maker within his organization. Therefore, you should view him as the guardian for all that relates to his projects. Many larger companies have a series of checks and balances in place. The producer must work within this system for his projects to run smoothly. These checks and balances typically include:

> **Technical directors.** These individuals will help ensure that a developer is technically able to undertake a specific project.
>
> **Sales and marketing.** This team will evaluate whether a product is marketable. Although it goes without saying that a game must look great and play well, there is a host of other factors that sales and marketing must consider when evaluating the marketability of a game. Some of these factors include market condition, competition, and timing to market.
>
> **The executive staff.** This group will make sure the product is consistent with the overall goals and guidelines of the company.
>
> **Legal/business affairs.** This organization will check to see that the deal meets corporate standards, and approve any contracts prior to signing them or beginning work.

Step 3: Know Your Producer

A producer is typically someone who likes to get involved in all aspects of the game development process. Recent information from Melanie Cambron (a.k.a. Game Recruiting Goddess) shows that 87% of all producers in the United States are male (Figure 2.6.1). There are numerous debates as to why there are not more female producers in the business; however, please note that this article is written by one of those few women who have chosen game production as a career.

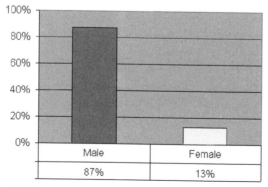

FIGURE 2.6.1a   *Percentage of male and female producers.*

As you can see in Figure 2.6.2, the average, experienced California-based producer earns about $80,000 per year. To put this in perspective, a teacher in the same city would make about 70% of a producer's wage.

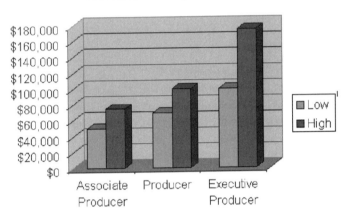

FIGURE 2.6.2 *Producer compensation.*

The Production Hierarchy

Understanding the hierarchy of the various production roles will help you decide where to invest your efforts in terms of networking, relationship building, making product pitches, and such. It will do you no good to invest time and effort in building a business relationship with someone who cannot influence decisions. It is important to keep in mind that the roles of a producer vary greatly by publisher. In some organizations, the producer is entrusted with a great deal of power and authority. In other companies, that level of power might only be available to the executive producer or vice president of development. Typically, the level of responsibility is directly related to the salary the producer earns. Do not let the title fool you, as each game company uses the "producer" title differently. Examples might be seen in a smaller game company where the title of executive producer is assigned. Those individuals might have responsibilities matching that of a producer at a larger publisher. Regardless of title, the producer is ultimately the person responsible for a title coming in on time and on budget. He will receive either the blame or credit for these accomplishments.

The organization chart shown in Figure 2.6.3 is an example of a typical production hierarchy. Expect this to vary by publisher.

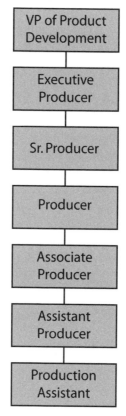

FIGURE 2.6.2 *Production hierarchy.*

The Five Types of Producers

Producers can be categorized into five distinct personality types. You can expect some overlap; however, these generalizations should help you in choosing the best way to deal with producers.

The five types of producers are the micro manager, the macro manager, the team leader, the creative producer, and the game designer.

The Micro Manager

You will find this producer to have excellent project management skills. He is very detail oriented and has a keen understanding of the processes involved in game production. The micro manager is sometimes better at identifying problems than at solving them, but given the proper authority and pre-production time, he will typically plan for contingencies and properly assess risk, thus saving you from unexpected problems later on.

To make the most of your relationship with this producer, you must use his passion for organization by involving him early in the planning stages. This producer is the master of follow-up and follow-through. He will read, digest, question, and reread every document you submit to him, especially schedules and plans. Therefore, have him provide templates and additional assistance in preparing these documents throughout the production process.

The Macro Manager

This individual is all about the big picture. He is a visionary, a franchise builder who might begin planning for a sequel long before the first title is completed, and typically quite adept at problem solving. This is because he constantly has his eye on the prize.

The macro manager has a solid understanding of all aspects of the videogame business and will be a valuable asset in navigating the publisher's organization. In working with this producer, you will obtain the best results by keeping your own focus on the details and letting him take care of the long-term plans. Remember that you must make that first game a hit before anything else matters.

The Team Leader

This producer typically gains the trust and respect of the development team by rolling up his sleeves and providing value wherever he is capable. He chooses to lead by example and strives to be liked by everyone on the team. The team producer can be easily spotted, as he can be found testing code for programmers at midnight, having coffee with the execs at 8 A.M. in an attempt to gain more budget money, and taking the art team to lunch. All of this is, of course, in addition to his regular producer job.

In working with the team producer, remember that it is important for him to constantly feel as if he is providing "added value." Therefore, take advantage of his desire to help and use his (often considerable) expertise wherever appropriate.

The Creative Producer

The title says it all. This individual comes from a creative background. He quite likely has very strong game design or graphic design skills. He thrives on the creative aspects of game production and does his job because of his love for games.

You will find that the creative producer provides invaluable contributions in terms of driving the vision of the product. Harness this energy early and you can have a solid foundation for building a winning product.

The Game Designer

Sadly, almost everyone has encountered this producer type, and his presence at a potential publishing partner can have long-lasting effects on your business.

Everyone knows how to spot the game designer, by the trail of battered and abused developers with nothing to show but cancelled games. Unfortunately, you might not have a choice about working with this producer. If you do encounter the game designer, you can get the best results by using an approach of consistency, respect, and thorough documentation.

Case Studies

To gain a practical perspective about the varying roles of a producer, we interviewed two veteran producers whose experience includes working for publishers such as 3DO, Activision, Eidos, Electronic Arts, and Midway. The individuals interviewed are Bill Hindorff and Mike Kawahara. Both of these producers have been in the business since the early days, and have in excess of 44 years of game production experience between them.

Quality, Not Quantity

A producer of console or PC titles is typically in charge of three to five projects at any given time. A project can be defined as a unique title for a specific platform. If a project is small in scope, such as with mobile games, the producer might have responsibility for even more, or, depending on the publisher he works for, he might have as many as 10 to 20 titles under his domain.

A Producer's Day

As you can see in Figure 2.6.4, a producer's day is typically spent making sure his projects are progressing according to plan. Topping the list of activities in his day is most definitely communication. These communications vary greatly depending on the status of the product and might include:

Bug list reviews. This typically happens first thing in the morning to understand the state of products in the alpha or beta phase.

Milestone schedule review. To keep on top of project status, a regular review of the milestone status is conducted by the producer with the developer.

Marketing plan updates. Keeping abreast of the status of marketing efforts and keeping the marketing group informed of how the game is coming along will help ensure the product gets the proper attention when it ships.

Product pitches. The product pitch process seems never ending to most producers. It is a constant cycle of creating and pitching project plans. Many of these pitches are built with the help of the targeted developer.

Negotiations. Negotiations are a large part of the producer's day. This might include negotiating additional features for his game, navigating a multimillion dollar development deal, or convincing the test department to close a particular bug.

Product review. There is a constant stream of meetings designed to update all stakeholders within a producer's organization on the status of his titles. The product review meetings are most important because each product and its status are discussed.

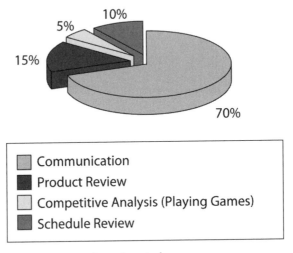

FIGURE 2.6.4   *A producer's day.*

Communication Is Key

It is important to note that the more effective producers will put communication with the developer and testers at the top of their priority list. Each producer interviewed told stories of inheriting troubled projects in which the developer was months behind. These projects were turned around in every instance because more effective communication was made a priority. Developers cannot succeed if they do not know how to meet the objectives of their publishers. Further, developers also need to feel that the project they are working on has visibility with their publisher and that their efforts will be rewarded at the end by effective marketing and sales programs.

The rest of the producer's day is split between reviewing schedules, seeking out and solving problems, and, of course, playing games. Each producer interviewed acknowledged that playing their and competitive products was always something they wished they had more time to do, but that this typically gets pushed aside because more immediate problems or priorities demand their attention.

A Producer's Dream

In addition to technical expertise, a producer will look for several other attributes in a development team:

Communication. Effective communication was most definitely at the top of the list. Being able to know when and how to communicate are essential traits in a developer.

Passion for making games. If you do not love your work, go do something else.
Willingness to take and act on feedback. Everyone needs to be able to take
criticism: it's what makes good games better.
Objectivity. Know when to escalate issues such as when a product is in trouble,
an individual is not meshing with the rest of the team, or a key milestone date is
not achievable. When you lose objectivity, things can quickly get off track. For
example, one story shared during the interview detailed how a development
team was falling apart. Milestones were being missed, the team members were at
odds with each other, and the lead developer had put in his resignation notice.
Why? Because one of the key contributors on the development team was not
capable of doing his job. Eventually, that producer and the programmer in
question were fired. The project had already missed too many key dates and was
ultimately cancelled.

Words of Wisdom

When asked to share their best advice with the development community, they had
some excellent words of wisdom to keep in mind:

Say what you are going to say. Say it. Say what you said. This is a lesson taught
in every communication class, but cannot be reiterated enough when you are
dealing with game development. Communication, follow-through, and follow-
up are essential in a successful producer/developer relationship.
Plan for everything to fall apart. Create a solid plan in advance; plan for it to
change and plan for everything around it to go wrong. Producers are keen risk
assessors. If they do not feel like you have planned for all contingencies, they
will not believe you are capable of succeeding. As you see the need for change,
raise the flag high detailing exactly what the costs of this change might be to the
schedule, budget, and team. Plan to do this early and often.
It is more work to make a bad game than a good game. Once the plans are set
in motion, each time a producer feels he needs to tune, tweak, and polish the
design, art, or gameplay, the bigger the opportunity for disaster. With the proper
team in place, much of this polishing will occur seamlessly with only the
occasional redirect. If a producer gets into a pattern of constantly changing or
redirecting resources, the budget and schedule (and typically the game quality)
will quickly get out of control.
Throwing more resources at a problem will not always fix it. There is a critical
path for everything. Do not shift resources from one project to something else
(that you deem higher priority) and expect to make up that time later. These
antics drive producers absolutely crazy.
Never throw good money after bad money. Some games should never make it
to market. This determination might not be accessible until a significant
investment has been made in the development process. Canceling those games

as soon as this fact is obvious is not only prudent for the publisher, but also very healthy for the development team, as they can focus on more positive work. All producers can tell stories of how they witness millions of dollars being thrown at a project that will obviously either never make it to market, or will never succeed in the market.

Success has many parents, failure is an orphan. If you have a successful project, people will come out of the woodwork to take credit. However, if your project fails, only the truest friends will stand by your side.

Conclusion

If you are trying to get your game produced by a publisher, get to know one or two of the producers at each of your target publishers. Stay in regular contact with them so they know your availability and projects. Frequent communication keeps you at the forefront when they are making a list of potential developers for their projects.

Once you have your product placed at a publisher, establish and maintain a positive relationship with your producer. Getting to know him will help you get the most out of that relationship.

Finally, as you are nearing the completion of your project with that publisher, make sure the producer knows you are ready to take on more work.

STARTUPS

3.0

Introduction

The game development market is extremely crowded. Of the thousands of games released every year, only a few hundred ever receive wide distribution, and a mere fraction of those earn significant profits. Both the publishing and the development sides of the industry are consolidating quickly. However, by far the most common cause of failure of new studios (and of new businesses in any field, for that matter) is insufficient preparation.

Time and time again, successful programmers, designers, and artists have left their jobs to create high-profile studios, only to see their new companies fizzle for lack of business acumen. For those who create startups with little or no prior industry experience, the odds of success are even slimmer. If you decide to start your own company, make sure that you have access to the right management, sales, and legal resources—preferably among the shareholders. Then, prepare a solid business plan, identifying an opportunity that you and your team are uniquely qualified to profit from, and you will be on your way.

The articles in this section describe ways to improve your chances of starting a company that will beat the odds and achieve long-term success:

- In Article 3.1, "Development Misery and How to Avoid It," freelance designer Sean Timarco Baggaley examines several of the common mistakes made by new developers and explains how to avoid them.
- In Article 3.2, "Startups: Don't Compete with *Half-Life 2!*," producer and agent Max Meltzer explains various ways in which startups can improve their odds of success by avoiding direct confrontation with the industry's powerhouses.
- In Article 3.3, "Writing a Business Plan for a Game Development Startup," François Dominic Laramée describes how to write a successful business plan.
- In Article 3.4, "Strategies for Staffing a Startup," games industry recruiter Grant Stanton explains techniques for optimal personnel selection.
- In Article 3.5, "Financing from the Buyer's Side: Evaluating and Acquiring a Game Company," veteran producer Tom Sloper explains the tricks and pitfalls of acquiring an existing game development company.
- Finally, in Article 3.6, "Financing Projects and Startups," independent studio owner Thomas Djafari describes the financing alternatives available to startups.

3.1

Development Misery and How to Avoid It

Sean Timarco Baggaley

stimarco@bangbangclick.com

It is common to hear of the great successes in our industry: the celebrities who have made millions from games and produced strings of hits. Yet, success is often not a good teacher. Many early game developers were successful as much through blind luck and serendipity as through judgment and management skill. In the 8-bit days, when development teams could be as small as one person, "management" was a dirty word, and formal business practices, aside from hiring an accountant, were rare.

Today, the industry has changed beyond recognition. Even the smallest of mainstream games can cost millions of dollars, and a developer wishing to go it alone is embarking on a dangerous path.

Successes are heavily advertised, but failure hires no PR companies: it is easy to point at what went right, but it is often far more useful to understand what—and why—a project went wrong.

The statistics—only one in five new businesses will succeed—speak for themselves. This is an average across *all* markets and industries: in a high-risk business such as game development, the success rate is often much lower. A glance at an early 1980s games collection reveals names that have vanished from the economic landscape: Quicksilva, Artic, Mikrogen, Hewson Consultants, Psygnosis, Ocean, Virgin Mastertronic, Firebird, MirrorSoft... All of them were major players in the UK during the 1980s, all of them are gone, absorbed by other companies or bankrupt. Each generation of hardware triggers a new cycle of shake-ups: budgets for games rise dramatically when new platforms are released, and under-funded developers and publishers usually go out of business as a result.

And yet many people still try to break in. Why? For the same reason people play national lotteries or gamble their savings away in Las Vegas: the rewards might be rare, but when you win, you can *really* win.

Success speaks for itself, so this article doesn't talk about success. It highlights the mistakes, the traps, and pitfalls that can beset the unwary.

Doing It Yourself

Managing any business is very hard work and is not for everyone, and there's no shame in deciding against setting up on your own if you feel that it is not for you.

If you've decided to forge ahead, you must first look at the basic rules of business management that apply to all businesses. Surprisingly, many managers have never run a business before. Granted, there has to be a first time for everyone, but this is not an excuse to just dive in at the deep end to see if you know how to swim.

Do Your Homework

If you want to run a business, or even if you've been asked to do so, it is your responsibility to learn how to do it. This isn't as onerous as you might think; contrary to popular belief, there's no real mystery to being a good manager. Being a *great* manager takes talent, certainly, but "manager" is a very broad job description. Great managers tend to specialize.

As with most jobs, the craft can be learned. Most adult education institutes offer courses in this area. If you have little or no formal training in the subject, a course in management and business studies is well worth the investment.

You should also take a class in basic bookkeeping and accounting. Although you will want to hire a dedicated accountant, it does help if you can understand what he's doing for you. (This ties in with the Golden Rule of Management, which we'll come to shortly.)

After you have done your research and studied the craft, you will have a far better grasp of what you're getting yourself into. The theory behind good management practices is easy to learn, but it can take a lifetime to master fully. One point to remember, however, is that management is much more about using common sense than making use of "magic bullets." There is no sure-fire way to management success, but knowledge, common sense, and a smattering of good luck will definitely help.

Make no mistake; running your own studio is a *massive* responsibility. Your own livelihood depends on your abilities, and so do any employees you hire.

Knowledge Is Power

Discounting the obvious issue of luck, about which little can be done, simple *ignorance* causes most new—and even some venerable—businesses to fail.

Ignorance does not mean "stupidity," although it is often mistaken for it. Ignorance means "lack of knowledge." It is clearly impossible to know everything about everything, but it is your *duty* as a manager to know what you *need* to know. Of course, finding out what you need to know is your first task, and many a startup has collapsed because of a failure to perform even basic research into your industry's target markets.

The Golden Rule of Management

Management is primarily about herding people. This is akin to herding cats: possible, but not easy. In reality, most people are generally nice, but they will often have their own agendas and desires that might not always match up with yours. It's your duty to understand how this behavior will affect your business.

The key to this is also the key to mastering management in any industry:

Learn enough about your chosen area of management to recognize problems when you see them.

This is the First Golden Rule of Management, and it means you can *never* stop learning.

Now, it might seem like you need to be an expert in everything related to computer games, but this is not necessarily the case. A good manager knows when and how to delegate: only rarely will the CEO of a company also wear the lead programmer and game designer hats. Instead, your job will be to hire people who can take care of the smaller details for you, leaving you free to work on the big picture.

CASE STUDY 3.1.1: A BRIEF HISTORY OF MS-DOS

When IBM came to Digital Research's door, looking for someone to write an operating system for their new "IBM Personal Computer," they were turned away. It was to Microsoft to whom IBM turned; a software company that, until then, had no experience with building operating systems whatsoever.

From that moment on, Digital Research's days as a colossus of the IT industry were numbered, whereas Microsoft, then just a tiny company in Seattle making versions of BASIC for home computers, has become the behemoth of the personal computer world.

However, the moral of the story is not "Digital Research's managers were stupid." They might have been ignorant, certainly—but they weren't "stupid."

No. The strangest act was to follow when IBM effectively signed away their crown jewels to Microsoft, agreeing to Microsoft's request—and it was merely a request at the time—that MS be allowed to license their own version of MS-DOS to other companies. IBM's use of off-the-shelf products to build their "Personal Computer" made the likelihood of clones appearing on the market very high. If IBM's management had understood more about the very computer industry they helped create, they would have tried the patent route, but they didn't. Along came the clones...and the rest is history.

Bill Gates wasn't being nasty or even immoral: Microsoft was a very small fish at the time and probably expected IBM to refuse their request. However, when someone hands you an entire market on a silver platter...

Microsoft's success didn't just make Gates rich: many of the developers at Microsoft at the time became millionaires as a result of Bill Gates' astute management decisions.

If you're setting up a large development studio with multiple projects, you will probably be dealing not with leads, but with producers who are in charge of those leads. In a small-scale venture, you might have to wear the producer hat as well as your manager hat. In each case, you will certainly need to have a firm understanding of exactly what is involved in game design and development.

In the games industry, this rule is applied by understanding what those programmers, artists, musicians, testers, and game designers actually do for a living. Again, you don't have to be an expert in these fields, but you do need to know enough to apply the Other Golden Rule:

"Communication! Communication! Communication!"

Interference and Communication

Interference is the enemy of all managers. It is your job to keep interference within your team or sector to the lowest level possible.

Interference usually interferes with communication. As soon as two or more people have to work together, the problem of communication arises. A major aspect of effective management is managing the lines of communication within your business. In this context, *interference* is anything that messes with that communication.

In very small development teams, it's usually possible to just turn to your colleague and ask him a question directly. As teams get larger, this becomes less workable: too many people talking to each other make for a very noisy and distracting environment. A lead designer can't design if he's being constantly assailed by department heads to discuss this or that trifling detail.

Communication forms the foundation of any business and can make or break it. Anything that messes with the team's communications, either internal or external, is *interference* and must be stamped out ruthlessly. Make no mistake: managing and maintaining your business' lines of communication and minimizing interference are *your* responsibility! Interference can cause all sorts of problems, not all of which are obvious.

Some types of interference are caused by tangible factors. For example, environmental obstacles, such as an office that is overcrowded, too warm or too cold to work in, will affect performance and morale. Unfortunately, the causes of interference are rarely so easy to spot.

Interference can manifest itself in the form of effects with no obvious cause. For example, morale might be gradually dropping for no visible reason. After some investigation, you may eventually discover an unsubstantiated rumor about the company going around the office. This type of interference can have an insidious effect on productivity, but can usually be countered by improving the flow of information between management and the people at the front lines. Of course, if the company's stated plans make no sense to your employees, you may find this too has a detrimental effect on morale. In such instances, you need to "sell" the plans to your own employees. (If you cannot make that "sale," you should certainly consider it a warning sign; your customers probably won't buy it either!)

The more transparent the communication, the easier it is for everyone to see what's going on. People are naturally wary of information hiding or obfuscation. Similarly, if you're deliberately interfering with your employees' jobs, they won't thank you for it. Morale will fall. Good people will leave. More naïve people will stay a little longer, but ultimately, no one will stay to the bitter end.

A more common problem is external interference from managers, producers, or others who have no real business messing with *your* people. Corporate politics are a fact of life. Nevertheless, your job is to prevent it affecting your team. For a producer, this usually means putting your foot down and saying "No!" to unreasonable feature changes and similar demands from those who have no business doing so.

As you can see, communication is a key part of management, regardless of your position in the management structure. You have to know how to communicate with your own colleagues and employees. Your business needs to communicate with its customers—both game players and publishers. Your business needs to communicate with marketing people, magazine reviewers, Web site building fans, new job applicants, and so on.

If you're not good at talking to people, *run*, don't walk, away from any and all management roles: you won't enjoy them. Even famous musicians hire PR people and agents when they can't face talking to people themselves.

Building Trust

Word-of-mouth marketing—also known as "viral" or "memetic" marketing—is the most powerful form of publicity available to you. The technique has the huge advantage of inherent trust: people lay a lot of store by their friends' recommendations, so if you can get those friends to recommend your game, you're onto a winner. You might not necessarily see first-week sales records smashed, but you can certainly ensure that your game maintains long-term interest. This makes word-of-mouth publicity particularly suitable for games with long shelf lives. This covers any game that doesn't rely primarily on cutting-edge technology to make it attractive to players: shareware card games and puzzle games are a classic case in point.

Of course, this form of marketing requires that you have a good game to sell. People simply won't recommend a lemon to their friends. If your game is truly dire, they might not even recommend it to their worst enemies.

Another problem this form of marketing poses is that it requires building a critical mass of support before you can see its effects. It takes a while after the initial release of your game for the recommendations to build up any noticeable momentum. Exceptions to this occur when someone with many useful contacts—and the means and desire to communicate with them—gets wind of your game. Many games developers will have been told about two of the most original games ever designed in recent years, Balasz Rozsa's *Elast-O-Mania* and Chronic Logic's *Pontifex* and *Triptych*, through their own contacts. Neither was advertised in the traditional way, but relied on word of mouth to build up that critical mass of support. It is often argued that this type of sales technique might be the future of many independent developers.

The power of the Internet has made this type of marketing by far the most effective for smaller developers. Hotmail, for example, grew from zero to several million accounts solely by attaching its "free e-mail" offer to all e-mails sent from its users. For larger developers, who are more concerned with making a big splash, the problem lies not with games players, but with the fact that you can't sell hot air: the games mentioned in the last paragraph were essentially self-funded, which is fine if the game is small in scale, but far harder to do if you're working on a multimillion-dollar project.

There is also a lot to be said for starting small and working your way up the scale. id Software did this in their shareware days: *Doom* simply wouldn't have been possible if they hadn't had the income from their earlier games to fund it.

Self-Marketing

The games industry is a small world in which to work. It's fair to say that pretty much everyone worth knowing knows everyone else worth knowing. Word gets around the industry grapevine very quickly, so you need to make sure that the words that concern you and your business are good ones. This means that word-of-mouth marketing also applies in your business-to-business relationships. If you build up a solid reputation for your company, you will attract more attention from traditionally conservative publishers.

If you plan to play with the major players rather than start with smaller, cheaper games, you'll need to look to publishers or other major sources of funding. This has the unfortunate side effects of (a) making *them* your customers, and (b) giving them a huge chunk of control over your business.

Giving away control is not always a bad thing, but as with most options in life, it needs to be analyzed in context. If you have absolutely no way of getting your game off the ground without funding, you will simply have to bite the bullet and sign. However, if you can recruit a board of directors full of savvy financial executives who know your business, they might be of great help to you—especially if this is your first attempt to run a business.

Covering Your Assets

In the games industry, as with most other storytelling media, the concept of *intellectual property* (IP) plays a huge part in your company's success. Your company's value is measured as much by its IP as by its physical assets. Peter Molyneaux and Les Edgar became millionaires because of the IP that Bullfrog owned. IP is valuable, but its value can be diluted. In Bullfrog's case, the IP included the "Bullfrog" brand as well as the games themselves. At its peak, a Bullfrog game was almost guaranteed high sales solely through the power of the name.

As Bullfrog became increasingly successful, producing a string of hits, Electronic Arts became more interested in the company. Eventually, they bought it lock, stock, and barrel. They paid the original owners and key personnel a lot of money to stay with the company for a few years, since Peter Molyneaux's name in particular was a "brand" in its own right, yet it was clear almost from the beginning that the "magic" had gone. From one point of view, the buyout could be seen as a failure, since the result was the end of Bullfrog and the gradual erosion of the IP's value, including the brand: within a few years, the name "Bullfrog" on a game no longer commanded the same sales it once did.

While the managers did well from the deal financially, they were clearly uncomfortable with what Bullfrog became after the buyout. Consequently, very few of the original members of the company remain there today, yet the original management team is still in the business, having set up new companies. From their perspective, the sale was a success: they have benefited from the transaction and advanced their careers in different directions. This is an example of planning for the long term.

Top Three Ways to Get It Wrong

Hindsight is a great teacher. It is easy to point fingers and laugh after the event, but it is unfair to those who at least *tried*. They made the effort, and that takes a lot of courage. The following is a short list of common mistakes that bring down most businesses, and not just those in the games industry.

Item 1: Don't Do Any Research

It's amazing how often people will take this type of risk. Failing to prepare adequately kills your business' credibility if the people you deal with see through your bluffing. Sure, talent and luck might get you through the tough times, but you will regret the mistakes that could have easily been avoided, the wasted money, and the bridges you will have burned.

Item 2: Place All of Your Eggs in One Basket

This is actually more subtle than it first appears. The obvious example comes from those developers who have made the mistake of focusing all their efforts on just one project. The problems occur when your publisher—who is likely funding your project— suddenly pulls out, gets bought up, or simply collapses into a morass of suspect accounting practices. Without some form of insurance, such as a second concurrent project with another publisher, your company is suddenly in deep trouble. Countless good developers have lost their businesses to this mistake over the years.

However, the single-project risk isn't the only example. Many developers have been badly stung by the practice of placing great portions of a project in the hands of one or two people. Lose those key personnel and you lose your project.

A good rule of thumb for analyzing this problem is the "hit-by-a-bus" question: "If this person should be run over by a bus tomorrow, how will it affect the project?" If the answer is, "We're doomed! Panic!" then you must remedy the problem *now*. Remember, these people don't have to be run over; they could resign, join your competitors, or even change careers tomorrow.

Item 3: Hire the Wrong People

"Manager" is a meaningless term without context. For example, a "project manager" and an "office manager" need very different skills. No one can possess all of the talents and abilities required to manage every possible mission.

A huge proportion of the games industry's managers come from nonmanagement backgrounds—often they are either ex-programmers or ex-designers. Neither role is particularly good at preparing you for management, yet the number of developers who have left one game development company to set up their own with little preparation is surprising. Some are successful, but they are exceptions, not the rule.

Similarly, many companies make the mistake of hiring a manager proven in one industry and expect him to be able to pick up all the nuances and quirks of another with little or no training. Managing a chain of grocery stores is not the same as managing a chain of development teams. There are similarities, certainly, but without that key understanding of how the industry works—of what it is all those people in the office actually do all day—it is all too easy to miss something that would be obvious to an experienced hand.

Conclusion

Starting your own games development company is hard work and can be very risky. It requires a massive commitment in blood, sweat, and tears. And forget about getting home at a decent hour: good managers are usually the last to leave.

- It's not about playing golf.
- It's not about fast cars.
- It's not about swimming in money.

It's about making a living. If you get seriously rich, great! However, you will have to do a *lot* of hard work first. Most businesses don't even survive the first three years of life. If you do survive for a while, you still can't afford to be complacent: Atari collapsed because of this attitude; and even the mighty IBM was brought to its knees in the late 1980s and nearly went under.

Business management, if done right, is a fantastic journey. It is hard, often thankless work, but like any of the really good careers, "it's how you get there" that matters.

If, after all this, you still want to go ahead and aim for the jackpot, go for it. But most of all: *enjoy the game!*

3.2

Startups: Don't Compete with *Half-Life 2!*

Max Meltzer

max@maxmeltzer.com

According to industry estimates, the development budget for Shenmue on Dreamcast was $26 million, while Eidos' *Hitman 3* cost $43.3 million. As of 2004, a typical AAA budget hovers around $10 million, and with the expectations of consumers being raised by the high specifications for the next-generation of consoles, the average game budget may reach $20–$30 million by 2006.

Given the sums of money involved, creating a new team and immediately securing an AAA development contract is quickly becoming impossible. This article describes alternative ways for a new team to carve their niche in the game development industry, establish a reputation, and position themselves for long-term expansion and success.

What Can You Do as a New Independent Studio?

Short of self-funding through government grants, loans, or investments, as Nevrax did for *Saga of Ryzom* and its $10 million budget, new teams can explore several alternative angles to enter the industry:

- Outsourcing Services
- Budget Games
- Middleware Creation
- Interactive TV Games
- Mobile Phone Games
- Educational Games
- Web-Based Games
- Mod Scene Development

Other articles in this book cover the outsourcing and middleware markets in depth; therefore, this one will focus on the others.

What Are Budget Games?

Budget games are developed inexpensively (in comparison to the rest of the industry) and are typically sold to the consumer at low prices. Once the domain of re-released titles nearing the end of their life cycle, the budget game market now includes a wide variety of first-run content, targeted to both personal computers and (since around 2002) to current-generation consoles.

There are two major reasons why budget games for consoles didn't achieve significant market penetration until relatively recently. First, console manufacturers shied away from inexpensive games for fear of brand damage, given that a glut of cheap, low-quality games is widely blamed for the collapse of the Atari VCS market in the early 1980s. Second, publishers worried that the manufacturing costs and license fees associated with console games were too high, considering the small profit margin they could earn on budget releases. However, as the market expanded and console manufacturers had success with inexpensive "greatest hits" collections, the situation evolved until first-run budget games became economically viable.

CASE STUDY 3.2.1: PLAY IT!

In Great Britain, a group of veteran industry executives formed Play It!, a company that specializes in publishing new games at budget prices for the Sony PlayStation 2. This was seen as a bold and risky move, but the risk paid off when Play It!'s title *America's 10 Most Wanted* reached the 8th position on the British sales charts in September 2004 and stayed in the top 20 for several weeks. In a hit-driven industry such as ours, the profits that Play It! earned on this single game were undoubtedly sufficient to fund development of several more titles.

The Future Market

Game marketers believe that the future market for budget games may resemble the market for independent films and independent music labels. In other words, budget games will remain a relatively small segment of the overall market, although as the total number of gamers (casual and hardcore) expands, more people may be willing to spend money to try out a cheaper title.

Potential for Entering the Market

As for independent films and independent music, the odds of a budget game breaking out into the mainstream and earning enormous profits are slim. However, it does happen: independent films like *Donnie Darko* and the original *Blair Witch Project* and games like *America's Top 10 Most Wanted* and *Roller Coaster Tycoon* are but a handful of examples. If and when your budget game achieves that sort of major breakthrough, you may be able to reinvest the profits in a larger production or use your track record to convince a publisher to fund your next full-priced project.

That being said, entering the budget market is getting increasingly risky, because producing even an average quality game could cost you anything from $100,000 to a $1,000,000 or more. Therefore, you will need some capital of your own or a strong financial backer, unless you come up with a game design that can be developed for a pittance or you assemble a team willing to work for a share of profits.

Unless you plan to self-publish, you'll also need to find a publisher, which means you'll have to go through the usual process that developers experience when they try to get full-priced titles funded or published. However, budget game publishers usually look for fully developed games before signing on, and they don't fund game development.

What Are Interactive TV Games?

Interactive TV games are available to digital TV subscribers, whose set-top boxes allow them to send e-mail, shop using the TV remote, change camera angles at live sporting events, order extra information about products featured in advertisements, and so forth. Interactive TV games are usually delivered either as a selection of games on a specific games channel or as a feature of a TV show where you can play along.

The Current Market

Interactive TV gaming is almost invisible in comparison to the amount of press the console and mobile phone markets receive, probably because the United States has only generated minuscule revenue from this segment of the market.

However, interactive TV gaming is thriving in Europe. Great Britain is reported by [Porter01-04] to have as many digital TV owners as they do internet Internet users, at 36% of the population, a proportion that is predicted to reach 50% within a few years. The television game show *Who Wants to be a Millionaire* already benefits from increased ratings thanks to interactive TV gaming, as viewers simultaneously vote for the right answer to questions from home.

However, as of late 2004, only half of these digital television owners have ever used any of the interactive facilities! Thus, while interactive TV games are available to the mainstream consumer, they have yet to achieve the kinds of market penetration statistics that will draw the attention of the rest of the games industry.

The Future Market

[Porter 01-04] estimates that, while the U.S. market is stagnating, it is expected to become the largest single market for interactive TV gaming by 2006, at which point annual European ITV gaming revenues are predicted to reach $1 billion. While these figures may be optimistic (many digital TV customers feel that interactive TV games have been forced toward them and that there isn't much demand for this sort of entertainment), the potential for interactive TV to become a viable platform for the more family-oriented games or to complement successful TV shows is quite real. The interactive TV game era is waiting for a major push from a top developer or publisher to get it started; analysts certainly think that the market will be there.

Entering the ITV Market

Interactive TV gaming is in a more precarious position than other sectors of the industry. Close analysis of the interactive TV market as a whole suggests that it is experiencing *intermediating change*, which [McGahan04] describes as a situation where relationships between providers and consumers are fragile. In this case, the problem is that the consumers' needs and wants do not seem to match the digital television providers' expectations very well, and the industry will have to adjust accordingly.

What Are Mobile Phone Games?

Games designed to be played on mobile phones are fast becoming part of the industry's mainstream. However, in this segment, the method of purchase is typically virtual instead of physical: consumers pay by credit card or by phone credit to download a game over the airwaves and save it permanently on their phones, rather than buying the game in a case over the counter.

Interestingly, and contrary to many expectations, the current valuation of the mobile phone games market stood at around $550 million as of late 2004, an increase of only $50 million since 2002, and unlike the rest of the games industry, the mobile phone market in Western Europe is experiencing rather sluggish turnover. Japan remains the most thriving market for mobile phone games playing and buying; thanks to more advanced devices and networks, Japanese consumers can purchase 3D games of a level of quality comparable to PlayStation 1 titles for about $11 each. Japan also benefits from having all the right technologies and networks in place to support the necessary client-side and financial streams for companies and gamers to use. On the down side, there is so much competition in the Japanese market that prices are being pushed down and companies are struggling to maintain profitability.

However, industry giants expect Western markets for mobile games to grow rapidly in the future, as demonstrated by Electronic Arts' decision to dedicate top development teams to this area and by over $100 million in investments announced by various publishers and developers in 2004.

The Future Market

The mobile phone market has always been recognized as one with huge untapped potential, so much so that analysts from the Wireless World Forum [W2F04] continue to predict a near quadrupling of overall market turnover to $1.93 billion by 2006 and an increase in the number of users of downloadable content from 32 million in 2004 to 220 million by 2009, which suggests that turnover may reach as much as $5.45 billion that year.

Meanwhile, the cost of developing a mobile phone game of expected quality is about $100,000 to $150,000 [Angell04]. Of course, that cost will rise with changes in technology and the market's quality demands. In addition, while developers and publishers used to be able to pick up licenses for next to nothing as the mobile market wasn't seen as profitable, the average price of a top wireless license is reaching seven figures.

Potential for Entering the Market

There is enormous potential for growth in this particular area of the games market in many parts of the world. Reports from [W2F04] suggest that both the American and Chinese markets will surpass Japan in turnover by 2009, although since these markets are still in their infancy, development costs are still within the grasp of many new development studios with limited financial backing.

The concern for new entrants is not only whether they can ship enough games to achieve profitability at this point, but also the progression of technology and the rising costs that will have to be sustained, in the same way developers have struggled with the technology increase in the console market. In addition, sales of wireless games are typically driven by name-brand intellectual property even more than the PC and console markets are.

Major publishers and developers of mobile phone games also understand the importance of establishing and retaining relationships with mobile phone manufacturers, operators, content providers, licensors, and non-game publishers. Such relationships can take time to build; without them, a startup will struggle.

Finally, developers should expect to have to release many titles to really benefit from the early years of the mobile market. As a startup mobile game developer, expect to have to build relationships with partners fast, and try to secure enough financial backing to get working on a range of games.

What Are Educational Games?

Educational games (or edutainment) are simply interactive games that intend to teach the gamers on both a conscious and subconscious level while they enjoy the "fun" factor of playing the game. Educational games are most often targeted toward younger audiences, who have shorter attention spans and would prefer to learn in the "fun" environment that games offer. (For some, educational games are fun in their own right and worthy of being played for the challenge; in these cases, learning sometimes happens on a subconscious level.)

The "serious games" discussed elsewhere in this book are a subset of the educational game world, typically targeted to adults.

The Current Market

Many publishers see the educational games market as "high risk, low reward," and try to keep their development budgets low to mitigate the risk. For new developers, this presents an opportunity for entry. And while edutainment receives relatively little press coverage, the children's educational software market alone is worth $2 billion a year, including software for home, schools, and systems.

The trend suggests that the market will only increase with the inclusion of more computers in schools and in homes worldwide. Meanwhile, businesses are more willing than ever to consider "serious games" as a means of educating their staff.

What Are Web-Based Games?

Web-based are (usually small) games available on the Internet, played in browsers, developed inexpensively, and usually paid for by a sponsor or a Web portal that wants to attract an audience. [Morris03] reports that Electronic Arts' Pogo.com Web gaming portal generates $12.5 million in annual advertising sales. However, by and large, attempts to charge subscription fees for access to Web games have failed, although some publishers have succeeded in generating revenue from online sales of "deluxe" editions of games that players can try out for free. [Morris03] indicates that Pogo.com may try the subscription model again in the future, using EA's development and marketing power to overcome consumers' reluctance to pay for Internet content.

Potential for Entering the Market

Web-based game development is an inexpensive proposition—one of the few areas of the industry in which "lone wolves" developing games in their bedrooms are still viable competitors. In addition, there are many skilled programmers from the sectors of Web design and Internet development available for hire, many of whom have spent lots of time developing Java content.

Indeed, the expensive part of Web game publishing is the marketing and brand awareness that is needed to get people to visit your Web site. Get yourself noticed by as many search engines as you can, and try to innovate to separate your site from the masses. Make sure you give a lot of thought to your domain name and aim to develop games and brands that are very catchy. In this market, good word of mouth is more important than any paid-for marketing.

What Is Mod Development?

"Mod" is the abbreviation of "modification." A game mod is content that changes an existing game to provide a new experience; mods can include new levels, characters, stories, or complete rewrites of a game's world, and are often created by fans of the original game from source code and tools provided by the original game's developers or publisher.

The Current Market

Millions of gamers download modifications of games every month. The only problem for the developer is that the downloads are free—legally, no mod can be sold, because the original content and technology is copyrighted by the game's developer and/or publisher. However, some mods have been successful in capturing an audience that the original game's publisher has released them commercially, *Counter-Strike* (which, by some accounts, was played more than the original game on which it was based, *Half-Life*) being the quintessential example. Indeed, Valve Software has said that sales of *Counter-Strike* have paid nearly half of *Half-Life 2*'s development budget!

Several other successful mods have been released commercially, helping their amateur developers turn into professional studios. Trauma Studios were amateur developers who created *Desert Combat*, a mod for EA's *Battlefield 1942* that dealt with modern warfare and was played in LAN venues and on the Internet more than the actual game itself. As a result of *Desert Combat*'s success, Electronic Arts and developers DICE acquired Trauma Studios and assigned a professional project to the team.

The Future Market

There was a time when publishers bought and released numerous mods, thus essentially getting a full game without having funded the development. This period is long gone, but the *Desert Combat* example shows that putting together a great team and developing a top-quality mod can be an effective way to earn a professional contract, however long the odds.

Conclusion

This article briefly introduced a range of game development scenarios and markets that are within the reach of a small startup company that can't afford to outspend *Half-Life 2*'s development team. New teams should reduce risk by entering a sector with lower risk and higher potential for company success and growth. Then, once they have achieved steady cash flow and a steady company, they will be in a much better position to move into PC and console development, if that is what they want.

Above all, remember that if you want to succeed as a development studio, you need to plan well and plan like a business. Analyze your markets properly, and most importantly, be realistic! One step at a time is the only way in the modern day.

References

[Angell04] Angell, M., "Plenty of Players in the Game Market," available online at *http://biz.yahoo.com/ibd/040928/tech01_1.html* .

[McGahan04] McGahan, A. M., "How Industries Change," *Harvard Business Review*, October 2004, pp. 87–94.

[Morris03] Morris, C., "EA to Charge Subscription Fees for Madden, Web Games?" available online at *http://money.cnn.com/2003/05/07/commentary/game_over/colum_gaming/*.

[Porter01-04] Porter, B., "Interactive Games" column available online at *www.newmediazero.com*.

[W2F04] Wireless World Forum, "Winning and Losing in Mobile Games," available to order at *http://www.w2forum.com/item2.php/1726*. 2004.

3.3

Writing a Business Plan for a Game Development Startup

François Dominic Laramée

fdl@francoisdominiclaramee.com

Preparing a business plan might well be the single most important action taken during a game development company's startup phase. Not only will the business plan help secure financing, the research process leading to it will strengthen the promoters' knowledge of the market, solidify their business strategy, and establish their credibility with clients and partners.

Multiple business plan formats, sharing much in content and structure, have been published over the years. [Gumpert96], [Touchie98], and especially [Bangs98] present several alternatives. The model described in this article is a hybrid modulated to the needs of game developers. The author has used variations of this model to write business plans for several successful clients since 1998.

The Many Purposes of the Business Plan

Your studio's business plan will come into play during all phases of the company's operation, in a variety of roles:

Strengthening your own convictions: The research leading to a business plan will help you determine whether the opportunity you identified really exists. If you want to start a motion-capture studio, and 8 out of 10 local studios you poll say they would use the service, you're on your way to success.

Identifying business opportunities: Sometimes, the research process itself will reveal ancillary sources of business you might not have considered. For example, while asking local publishers about their interest in full-service game development, they might tell you that their existing stable of developers is in dire need of extra 3D animation help; adding a 3D team for hire to your studio's assets could therefore increase profits.

Guiding your strategy: Once you have identified key opportunities, the business plan will help you pursue them effectively—and avoid distractions.

Establishing partnerships: A credible business plan will help you recruit key employees, secure publishing contracts, obtain a favorable lease, negotiate credit, and so forth.

Securing debt and equity financing: Since the safety of (and return on) their money is paramount to them, bankers and investors will base their funding decisions on the viability of the business plan.

Selling the company: Finally, if you ever want to sell your studio, a business plan showing a viable long-term strategy will be your most important asset, especially if the buyer is not intimately involved in the interactive entertainment industry.

Therefore, the business plan should be created before the studio's launch and updated on a regular basis (at least twice a year) as long as the company is in operation.

The Business Plan's Contents

A business plan is an organic document. It can and must be tailored to the needs of the person or organization to which it is being presented. For example, if your business is applying for a bank loan, the banker will be far more interested in seeing how you will generate a regular positive cash flow (and therefore be able to repay the loan on time) than in your long-term growth process, while an angel investor will focus on the exact opposite.

That being said, most business plans need to include:

Front materials: A cover page, executive summary, and table of contents.

Market information: A general description of the state of the industry, the niche you want to carve for yourself, and the clients who will buy your products and services.

A description of your company: Your own track record, key members of the team, your staffing plans, and the outside resources to which you have access.

Your development plan: Growth objectives, research and development, other markets you wish to expand into, and risk management.

Your financial plan: How much money you need (and when), your cash flow and earnings previsions, and your capital structure.

Assorted supporting documents: Personal résumés, letters of intent, and so forth.

Length

The complete business plan should not exceed 50 pages (preferably 30), starting with a 2-page executive summary and including 10 to 15 pages of financial statements and supporting documents. This is often insufficient to discuss everything that you feel is relevant; however, not every reader needs to see every piece of information, so you can assemble the 30-page document you submit on a given occasion from substantially more material. Case Study 3.3.1 discusses ways to do this effectively.

CASE STUDY 3.3.1: MODULATING THE BUSINESS PLAN

Once you have written all of the material that belongs in your business plan, you can assemble different versions of the document for different purposes. For example:

To secure a work-for-hire contract with a publisher: Emphasize the team and any staffing growth plans (publishers like to establish long-term relationships), leave out the intellectual property except technology, and skim over financial predictions.

To secure a bank loan: Include extensive personal information, make sure that your cash flow forecasts minimize fluctuations, and expand the section on risk management. De-emphasize long-term development.

To define internal strategy: Prepare extensive market research, alternative financial forecasts based on different development scenarios, and leave out team info.

To obtain equity investment: Insist on development plans and on how you will retain your key employees. In your market analysis, insist on emerging trends with long-term sustainability.

To obtain venture capital: Identify a critical shortage in the market. Show enormous earnings growth potential within two to three years. De-emphasize risk management, except where it concerns very short-term cash flow.

To recruit key employees: Leave out most of the market description (unless hiring outside the industry) and the financial data, and emphasize the company profile and the development plan.

The Market, and How You Fit into It

This section of the business plan might be the most important, because it shows *why* your business should exist in the first place. Avoid the temptation to skimp on it to save pages for the financial forecasts: in the eyes of the shrewd investor, cash flow statements without a credible market opportunity are worthless.

Your Products and Services

First, describe what your company will do, and how it will distinguish itself from the competition. Examples of unique distinguishing characteristics might include:

Exceptional talent: Do your partners and you have marketable industry credentials, advanced degrees, or unusual backgrounds?

Unique intellectual property: Have you developed characters that focus groups have identified as the next Pokémon? Or have you secured an exclusive license to an upcoming film franchise's gaming rights?

Financial advantages: Will you be able to develop better games for less money than the competition? Why? Is the cost of living very low in your state or country? Is your national government subsidizing high-tech companies?

Geographic specificities: Is your studio located in a high-density game development area, with plenty of competent talent available to be hired? Or are you the only game company in an area teeming with exceptional 3D artists?

Current Market Conditions

Telling the reader that the games industry's total sales have experienced double-digit growth every year since 1980 is not enough: you must also demonstrate knowledge of the specific segment(s) you are attacking. Who are your customers? Are they used to buying what you propose to sell? If so, is there room for additional suppliers? If not, how will you convince them of the benefits of leaving their current partners to do business with you?

The best way to do this is to identify an obvious need in the marketplace. For example, if you want to start a game programming school, ask local companies how long it takes to fill an opening, how many technical positions they have available, and how many more art and production jobs they would be able to create if there were enough qualified programmers to fill the team. (In some countries, the answer to that last question might help you secure funding from government agencies.)

You must also identify trends that support your approach. If you want to develop games for publishers on a work-for-hire basis, show that licensed properties account for an ever-increasing percentage of the best-sellers list on your platform of choice. If you prefer to create your own characters, show that the market for intellectual property of their kind is large, growing, and/or underserved. Be precise, and aim where the competition isn't too strong: while there is a seemingly inexhaustible demand for fantasy, the teenage-wizard-at-boarding-school-in-England subgenre is probably saturated until at least 2010.

Your Marketing Strategy

Finally, demonstrate how you will carve your own niche in the difficult game development market. Have you secured the services of a reputed agent? Will you begin by developing a low-cost, low-risk title that can be played on personal digital assistants (PDAs) or mobile phones, and use it as a calling card? Will you focus on a narrow segment and establish yourself as an unquestioned leader—like id Software for first-person shooters and Maxis for simulations—or will you develop an entire line of complementary sports games and distribute them on all major consoles?

Your Company

Having identified an opportunity in the marketplace, you must now prove that you and your partners/employees are qualified to turn that opportunity into a profitable business. This section will establish your credibility in this regard.

Promoters

Identify the partners who will be involved in day-to-day operations by name, and describe the skills they bring to the company.

Insist on expertise in three major areas: management, sales, and game development, in that order. [Bangs98] states that 92% of all business failures in *any* industry are caused by managerial incompetence or lack of industry knowledge. Bankers and investors are understandably wary of funding companies that they perceive as deficient in these areas. Also remember that most of the people who will read the business plan know nothing about the games industry, except what they might have read in the mainstream press—and that coverage is rarely flattering. Thus, to maximize your odds of securing capital, your core team should include:

- A proven business manager, preferably with a finance background
- An experienced salesperson with solid industry contacts
- A game designer or producer with multiple titles to his or her credit
- A lead programmer, also with multiple industry credits

Of course, it is possible to rely on the support structure described in the next section to fill a gap in your expertise, but this is the optimal combination, because investors love it when people who hold long-term stakes in the company occupy the key positions.

Support Structure

Few startups, if any, can count on promoters with all of the skills necessary to succeed. The "Support Structure" section of the business plan lists the employees and external resources that will complement the promoters' knowledge, including:

- One or more senior software engineers
- A lead artist, if he is not among the promoters himself
- A law firm and/or agency with entertainment industry experience to represent you in contract negotiations

- Members of the board of directors and/or advisory committee
- Auditors and other consultants
- Local schools and research institutes
- Chambers of commerce and other business associations
- Laws and regulations that favor the games industry in your local jurisdiction

Staffing

Then, describe your initial team in these terms:

- How many people will you hire?
- What will their jobs be, and to whom will they report?
- What salaries and benefits will you offer? Are you going to pay above or below the industry average in your area? Will you implement a stock ownership plan to minimize employee turnover?
- Can the local market provide you with enough qualified talent? If not, what type of training will you have to invest in?

Production Plan

Finally, describe how you will organize the studio's operations. Will you have a single unified team? Multiple projects based on the same engine? Three independent product lines?

Remember that generating positive cash flow early and regularly is important for investors. When seen in that light, a single group working on the same AAA game for three years is not very attractive. You might have an easier time securing capital for a larger company that can release two mobile games every quarter and a major console title every Christmas season.

Development Plan

The development plan describes how you envision your company's evolution over the next few years. In traditional businesses, the development plan usually covers five years; for a game studio, it is very hard to make predictions more than two to three years in the future with any credibility, so a two-year plan will usually be sufficient.

Research and Development

Explain your company's technological strategy. Will you develop in-house engines, license technology developed elsewhere, or take advantage of industry standards such as Macromedia Flash? Do you plan to use technology as your competitive advantage? If so, will that competitive advantage lie in visual quality, character behavior, or faster development? If not, where will you put the emphasis: art, design, or writing?

An aggressive but sound research and development plan is a high-risk, high-reward strategy. While success might bring enormous profits, there is always the chance that you will find yourself, years into a new engine's development, with technology that fails to bring the expected competitive advantage. Therefore, such a strategy will attract venture capitalists, but will scare loan officers away.

Growth Targets

Is your goal to keep your company small and easily manageable, or do you want to turn it into an industry powerhouse? Do you want to concentrate on a single platform or develop for all major consoles at the same time? Do you want to become your own publisher? Handle your own distribution? Exclusively online, or in retail stores as well? Or do you intend to take the intellectual property you develop for your games and turn it into a TV, comic book, and merchandising franchise?

Again, an aggressive growth strategy is attractive to equity investors, but perceived as risky by lenders.

Risk Management

The best business plans demonstrate knowledge of the common sources of failures in the industry, and explain how the company will maximize its odds of defeating them. For example:

- Many experienced game developers leave the industry because they can make more money and work shorter hours elsewhere. How will you retain your key staff?
- A small number of hit games earn enormous profits, while most projects lose money. How will you minimize your financial risk?
- The industry suffers from a high employee turnover rate, especially in active areas like California and Texas. How will you keep your teams intact throughout long projects?
- As the industry grows ever more concentrated, the number of potential publishers for your games shrinks every year. How will you get your games to market?
- The average AAA game budget reaches millions of dollars. How will you minimize your costs and still have a chance to compete for consumers?

Convincing answers to these questions will show that you are ready to face the challenges of the marketplace.

Also note that local circumstances might influence your vulnerability to these risks, or even spawn others. Study your state or country's tax code (especially the provisions on tax incentives for R&D and investment in technological ventures) and job market thoroughly.

CASE STUDY 3.3.2: CREATIVE RISK MANAGEMENT

Nothing impresses investors quite as much as a proactive, original approach to minimizing the risk of failure. Here are a few examples of strategies that can increase your odds of success:

- Send employees to teach at local colleges and universities, where they can recruit the best students.
- Participate in work-study programs.
- Implement a profit-sharing plan; this retains key employees more effectively than stock options, because few game companies ever make it to the stock market.
- Pool resources and/or trade services with other companies to eliminate the costs associated with the hiring/layoff cycle.
- Enforce a strict upper limit to the duration of the workweek to maintain morale and avoid employee exhaustion.
- Establish strong relationships with the local mainstream and business press to gain notoriety in the financial market and attract quality employees.
- Mix and match project types and durations to generate regular cash flow.
- Involve employees in every project, if only for a couple of weeks, to create a sense of unity.

Financial Planning

Most companies write business plans to obtain financing. Others do it to secure contracts and partnerships. In both cases, a sound money management plan is of the utmost importance.

Types of Financing Deals

If your studio needs funding, you must determine which type of financial arrangement between you and your backers will be most appropriate. There are three general categories of funding you might solicit:

Debt. This category includes credit margins, "bridge loans" allowing you to cover cash flow shortages until a milestone payment arrives, bonds, and mortgages. Lenders avoid risk, and they want to get their money back (with interest) on a precise schedule. Therefore, debt funding is easier to obtain if you already hold a letter of intent or work-for-hire contract from a publisher, or if you are willing to offer significant collateral (e.g., a house) to secure the loan.

Equity. Family, friends, financial angels, and some investment funds might be interested in providing a studio with long-term capital in exchange for a percentage of ownership—and thus a share of future profits. Equity investors might be willing to accept a higher risk factor than lenders, but mavericks beware: while any business failure is painful, one that destroys your relationship with loved ones will be much worse. As a rule, investors will expect to earn back their seed money within two to three years and receive a 25% to 40% return thereafter.

Venture capital. Some investors specialize in high-risk, high-payoff companies. A typical VC contract involves the studio selling a percentage of its stock to the investor at a certain price and buying it back later at a higher price so that the venture capitalist will be out of the picture within 3 to 10 years. Usually, VC is only available to companies with *extremely* high potential—for example, those that hold the rights to a breakthrough technology or show immediate stock market perspectives. At the height of the dot-com bubble, VC firms expected 100% to 500% rates of return on their investments within one year.

Depending on your company's business model, some of these types of financing will be easier to obtain than others: venture capitalists have little interest in stable, low-growth companies, while banks will not risk large sums unless the loans are secured by contracts with well-defined milestone payments.

Pro Forma Financial Statements

To convince potential investors and partners of your company's potential, you must demonstrate financial viability. To do so, you must provide the following statements:

Cash flow statement. This document lists cash receipts and expenditures, demonstrates your company's liquidity, and shows how much external funding you will need at any given time. Table 3.3.1 shows a simple cash flow statement. Don't forget to take trade show expenses and representation into consideration!

Earnings statement. This document summarizes sales, costs, and profitability. It differs from the cash flow statement in several important ways; for example, sales are "earned" as soon as they are closed, but accounted for in the cash flow statement only when the invoice is paid. Table 3.3.2 shows a simple earnings statement.

Balance sheet. This document summarizes a company's assets, liabilities, and book value. Since game studios rarely own many assets except quickly depreciated computers and software, this statement is less important for you than for a traditional business such as a manufacturing plant, but lenders in particular will still want to see it, because they can seize assets if you default on your payments. A 1:1 ratio of cash and accounts receivable to short-term (one-year) liabilities is considered comfortable.

The business plan should include monthly statements for the first year, and quarterly statements for the next two years.

Your Financing Proposition

Having prepared your cash flow statement, you know how much external funding you will require to support your operations. It is now time to propose a deal to your

Table 3.3.1   Simple Cash Flow Statement (Simple Studios Inc.)

Receipts	Q1 2005	Q2 2005	Q3 2005	Q4 2005	Q1 2006	Q2 2006	Q3 2006	Q4 2006
Equity funding	$250,000.00	$0.00	$0.00	$0.00	$0.00	$0.00	$0.00	$0.00
Milestone payments	$0.00	$100,000.00	$100,000.00	$200,000.00	$100,000.00	$100,000.00	$200,000.00	$0.00
Royalties	$0.00	$0.00	$0.00	$0.00	$0.00	$150,000.00	$150,000.00	$150,000.
Tax credits	$0.00	$20,000.00	$20,000.00	$20,000.00	$20,000.00	$40,000.00	$40,000.00	$40,000.0
Govt subsidies	$100,000	$0.00	$0.00	$0.00	$150,000.00	$0.00	$0.00	$0.00
Total	**$350,000.00**	**$120,000.00**	**$120,000.00**	**$220,000.00**	**$270,000.00**	**$290,000.00**	**$390,000.00**	**$190,000.00**

Expenses	Q1 2005	Q2 2005	Q3 2005	Q4 2005	Q1 2006	Q2 2006	Q3 2006	Q4 2006
Rent and suppliers	$8,000.00	$8,000.00	$8,000.00	$8,000.00	$10,000.00	$10,000.00	$10,000.00	$10,000.00
Capital expenses	$100,000.00	$0.00	$0.00	$0.00	$100,000.00	$0.00	$0.00	$0.00
Salaries (burn rate)	$120,000.00	$120,000.00	$120,000.00	$120,000.00	$240,000.00	$240,000.00	$240,000.00	$240,000.00
Income tax	$0.00	$0.00	$0.00	$100,000.00	$0.00	$0.00	$0.00	$0.00
Total	**$228,000.00**	**$128,000.00**	**$128,000.00**	**$228,000.00**	**$350,000.00**	**$250,000.00**	**$250,000.00**	**$250,000.00**
Quarterly variation	$122,000.00	-$8,000.00	-$8,000.00	-$8,000.00	-$80,000.00	$40,000.00	$140,000.00	-$60,000.00
Cumulative	$122,000.00	$114,000.00	$106,000.00	$98,000.00	$18,000.00	$58,000.00	$198,000.00	$138,000.00

Table 3.3.2 Simple Earnings Statement (Simple Studios Inc.)

	Q1 2006	Q2 2006	Q3 2006	Q4 2006	Total 2006
Milestones and royalties	$400,000	$250,000	$200,000	$1,200,000	$2,050,000
Development costs	$350,000	$350,000	$350,000	$350,000	$1,400,000
Gross margin	**$50,000**	**($100,000)**	**($150,000)**	**$850,000**	**$650,000**
Overhead	$100,000	$100,000	$100,000	$100,000	$400,000
Gross profit	**($50,000)**	**($200,000)**	**($250,000)**	**$750,000**	**$250,000**
Income tax	($7,500)	($30,000)	($37,500)	$112,500	$37,500
Net profit	**($42,500)**	**($170,000)**	**($212,500)**	**$637,500**	**$212,500**

prospective financial partners. Do you ask for a single equity investment in the entire amount, or are you willing to bring in multiple partners? What percentage of your stock are you willing to offer in exchange? If you prefer a loan, venture capital, or a combination of both, what interest rate are you willing to pay?

As a general rule (with many exceptions), angels and funds don't like to provide a disproportionate share of a company's money: they are more comfortable if the principals and/or a number of other institutions participate as well. However, venture capitalists often demand a high percentage of the stock, or provisions that let them increase their ownership (and ultimately wrest control from the promoters) if the company fails to meet the expected buyout schedule.

Capital Structure

List current owners and debtors, their stakes in the company, and their roles in its management, if any. A second table showing the situation after the proposed funding must also be provided.

In addition to the principals' investments in the company, you might also want to declare the salaries they will be receiving until the company releases a title or signs a publishing contract. Investors tend to frown upon promoters who pay themselves generously at this stage, so you might have to prove your commitment to the company by taking much less than you could be making as an employee elsewhere; your payoff is supposed to come later.

CASE STUDY 3.3.3: MINIMIZING THE COST OF MONEY

An overly aggressive venture capital buyout can cripple a company. So can deteriorating relationships between dissatisfied shareholders. Common sense dictates that game studios should cap the potential negative impacts of outside capital influxes, by minimizing the amount of money they have to bring in and/or by cutting on the premiums they have to pay for it. Here are a few ways to do so: →

Select venture capital partners who are accredited by fiscal authorities. In some jurisdictions, VC firms receive tax credits on risky investments; if this is the case in your state or country, you will not have to guarantee as high a rate of return to secure an investment.

Find alternative suppliers. If you can bear the risks associated with a nonstandard 3D animation package or programming environment, their suppliers might be willing to sell them at a substantial discount to gain a foothold in the games industry.

Lease instead of buying. In some jurisdictions, lease payments are 100% tax deductible, while purchased equipment must be depreciated over several years even if they are paid in advance. Computers, office furniture, and some software packages can be acquired this way.

Consider a second mortgage. If you are going to have to put your home up as collateral on a business loan anyway, why not get a mortgage and invest the money in the company? Mortgage rates are often lower than those granted on business loans.

Cross-subsidize. Accept work-for-hire deals, subcontract your workforce to other companies during downtime, and use the income to pay for your own original development projects.

Sweat equity. Some employees might be willing to work for less money at startup in exchange for a share of the company's stock. Unfortunately, this mechanism is often abused; projects advertised on industry Web sites routinely ask for several months of unpaid work (in one case, as much as *three and a half years*) in exchange for vague promises of regular employment—no stock—in the future. Remember that you always get what you pay for.

Supporting Documents

Finally, append any document that could help sway the reader's decision in your favor: personal résumés, personal balance sheets, letters of intent and contracts from publishers, leases, awards received, a description of the company's intellectual property, and so forth.

Conclusion

A well-crafted business plan is a management tool, a calling card for the company in negotiations with publishers, and the single most important factor in obtaining financing for your projects. Do not underestimate its impact.

Above all, remember that your business plan must capture your company's unique personality: write it in a lively, attractive style that shows that you belong in the entertainment industry. Best of luck!

References

[Bangs98] Bangs Jr., D. H., *The Business Planning Guide*, 8th Edition, Upstart Publishing Company, 1998.

[Gumpert96] Gumpert, D. E., *How to Really Create a Successful Business Plan*, 3rd Edition, Magazine Publishing, Inc., 1996.

[Touchie98] Touchie, R. D., *Preparing a Successful Business Plan*, 3rd Edition, Self-Counsel Press, 1998.

3.4

Strategies for Staffing a Startup

Grant Stanton

grant@TSCsearch.com

Perhaps in no other industry short of motion pictures is there such a direct correlation between the success of the product and the staff involved. There is a vital creative element involved in games development that sets it apart from other software products, and being successful in this young and volatile industry requires brilliant and fanatically dedicated staff. The most promising game concept or license can fail as a product in the hands of a lackluster studio.

As recently as the early 1990s, the industry was witness to successful startups born at home by a few young entrepreneurial spirits that created games like *Castle Wolfenstein* and *Myst*. In recent years, rocketing development costs and the size of the teams required to create a sophisticated competitive product have created a substantial barrier to entry for this form of genesis. Most often, today's startup falls into one of two broad categories.

The most common genesis of a developer is when a few key employees depart from an established studio to form their own company. In this case, they typically capitalize on their contribution to a successful title to secure funding and contracts. The most common error made by the first type is that they don't take the management responsibilities seriously enough. They just created a hit game, how hard could managing a studio be?

The other less common origin for a studio is when a company well established in a similar field—like motion pictures or software application development—decides to expand into games development. The latter type usually puts too much faith in the management techniques that have served them well in other industries.

In staffing a new venture, your candidate pool (available applicants to choose from) will consist chiefly of two groups: *active* candidates, people who are unemployed or actively looking for a new job, and *passive* candidates, candidates who aren't actively looking to change jobs but are still interested in opportunities to advance or improve their careers.

In this article, we discuss strategies for sourcing, screening, interviewing, and hiring both types, as well as how to avoid some of the common staffing pitfalls that young studios face.

Creating Job Descriptions

This crucial first step in the hiring process is often not given the full attention it requires, and when not thoroughly implemented is the primary cause of a hiring process going awry. Without a clear, complete, and detailed job description to reference, the hiring decision is often made on an emotional level, based on whether they *like* or *feel good* about a candidate rather than determining who is best qualified according to the needs and requirements of the position.

The following is a summary of the five fundamental steps to creating a job description:

1. **Determine the hiring manager.** Who is going to make the actual decision to extend an offer? Ideally, there should be just one person responsible for making the final hiring decision. If this is not practical, then it is important to restrict the number of people involved to as few as possible. You can certainly use the entire team in the interview process and consider the resulting input, but the actual decision of whom to hire is critically important and should not be put to a "team vote" any more than other important management decisions. Imagine taking your entire family and extended family along to buy your next car and allowing everyone to have veto power in the decision. Do you believe you would end up with the best car for your needs, or just a car that everyone agreed on? It is the team leader or manager who has the best perspective and understanding of what the needs are that this new hire will address. In business, only the people most qualified to make a particular decision should be empowered to do so.

2. **Determine what the needs are.** What are the specific needs that this position will address? Make sure that everyone involved is in agreement as to these needs.

3. **Position responsibilities.** What responsibilities will this person have? What will this person be expected to accomplish? What specific tasks will this person perform on a daily and weekly basis? What management or leadership responsibilities will this person have?

4. **Required skills and bonus skills.** Clearly define the necessary skill-set to succeed in the position. Also determine what skills would be an additional benefit, but are not a necessity.

5. **Personality.** Are you looking for a strong leader? A team player? Someone who works independently? Someone adept at resolving conflict? Determine what personality traits or attributes would have the most bearing on a candidate succeeding in this position as well as the company as a whole. Now is

the time to determine what type of individual you are looking for and what type of individual works best in your company culture.

Your completed job opening document should include job title, who this position reports to and who would be reporting to them, hiring authority, responsibilities (this includes both duties that would be performed on a daily basis and longer-term objectives for this position), skills required, skills that would be beneficial, a brief sentence or two about beneficial personality attributes desired, and finally, a salary range.

Make sure that you have created a job description that can be done by one person. Sometimes, managers amalgamate several distinct positions' needs into one. Care should be taken that a job description doesn't become a wish list that no one candidate could fill. When the document is completed, revisit the hiring authority(s) to make sure everyone is in agreement. This is a very important step. Everybody might agree that you need a technical director, but there might be several different opinions as to what exactly a technical director does and is responsible for.

Strategies for Finding the Candidates

The videogames industry is in a growth cycle and the best development talent is in constant demand. The worth of a studio is in a large part determined by the caliber of its development staff. In an industry with such a high demand for talent, a new studio should not rely exclusively on advertising and should be both creative and aggressive in their recruiting efforts.

Advertising: This is the most obvious method. There are numerous avenues to consider with advertising, from print to the Internet. There are trade magazines published specifically for the game development community as well as the computer graphic arts community. On the Web are game developer forums and Web sites to consider as well as a few private sites in the developer community that will post job ads free of cost to developers they trust. While simple advertising will likely produce the largest quantity of applicants and the occasional diamond in the rough, it should be mentioned that often the majority of the respondents are either inexperienced or looking to break into the games industry rather than experienced veterans.

Networking and trade shows: Talk to friends and employees, ask whom they know. Attend trade shows like E^3 and the CGDC and let people know about the exciting projects you are working on.

College recruiting and internships: Today's colleges are producing some brilliant young engineers and artists. Many a startup owes their success in part to their proximity to a college campus; Raven—University of Wisconsin, Volition—University of Illinois, Redstorm—University of North Carolina, Turbine—MIT, and so forth. As the games industry matures, more and more colleges are developing curriculums with games development in mind, and then there are schools that specialize in games development like Digipen and Full

Sail. Many of these students actually have exposure to console development even before they graduate. An enthusiastic student intern or recent graduate with the essential skill-set and a fanaticism for games can be a terrific addition to your team.

A professional recruiter: Using a professional recruiter seasoned in the industry is the most efficient and direct method of sourcing the entire applicant pool, not just the candidates who are actively looking. A good recruiter will champion your studio in the games community and aggressively pursue the passive candidates. Passive candidates are not unemployed, not unhappy, not reading the want ads, and represent the majority of development talent. If your studio has something exciting to offer, it is the professional recruiter who will be proactive and make sure the right people know about it. Some recruiters in the games industry even offer special fee arrangements to startups. The recruiter you select should know the industry top to bottom, have an extensive network of contacts, and have a good reputation within the games community.

Reputation: This is an often-overlooked facet of recruiting in the games industry. The games development community is very closely knit. Consequently, news travels fast. Good development staff is in high demand, so a good candidate has many choices. The caliber of talent that you attract will have a great deal to do with how your studio is perceived in the games community. Your reputation will, in part, be based on the founders' reputations, the quality of game you are producing, your studio's work environment, and studio culture. This can be both an advantage and a disadvantage when creating a startup. It is difficult to repair a poor reputation. Take special care with your burgeoning reputation in the community and treat all applicants graciously.

Screening and Qualifying Applicants

Sorting through large quantities of mostly unqualified applicants can be daunting. These days, the résumés will arrive primarily via e-mail. For the sake of organization, dedicate an e-mail address just for applicants (e.g., Jobs@Newstudio.com). Set up an auto response that is sent to every e-mail received at that address thanking them for applying and letting them know their résumé will be reviewed and thoroughly considered for open positions.

Discipline yourself not to make judgments about a candidate based on résumé format or composition. Remember, you are not hiring someone for his or her résumé writing skills. The résumé is not the candidate. If the résumé is difficult to understand or leaves you with more questions than answers, but the candidate looks like a possibility, then a telephone screen is warranted to find out more.

The Telephone Screen

The telephone screen is not an interview and shouldn't be confused with one. It should be used to clarify information on the résumé and the qualification of a potential interview. A telephone screen is a friendly, brief, fact-finding conversation designed to determine whether someone is qualified to do the job. A face-to-face interview is for determining whether this is the actual person you want to hire.

Key Questions

There are questions that are appropriate for a telephone screen and questions that are best left for a face-to-face interview. How do you distinguish between the two? Here are some examples.

- **Phone screen question:** What is your current salary situation?
- **Interview question:** What are you looking to earn?

This question should be left until the end of the interview process. Asking a candidate to commit himself to a number before he has been fully briefed on what your company has to offer and the specifics of the position doesn't benefit you or the potential hire. You want a chance to sell him on the position and your company before asking what salary he is looking for.

Phone screen question: I see that you used C++ at your last employer. How many years have you programmed in C++? How would your rate your skill level with C++?

The candidate can answer this type of concise question with just a few words. The answer speaks directly to whether the individual is qualified to perform the essential duties of the position.

Interview question: Where do you see yourself in five years?

This question pre-supposes that the candidate has the necessary skills for the position and is probing big-picture considerations such as ambition and motivation. These traits are difficult to detect over the telephone and are best gauged in a face-to-face setting.

Phone screen question: How many people do you currently have reporting to you? Or what is the most number of direct reports you have had?

The answer to this question can be as brief as one word and still give insight and context to management skills described on the résumé.

Interview question: Describe your typical workday or workweek.

Asking this question during a personal interview allows the interviewer to watch for changes in the candidate's enthusiasm level and demeanor while he or she describes different daily tasks. This can tell you which tasks he enjoys or feels confident at and which ones he doesn't.

Verifying Candidates' Skills

Okay, so you find a candidate with the right skills on his or her résumé. How do you confirm these skills? References are one way, but if the candidate is currently employed it might be difficult to check references without compromising his or her situation. If you can speak with references, due to legal concerns, references most often offer very few specifics beyond dates of employment and title.

How can you be sure the candidates are as skilled as they claim to be on their résumé? The games industry has evolved some analytical methods of assessing skills:

Code samples: Samples can tell you a great deal about someone's coding style. Does this programmer just make the code work, or is the code "concise," "creative," and optimized. Be specific about what type of samples you are interested in seeing. The drawback here is that sometimes a programmer cannot share his best work because of intellectual property and nondisclosure agreements (NDAs). If the programmer doesn't feel that he has samples available that he can share that meet your specifications, then a code test can help.

Code tests: Code tests can be given in place of or in addition to code samples. Before a code test is devised, careful thought should be given as to what skills should be tested. Remember, the type of candidate you are looking for is a games enthusiast, dedicated to his or her project and is most likely working ridiculous hours. The test should consume the least amount of time as possible while still being able to gauge the necessary skills, or lack thereof, that you are screening for.

Math tests: Math skills are crucial to a programmer creating game worlds/environments and the virtual physics that govern them. Math tests are not as common as code tests, but there are studios that feel they are a very useful screening tool for certain engineering positions.

Demo reels: Demo reels have taken on such importance for artists in the videogames industry that virtually all development studios will not even consider an artist without one. Reels and portfolios come in various forms, ranging from VHS tape to CD-ROM. Unfortunately, some artists have difficulty assembling their best work without violating agreements with past and current employers. Avoid misjudgments by asking potential art hires to include a brief guide to their demo reel explaining what tools were used and a description of precisely what they were responsible for in the demo.

Art tests: Art tests can be designed to ascertain artists' general skills. They can also gauge aptitude with a particular graphics package. While not yet industry wide, art tests are gaining in popularity.

Interviewing

It has been said that interviewing is more of an art than a science. It is a wonderful professional skill to develop, allowing you to elicit important information about someone without making him feel "handled" or uncomfortable. Before the interview, thoroughly review the candidate's résumé and compose a list of questions germane to the job being interviewed for. The interviewing process can be a stressful one for both the interviewer and the interviewee. The more relaxed and unguarded both you and the candidate feel, the more you will learn. Show the candidate around the studio. Ask how the drive was. Make small talk for the first few minutes before getting down to business.

Preparing for the Interview

If more than one person will be meeting with a candidate, talk with everybody prior to the interview and come to an agreement as to who will cover what areas. Otherwise, you risk having an individual having to answer the same questions, possibly with some fairly involved answers, four or five times in one day. This can frustrate a candidate and make your company appear disorganized.

Some people will come prepared with a list of questions about your company. It's acceptable to offer brief answers to applicants' questions during the interview, but if the applicants ask a question that warrants a lengthy answer, make note of it and explain that due to time constraints you will answer their question toward the end of the interview. The goal is to learn as much about the applicants as possible. You want to keep the focus on them and keep them talking.

Selecting Interview Questions

Avoid obviously illegal questions about ethnicity or family situation. Several books have been written based simply on compilations of hundreds of interview questions. Prepare a list of questions before the interview and give some thought as to how you want to phrase the questions in order to get the specific information you are looking for. Beyond the position-specific questions, technical and otherwise, here are a few staple questions to consider asking:

- "Why did you leave your last employer?" Or, if the candidate is currently employed, "Why are you looking elsewhere?" Keep in mind that if a recruiter was responsible for sourcing the candidate, the candidate might be there for no other reason than the recruiter has convinced him that it was an opportunity not to be missed.
- "Describe your typical workday? Your typical week?"
- "What was the biggest professional challenge you have faced? How did you go about tackling it?"
- "What do you feel it takes to be successful as a (position title)?"
- "In what type of environment or culture are you most productive?"
- "What type of environment or culture do you not work well in?"

- "What kind of games do you like to play? What is your favorite game and why?"
- "Professionally, where do you feel you could use the most improvement?"
- "What is your greatest professional strength?"

In addition, don't hesitate to ask a few "Why…" oriented questions. These questions speak to what motivates someone and offer an insight into their reasoning processes. For example:

- "Why did you take the job at your current/last employer?"
- "What made you choose to use (Maya, RenderWare, etc.) on your last game?"

When you have gotten the answers to your questions, revisit any questions the applicant might have had during the interview and offer him a chance to ask more.

Finally, keep 5 to 10 minutes at the end of the interview to sell your company. This is crucial, even if you don't intend to hire the candidate. You want everyone who interviews with your company to leave with a positive impression of the interviewing process and your studio as a whole. If the candidates believe that your company is a great place to work, they will encourage friends in the industry to interview with you as well. If the candidates have a negative impression of your studio, then they will discourage friends and colleagues from applying. Think about what makes your new studio special and how you want to communicate it.

After the Interview

Immediately following the interview, while the candidate's answers are still fresh in your mind, take a few minutes to write down your impressions of the candidate and flesh out any notes that you didn't have time for during the interview.

Making an Offer

If you are confident that you have found the right person, move as quickly as possible to offer the job. If you are just working out the details of the offer, then let him know an offer will be coming. This will help reduce the risk of the applicant committing to another company before you have a chance to conclude the deal..

Extend the offer by telephone first. Once the candidate has committed to a verbal acceptance, have other employees whom he met with call or e-mail to congratulate and welcome him aboard. It is important that the new hire feels good about the decision—and fully committed to your company. Otherwise, there is a risk he might accept a counteroffer, especially one coming from his current employer; after all, no organization likes to lose a good talent. The bottom line: don't simply register the acceptance and then wait for the new employee to show up a few weeks later. Stay in touch; make him feel like a member of the team as quickly as possible.

Offer letters vary, but should contain:

- The position title and to whom it reports

- Salary and bonus, royalties or option details
- An explanation of what benefits the employee will be eligible for, such as insurance, health, dental, profit sharing, 401k, and any other notable benefits
- A tentative start date and a summary of what conditions the offer is contingent upon (e.g., physical, drug test, reference checks)

Include an expiration date by which the candidate must accept the offer. Giving the candidate two to five days to think about it is usually sufficient; extend the deadline only at his request.

Finally, send the offer sheet in two copies (one for the applicant to return, and one for his own personal files) and a signature line for the human resources manager and the new hire.

Conclusion

In this industry, a love of games, intelligence, and enthusiasm are the most important qualities that you should look for in a prospective hire. An intelligent and enthusiastic candidate learns rapidly, invests himself in his work, and will pay for himself several times over in a short period of time.

The competition for top talent in the games industry is fierce. When you find a good candidate, be aggressive. Move the process along as quickly as possible. Whom you hire is the most important decision you can make in starting a new company. When you are are successful in choosing people who share your vision and enthusiasm about what kind of company you are creating, you have gone a long way toward assuring success.

3.5

Financing from the Buyer's Side: Evaluating and Acquiring a Game Company

Tom Sloper

tomster@sloperama.com

The information in this article is based on the steps taken in evaluating a potential acquisition that did not come to fruition. By reading this article, you will learn about the various processes involved in evaluating and eventually acquiring a company.

The Target Company and You

The process begins when you find a company you think you would like to buy (or when the company's current owner thinks he would like to sell it to you). A preliminary conversation sets things in motion. You and the company's owner discuss whether a deal can occur, including a range for the acquisition price. In our case, the business' owner initiated negotiations. An initial meeting revealed that the seller's target price was twice what the buyer had in mind, but the parties did agree that they would probably be able to negotiate a deal in that range.

The Emotion Factor

The first thing to keep in mind as you begin the acquisition process is that emotions play an important role in acquiring a business, both for the buyer and for the seller. The buyer is buying a job, a new career, almost a new persona. The seller is selling the product of many years of hard work, and he wants to see the business go to someone who will work equally hard at keeping it successful.

It's important, though, that you not allow your emotions to win over your better judgment. If the deal is going to cost too much or otherwise turn problematic, you need to be prepared to walk away from it.

The Business Plan

The first step once you've decided to acquire a company is to work on your business plan. As explained in Article 5.2, "Managing the Development Process," you have to make a plan.

The business plan is not only a document that you will use to define what you will do with the company. It is also a plan used to get capital for acquiring the business. Your business plan also helps you set priorities and define, in concrete terms, the reasons for (or against) acquiring this particular business.

Without a solid plan, life usually conspires to prevent you from getting where you are trying to go. The very act of planning, though, lays the groundwork for a flexible approach to a process. Almost assuredly, things will work out somewhat differently from your well-laid plan, but you absolutely have to have a solid plan before proceeding. The process of developing the initial plan helps later on, when the plan has to be adapted to deal with changing circumstances.

Outlining the Plan

In the first section of the plan, you should describe your plan for the business itself. Some of this is covered in better detail in Article 5.2 in this book, and it is recommended that you read that article as well.

- **Describe the company, its products and services, its focus.**
- **Accomplishments of the company under the current ownership.**
- **Growth opportunities under your ownership after acquisition.**
- **Marketing aspects:**
  - Who the company's customers or clients are.
  - Your plan to step in and take over those relationships—how you will keep them and strengthen them.
  - What steps you will take to get more clients.
  - How you will maintain the balance, not taking on more than you can handle.
- **The competition:**
  - What other companies are doing what this company does.
  - Strengths and weaknesses of the competition. What lessons can be learned from those competitive operations.
  - Your plan to make your company successful and unique in that competitive environment.
  - Analyze current trends, and their implications for your venture.
- **Operating procedures:**
  - Location: Where you will operate the business, and why.
  - Space: What kind of space the business needs.
  - Accessibility: For employees, for clients, for courier services, etc.
  - Hours of operation.
  - Building security.

- **Personnel and staffing:**
  - Job descriptions and job titles: Number of employees in each. Name the employees if possible.
  - Salaries, benefits.
  - Staffing schedule.
  - What is the "business personality?"
- **Transition plan:** When the acquisition occurs, will you be suddenly replacing the current president, or will there be a gradual transition?
- **Goals and objectives.**
- **Future opportunities.**
- **Risks:** You have to be brutally honest in considering what kinds of things could go wrong, the likelihood of them happening, and what some contingency plans might be in case they do happen.

The preceding is a very brief description of what goes into Part I of your business plan. It is recommended that you get a good book on business plans; see this article's *References* section for suggestions.

Financial Data

Part I is written in prose style, but Part II of your business plan is presented in spreadsheets, charts, and graphs. Here you get into the real nuts and bolts: how much it costs to run the business, and how much money is to be made.

First, analyze and show the financial history of the company under current ownership. Banks want to see at least three years' history, and they want to see a pattern of profitability. If the company has not been profitable, then they'll see it as a bad risk. If you have a plan for turning that around, it had better be a really good one—and very convincing. You'll have to overcome skepticism and (worse) entrenched bank policies.

Analyze what it costs to run the business per month, per quarter, and per year.

- **Personnel costs:** Salaries, benefits, raises.
  - Office rent or building purchase payments
- **Utilities and ongoing expenses:** Electricity, gas, water, trash removal, cleaning service, telephone, Internet access, Web hosting.
- **Capital expenses:**
  - Computers, printers, scanners
  - Telephones, faxes, answering machines
  - Teleconferencing equipment, projectors for presentations
  - Desks, chairs, filing cabinets, credenzas
  - Conference tables, chairs
  - Coffeemaker, refrigerator, microwave, toaster
- **Supplies:**
  - Printer ink, printer paper
  - Pens, pencils, erasers, staples

- Batteries
- Coffee, sweetener, creamer, filters
- Cleaning supplies
- **Analyze where the money comes from:** Development milestone payments, royalties, direct sales.
  - How much
  - How often
- **Break-even**
- **Desired profit margin**
- **Profit & Loss analysis after acquisition**
  - Year One—per month
  - Year Two—per quarter
  - Year Three—per quarter

Evaluating the Company

It might or might not want to be part of the business plan document itself, but you need to evaluate the business. This can be a difficult part of the process, because no two companies are alike, and standard guidelines you might find won't necessarily apply. Each bank uses its own valuation methods, and nobody wants to tell you what that method is.

In this case, three different valuation methods were used and then averaged together. The three methods were as follows:

- Thirty percent of annual sales. (Source: [BizStats02]).
- Five times EBIT (Earnings Before Interest and Taxes). (Source: [Robb95])
- Earnings (EBIT) times two, plus inventory. (Source: [SCORE02])

The desired and maximum purchase prices were set based on the average of the valuations yielded by these three different methods.

Adapting Valuation

The target company is a retail game business, so the valuation methods that were used were based on factors such as sales and inventory. Different valuation methods should be used for a game development company.

The concept of EBIT (Earnings Before Interest and Taxes) applies to any business. Put succinctly, EBIT represents all profits (income minus deductible expenses) before interest and income taxes are deducted.

You will also need an asset breakdown: what exactly are you buying, and how much is every piece of that puzzle worth. A little creativity might be needed here, because it is likely that some of the price that will be paid will be above and beyond the tangible assets. That "above and beyond" money is usually called "goodwill." However, if your loan goes through the U.S. Small Business Administration (SBA), there cannot be any goodwill built into the purchase price. Therefore, you have to find other reasonable assets and assign them value. An example of such a valuable but intangible asset is a Non Compete Agreement, which states that the current owner or president cannot start a new game company (taking the most valuable employees with him) and compete against your new enterprise for at least two or three years. Determine how much such an agreement might be worth, and add that to the asset breakdown. Alternatively, perhaps the current owner will agree to consult exclusively for you for the first two years after the acquisition.

Figure out your capital spending plan. How much money do you need to buy furniture, equipment, business licenses, office lease deposits?

What is your "startup nut?" How much money do you need to buy the business and run it until you're past the transition period and the company is making a profit?

These figures tell you how much of a loan you need. You will be expected to inject some of your own capital into the acquisition. Expect this to be at least 25% to maybe 30% or more, depending on bank policy.

Figure the loan payments into your Profits & Losses and Cash Flow statements. The interest payments go into the P&L, while the principal payments go into the Cash Flow.

Completing the Picture

Part III of your business plan is all about the current owner and you. The business plan needs to paint a complete financial and professional picture of both parties of the deal—the buyer and the seller—and why the banks should want to loan the money for the deal to happen.

The banks want to see that you are stable, capable, reliable, and responsible. You have to have an up-to-date credit report and FICO score. A FICO score is a number that rates the individual's likelihood to repay a loan. A high number means you are a good credit risk. Use myfico.com, equifax.com, or one of several other Web sites to obtain this data. Each bank will also have its own Personal Financial Statement forms they'll want you to fill out. They're taking a big risk on you, and they want to feel comfortable about taking that risk.

Other supporting documents that will need to be attached to the business plan are your résumé and the company résumé of the acquisition target. Specifically, you will need to include the past three years' corporate tax returns for the acquisition target, as well as your own personal tax returns.

Putting the Plan to Work

Your business plan is finally done. It's a masterpiece, and it was hard work to write. Still, in the end, the business plan is just a tool. Once you have written the plan, it's not as if everything else will fall into place. However, completing the plan is an extremely important step in the process, and you should give it your best effort.

Getting the Loan

There are various sources for obtaining business loans, including the Small Business Development Center (SBDC) and your local bank. The SBDC program is administered by the U.S. SBA. Their mission is to provide management help to small business owners (those who currently own or are working to own small businesses).

However, going through the SBA is usually very slow, and it seems that the program is geared primarily to aid minorities and veterans. As mentioned before, one of the major documents required by the banks is tax returns for the company you are purchasing. Companies need to have at least three years' worth of tax returns in order to be considered stable, and our target company only had two years of returns. You need to check with your bank or financial institution to determine exactly what paperwork they require, but keep in mind that it's a long process that requires a lot of follow-up.

Contracts and Due Diligence

Another major part of the purchasing process is the contract and due diligence review. There must be a Buy-Sell Agreement between the buyer and seller. This agreement should cover all the rights and obligations of both parties, including delivery of intangible assets covered in the Asset Breakdown as mentioned previously. It's a truism that the seller is the one who controls the price, but it's the buyer who controls the terms. Although a particular business is offered for sale, there won't be a sale if the buyer doesn't come up with the seller's desired price. Once the seller agrees to an offer, though, it's the buyer who holds the position of strength; the money won't be changing hands if the seller doesn't agree to the buyer's terms.

"Due diligence" means that the buyer has accountants and other experts in the area review all business documents to ensure that they are factual and reflect the actual costs and revenues of the company. If anything is found to be false during this phase, the deal can be canceled, or the seller might be given time to remedy the problem. Do not underestimate its importance; many high-profile corporate mergers collapse at this point.

Advisors

Typically, you should have a CPA, a lawyer, and a businessperson as your advisors.

You should seek a CPA who is familiar with business acquisitions. The same goes for your lawyer. You probably don't need the lawyer until you are ready to write the contract, but you should at least get him lined up in advance. The CPA you will want even earlier in the process—you'll want his feedback on your business plan, before sending it out to banks.

SCORE stands for "Service Corps of Retired Executives." These are folks who have learned a lot about business and volunteer their time to help neophytes in any way they can. A SCORE counselor can help you evaluate the target business, for example.

Good advisers are tremendously important. When the result of an action comes back, you have to make a decision, and quickly. The thinking of others will be extremely valuable in this process. Each adviser adds his perspective on the matter. These different points of view will help you arrive at a better-informed decision than if you just proceed based on your gut reaction. In our case, although the buyer very much wanted to buy this business, there was group consensus that this deal was not going well. Intellect wound up winning over heart. (Why is this section blue?).

Conclusion

Buying a business is a good way to become a business owner. However, emotions can get in the way of making the best decisions, both for the seller and for the buyer. As with any important venture, planning is vital. You'll need money to buy a company, and if you're not a minority or a veteran, perhaps the conventional bank business loan might be better than trying to go through the SBA.

References and Additional Resources

[Bischof &Pucket96] Bischoff, W. R. and Pucket, G. Douglas, *Guide to Buying and Selling A Business*, Practitioners Publishing Co., 1996.

[BizStats02] BizStats.com, "Rules of Thumb for Valuing Small Businesses," available online at www.bizstats.com/rulesofthumb.htm, 2002.

[McKeever99] McKeever, M., *How to Write a Business Plan*, Nolo Press, 1999.

[Robb95] Robb, R., *Buying Your Own Business, Adams Media Corporation*, 1995.

[SCORE02] Service Corps of Retired Executives, available online at *www.score.org*, 2002.

[Yegge96] Yegge, W. M., *A Basic Guide for Buying and Selling a Company*, John Wiley & Sons, 1996.

3.6

Financing Projects and Startups

Thomas Djafari

tdjafari@activision.com

With every year, games become increasingly expensive to develop, the amount of work to handle becomes larger and larger, and while good planning and a well-controlled production will save you money, you still need lots of cash.

Ironically, it turns out that keeping the team together throughout the project and actually turning a profit might be harder than getting the initial funds.

The goal of this article is to illustrate the various sources of financing you can use for your project, how they work, and what the people who will decide whether to fund your team are looking for when evaluating your project.

Risks versus Returns

This is the single most important consideration, and one of the cornerstones of any business. The higher the risk, the higher the expected return must be; the larger the investment, the more important it is to keep risk low, or at least manageable.

All investors will need to evaluate the risks associated with your project. Provide them with the right information to allow them to evaluate the potential risks versus the potential returns of your venture.

In general, videogames are considered a risky investment. Compared to some other domains, they carry a relatively low cost in equipment and a very high cost in human resources, which is what investors tend to shy away from. While it is possible to recover assets from a failed project and reuse them or resell them, the money gone in salaries is a loss; when making videogames it represents the largest chunk of the budget.

Another concern is that many games lose money. A good product is not enough: you also need good marketing, because companies are competing for shelf space in retail stores. Generating expectation from the customers, as the movie industry has done for years, has become indispensable. From an investor's point of view, there are many ways in which this process could go wrong.

What Matters

You have a game concept, and possibly a team. Investors have money and questions.

A financing deal has to be built on a win-win agreement. Building a product with someone else's money requires a strong and honest relationship between the parties. Answering each other's questions is the key to a good start.

Risks Are Everywhere

Software development is very hard to plan. Unexpected problems—hardware failures, employee turnover, and so forth—keep cropping up at the most inopportune moment. Your design should be structured in such a way that it minimizes risk, and you must prove to investors that you have taken all of the steps necessary to do so.

It is very important to be completely open and honest at this stage. All parties involved need to know what parts of the development carry the risks, how to handle them, and so forth. For example, the technology to be used has to be discussed in detail; using preexisting engines or building on a previous game carries much less risk than rewriting code from scratch, even if it means more work.

Fallback Plans

Plans fail. Seemingly perfect ideas sometimes turn out to be wrong. And things sometimes just don't happen as expected.

Nobody is expecting you to deliver a problem-free project. However, investors need to know that you're ready to handle the problems as they arise. Take the right steps to minimize the risks, and prepare multiple fallback strategies to account for the possibility that part of your design might be cancelled, that you might lose a part of the team, suffer technical or planning problems, or that an unannounced competing title might change your own game's market conditions.

Experience and Knowledge of the Industry

Dealing with a company familiar with the games business is definitely easier for everyone involved. If your investor is not also your publisher, relationships can become slightly more complicated, especially if the funding company has no prior games industry experience. If that is your case, question the investors about their motivations for entering the games market and try to understand their culture and goals.

Commitment

All projects go through hard times. For an investor, it is sometimes easy to bail out, leaving you with very little recourse, no matter what the contract says. Keep in mind that contracts are not much more than what arguments revolve around in courts if things go wrong, and that the investor has more money to fight legal battles than you do.

In practice, completing the project successfully will require you and the investor to be more flexible than what is specified in the contract. As long as both parties are committed and on good terms, this is the way every project goes. Therefore, before signing with an investor, make sure that they are as committed as you are. Ask the tough questions: Are they going to concentrate on a couple of projects, or do they run a myriad of them at the same time? If your game is just 1 out of 100 projects for them, it probably won't hurt them much to cancel it for any reason they please. Ask them to demonstrate a strong interest in your project and team.

Flexibility

Don't be afraid to ask the prospective investor about their plans if the game slips, and if they'd be open to prototype some ideas that might change the nature of the product. While the answers to these questions will need to be detailed in the contract, it is a good idea to understand the intent of what the other party is looking for as early as possible. Do they want a specific game to fill a niche, or just any good game with a chance to compete in the marketplace? Learn from other developers who worked with that investor.

How Solid Is the Company?

Even a good deal is not worth much if the company disappears in the middle of your project. It is important to do your homework and then question them. You'll have to get involved with their politics and listen to their employees as well as other developers before you can determine if you want to do business with them. Remember that a single replacement on the board of directors can make the difference between saving and canceling your project, and that this type of situation is out of your control. In addition, don't forget that the financial situation of the investing company's subsidiaries, parent company, or other branches might also affect you.

Publisher Funding

So far, we have covered all the essential points that will need to be discussed with a source of financing. But where do you go now? To whom should you talk? The most common option is to sign with a game publisher, but it is not the only one. Here are some of the issues that might arise when negotiating publisher funding.

Control

The publisher will want to assume the role of producer [McGilvray05]. This is usually a good idea because their knowledge of the market is probably better and more current than yours is. The producers working for large companies are usually very knowledgeable and can help you make your product appealing to a larger audience, help with gameplay tuning, and so forth. However, the contract must set boundaries delineating what can be changed by the publisher; otherwise, the number of features might double in a month, and your project plan quickly becomes obsolete.

Manage relationships with the publisher well. The team will lose some power over their own game; make sure they know it is for the project's greater good.

Ownership

Ownership is a very important and controversial topic. Typically, the publisher will want to own the technology used in the game, which will allow them to legally reuse it without paying you extra sums. If your game is almost ready and you have other opportunities elsewhere, the publisher will be the one making concessions in this area; otherwise, you might have to give up ownership of the software. At the very least, make sure you get a percentage of the profits they earn from reusing your work.

Protecting Your Team

Get a minimum number of units sold guaranteed in writing. A publisher buying a product that competes with their franchise title and never releasing it, in order to protect their sales, is a nightmare scenario that rarely happens but one that you must be protected against. Make sure your contract guarantees a release in stores and a minimum marketing budget, and negotiate a "kill fee" to protect yourself in case of cancellation.

In addition, of course, make sure that the milestone payment schedule is structured in such a way that you will never experience cash flow shortages. Since checks won't be mailed until the publisher has approved a milestone delivery, build the delay into your plan.

Going through a Venture Capital Company

Foregoing publisher funding to sign with a venture capital company is a radically different experience, with higher risks for you—but also higher potential rewards.

While working *with* a publisher is pretty much like working *for* a publisher, dealing with a VC company is like having a partner—but one that doesn't share your priorities.

In addition to a good team and a good game idea, you need a solid business plan to obtain capital. Capital investors are buying a share in your company, not just in one project; they must be confident in your long-term plans before they open their checkbooks. Preparing a business plan requires significant work; hiring a professional to write yours might be money well spent. See [Laramée05] for details.

Selecting a VC Partner

Most VC companies are not interested in videogames. Unfortunately, game projects are too expensive for very small funds, and not large enough for most companies that deal in the stock market. Moreover, since a game might take two or three years to yield revenues, it is hard to reconcile investment in games with the typically very short-term horizon of venture capitalists.

If a VC company initiates a dialogue with you, it will be extremely different from what you get with the publishers. Since you will be asking for "seed money" to create a demo, or maybe even for enough money to develop the entire product, they will question your ability to deliver the game, how you plan to sell it, and what they can get back if everything fails. Since they are not from the games industry, they might rely on publishers you choose with them to evaluate the product itself, and they might get involved in negotiating the publishing deal. For example, the VC might pay you to develop the game and receive the milestone payments from the publisher; this protects you from cash flow fluctuations, but at the cost of an extra middleman. They will also control expenses very closely, thus forcing you to stick to the plan instead of doing research—to a VC company, a decent title delivered on time is preferable to a better product that costs more than expected and therefore reduces the calculated return on investment.

Going Private

Individual investors might also be interested in putting their own money into ventures like yours. Moreover, they may not be as difficult to find as you might think. For example, owners of small to medium-sized businesses might be willing to diversify their portfolio and risk small amounts of money in projects such as videogames.

In practice, individual investors will rarely provide more than what is needed to build a prototype, which brings you back to the original problem: finding a publisher. Funding a complete project from beginning to end is out of reach for most individuals. Therefore, this is a quick method to get started on a game, but it is not suitable for large projects.

A word of warning: since individual investors are usually not very familiar with the industry, they might not be prepared to deal with the types of problems that every project encounters, such as delays when developing the demo, finding the publisher, signing a contract, and so forth. Make sure there are no misconceptions, or the relationship can quickly sour.

Banks

Banks lend money to people who have money. It is easier to get $500,000 from a bank if you bring another $500,000 as collateral than it is to ask for just $50,000 empty handed. Therefore, banks cannot be realistically considered a standalone funding resource; instead, you should use bank loans as a complement to your core funding.

For example, it is possible to secure an advance from a publisher and finance the rest of your development with a bank. This can be very useful, as the lower publisher advance might allow you to negotiate better royalty rates.

The bank can also provide a credit margin to use as a buffer when the schedule slips or milestone payments don't arrive in time. A good credit margin also comes in handy when beginning the next project while awaiting royalties.

Conclusion

Getting funding for a project is not nearly as difficult as getting the project done. It is, however, very time consuming, and the process can take anywhere from three months to a year.

Getting professionals to help can be invaluable. Involve a lawyer who is familiar with intellectual property laws when discussing your contracts. Agents can also help represent your team; meeting people and shopping around for a publisher is a tough job, not to be taken lightly, and a good agent with the right contacts and knowledge of all the pitfalls can make the difference between success and failure.

One word about ethics: there is nothing wrong with getting publishers and funding companies in competition with each other—it is actually the best way to go—but commitments are not to be taken lightly. Verbal agreements are binding. Do not promise something you can't deliver.

It is difficult for developers who are passionate about their product to change their focus from making the best game to making the most profitable game. However, remember: it is what investors expect of you.

References

[Laramée05] Laramée, F. D., "Writing a Business Plan for a Game Development Startup," *Secrets of the Game Business*, 2nd Edition, Charles River Media, 2005.

[McGilvray05] McGilvray, M., "The Producer, Friend or Foe?" *Secrets of the Game Business*, 2nd Edition, Charles River Media, 2005.

4

BRINGING GAMES TO MARKET

4.0

Introduction

You have built a solid company, with an impressive business plan that has seduced investors and allowed you to secure enough private financing to develop your first game. Or maybe you have created a spectacular demo and are ready to show it to publishers. Or have you completed a project and decided to sell it online yourselves? Good; you have taken the first step toward success. Now comes the most difficult part of the operation: taking the game to market.

The game publishing market is highly concentrated, with only a few dozen large publishers accounting for the overwhelming majority of sales, and getting more so every year. Retailers have limited shelf space, and will only open it to games they perceive to have reasonable expectations of success. Players get bombarded with information about new games every day; how will you make sure that yours is the one they remember?

Most developers' marketing effort is essentially limited to what is needed to obtain a publishing contract. For self-publishers, the job expands to public relations, customer service, and maybe even direct sales. How do you go about ensuring that your company signs with a publisher at advantageous terms, or that your downloadable game emerges from the masses of its competitors to become a cash cow for years to come?

The articles in this section of the book describe the work that goes on behind the scenes while the artists, programmers, and designers are busy creating their magic.

- In Article 4.1, "Psychological Profiling: Entering the Mind of the Game Player," designer and producer Steve Bocska explains how his team analyzed consumer psychological profiles and guided their game design accordingly.
- In Article 4.2, "Showing Publishers What They Want to See," game agent Jay Powell explains what publishers expect to see from a developer who is pitching a project, and how to maximize your odds of securing a contract.
- In Article 4.3, "Securing a Development Contract: The Art of Pitching," producer Ed Bartlett brings further advice on ways to secure a publishing contract.
- In Article 4.4, "Introduction to Contract Negotiation," Jay Powell explains techniques that developers can use to negotiate a contract effectively.
  In Article 4.5, "Effective Development Contracts," games industry attorney Thomas Buscaglia examines the clauses found in typical development contracts, and explains how to negotiate deals that protect your interests.
- In Article 4.6, "Pros and Cons of Worldwide and Country-by-Country Deals," Jay Powell discusses the comparative advantages of signing a world-

wide publishing contract with a single partner, versus multiple partnerships with national publishers.

- In Article 4.7, "The Whys and Wherefores of Game Agents," Borut Pfeifer, co-founder of independent developer White Knuckle Games, explains the pros and cons of hiring an agent to represent your company in negotiations with publishers.

- In Article 4.8, "Public Relations: Making the Most of the Gaming Press," Beverly Cambron, president of game public relations firm Rocco Media, explains how to build good relations with the gaming press and use them to improve your title's notoriety.

- Finally, in Article 4.9, "Techniques to Increase Upsell for Online Games," Mason McCuskey, president of independent developer Spin Studios, explains how self-publishers can optimize the online sales of their own games.

4.1

Psychological Profiling: Entering the Mind of the Game Player

Steve Bocska

strategus@shaw.ca

Even with all the recent technological advances in consoles, perhaps one of the most exciting innovations in game development can be found in a theory of design that looks into the psychological motivations of the targeted game player.

There is a variety of useful ways in which game developers and publishers can categorize consumers and analyze these "clusters" to develop a deeper understanding of what motivates their behavior. Using *CSI: Dark Motives* and *Simpsons: Hit & Run* as case studies, this article examines various analytical and profiling techniques that can be adopted in the design and targeted marketing of video games. Using these same methods, designers can also better anticipate gamers' wants, fears, expectations, and preferences toward creating games that uniquely target specific consumers.

The Gamer Landscape: A Primitive View

The gaming landscape is the most varied and complex it has ever been. Gamers today can be as young as toddlers and as old as seniors. They are geographically, ethnically, socially, culturally, and economically diverse. Why, then, do most publishers and developers in the videogames industry continue to assume that it is suitable to distill the gaming audience down to just the broad, high-level categories of "casual" and "hardcore?"

While the answer can be in part attributed to a stubborn reluctance to admit that a finer resolution of market segmentation exists, the outright unavailability of data and ignorance of statistical techniques available are other huge contributing factors. Without the data or expertise to describe, group, and analyze game-buying consumers, we, as developers and publishers, are forced to resort to speculation and conjecture when trying to identify consumer clusters and profile their behavior. Despite the videogame industry's preoccupation with state-of-the-art technology, we nonetheless remain virtually prehistoric in our grasp of consumer clustering and behavior relative to most other consumer product industries.

Some worthwhile "baby steps" have already been taken in the direction of classification. A simple analytical methodology was proposed by [Ip02]. It suggested a survey using Likert scale data (e.g., ranging from strongly agree to strongly disagree) where participants would assign self-ranked scores to 15 weighted factors ranging from their degree of technological savvy to their tolerance for frustration. They proposed that five discreet categories of game player typologies would emerge: ultra casual/nongamers, casual, transitional/moderate, hardcore, and ultra hardcore. These typologies, they predicted, would approximately match the exponential distribution in Figure 4.1.1.

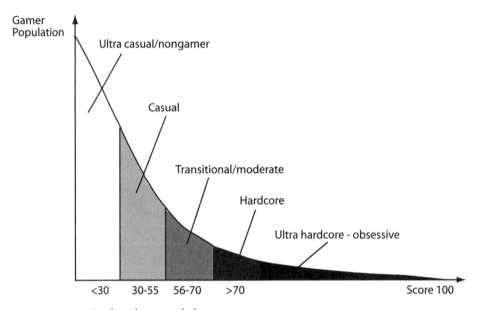

FIGURE 4.1.1   *Predicted gamer-dedication scores. (© Copyright Ernest Adams, Barry Ip, 2004.)*

This approach is useful as a starting point for further discussion, but extremely limiting in its ultimate value. Their continuum, even if validated, does not provide much useful insight into the true clustering of these groups, nor their specific preferences for gaming genres, price points, or features. Even though it's a good first step, it's still nowhere near enough to suit our purposes.

To leap forward, we must consider the concept of clustering, for which there is a wealth of statistical techniques and marketing tools available to generate salient and meaningful consumer data. For example, simple mathematical measures (tree clustering, block clustering, and K-means clustering) can help objectify classification schemes and group consumers statistically, preventing overly generic and broad gamer categories—such as "casual" and "hardcore." Discreet choice and conjoint analysis are both effective tools for breaking down these clusters into relevant sales metrics that can help in developing a successful product design, optimizing the bundling of features, gauging demand for specific features, and identifying monetary tradeoffs buyers are willing to make for specific features.

Personality Profiling

After Radical Entertainment, a Vancouver-based developer, shipped *CSI: Dark Motives*, the CSI development team rolled right into preproduction for *CSI: Miami*—another PC mystery adventure game with a decidedly mass-market appeal. Frustrated by frequent disagreements about the "optimum feature set" throughout the production of *Dark Motives*, the team's goal became clear: to create a baseline of understanding and agreement among every person involved in making the game about who the target audience was—and more importantly—reinforce the notion that the team was not making the game for themselves, but for the target audience. Consumer behavior research would help shape the design direction of the game, encouraging the publisher and even individual team members to make extensive use of psychological profiling when considering potential features and discussing design alterations.

The CSI property is one of the rare examples of a license whose appeal has a decidedly female skew—approximately 60%. Yet, the team recognized the need for type profiling over just a simple gender analysis of preferences. According to Radical's Kirsten Forbes, producer of the title, "There's much more variance in gaming preferences *within* genders than between them. Just because you're female doesn't make you automatically indifferent to RPGs or shooters. Gamers can only truly be defined by their psychological profiles." The team researched several different profiling tools and ultimately chose the Myers-Briggs Type Indicator.

CSI and MBTI

The Myers-Briggs Type Indicator (MBTI) is designed to identify a person's psychological type as it relates to his or her preferences for taking in information, making decisions, and degree of extroversion [Myers85]. These preferences are translated to a psychological or personality "type." The theory of psychological type says that people with different preferences naturally have different interests, perspectives, behaviors, and motivations. Awareness of these preferences would help the team create a game that had features the target audience craved and avoid those that annoyed them.

Fortunately, a designer on another project at Radical happened to have an academic background in clinical psychology. Through the course of several meetings, Josh Mitchell helped the *CSI: Miami* team break down the potential audience into several key groups based on little more than professional insight and feedback from reviewers and discussion groups about the previous CSI game. Using his considerable depth of understanding of the Myers-Briggs psychological categories, Josh was able to identify five typologies (listed in Table 4.1.1) that seemed to match the kinds of gamers who were expected to be attracted to the game.

Table 4.1.1 *CSI: Miami* Player Taxonomy and Purchase Share Estimates

Player Type	Estimated Purchase Share	Myers-Briggs Indicator
CSI fan (learners)	60%	Extravert, Sensing, Feeling, Judging
CSI fan (gawkers)	10%	Extravert, Sensing, Feeling, Perceiving
Gaming enthusiast	10%	Extravert, Sensing, Thinking, Judging
Puzzle gamer	10%	Introvert, Sensing, Thinking, Perceiving
Mystery fan	10%	Introvert, Intuition, Thinking, Judging

Myers-Briggs Type Indicator Glossary

Extravert: Attempts to get into the outer world of people; compelled to analyze, organize; focus on enjoying, using, and tolerance.

Introvert: Prefers the world of concepts and ideas; compelled to analyze or organize their inward life; enjoys relating situation to past experience or knowledge.

Sensing: Leans toward reality; prefers not to play hunches; pays close attention to surroundings; focus on the actual/here-and-now.

Intuition: Driven by possibilities; likes using imagination; has clear vision of the expected outcome; responds to inspiration and a desire to see dreams come true; less interested in measuring results in the real world.

Feeling: Concerned about perspective and feelings of others; looks for relational harmony; focus on people skills, warmth, and friendliness; leans toward empathy and compassion; may minimize the importance of facts.

Thinking: Frequently uses logic or principles; compelled to look for truth; focus on understanding; tends to organize, sum up, or categorize; leans toward the measurable or objective; may minimize the importance of human values and feelings.

Judging: Likes drawing conclusions/closure.

Perceiving: Likes continued thinking and listening.

Admittedly, this is a somewhat ad-hoc approach. And while the first choice would have been to solicit a huge sample of focus testers, cluster them by gaming preference, and subject them to the Myers-Briggs test, the team quite simply didn't have the time or the resources to do so. Still, the outline generated for *CSI: Miami* was more insightful than any other audience profiling previously attempted at Radical.

The next step was to take these typologies and make them part of the common vocabulary among team members and between Radical and the publisher. Through a series of discussion and exercises, the team was able to validate—in principle—the assumptions made about the proposed typologies and even obtain estimates from the publisher about what their anticipated purchasing split would be among the different groups. The result was a simple taxonomy that would capture the gameplay preferences and styles of the audience profile, outlined in Table 4.1.1.

The benefits of this activity were immediate. First, team members now had a much clearer understanding of the intended audience of the game, making it easier to put their interests first. Second, all design considerations could be evaluated against their impact on each of the various profiled segments—both positive and negative. This was vitally important for balancing features in the game, as it was recognized that there would be an unusual blend of interest received from both mass-market and fanatical adventure gamers—a typically incompatible mixture. Finally, because there was a mutually accepted reference of the demands and preferences of the target audience, it became an invaluable "tie breaking" tool when arguing about eleventh-hour feature priorities.

There are many in-game examples of the impact this profiling had on the selection and design of gameplay features. For example, the large proportion of "sensing" types in the analysis—who typically "prefer not to play hunches"—required that a greater emphasis be placed on designing a comprehensive, yet accessible, tutorial. The previous two *CSI* games included a tutorial that was integrated directly into the first case. However, this was deemed too limiting and inaccessible for those "sensing" types who wanted to refresh their skills at a later point in the game. Thus, the tutorial was ripped out, redesigned, and created as a standalone level accessible from the Main menu.

Recent Advances in Psychological Profiling

Some encouraging strides have recently been made in the area of profiling, especially as it relates to using Myers-Briggs typologies in building a better understanding of the unique needs of various audience clusters. International Hobo, a games design and narrative consultancy, has been extensively researching this area recently and has generated some insightful reports and findings [Hobo04]. Their research has already uncovered some interesting relationships that are bound to have far-reaching implications with respect to game design and audience segmentation. First, they grouped the eight Myers-Briggs axes (Introvert/Extrovert, Sensing/Intuition, Thinking/Feeling, Judging/Perceiving) into four paired types, based on similarities in their game-playing habits:

> **Type 1 (Thinking/Judging):** Consists of ISTJ, INTJ, ESTJ, ENTJ.
> **Type 2 (Thinking/Perceiving):** Consists of ISTP, INTP, ENTP, ESTP.
> **Type 3 (Feeling/Perceiving):** Consists of INFP, ENFP, ISFP, ESFP.
> **Type 4 (Feeling/Judging):** Consists of ESFJ, ISFJ, ENFJ, INFJ.

Using survey data and thorough follow-up case studies, they were then able to further investigate these groupings to determine the nature of each type's tastes and preferences in gameplay. They then applied these four typologies to two familiar theoretical demographic categories—Casual and Hardcore. The result was eight final "Demographic Game Design Clusters" grouped under four key headings: Conquerors, Managers, Wanderers, and Participants.

Their findings to date are fascinating, showing how high-level personality type similarities can trickle down through the demographic clusters and provide useful "style of play" generalizations, specifically between so-called "casual" and "hardcore" categories. For example, the casual "Wanderers" cluster (Feeling/Perceiving) suggests they have a preference for relaxing, easy games where there is a strong feeling of ongoing accomplishment, such as *The Sims*. However, the complementary hardcore "Wanderers" are avid gamers who play more frequently, are interested in aesthetic appeal and good story but often find current games too hard—these are prime candidates for cheat codes.

The Typology Filter

Encouraged by the success of simple profiling in improving the understanding and agreement about the game design, it seemed logical for Radical to extend its influence to another, larger project. While nearing the end of the production cycle for *Simpsons: Hit & Run*, Radical faced the task of building a design foundation for the team's next project. At the time, it was erroneously assumed that this new project would be a similar kind of open-world driving game. Nonetheless, the exercise—as outlined next—turned out to be extremely useful, as it solidified the use of consumer profiling at Radical and confirmed its value in reducing the all-too-often abundant ambiguity and confusion during the preproduction phase.

Collecting Ideas

Developmental exercises during preproduction can be a mixed blessing. While it is certainly exciting to facilitate an eager room of exceptionally talented designers toward creating a monstrous list of good ideas, it is nonetheless emotionally exhausting to have to filter all of the great ideas down to only those that have strong consumer viability and can fit reasonably within a 16-month production schedule. To streamline the process—while still keeping it relevant—Radical adopted a three-phased strategy combining free-form brainstorming with consumer profiling to generate a filtered list of realistic and achievable features for the next game.

The first phase was a pure brainstorming session to collect as many good ideas as possible from the design team and categorize them within the feature framework of the current game design and engine. This phase was understandably chaotic, with great ideas furiously bantered around the room and the biggest challenge being trying to record them all. Brainstorming exercises like this tend to generate a wealth of exciting and high-potential suggestions. The downside is that participants have little or no discipline or reality checking—in fact, any brainstorming session facilitator worth his engagement fee at this stage should be *actively discouraging* any nay-saying or "black hat" criticism [Bono99]. Still, the result is usually a voluminous collection of ideas that unfortunately reflect the blue-sky gameplay cravings of the designers more than the target audience of the game.

Current research suggests that employing multidisciplinary specialists in such creative sessions is more likely to produce breakthroughs of unusually high value—superior even to the best innovations achieved by conventional approaches [Fleming04]. Ironically, though, they also tend to generate a higher number of insignificant innovations and even fewer average ones. Bearing this in mind, the next step was counterintuitive—the designers expanded the already unmanageable feature set even further by proposing it to an interdisciplinary cross-section of peers, from artists to programmers to testers. Following yet another brainstorming session, they felt they had completely exhausted their capacity for raw suggestions. The resulting collection of ideas for the next game was impressive, yet at the same time unmanageable and daunting, as shown in Figure 4.1.2.

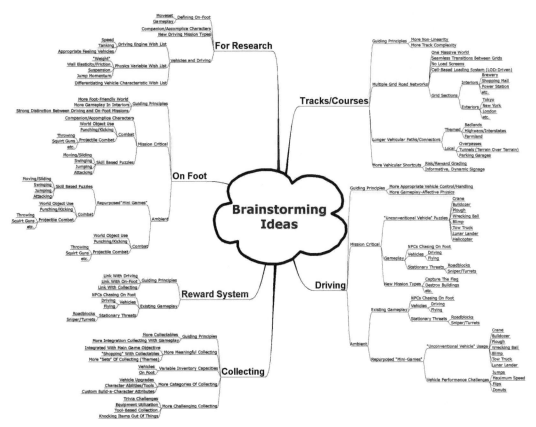

FIGURE 4.1.2   *Chaotic and overwhelming outline from the original design brainstorming suggestions.*

Creating the Filter

The second phase of the process was to create a "design filter" based on consumer profiling through which the ideas would be screened down to only those that should be found in a game targeted to the particular audience in question. This was the most academic part of the process, but somewhat ironically, also the least rigorous and scientific. Once again, the framework for the filter would be created by a simple mental exercise by the Radical designers. The potential audience was broken down into several key groups, this time based on professional experience and the first-hand insight gained from monitoring dozens of hours of focus testing conducted on *Simpsons: Hit & Run* during the final stages of production.

It was concluded that players who found themselves drawn to this title would likely fall into one of four fairly broad categories: platform gamer with inventive/rational tendencies, platform gamer with competitive tendencies, collectors, and driving game players. While this classification was interesting, it was still not yet very useful. What was required was greater insight into their preferences, fears, expectations, and desires. The next step was to assign behavioral psychology classifications to four categories, as shown in Figure 4.1.3.

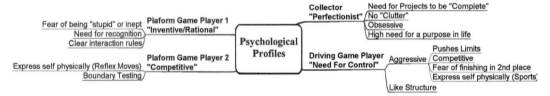

FIGURE 4.1.3 *Psychological classifications of target user categories.*

For those with preferences for platform gaming, there were two distinct behavioral types: "Inventive/Rational" and "Competitive." Players who primarily enjoyed searching and finding collectables (like the collector cards in *Simpsons: Hit & Run*) were profiled as "Perfectionists," while those who enjoyed the thrill of fast driving were assigned the label "Need for Control." Once again, even this simple profiling gave the Radical design team unprecedented insight into the possible preferences, fears, and needs of the target audience. The next step was to apply this knowledge to the framework of the design.

Applying the Filter

Armed with the newly created filter, the team moved into the third and final phase—applying it to the original mind map of brainstorming ideas to pare it down to something more manageable. As a group exercise, they reviewed each of the "branches" from the original collection and passed them through a simple test: does this feature

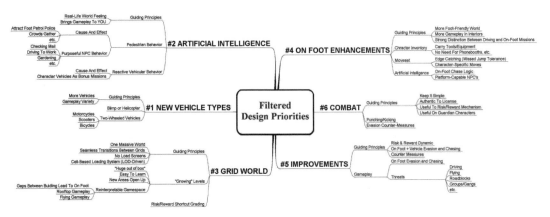

FIGURE 4.1.4 *Filtered design brainstorming suggestions: a manageable feature set.*

or idea conform to the expectations of any of the player types identified in the profiling exercise? Very frequently, the answer was "no"—a clear sign that the team had slipped into the all-too-common designer mindset of making games for themselves instead of for the average gamer. By the time the filtering was complete, the team had screened out dozens of inappropriate ideas and ended up with a design feature set that was not only focused on meeting the demands of the intended audience, but also workable within the proposed production schedule, as shown in Figure 4.1.4.

As mentioned earlier, this game was never created—another project was eventually assigned to this team. While the effort of defining this particular feature set seems to have gone to waste, the value of creating a profiling initiative and methodology has not. Radical now employs an even more rigorous approach to analyzing its target audience for *all* of its games. The most recent of these "audience analysis" documents was a comprehensive 15-page report that thoroughly analyzed the motivations, compulsions, and fears of each targeted audience segment for an upcoming title.

Conclusion

Even with so many recent technological advances within the videogames industry, there still seems to be a pervasive lack of sophistication when it comes to understanding the "gamer" consumer. Indeed, many games are still created with the stereotypical male 18–35-year-old gamer in mind—without any thought as to whether this should even be the primary audience. In addition, there has been a "coarse" approach when segmenting these consumer groups—often relying on broad categories such as hardcore or casual—without looking deeper into how more specific consumer preferences might help to shape game design. Other industries use a multitude of tools to understand that "sweet spot." Drawing upon demographics, psychographics, and perceptual mapping, these industries have a long history of successfully launching and marketing products that are well received by their intended audience—a lesson for us all. When more complex profiling is undertaken within the videogames industry—for example, creating typologies from such tools as the Myers-Briggs tests—publishers and developers will begin to better understand the unique needs of the various audiences, and possibly even create useful "filters" to help keep a team focused on the consumer and reduce design ambiguity.

References and Additional Resources

[Bono99] de Bono, E., *Six Thinking Hats*, Bay Back Books, Boston, 1999.

[Fleming04] Fleming, L., "Perfecting Cross-Pollination," *Harvard Business Review*, September 2004.

[Hobo04]International Hobo, "Demographic Game Design," International Hobo Ltd., Manchester UK, 2004.

[Ip02] Ip, B. and Adams, E., "From Casual to Core: A Statistical Mechanism for Studying Gamer Dedication," available online at *www.gamasutra.com/features/20020605/ip_01.htm.*

[Moore91] Moore, G. A., *Crossing the Chasm*, HarperBusiness, New York, NY, 1991.

[Myers85] Myers, I. and McCaulley, M. H., *MBTI Manual*, Consulting Psychologists Press, Palo Alto, 1985.

[Wedbush03] Wedbush Morgan Securities, "The Great Console Cycle Myth And Other Tall Tales," *Industry Report*, May 2003.

4.2

Showing Publishers
What They Want to See

Jay Powell

jep@octagon1.com

With the growing need for titles to fill release schedules for consoles, handhelds, and the PC market, developers who can present publishers with the best package possible maximize their chances of securing a deal. This article reviews some of the basics of package submission, and presents a few of the new requirements that are being instituted by some of the world's top publishers.

Product Information

The most important part of a package will be the information on the product itself. A submission will be reviewed by a variety of departments and people within the larger companies, so it helps to provide information targeted toward each group. While the acquisitions group will need to know about the overall concept of the game and its expected budget, the marketing group will be interested in reasons why the game will sell, and the testers will need as much information as possible to properly evaluate the title.

Game Overview

Start building the package with a brief overview of the game. This should be kept to 10 to 15 pages, because it is meant to convey a high-level view of what the game is about.

The acquisitions manager and marketing departments are the primary audience for this overview, which should include a detailed concept of the game, a description of its look and feel, gameplay details, a timeline for completion, the target platforms, and a budget. These are the most important points in the evaluation of any game being submitted today.

Sell Sheet

Include a one-page sell sheet in your package to give everyone at the publisher's office a very quick and concise overview of your game. This sheet should contain several screenshots to show the "feel" of the game, five or six unique selling points, a high level concept, system requirements, and what ESRB rating you expect the game to receive. Do not make the mistake of including features in your unique selling points; save features for your 10- to 15-page game overview and concentrate here on the things that truly make your game different from others in the genre. Keep this information to one page, as your main target is the marketing and sales division of a publisher. You want the decision makers at the company to quickly be able to get a good feel for what you are doing.

Technical Design Document

Prepare a technical design document, which will serve as a companion to the overview. This document should describe the specifics of the engine being used for the game. If the engine is unique, the document should compare it to the other engines that are on the market: let the publisher know why yours is better or worse, and in what areas. If an existing engine is being licensed, the document should state the changes that were made to the existing code to make this game stand out technically. Regardless of whether the engine is proprietary or licensed, the publisher will need to know how it compares to the engines powering the best-selling games on the market. Deals have been closed based on engines alone, so this is a key part of your package.

This document is also the place to outline the steps for porting a game from one platform to another. Publishers will want to know if this step has already been planned for, or if a separate version of the game will have to be developed from the ground up.

Finally, if you are presenting a PC game, do not forget to include the end-user system requirements in the technical design document. Publishers will need this information to determine the price point and demographic of a mass-market game and make sure that there will be a large enough install base of users with your requirements to make a release viable.

Project Outline

The next key components of a package are a time scale for the game's development, and the budget involved.

This document should describe the content of the milestones in detail, tell when they will be accomplished, and specify how much money is due after each of them. Extremely detailed budgets are not often required at this point, but if the publisher is going to be investing a large amount of money into the title, they will want to make sure it is justified.

One thing to remember about a budget is that once a title is evaluated for quality, the publisher will create a profit and loss spreadsheet (P&L). This P&L will determine how profitable the game will be, based on sales projections. The more that a developer knows about the publisher's business model, the easier it is to work out a deal that is profitable for both parties. To help the publisher, include sales figures of similar products if you have access to this information. Such figures let the publisher know that there is serious consumer interest in the type of title being presented, and what to expect at retail when the title is released.

Remember to keep the budget and timetable reasonable. If there is any uncertainty in the "industry norms," consult with other developers to see where they have had success.

Localization

Include as much information as possible about the game's localization costs. How many words are there in the game and in the manual? How much dialogue? How many actors are needed to contribute to the final product? Any international publisher will need to include this information in their P&L, as this is additional cost that they will need to invest in the game.

This document is also a good place to add any copyright information necessary for the game. If the intellectual property is licensed, make sure to include the appropriate documentation. For more information on the legal aspects of a submission package, see [Powell05].

Game Demo

The most important part of the product information section of the package is the game demo itself.

An effective demo will highlight the key selling points of the game and show them to the publisher. The demo should accurately depict the game's user interface and the engine that will be used. Many developers make the mistake of creating a demo on a freeware engine and promising a product based on an engine they have yet to license. This does not help the publisher, as they cannot see an accurate depiction of the graphics and environments of the final product. The demo should also include at least some of the artificial intelligence (AI) that will be present in the game. Strong, accurate AI is a key feature in videogames today; a publisher wants to know that the product they are purchasing will be up to the industry standard. Most importantly, the demo should be polished and stable. A demo that crashes repeatedly or fails to deliver components that the publisher is expecting has a much higher chance of being rejected.

Every publisher is going to have their own idea of what should be included in the game demo, so there is no "sure bet" as far as content is concerned. In an ideal world, the developer would be able to show the entire game and have the publisher make their decision based on that. Obviously, this is rarely possible, but at the very least, the demo should contain:

- Unique selling points the developer has identified in their game.
- Accurate depiction of the user interface.

- Multiplayer play if included in the final game.
- Technically sound gameplay. The art may not be 100% complete, but the game should operate smoothly.

Ask yourself if your demo accurately represents the game you want to make. If you are not happy with the demo, chances are the publishers will not be either.

If it is impossible to create a demo, at least include a movie that shows the same key points that the playable demo would.

Competitive Analysis

The final aspect of the product portion of a package is the competitive analysis. In addition to the sales figures of similar products, developers must look to the future. Let the publishers know which similar games will be released at about the same time as yours.

This research will also help identify which publishers to approach with a game. Sending a game to a publisher with a competing product may give away some of the key selling points that the competing title is lacking. Explain why your own product is better than competing games. A list of features in the engine, design, and gameplay of all competing products should be compiled, to let the publisher know immediately which are included in your own game, which are on the "nice to have" list, and which will not be in the game at all.

Developer History

The second half of a complete submission package will discuss the team creating the game, their history, and their strengths.

This portion of the package must prove to the publisher that the team can complete the product and that it will be up to industry standard when finished. Many publishers require that the team members of a development project be named in the contract to guarantee the quality of the final product.

Establishing the development team and providing the publisher with this information will be a great asset, both for this project and for your company's long-term future. Often, publishers will approach teams whose projects they have rejected with the opportunity to work on an intellectual property they have acquired.

Track Records

Packages should always include the track record of both the team and the individual team members. Include a description of all the titles that have been shipped by the company, the platforms on which they were released, and their sales numbers if possible. A history of being on time and under budget is a major asset in this industry; if your team has met this kind of success, bring it to the publisher's attention immediately! Even a title that sold poorly shows the publisher that the company can complete and ship a title. Publishers can research this information anyway, so it is a good idea to provide it up front in the package.

If the company is a startup, or has new team members, a complete breakdown of the titles each person has worked on in the past and of his or her role in that development should be included. Having the lead programmer or artist from a successful project working on your game carries much more weight with a publisher than hiring someone who provided very little input on the product.

Team Breakdown

The package should state how many people are involved in the project and the roles of the people involved. This information helps the publisher evaluate the budget of the game and the potential weak spots. Some genres or platforms need more artists or programmers than others, and publishers need to know that members of a development team are sensitive to this and are prepared for what they are about to begin.

The number of people employed by a developer can also provide information on the company's financial stability. Publishers are more comfortable dealing with teams that have business experience and have proven themselves capable of balancing budgets. Along the same lines, developers that have stayed together for long periods of time and show significant amounts of company loyalty and unity catch the eyes of publishers more often.

Unique Technology

Finally, let the publisher know if you have any unique technology that you can bring to the table. Whether the technology is a complete engine or a modification to an existing engine, it is a powerful incentive and could be the key to signing the deal. Publishers always want to be a step ahead of the competition, and a technological edge is the best way to do it. If possible, show these unique features in your demo.

Package Presentation

How a developer presents a package can be just as important as the contents of the package.

All submissions should always be as professional as possible. Publishers see hundreds or thousands of submissions a year. A package that looks great, with professional printing and binding, will attract a publisher's attention before the game is even reviewed. In today's industry, where developers come and go every day, publishers want to find professional teams who they feel can properly manage a business as well as a game project. Having a professional-looking package on the publisher's desk will help build this credibility.

CASE STUDY 4.2.1: SUBMISSION PACKAGE CHECKLIST

Here, again, are the components that should be included in your package:

- Game overview
- Sell sheet
- Technical design document
- Project outline
- Localization information
- Game demo
- Competitive analysis
- Team and team member track record
- Size of team with breakdown for programming, art, etc.
- Information on unique technology

In addition, you may add:

- Copies of any press the game has received
- PowerPoint presentation summarizing the entire package
- Videotape version of gameplay and movies

Conclusion

The submission package you send to a publisher could be a first and last chance for a deal with that company. The old saying about never getting a second chance to make a first impression could not be truer in this industry.

Your package should strive to answer every question a publisher could possibly have and even some they do not. Once a publisher rejects a project from a developer, it is very difficult to get them to look at that project again, so make certain that all the features and benefits of the team and project are plainly stated in this package.

References

[Powell05] Powell, J., "Introduction to Contract Negotiations," *Secrets of the Game Business*, 2nd Edition, Charles River Media, 2005.

Securing a Development Contract: The Art of Pitching

Ed Bartlett

ed@hivepartners.com

Gone are the days when it was possible to sign a development deal from a handful of buzzwords shouted during a post-E3 party. With team sizes, development schedules, and product budgets on a seemingly unstoppable upward trend, and a noticeable bias toward what publishers consider "safe" products such as sequels and licenses, pitching new products to publishers is becoming increasingly unpredictable, complex, and frustrating, particularly for smaller, lesser-known teams.

This article looks at the pitching process in detail and explains the rudimentary criteria that should be fulfilled to maximize the impact of your pitch and help speed the signing process.

What Is Pitching?

pitch[1] (pĭch) *v.* pitched, pitch·ing, pitch·es *v. tr.*

1. A form of words used to persuade.
2. To attempt to promote or sell, often in a high-pressure manner.
3. Set or aim at a particular level, target, or audience.

Almost every industry has to pitch for work in some way, shape, or form, and this applies particularly to creative industries, in which companies compete against others in their sector for key accounts and contracts.

Pitching is the established way for a client to evaluate exactly what an individual, team, or company can offer them in terms of services and skills by allowing them to prepare a highly specific presentation containing not only details of any relevant products, but also important peripheral aspects such as background and company history, staff profiles, and previous work samples.

In the case of videogames, publishers have limited budgets and resources allocated for each quarter, so even if their game concepts are different, developers are still competing for a slice of the same pie as well as regularly pitching directly against each other for "work for hire" deals, usually based around publisher-owned intellectual properties (IPs) or licenses.

Numerous pitch types take place within the videogames industry, ranging from middleware vendors touting tools and technology, to publishers selling their latest lineup to retail, but in this article we will concentrate on the most nebulous of pitch type: developer deals.

Deal and Product Types

Before touting your development skills, it is important to understand the different deal and product types on offer.

Deal Types

Work for hire. The most straightforward of contracts, this "cash for content" deal generally sees developers pitching for the right to work on one of the publishers own IPs or acquired licenses. Publishers are looking for emphasis on professional production techniques, stability, and a proven team or track record. "Work for hire" teams rarely secure more than a basic royalty rate, although many such deals involve working on franchised or licensed products, which tend to have a greater potential of realizing royalties for the developer.

Prototyping deal. As publishers look to minimize their long-term development risks, many are starting to offer prototyping deals. Here, the publisher pays the developers' costs, or "burn rate" for a short period of time (usually three to six months) to allow them to produce a more detailed "proof of concept" demo to evaluate before making the final decision on a product. Some publishers also use external development teams to create prototypes of games they intend to develop internally rather than tie up their own teams, in which case the developer will factor a larger percentage profit margin into their burn rate.

Development deal. The most common deal type, where the publisher funds a new product through a royalty advance, a set number of milestone payments to cover development overheads, and an agreed royalty rate once the publisher has recouped the advance.

Publishing deal. Effectively a marketing and distribution deal, here the developer approaches the publisher with a finished or near-finished product, negating the publishers' risk as much as possible and maximizing the opportunity for the developer to negotiate a substantial advance and higher-than-average royalty rates. With the massive budgets and protracted development cycles of modern AAA titles (publishers grade products internally according to their quality and sales potential, with AAA at the top of the scale), the straight publishing deal is now the Holy Grail for all but the biggest and best developers.

Product Types

It is important to consider that the parameters of any potential deal will also be dictated to an extent by the type of product in question.

> **Original IP.** A developer approaching a publisher with a totally new, untested IP needs the sharpest of pitches to convince publishers of its merits. Publishers regard new IPs as the biggest risk, as they are an untested and therefore unknown quantity. The risk factor is exacerbated if the product is devoid of a compelling character, environment, storyline, or gameplay "hook" for the marketing department to work with, which is why it is increasingly important for developers to consider such factors from inception.
>
> **Third-party IP.** Usually a work for hire deal using one of the publisher's own IPs, the developer must be able to deliver a quality product according to rigid schedule and budget guidelines.
>
> **Third-party license.** Licenses are still very hit and miss within the games industry, and the pitching process for licensed products generally reflects that, as the developer often has to please both the publisher and the licensor. The majority of licensors have little or no knowledge of the games industry or development process. Therefore, where some licensors will require a creative solution, requiring the developer to rework the subject matter for a gaming audience, others will demand that the IP remains untouched. Many simply don't know what they want. Fortunately, most publishers are now securing more control over licenses before commissioning them for games, and some licensors are even securing a developer and creative brief before approaching the publishers.

The Fundamentals of Pitch Preparation

While there are a number of different types of pitch, they share the same core structure needed to provide the publisher with a well-rounded overview of any potential product or deal. The following section outlines the main stages in detail, giving hints and pointers along the way.

Researching Your Concept

When developing any new product, research plays a fundamental part, and videogames are no exception. It's one thing to have a great game idea, but the sooner you gather hard facts on potential competitor products, consumer demographics, and platform statistics, the easier it will be for you to create a concise pitch that will convince the publisher that your product is more than just a good idea.

Start by looking at products that are broadly similar to your "high concept," and then compare and contrast your unique selling points (USPs). Look at which publishers tend to favor that genre of game and get your hands on platform- and territory-specific sales figures, marketing information, and any relevant press coverage for competitor titles.

It's important even at this early stage to consider how you will differentiate your product from similar titles, and if it's highly original, how you will make the most of its features and establish it as a unique brand in an overly saturated market. A frightening number of developers never consider marketability, positioning, and brand development, and are all too happy to leave such important details to the publisher, even after a deal is clinched.

Preparing Documentation

It is very likely at pre-pitch stage that you will have a short, concise document outlining the fundamental elements of your concept. Until fairly recently this was all that was required when pitching new products. Nowadays, however, publishers are keen to read more deeply into your game mechanics and theory.

Feature-creep has cost publishers countless millions in the past, so the more concrete a design they can see in place from the beginning, the better. A good idea is to create two separate documents: a marketing/concept overview document and a design document.

Marketing/Concept Overview Document

This document is for people who do not have the time or need to digest every ounce of your game design, but rather need a concentrated "shot."

It should ideally weigh in at less than 20 pages, starting with a concise, accurate, and informative overview of your concept including positioning, and subsequently detailing in a similarly concise manner elements such as:

- Storyline
- Setting
- Characters
- Key features
- Competitor analysis
- Bullet-pointed USPs

The concept document should also be fairly graphical. Avoid filling entire pages with text; instead, try interspersing text with attractive concept and early game art.

Design Document

The nature of a design document tends to vary from game to game, designer to designer, and company to company. At the pitching stage, our advice would be to focus your designers' time on documenting, explaining, and illustrating only the *key* functionality, including:

- Control features
- Game and level progression
- Graphical themes
- Core game systems
- Any unique, unusual, or important functionality

Unlike the concept/marketing document, the design document needs only to be graphical when illustrating gameplay features.

Creating a Demo

The "proof of concept" demo has fast become the most important aspect of pitching to publishers. Demos themselves have evolved from simple technology prototypes to impressively feature-complete previews of what the final game will offer.

With development costs escalating as they are, assigning even a small team to a demo for just a few months can cost developers dearly, especially as there are no absolute guarantees that their game will get signed, regardless of its quality. Indeed, many a developer has gone out of business during the crucial pitching process. For these reasons, it is essential that you plan carefully and extract the most value for money or "bang for buck" from your demo.

Planning

As with a full product, it is vital when creating a demo that you plan in advance the time and cost factors. This involves working out exactly which features you intend to implement, and not necessarily what you think should be in the demo but rather what the publisher will want to see.

At demo stage, publishers nowadays are rarely moved by amazing graphical routines. What they really want to see is proof that your core game systems—particularly those that are new or different, or that feature strongly in the USP list—work as planned.

Consider the first presentation of your demo and if at any point you would have to say to the publisher "now imagine…," then you need to do more work. Never take for granted that other people will have the same vision of your concept as you do.

Once you have an understanding of what is required for your demo, you should sit down with your department heads to prepare a schedule. Again, be realistic. Always remember, there are no guarantees that you will ever sell your game or recoup the cost of creating the demo, so while an increased content and quality level within the demo presents a stronger case to publishers, if you still fail to secure a deal your financial loss will be even greater. Pitching is a very delicate balancing act.

Choosing a Platform

Another key consideration when preparing a demo is the target platform. As the vast majority of development work is done via the PC, this is for many the obvious choice, but not always the best one. Presuming that you have researched your concept, you will have a fair idea as to the platform(s) that best suit it. If your primary shelf keeping unit (SKU—i.e., version) is console-based, however, most publishers will want to see the demo running on that platform before committing, both to show that you are a registered developer and are capable of creating content for that platform, and that the key features you are including are possible within the fixed limits of the target hardware.

If you are already in possession of the necessary equipment, this is less of a problem. However, for startups and PC-only developers, both the time and cost of obtaining hardware and finding experienced staff must be taken into consideration. If for any reason it is not possible to develop your demo on target hardware, then consider options such as keeping your PC content in line with console specs, show demo footage running on a TV, and develop your control system using one of the many console joypad adapters on the market so that at least the publishers can feel as though they are playing it on the relevant system.

Using Middleware

Middleware is one of the biggest stories in recent development history and has in a short space of time evolved from simple component software such as video codices to complete game engines at the bleeding edge of technology.

Middleware can greatly enhance your development process—RenderWare Studio, for example, can be used to develop simultaneously for PC, PlayStation 2, Xbox, and Game Cube. Moreover, such software is especially useful when developing your demo, as they already contain much of the core functionality you will require, thus allowing you to concentrate your limited time and resources on implementing the key features.

Bear in mind, however, that middleware is not a magic cure for all game development issues, nor is it suitable for all developers and all games, and time saved at the demo stage might be lost later in development. Unlike proprietary technology, when using middleware, you are never 100% in control, and middleware vendors work to different ideals and deadlines than your team and product do.

Although many publishers are warming to middleware solutions thanks in part to the success of games such as *Grand Theft Auto 3*, some still favor developers with proprietary technology, and others even have exclusive deals with certain vendors or buy licenses in bulk. This also needs to be taken into consideration when deciding on your technical solution.

Schedule and Budget

Although a detailed schedule and cost analysis are rarely required until after the initial pitching stage, you will obviously be required to give the publisher some indication of the cost of the product, and at the very least an estimate of the quarter of the year in which you will deliver it.

Diligent developers will create accurate breakdowns as early as possible using spreadsheets specifically designed to allow fast and accurate assessment of project budgets using predetermined hardware, software, and overhead figures. It is also useful to develop two different breakdowns detailing the game features you can deliver on varying budgets. This shows that you are flexible, and can save a lot of time at the negotiating stage. Most publishers will naturally try to knock down your price, so always go in slightly higher than necessary without pricing yourself out of the market.

CASE STUDY 4.3.1: TEAM 17

The pitching process has changed dramatically since the early days of the industry. We asked veteran Team 17 creative director, Martyn Brown, how they have adapted over the years.

Q. How has the pitching process changed for developers over the years?

"The most apparent change is the risk assessment and due-diligence carried out by publishers nowadays. A few years ago, pitches were relatively simple, brief, and to the point. The industry has matured; no matter how good the developer, you need a commercial or business manager to help with the pitching process."

Q. What types of materials do you prepare before approaching publishers?

"We prepare many items, from the obvious game design overview and concept materials to a business plan, sales forecasts, and marketing ideas. This can differ from publisher to publisher depending on their individual approach and prior requests."

Q. How many publishers do you approach initially, and what do you look for?

"I think in the current marketplace only a handful of publishers are capable of doing justice to our titles, so we approach only the major players, most of whom are U.S. based. In terms of publishing, we look for security, presence in the marketplace, distribution capability, and how we can fit into their 'machine'."

Q. Do you tailor your pitches to the individual publishers?

"We produce a main core of generic presentation materials that the majority of publishers will see. We have produced publisher-specific content where it is applicable or it has been requested. However, I think it's important to have a well-covered, well-rehearsed pitch in terms of consistent content." →

Q. What do you think is the most important thing a developer can offer a publisher?

"There are a number of things that are vital to a successful pitch, and I would personally think that the ability, organization, resources, and reputation of the developer are first and foremost.

"A prototype that reassures publishers on technical implementation (upon the core platform where possible) is also extremely useful since few, if any, original pitches are made on concept ideas these days. In all cases, developers need to identify areas of publishing risk and allay those fears."

Product Presentation

Before making contact with publishers, you should create a digital presentation using software such as Microsoft PowerPoint. This presentation should be used as the first point of contact for anybody evaluating your game. Its purpose is to educate newcomers to your product in the most concise and attractive way possible, leaving little of your ideas for the game open to interpretation, but without going into design-doc-size detail.

The basic structure of the presentation should be fairly similar to that of your cut-down concept/marketing document, but with bullet point summaries replacing paragraphs of text.

Using no more than a single slide per heading, and following a similar order, key content should include:

Introduction. The first few pages should include an attractive title page and suitable game-related imagery and company logo branding; an introductory paragraph outlining your new concept focusing on the storyline, game genre, target audience, and platforms; the top two or three features that make the game stand out; and a page detailing your perception and research on the market for such a game and why you believe your particular title will be successful. Be wary of making any overly assertive assumptions at this stage.

Sales figures. If your product is part of an illustrious franchise and boasts fantastic sales figures, be sure to insert them early on to get the publisher's attention. If you can break them down per SKU and per territory, all the better.

Game features and USPs. The next several pages should cover all key game features in a purely bullet-pointed fashion, starting with engine and technology details, focusing primarily on the core gameplay and single-player features, and ending with an overview of any multiplayer features, if applicable.

Visuals. At this point in the document, you should break the monotony of pages of text by showing off two to three pages of concept art, game models, screenshots, and videos, depending on what you have available. Line them up neatly as thumbnails within the presentation and link them to full-size versions on the CD so they can be experienced in their full glory.

Press coverage. Developers are increasingly using the specialist press as a tool to help secure deals by releasing details of the game almost from inception. If you have any positive press coverage, it's good to include links and details to help marketing teams gauge potential press and public opinion.

Competitive analysis. The worthiness of a competitive analysis depends largely on how far from completion your product is. If you are at the start of an 18-month development cycle, it is unlikely you will have an accurate picture of the games with which your product will eventually compete. However, at the very least it is worth listing key titles in the same genre, and briefly comparing and contrasting key features and USPs.

Demo. If you are including playable code with the presentation, you should link the appropriate file into the presentation to ensure that the publisher is aware of that fact, and allow them to install the program before continuing with the presentation. If you are not including playable code, you should at least attempt to supply a crisply edited video clip of your game or technology in action to whet the appetite.

Company profile. At the end of the document, you should include a brief company profile, including a list of software and any relevant links, allowing the publisher to find out more about you without having to ask.

Thanks to its digital nature, this simple presentation can be duplicated onto numbered CDs, at which point your art team can create a realistic mockup of a box cover, CD label, and insert that can be printed on photo-quality paper and slipped into blank CD boxes to look like retail product.

You might also see fit to include any other relevant info on the CD, such as design documentation and schedule breakdown, all of which can again be hyper-linked into the main presentation to ensure that they are not overlooked on the disc. Be sure to include any necessary software needed to allow the end user to view the presentation, and a "read me" file containing detailed instructions. Before duplicating a CD, get someone to test it as an end user to ensure that everything is clear and works as it should.

If executed well, you can be sure that such a package will garner attention and interest when it hits the publishers' in-box. It is also a good idea to send several copies to each publisher that you are courting, allowing them to instantly forward copies to other territories, and thus speed up feedback response times.

Choosing a Publisher

Once all of the key components of your pitch are in place, the next step is getting publishers interested. It is a dramatically different story approaching a publisher with a new product as an established developer compared with, say, an untried startup team. However, most publishers will be happy to explore every product they are offered lest they overlook the next *Tetris* or *Tomb Raider*.

Once you get this opportunity, it is up to you to grab their attention and hammer out a deal.

Publisher Pitch Expectations

Although different publishers will place emphasis on different features, the main requirements are universal:

- A marketable concept with even a hint of originality, preferably with at least rudimentary multiplayer elements
- A solvent, trading company, preferably with a relevant track record
- Design documentation
- A team, or at least key team members
- Playable demo
- Schedule and budget estimates

Publishers are becoming increasingly adverse to risk, so your pitch has to convince them that your product merits the time and financial investment that you are seeking as well as allay any fears that the game might not be completed successfully within the specified timescale and budget. You might have the best new game idea on the planet, but if you only have half a team and a wildly ambitious schedule, you cannot hope to find a deal.

Choosing Publishers

Pitching new products can be a long and arduous process, and you can often spend a number of months in negotiations with a publisher only to fall at the final hurdle and find yourself back at square one. As such, it is important to pitch to more than one publisher simultaneously. Of course, the extreme example of this is pitching to every publisher at once. However, this too can be fraught with problems—not to mention incredibly time consuming, tiring, and confusing!

Many developers will already have relationships with one or more publishers, either from current or previous products, and some might even have "first refusal" clauses on new products in their active contracts. However, this is by no means a guarantee of interest, so you should continue to court other publishers as well, providing you are not bound by a nondisclosure agreement (NDA).

The best path when pitching a new product is to put your ear to the ground and find out which publishers are currently on the hunt for new products, and (obviously) who has money to spend. It is also worthwhile to compile a list of publishers who tend to favor your game genre when deciding whom to approach.

Making Contact

Once you have decided which publishers to target, the next step is making contact. Contacts are an invaluable part of game development, and you should seek to build them as quickly as possible. Make a point of visiting industry trade shows and parties, exchange as many business cards as possible, and spend time cataloguing the names and addresses of publishers throughout the territories to save time. This information can often be found in trade magazines such as *Develop* and *Game Developer*, and where there are blanks, feel free to call the publisher directly and establish who their contact is for new product.

Cross-Territory Pitching

When dealing with publishers whose primary operations take place on another continent, you will need to consider whether to pitch in your territory or directly to the heart of the company.

Again, there are no hard-and-fast rules to this—some publishers will specify that you contact their representative in your territory, whereas others will happily work with you directly.

While the obvious downsides are different timelines and the logistics of setting up meetings, the ultimate decision on new products often comes from the publisher's global headquarters. Therefore, by taking the direct approach in many cases you can effectively cut out the "middleman," saving yourself yet more time, effort, and money.

Once you are ready to make contact, open with a polite telephone call to introduce you, your company, and your product, and ascertain whether they are interested in opening dialogue. If the results are positive, you should then arrange delivery of your presentation to allow evaluation by the publisher, and a suitably timed follow-up meeting. If you do not already have them at this stage, try to get hold of all relevant contact details, including e-mail, direct line, and mobile phone numbers. You will see why this is particularly useful later.

Follow each telephone call immediately with an e-mail thanking them for their time and confirming any arrangements discussed. If you have arranged a meeting, make an effort to offer information such as studio location rather than waiting to be asked for the directions, and never double-book appointments. Different publishers will want to spend varying amounts of time with you when visiting your studio, so wherever possible, set aside at least half a day per meeting.

Making a Pitch

When pitch day arrives, again, preparation is the key. If you do not appear confident, organized, and in control of something as simple as a meeting, how can you expect a publisher to trust you with a complex, lengthy development process?

Publishers like to see clean, well-organized offices, but anything overtly flashy will trigger alarm bells about your overheads and how much of your burn rate is actually spent directly on development.

It is fairly common within the industry for staff to work flexible hours, but when you are expecting a publisher visit it is vital that all staff are present, particularly the key staff members who will usually be required to say a few words during the studio walkabout.

Ensure the day prior to the pitch that all documentation is printed and bound, and any demos, presentations, and machinery are updated and running smoothly in the required location.

Meeting rooms should be kept cool, so that your visitors won't feel sleepy. Any unrelated materials and whiteboard markings should be covered or removed from the room.

Just before the representatives are due to arrive, grab a handful of business cards and ensure that all mobile phones are switched off and external calls are diverted.

First Impressions

Remember:

- Make a mental note of representatives' names beforehand and be sure to use them correctly.
- Offer a firm handshake, a smile, lots of eye contact, and a selection of beverages.
- Don't jump straight to business; try to connect on a personal level first.
- Remain confident at all times. Remember, this is your product and it is your job to set the pace.
- Avoid appearing overly somber and business-like, but conversely, don't attempt your latest stand-up routine.
- Avoid making negative comments about past or present projects or partners.

Order of Play

Creative meetings are at their best when organic in nature, but where business is involved, it is important to have at least a basic order of play. Expect the natural progression of such meetings to be as follows:

1. Show and tell. Start with a mutual exchange of company-related information such as studio locations, staffing, head count, current products and performance, and future plans.
2. Presentation. Go through your presentation with the publisher. Now that you have their undivided attention, feel free to expand verbally on each point—within reason! If you have playable code, end the presentation by showing them the game in action and allow them to try it.

3. Studio walkabout. Before discussing the finer points such as deal terms, take a break and show the publisher around the studio, allowing them to gauge how you work. Obviously, for bigger studios it's not feasible to meet every staff member individually, but be sure to stop and talk with key staff, and where possible, show work in progress on both the game you are pitching and any other products in development.
4. Fine print. Upon returning to the meeting room, you should now broach the subjects of schedules, budget, and any important contractual terms. At this stage, most publishers will simply require a cash figure and delivery date, but some might want to go into more detail—so be prepared!
5. Winding up. It is incredibly rare that a publisher will commit, even verbally, to a product at this stage. If you're lucky enough to have in attendance someone with the authority to do so, he or she will usually still need time to discuss matters internally, especially if any new issues arose during the meeting. All you can do now is thank them for their time, ensure that they have all the necessary information, and show them out.

CASE STUDY 4.3.2: ACCLAIM

As the complexity, costs, and gestation periods of new titles increase, publishers demand to see more of games and their developers before signing deals. However, are they asking too much? Jeremy Chubb, Acclaim's product development manager, international, reveals his expectations.

Q. First impressions are important, so how should developers best approach you?

"It really shouldn't make any difference, although arriving on a packed and noisy stand at E3 brandishing design documents and business cards probably isn't the best approach. Most publishers are bombarded by requests for meetings a couple of months before trade shows, and schedules tend to be packed by the time the show starts.

"An e-mail with some basic assets introducing the pitch/studio is an ideal start, and a call to make sure the e-mail got through to the right person is recommended."

Q. What are the different stages of the evaluation process, and what is required of the developer?

"This depends on how far along the project is. Concepts reviewed can range from single-page designs from unknown startups to complete games from the greatest developers in the world, and the process is different for each.

"A general approach for a new developer with an unknown game on new technology might look something like this: →

1. **First contact.** A telephone call or e-mail just to quickly outline the proposed project, exchange contact details, and arrange a follow-up visit. Inquiries should target product development/new business development staff or producers.
2. **Pitch.** A follow-up visit to the publisher to pitch the game comes next. Here, the developer needs to get the game across as imaginatively and efficiently as possible. Aim for a 40-minute presentation.
3. **Evaluation.** The pitch, including available assets, is internally presented to a brand/marketing group for initial feedback. Issues relating to market potential, projected marketing costs, brand opportunities, licensing, and competitive analysis are investigated.
4. **Studio visit.** Based on initial interest, producers will visit the studio to assess the developer's technology and management of the project.
5. **Feedback.** Feedback from acquisition, producer, and brand manager are presented to senior executives.
6. **Final pitch.** Presentation of the game to senior executives. This is the final pitch to the top brass. Make or break on the project.

"It's very rare for this to actually be the case, though. An experienced developer with a recent hit and a great concept can expect to walk straight into a senior executive meeting. Similarly, a near-final game can be appraised very quickly. Many games are developed based on an existing relationship with a studio and publisher. Z-Axis' Aggressive Inline was signed based on the studio's success with Dave Mirra BMX 2, and Criterion signed Burnout 2: Point of Impact based on the huge success of their excellent first game."

Q. Do you have a preference for people using their own tech or using middleware solutions?

"There's no real preference. *Burnout 2* and *GTA3* are great examples of middleware generating great sales.

"The benefit of using middleware is that it allows developers to get playable demos up and running quickly and cheaply, particularly on new hardware. Publishers warm to proof of concept like nothing else, and particularly for smaller developers, this can be the best approach."

Q. What would be your definition of the perfect pitch?

"I recently saw the perfect pitch. The developer had worked hard to create assets for everyone concerned and had taken advantage of early feedback on the design, cost, and timelines. The result was a final meeting to pitch to senior executives at the publisher. They arrived an hour before the meeting to set up the room and ensure that all the equipment worked on cue. It was a 45-minute pitch detailing the following:

For senior executives, a PowerPoint presentation of the concept and overview document containing: $\rightarrow$

- Company background and team experience, including brief demos of previous, relevant games
- Concept competitive analysis
- USPs
- Key gameplay elements
- Example level walkthroughs
- Basic scheduling and cost breakdown
- Concept art and renders
- MPEG video combining in-game and FMV (full motion video) footage to illustrate the overall feel of the concept
- Two-level playable demo illustrating key elements in action
- Mockup screenshots estimating the final quality of the game graphics

For producers:

- Complete design documentation
- Detailed scheduling and milestone information
- Exact cost breakdown

Q. What are the most common mistakes developers make when pitching?

"Too many developers pitch an approximation of a concept, rather than a clearly defined game. Knowing that the publisher will want creative input, developers are often overly cautious in developing their ideas.

"It's no use answering questions like 'how much will it cost?' with 'how much do you want to spend?' or 'what's the play-through time?' with 'as long as you want.'

"Publishers are most attracted to groups with a clear vision and total understanding of cost and schedule details."

Q. What is the single most important thing a developer can bring to the table?

"Experience. There's no substitute for a proven track record in the chosen genre."

The Waiting Game

It is notoriously difficult to gauge how successful a pitch has been. Some publisher representatives will talk candidly and excitedly about your product, often expressing how delighted they would be to sign it. However, this generally indicates that they aren't personally in a position to do so, and therefore their excitement should not be misconstrued as acceptance.

Equally, other publishers might leave stony faced having hardly said a word, but this too should not be misconstrued as rejection. It can take time—sometimes months—for publishers to make a decision on a product. Many people in numerous territories are involved in the process, so don't expect an immediate answer.

You should follow up your meeting with a courteous e-mail thanking the representatives for visiting and that you look forward to their feedback. Do not worry if you don't get a response; like developers, publishers are extremely busy people, and in the same way developers hate to be hassled by vendors, publishers don't take kindly to persistent pressure.

If you have pitched to multiple publishers simultaneously, the wait for responses won't be quite as intense, and if you start getting further interest you can use this as gentle leverage with the remaining publishers.

Unfortunately, some publishers are known for simply not responding, and in this case, remember that a telephone call is far harder to ignore than an e-mail. Here lies the importance of noting your correspondent's direct line or mobile number during the contact phase.

Conclusion

As you can see, pitching has become a long, drawn out, and complex process and should never be taken lightly. Rather than being part of the overall development process, think of it as a development process in its own right.

Planning is absolutely essential, especially because development at this stage comes straight off your top line, so any time and effort wasted merely increases your overhead and adds to the already prevalent risks.

While following these guidelines gives no guarantee of success, at the very least it will help you to maximize the effectiveness of your pitching process and minimize the time wasted both internally and when awaiting feedback… And as we all know, when it comes to game development, time really is money.

4.4

Introduction to Contract Negotiation

Jay Powell

jep@octagon1.com

Contract negotiation is never fun, and as a general rule, the bigger the publisher, the longer the process will take. This article outlines the major components of any contract between a publisher and a developer, and discusses how to structure a deal that will be beneficial to all parties.

Preparing for Negotiation

There are two key questions that you must answer prior to any negotiation:

- What does my team need in a contract?
- What is our negotiation position?

Knowing what the team needs from the beginning will help you establish a negotiation position. Look at several factors before you start talking about a contract:

- What is the lowest budget on which we can finish this game?
- What intellectual property rights need to be retained? Characters, worlds, technology, etc.?
- What royalty rate is expected?
- How much development time do we still need to finish the project?

These are a few examples, but a developer who does not need very much money to complete the game is in a much better position than one who will have to rely on deep commitments and investments from a publisher. By knowing what portions of a contract you can give way on, you stand a much better chance of winning the points in which you are really interested. Contracts for developers who only want to get their finished game in the market with a launch and great marketing will have little in common with contracts in which a developer is seeking a publisher to fund a multimillion-dollar budget.

Obviously, teams with a stronger starting position can look forward to better contracts. It is easier to get the terms the developer is seeking if the developer has already demonstrated an ability to do what they promise. By knowing the needs of the team in advance, a contract can be tweaked and polished to benefit the developer and publisher and then lay the groundwork for a satisfying relationship. For example, some developers find that it is worth the lost advance to take a higher royalty rate and guarantee more marketing dollars for the game. This is the kind of decision that should be made early in the process.

Advances

One of the first questions a publisher will ask is, "What is the price?" The answer to this question will depend on the type of deal for which you are aiming.

With a development project, the response is quite simple: the price is the budget you have calculated. Be certain that your budget is realistic. When publishers are asked to invest a large amount of cash into a project, they will be very careful in evaluating budgets. Developers should be aware of the typical price for a game in the genre and platform they are targeting, and be prepared to provide interested publishers with a list of the people on the team, their experience, and their role in the project. This will help substantiate the budget being presented.

Also consider the relationship between advances and royalties. Typically, the higher the advance, the lower the royalty. Publishers want to make sure the game will be profitable for them. The actual budget for a publisher can be twice as high as the developer's advances when marketing, shelf space, manufacturing, technology support, and other factors are calculated in.

Net Receipts

If you are seeking a distribution deal for the game, or licensing a product that is near completion, more research could be needed. Know from the beginning how much revenue you need to recoup on the project, find out how similar titles have sold in the territory you are discussing the contract for, and base your initial proposals on these numbers.

A licensing deal for a full-price product should usually come to $4 to $6 per copy sold. If the publisher wishes to base royalties on a percentage of *net receipts*, aim for 25% or higher, and pay careful attention to the definition of net receipts in the contract or letter of intent. The more a publisher is allowed to subtract from gross sales numbers, the lower the royalty will be, regardless of percentage. Net receipts should usually be defined as the amount billed by the publisher for the sale, lease, or license of each product, minus a deduction for credits or returns that should not exceed 15%. Do not allow publishers to deduct expenses like manufacturing, insurance, shipping, withheld taxes, and marketing from the net receipts. There may be resistance to the marketing and manufacturing deductions; if so, at least put a cap on the recoupable part of this budget.

Helping Publishers Helps Developers

Publishers will use a Profit and Loss sheet (P&L) to decide if a project is feasible from a financial perspective. If you are seeing real interest in the project from the publisher but the budget seems to be out of reach, ask the publisher how you can make the deal work. It is always better to take a little less money up front and work with a publisher who is enthusiastic about the team and believes in the project than it is to take more money and risk being just another title in a catalog.

Many variations of the payment schedule can be implemented to help a publisher. Developers who are financially stable can spread the payments over a longer period of time, although all advances should be paid no later than 60 days after the game ships to retailers. It is also possible to lower the advance in exchange for a higher portion of the royalties. This shows the publisher that a team has complete confidence in their product and that they are willing to prove it in the contract.

Be honest and open with the publisher. They should understand the needs of their partner and work to make a contract that makes everyone happy. Large egos or unrealistic expectations can be a severe hindrance in negotiations.

For a straight distribution deal, the payment schedule is well defined. There are still milestones to be met, but they are consistent across all distribution or licensing deals. When a developer has nearly completed a game and does not need funding each month, they should expect to negotiate payment based on the following list of milestones:

- Signature of letter of intent
- Signature of contract
- Receipt of gold master by the publisher
- Receipt of localization kit by the publisher
- Receipt of localized gold master by the publisher
- Release of the product
- 30 days following the release of the product
- 60 days following the release of the product

Royalty Rates

The royalty rate is the second half of the monetary equation. As mentioned earlier, advances and royalties are directly related and should be negotiated at the same time.

There are many factors involved in the calculation of the royalty rate, but as a general rule, it should never fall below 15% for a PC title. The higher the better, of course, but most developers will find that they will ultimately see around 25%. Console titles can be a little more difficult, as the console manufacturers take their share as well. With most consoles, developers will see a royalty of between $2.00 at a $19.99 price point and $10.00 to $12.00 for a full-price release. Some of these rates may seem low, but the sales volume of console games versus PC games will certainly make up the difference.

Be very careful when negotiating console contracts. Find out whether the publisher is factoring the console manufacturer's royalty into the net receipts. If the manufacturer's cost is deducted prior to the division of royalties, a much higher rate should be sought.

Sublicensing

If the publisher does not have direct distribution in some territories, negotiate a separate royalty rate for these deals. Otherwise, you may have to make do with a small percentage of a small percentage.

If the publisher plans to sublicense the game, aim for a royalty of 50% of their net receipts from these territories. Be especially aware of companies that promise "developer friendly" royalties in the 35% to 50% range. If contract terms look too good to be true, they probably are.

Ask how the distribution is handled, and contact other developers who have worked with the publisher. This question is important in any case, but especially important here. Most publishers will not give a hard number when it comes to the amount paid out to other developers, but most of the time a friendly call to the developer will yield that information and an accurate account of how the relationship with the publisher is working. If the situation is still unclear, negotiate a set dollar amount per copy for the royalty instead of a percentage. Protect yourself against the possibility that the publisher might not find a sublicensing partner in a particular territory. Insert a clause that states that, if the game is not released within a specific period of time after the first market release, all rights for the unreleased territories revert to you.

Other Options with Royalties

When a flat royalty rate is negotiated, be sensitive to the realities of the retail market. If the retailers demand a price drop, the publisher may not be able to afford to continue to pay the same royalty, and the title will be completely removed from the shelves. Always be prepared to renegotiate the rates in these situations.

You may want to look at the option of escalating royalties as well. In the initial discussions with publishers, find out how many copies the publisher must sell to break even on the title and reach an acceptable profit. (Merely making a profit will not usually sell a publisher on a game: as with any business, companies need to show a certain percentage profit to "green light" a project.) Then, discuss the option of having the royalty increase when the project breaks even, and again at certain sales milestones or when the publisher achieves the profit they anticipated. This rewards both companies for a job well done. Some of the greatest games made will not sell well if the publisher does not market and sell the title properly. Great success should be viewed as an achievement by both companies, not just one.

A frequently overlooked portion of the contract that will affect the royalty rate is the number of copies that a publisher gives to the media and retailers as samples. These promotional copies will generally hurt the publisher more than the developer, as they are manufacturing copies of the game on which they receive no revenue. While getting the word out about a game is useful, free copies should be limited to around 100. As with many other aspects of the process, you should discuss this with the publisher and see how many free copies they typically send out.

Localization

All developers should begin planning for the localization of their game very early in development. By the time a game is ready to be shown to publishers, it is usually too late to change the underlying code. Games should be prepared for double-byte characters from the very beginning of development. Care and attention should also be given to languages such as German, which requires more characters per word than others. Failure to support languages such as these will certainly result in lost revenue: Germany is the second largest Western World market (behind the United States) for videogames, and Asia is fast becoming a major market for PC games as well as console titles. Korea, in particular, has excellent support from its government for the gaming industry; the country is home to scores of publishers and literally thousands of developers.

Localizing Content

Aside from simple language issues, actual content must be carefully examined as well. Many countries are becoming more vigilant against violent videogames. Korea, China, and Germany already have strict laws regarding videogame content; these laws focus on violence and little else. Videogames in Germany cannot show violence toward people at all: for example, enemies in shooters must be robots or aliens, and they cannot shed red blood when shot. Germany also has very strict laws regarding the portrayal of the Third Reich or Nazi propaganda in any way. Conversely, the U.S. market is more concerned about sexual content than violence, and censorship happens at the retail level as opposed to government committees.

Localization Responsibilities

When developers approach publishers with games, the cost and job of localization need to be carefully examined. The contract should state that the publisher will pay for and provide localization for the game, and that the developer will be responsible for the integration of the localized content into the game. In practice, the developer will send all text and art that needs to be localized to the publisher. The publisher will then translate these files and return them to the developer, who will create a localized master of the game for each language. Occasionally, publishers will want to do all the work themselves; only agree to this if you have an excellent relationship with the publisher, because it usually involves giving them access to the game's source code.

Marketing

Marketing can make or break a game. Some of the best games in recent memory did not sell well, due to insufficient or bad marketing. Do not overlook this part of the contract.

Research the publisher's past marketing campaigns and request a marketing proposal prior to signing the contract for the game. This marketing proposal should outline what the publisher plans to do for online, print, and possible television marketing, along with the budget allocated to these plans. You need to know the publisher's strategy to secure prime shelf space and end caps (the spaces on the end of shelves that are shown in the aisles of a store), and how the game will be sold to the retailers.

Marketing costs for a game today can range from $150,000 to well into the millions for some AAA titles. Obviously, the more a publisher will commit to the marketing effort, the better, but this amount will buy a title a good campaign. Pay close attention to how the money in the budget is allotted; a good box design by itself can cost $10,000, so make sure the money is well spent. Finally, do not allow this money to be recoupable against your advances: this is the publisher's cost of doing business, not yours.

Name Recognition

Developers should always make sure that a clause in the contract states that the logo for their company must be displayed any time the publisher's logo is shown, and that it should be the same size. Consumers are more likely to build brand loyalty to a developer than they are to a publisher. Even when a major publisher franchise is handed to a different developer, there can be uncertainty in the minds of the consumers. By guaranteeing that your logo is shown with the publisher's, you can invest in your future in two ways:

Consumer recognition. Even if a different publisher handles your next game, the public will remember the quality of your previous titles and be interested in this one.

Publisher recognition. Other publishers will take note of the great job you did on a particular game and pay close attention to you down the road.

Both of these points of recognition could result in opening doors that were closed earlier, or in contracts from publishers to work on licenses they have secured. Finally, once a developer is known to have shipped a best-selling game, their negotiating position is much better for the next contract.

Supporting the Publisher

Finally, developers need to remember that to ensure excellent marketing, they must support the publisher. The publisher is going to need artwork, demos, selling points, and time from the developer to create the appropriate buzz for a game.

Most publishers will want to start marketing a game no less than three months from launch. If a publisher wants to rush a title to market sooner than three months from signature, the developer should closely evaluate the situation and make sure they are making the right decision. In this pre-launch period, the publisher may bring the press to the studio; the team should make sure that the producer knows the game inside and out, because he or she will be handling the majority of the press inquiries and needs to know exactly how to sell the game. It is also a good idea to have the art assets ready for marketing and packaging, and to prepare a list of frequently asked questions and answers to help the publisher with typical queries.

This work will help the publisher properly support the game. Without serious support, the game will fail at retail, regardless of its quality. Know from the beginning of the negotiations how the publisher plans to support the game, and provide any help that is necessary to assist the publisher with this support.

Intellectual Property and Technology Rights

Negotiating who retains the rights to what assets can be one of the trickiest parts of the entire process. The publisher will want to retain all rights from the beginning, but you should be very careful with what you give away.

The *intellectual property* (IP) rights to the game will most likely end up in the hands of the publisher. Contracts that prevent this are possible, but not very common. In this context, IP includes the names of the game and its characters, the story, trademarks and logos, artwork, and music.

You may want to push harder to retain IP rights if the game is a role-playing game (RPG) or involves a world into which the designers have put a lot of effort. However, if you cannot retain the rights, you should at least be compensated for them, and a clause should be placed in the contract stating that you have first rights to develop any sequels or spin-offs—and a last match option, meaning that if you are willing to perform the work under the conditions that the publisher is about to sign with another team, the assignment is yours. This may be the best possible situation: a publisher will have more incentive to promote a license they own, but you should simply make sure your team continues to develop the property.

As with the marketing and sales of the game, if the publisher is not using the rights, they should revert back to you.

Technology Rights

Technology rights are a different issue. The developer should always retain these rights, especially if the engine was created in-house, because licensing the engine underlying a successful game can provide a significant stream of income. With this in mind, document the engine from the beginning of development, and make sure all tools associated with the engine are easy to comprehend.

Developers will not want to devote a lot of resources to engine support unless a serious amount of revenue is being generated through technology licensing. Good game engines can sell for $250,000 to $500,000, plus a 2% to 5% royalty on net income. With this added revenue, developers can easily begin additional projects and support a small staff to help other developers with questions. Tools will also be necessary if an editor is shipped with the game; an avid community of players developing new content ("mods") for a game can greatly increase its shelf life, but if the consumers do not comprehend the editing tools, it will be no benefit at all.

Note that the publisher may wish to impose an exclusivity clause on the games developed with your new engine. If the technology is groundbreaking, the publisher will not want a competing title to be released that may damage sales. This is a common request, but developers should make sure that the term of exclusivity is realistic; it should not exceed six months from the launch of the game.

Term

The final major component of a contract is the term and the rules governing its extension. Some games can have a very long shelf life, and publishers will plan for this entire life when they are working with their P&L statement. A game that releases at a $49 price may see sales at $39, $29, $19, and $9 before it is officially pulled from the shelves. Even at this point, the game could be bundled with similar titles for additional revenue.

To give the publisher the time they need to run a game through its complete life cycle, a term of five years is standard. If the game is still selling at this point, contract extensions should be added, at one-year increments.

By cutting the term of the contract short, a developer runs the risk of losing sales that a good publisher can extract from games that are four or five years old. However, as with many other points in the contract, if sales are nonexistent for a period of time, usually three months, the rights should revert back to the developer. It may be possible to find a partner who can revive the sales using tactics or connections that the primary publisher did not have.

Points to Avoid

The following are points to be aware of and to avoid when negotiating a contract.

Cross-Collateralization

Developers should always be extremely cautious of this term. There are situations when cross-collateralization can be beneficial, but for the most part, it should be avoided.

Cross-collateralization will only fall into a contract when more than one title (or more than one version of the same game for more than one platform) is being sold. If a contract includes the cross-collateralization of two different games, the publisher will not be responsible for paying royalties until the guaranteed number of units is sold through a combination of the sales for both titles. For example, if a publisher guarantees 500,000 units of two games, they would need to sell 400,000 of one and 100,000 of another in order to meet their commitment. This is a poor situation for the developer because they would already be seeing royalty checks for one game if the contract were negotiated in a different manner.

For contracts containing two different games, each game should have its own guarantee for units. This prevents a publisher from holding royalties on a strong-selling game to make up for a lack of sales on the other. If the example used here were negotiated to say that there was a 250,000-unit guarantee for each game, the developer would have already seen a significant amount of royalties for the title that sold 400,000 units.

Cross-collateralization can be useful when a title is released on several platforms. Developers should still be very cautious, but having one platform cover for the lack of sales on another is not nearly as bad as the two-game situation. For one thing, it may be the best way to obtain funding for development on a new platform, and the expertise gained can be worth the financial risk. Agree to cross-collateralization in this case as a last resort, but do not avoid it as earnestly as with two separate games.

Management Fees

On rare occasions, publishers try to insert the deduction of management fees, trade shows, travel expenses, and such items into the contract, usually under the definition of "net receipts." Under no circumstances should you agree to these terms. Publishers should always be responsible for these costs, and unless they are going far out of their way for a game, there is no reason for the developer to pay for them. The publisher has complete control over these expenses, after all.

Canceling without Warning

Make sure that a clause is inserted to protect you in the event the publisher decides to cancel a project with no warning. This happens quite frequently in the industry, most often when the publisher is purchased and the new owner has a competing project or no interest in the game.

A protection clause should state that in the event of cancellation, the publisher must pay the current and next milestones of the contract to the developer. This gives the development team sufficient time to find a new partner and does not leave them in a situation where they are instantly out of cash.

Protecting Your Team

There have been cases of publishers recognizing great talent in a team and hiring those members away for their own internal teams. All contracts should state that the publisher will not hire any member of the development team from the company during the process and for a set period after release. This clause is even easier to insert in a contract if the publisher wants to define the team members for a project in writing.

Besides, any publisher who would poach staff is one you would not want to work with in the future. This clause is also a good test of the potential partner's good faith.

No Defined Time Restraints

Finally, make certain that each milestone's acceptance and payment is tied to clearly defined time periods in the contract. For example:

- "Payment is due within five days of milestone acceptance."
- "Publisher has five business days to review the milestone or the milestone is considered accepted."

For all deliverables, define a due date, a time table for review and response, and a set amount of time for corrections. Including these definitions in the contract ensures that payments are made swiftly and that nothing is lost in the shuffle.

Conclusion

There are countless numbers of points a company can negotiate in a contract. The ones selected here are the key points that a developer would be certain to focus on.

The most important thing to remember is to know what the company or team needs. Then, remember that the company you are negotiating with will be your partner for some time to come. It does no one any good to start a long relationship on bad terms because of an acrimonious negotiation.

4.5

Effective Development Contracts

Thomas H. Buscaglia, Esquire

thb@gameattorney.com

The development contract is a written agreement between a developer and a publisher that establishes the rights, duties, and obligations of the publisher and developer to each other. Development contracts cover the various issues involved in the developer/publisher relationship, including the funding, production, marketing, distribution, ownership, and ongoing obligations of the parties. This article looks at the many clauses of the usual development agreement and examines in detail some of the more important provisions in these contracts. We conclude by discussing strategies that might help a developer get the most they can out of a contract, based on their relative bargaining power.

How It Works

Publishers, those in the business of selling games, have no interest in ideas. They want teams that have what it takes to turn those ideas into reality. Once a publisher has sufficient confidence in the developer's ability to deliver a profitable game, the publisher will fund the development process and share the fruits of the commercial release, after their investment is recovered in accordance with the contract.

The method used to accomplish this is a combination of advances and royalties. The development budget and royalty rate are essential parts of every developer contract.

Payment Schedule

The total advances under the contract are divided into a series of payments. The publisher advances money to the developer throughout the development period based on a series of production milestones. This system of milestones is established to allow a publisher to protect their interest by requiring the developer to deliver ongoing builds of the game for evaluation and approval during the course of development, while the advance payments allow the developer to work in relative financial security. The failure of a developer to satisfactorily meet their milestones can result in a termination of the contract and the end of any further payments by the publisher to the developer.

Royalties

Royalty rates are calculated from the net proceeds of game sales, after the publisher's costs related to the production, manufacture, and distribution of the game have been deducted. The developer's portion of royalties is first applied to "recoup" the advances the publisher made to the developer. After all advances have been repaid from the developer portion of the net receipts as defined in the contract, royalties begin to flow through to the developer.

How It Starts

To convince a publisher to fund a project, a developer must prove not only that the game has commercial merit, but also that the developer has what it takes to deliver the game on time and in acceptable form. The developer prepares a comprehensive demo of the game that adequately displays the environments, characters, technology of the game, and game playability. In addition to the demo, a project document or "game bible" that sets out in detail all the elements of the game is presented. These elements include the backstory, characters, level shots, graphics and design elements, and any other content necessary to the game, especially those that are in addition to the ones included in the demo.

The Letter of Intent

Once the publisher (or publishers) decides to try to sign your game, the negotiation of the basic terms begins. If negotiations are successful, they might result in the execution of a letter of intent. This is a temporary agreement outlining only the most basic terms (e.g., advance, royalty structure, and delivery date) and stating that the parties intend to negotiate a full-length contract in good faith.

At this point, the publisher will probably prepare and deliver their "standard" developer agreement. Don't let the term "standard" fool you. Many fill-in-the-blanks contract terms are negotiable, depending on the relative bargaining power of the parties. While you might be inclined to just sign the contract and get on with what you love to do, which is make your game, some patience and tenacity can have a substantial positive impact on the final terms of the agreement.

The Importance of the Contract

Game development contracts range in length from 8 to 30 pages. These are important documents and should not be treated lightly. Ultimately, the quality of your developer contract is essential to the success of the project and the long-term viability of your entire career as a developer. Therefore, the negotiation of the contract's terms should be treated with the same care you treat your code or artwork. Even if your team has an agent who has been assisting you in negotiating the terms of the contract, entering into an agreement like this without having a qualified attorney review and assist in the negotiation of the details can result in serious problems later.

As we discuss in detail later in this article, development agreements cover a broad range of issues. In addition to the milestones and payments, the development agreement describes the submission and approval process in detail, and, more important, specifies any transfer of ownership of the elements that comprise the game. For example, publishers require most new developers to relinquish all of the intellectual property (IP) in the game to the publisher. In this context, "intellectual property" usually includes the game code, game name, concept, images, characters, backgrounds, textures, and all other marketable assets that go into the game. It might also include any tools created by the developer in the process of making the game. When and how this property transfer occurs should be well delineated and set out in detail in the contract.

Of course, in some cases much of the intellectual property used in the game might already be owned by the publisher or licensed to the publisher by a third party. For example, games derived from movies, expansion packs, or second or third releases of games already published might already be owned or licensed by the publisher. In these cases, the development agreement will instead delineate the scope of the developer's right to exploit the property. In addition, if any third-party software such as game engines, software development kits, or middleware is involved in the development of the game, the contract terms will spell out who is responsible for acquiring the rights to this software, as well as who retains the right to use them during the development period and upon completion of the game.

Finally, just like any other business contract, development contracts contain numerous general provisions that lay out in detail what will occur if any specific contingency occurs. These contract provisions deal with more mundane issues such as who is responsible for quality assurance and testing, localization of the game, publicity and marketing, rights to proceeds from ancillary products such as dolls and lunch boxes, areas of distribution, insurance requirements, confidentiality and nondisclosure agreements, nonsolicitation agreements, notices, assignments, waivers, and even what will occur if one of the parties files for bankruptcy or is forced into bankruptcy. In addition, of course, the contract will specify where and how any disputes that might arise will be resolved.

The Standard Sections

Let's look at the sections usually included in development agreements.

Preamble or Recitals

The preamble is where the identity of the publisher and the developer as well as the effective date of the agreement are set out.

Definitions

The first formal section of the contract is usually the "Definitions" section. This section identifies the specific way in which certain terms are used throughout the remaining text of the contract. These terms are then capitalized throughout the contract so that the readers can identify them as being specifically defined terms.

Term

The term of the agreement sets the length of time during which the development agreement is effective. It might also include other specific responsibilities concerning events that occur within that time period.

Territory

This section identifies the different countries or geographic areas covered by the sale and distribution obligations of the publisher under the agreement. It is not uncommon to have agreements with several companies in different territories to facilitate worldwide distribution of a game.

Ownership and Licenses

This important part of the agreement will establish ownership of the game content and of related intellectual properties. In addition to actual game content, this section will typically resolve ownership of any trademarks associated with the game, such as the game's name, logo, character names, fictional locations, or any other unique matters essential to the game.

The Obligations of the Parties

Usually, the developer's obligations are set out in one section and the publisher's obligation set out in another. However, these obligations might be included in a single section of the contract. Either way, this section of the contract sets out in detail the responsibilities of developer and publisher to each other. The developer's duties under the agreement generally include specific details regarding the dates and content of each milestone. The duties of the publisher concern advance payments, royalty payments, testing, promotion, and distribution and sale of the game; in some cases, the contract will even specify the promotion and advertising budget that the publisher will spend on the game's marketing.

Finally, provisions concerning any rights regarding sequels and ancillary products might also be set out in this section.

Notices and Credits

Everyone involved in the game wants to be recognized. This section sets out in detail exactly how the identity of the developer and publisher, as well as distributors or licensees, will be displayed in the game and on game advertisements and packaging.

Warranties

Warranties are the legal guarantees and assurances that each party sets out in the contract. These include the absolute rights that each party has in whatever they are contributing to the project. For example, the developer must warrant that it owns or has an appropriate license to use all of the content in the game that is being delivered to the publisher. Similarly, the publisher must warrant that it has all rights to any materials or content that it is providing for inclusion in the game or the game packaging.

Indemnification

Indemnification is the obligation of one party to a contract to cover the losses of another party incurred as a result of any acts or omission by the first party. For example, if the developer did not actually secure ownership of all of the intellectual property contained in a game, then the developer would be responsible for any losses incurred by the publisher as a result of that failure in ownership. Similarly, if the publisher did not own a trademark that was to be associated with the game and it resulted in a loss or a lawsuit, the publisher would be required to defend a lawsuit and cover any losses incurred by the developer.

Confidentiality

Confidentiality provisions assure that the confidential information conveyed between the parties, as well as the terms of the agreement itself, are keep confidential both throughout the term of the agreement and for a reasonable period thereafter.

Nonsolicitation

Many development contracts prohibit either party from soliciting employees from the other. This prevents a publisher from "poaching" talented employees from the developer either during the course of development or after the completion of the game. Such provisions can be very important for developers wanting to maintain development team integrity.

Termination

This important section identifies and details the situations in which one party can terminate the contract, and the procedures to follow to do so. Termination clauses typically include failure of either party to meet their specific obligations under the agreement, matters beyond their control (acts of God and war), and even financial matters such as the bankruptcy of one or the other parties. Many of these provisions contain a time limit within which the breaching party can cure the breach without the contact being terminated.

General Provisions

General provisions, often referred to by lawyers as the "boiler plate," are the general terms of the contract regarding everything from the assignment rights, notice of the parties to each other, effect of the headings, execution of the contract in counterparts, remedies, and provisions regarding arbitration, attorney fees, and what state's or country's law applies to the enforcement of the obligations under the agreement.

Contract Addenda and Attachments

In addition to the main portion of the contract, for ease of drafting, attachments to the contracts set out the specific terms unique to the deal. Some examples of matters often detailed in these addenda include:

> **Specifications:** Setting forth the game title and general specifications.
> **Milestones and payments:** Identifying in reasonable detail the time (either a date or number of weeks from execution) for each milestone delivery and payment, what deliverables are included in each milestone, and how much money will be paid upon delivery and acceptance of each milestone.
> **Additional deliverables:** Things such as screen shots, promotional demos, downloadable demos, and other promotional materials.
> **Additional agreements:** Any secondary contracts regarding conveyance of intellectual property rights, and specific confidentiality agreements to be signed by all of the members of the team.
> **Localization:** What specific languages the game will be delivered in and who is responsible for the localization.
> **Personnel:** Identifying by name and address all essential team members involved in the development.
> **A signature page:** The names and titles of the people who are entitled to sign the contract, along with the date of the contract's execution.

Contract Form and Tone

All contracts are different, but most contain the various sections listed in the preceding section. The details will vary from publisher to publisher. Some developer contracts have a lot of technical legal language. Others are worded in "plain language." Each type has its advantages and disadvantages. Formally written contracts are, at least in principle, more exacting, and therefore better delineate the duties and responsibilities of the parties. However, they are often difficult for anyone other than lawyers to understand. Conversely, reader-friendly "plain language" contracts might be easier to understand for a nonlawyer, but harder for a court to enforce due to loose construction. Ultimately, it is the publisher who starts the contract negotiation, so it will be the publisher who decides the basic tone and format of the agreement.

Effective Contracts

Now that we have covered the basic business relationship and different elements that go into a development contract, let's get down to what a developer can do to ensure the success of their development agreement. Of course, the quality of the deal that the developer is able to negotiate is directly proportional to the publisher's desire to obtain the game and the publisher's relative comfort level in the economic success of the game on release. Therefore, if you are id Software or Lionhead Studios, you will probably be able to negotiate extremely favorable terms, retain all IP rights, and get a huge royalty percentage. Similarly, if the development team has a desirable product and a highly qualified team, favorable terms can be reached. However, if you are trying to negotiate a development contract for a game that the publisher perceives as being high risk, your ability to obtain favorable terms is not good. Let's look at some specific goals to strive for in your developer contract.

Setting the Net

Ultimately, it all comes down to royalties, and royalties come down to royalty rates. Royalty rates can range from below 15% to above 40%, depending on the development team, the publisher, and the game product. However, other issues come into play besides percentages.

Royalties are defined as a share of the "net" profit to the publisher. The contract should set out in detail exactly how this "net" is calculated. These provisions are often complicated, and a close examination is important to make sure that the publisher is not deducting expenses that it should be absorbing into its own cost of doing business. In the end, the definition of the net profit can be even more important that the percentage.

Indeed, the "net" should be the net profit derived from sales of your game after the publisher has deducted costs related to the development of the game. Therefore, deducting costs such as software development kits, licenses, manufacturing costs, discounts, freebies, returns, and distribution expenses is appropriate. However, these deductions should be limited to variable costs directly related to your game. The publisher's costs for advertising and promotion, marketing, inventory storage, internal operations, or what is being spent to promote the publisher itself should not be included.

Royalty Run Up

Escalating royalties are an excellent method to capitalize if your game really hits it big. The nicest thing about escalating royalties is that they only apply once the game's sales have reached a point where the revenue stream is pure profit for everyone. Once the publisher has recovered all of his costs, including those that are not included in the deductions that establish the net, the game becomes extremely profitable for the publisher. And increasing the developer's share of the additional profit is both reasonable and appropriate.

Here is what it looks like. Let's say that the initial royalty rate is 20%. After the initial 150,000 units are sold, that rate increases to 25%. Then, if the sales go up another 150,000 units, the percentage goes to 30%, and so on up to a maximum rate of 50% for sales over 1,050,000—a total that is both phenomenally high and very unlikely. Rarely, some contracts even call for this higher royalty rate to be applied to all sales retroactively, and not just to those above the threshold.

The main point of escalating royalties is that these higher sale numbers signify an exceptional product and a much higher return for the publisher. Therefore, publishers are more likely to share a larger proportion of the sales at that point.

Avoid the Slide

Even the greatest games end up in the discount bin eventually. Publishers sometimes seek to have the developer's royalty percentage decrease as the price of the game goes down.

Avoid this at all costs. Keep in mind that your game has already been paid for and that most if not all of the marketing has already occurred. Consequently, there is no rational basis for the publisher not to share the net profits here at the same percentage as they did at the beginning of the project. After all, they are "net" profits. In fact, there are some good arguments to be made for increasing the developer's royalty percentage on the discounted games, since by then the publisher's costs associated with the game might have already been fully recovered.

Lunch Box Bonus

Ancillary products and product placements can create substantial profits for everyone—and at no additional cost. A savvy developer should demand a higher royalty for these secondary revenues, hopefully at least twice the base royalty rate set for the game itself.

If possible, you should also include a time limit on the exploitation of ancillary products derived from your game. This way, if the publisher does not pursue these ancillary revenue sources within the set period of time, you will be able to do so yourself.

When Things Go South

The termination provisions are, not surprisingly, contract terms that should be examined very carefully. As with all of the important provisions of the contract, make sure that they are mutual, within the boundaries of reason. While your company might be much smaller than the publisher, there is no reason to assume that they are less likely to run into problems. Publishers go bankrupt or sell off their assets all the time.

Try to include provisions in the development agreement that call for the reversion of all of the game's assets and obligations to the developer if the publisher goes into bankruptcy or receivership. Even in contracts where the agreement calls for a conveyance of all your intellectual property rights in the game to the publisher, postpone the transfer of ownership of the game's assets until the final payment. This will help avoid your game being pulled into the publisher's bankruptcy estate, which would make the ultimate completion and distribution of the game beyond your control.

Get It Back

Make sure that if the publisher drops your game or decides not to market it within a reasonable period of time, all rights revert back to you so you can try publishing your game with another company.

Space It Out

Contract provisions regarding material breaches often allow for a period to cure such breaches. Make sure that this period is as long as possible; if the publisher offers 10 days, ask for 30 or even 60. That way, if you receive notice of a breach, you might have that extra week, or month, you need to save your project.

Stay Loose

Flexibility in milestones is also something that can help when a project starts to get away from you. An overly rigid definition of milestones creates a contract that might not remain viable throughout the project. We often hear publishers complaining about slippage in milestone dates. While slippage in milestone dates hurts the publisher, it hurts the developer even more. As delivery dates slip, the period of time it takes to develop a game lengthens. As a result, fixed costs such as payroll, rent, and so forth continue to accumulate for the developer. Therefore, the extended time between milestone payments can make payroll, rent, and other financial responsibilities of the developer difficult if not impossible to meet.

One good way to insert flexibility in a contract is to have the development schedule and milestone definitions subject to revision at the delivery of each milestone. This can really help when new technologies, market changes, and other unexpected issues come up. Keep in mind that it is in everyone's best interest to have the game delivered in a timely manner and in acceptable form. Therefore, this sort of flexibility is good for both the developer and the publisher.

Keep It Simple

Multiplatform deals are becoming increasingly common. However, as far as contracts go, the more components in the contract, the likelier it is that something will go wrong.

For example, a PC/Xbox deal might look very appealing. However, if 75% to 80% of the work is related to the PC game development, but over 50% of the revenue is tied to the Xbox version, a simple thing like Microsoft either lagging or denying approval of the game could spell disaster for the developer in mid-production.

Make sure that only the appropriate share of the development advances is tied to each platform's SKU. Remember that the purpose of the advance is to fund the creation of the game. The work needed to develop each component should be the basis for the apportionment of advances, not the potential return, especially in a situation where a third party has the ability to substantially delay or even kill the project and there is nothing the developer or the publisher can do about it.

One at a Time, Please

Publishers also like to tie one game contract to another by cross-collateralization when acquiring two or more games from the same developer. What that means is that the set-off costs being accrued on one game for the publisher are applied to the royalties on the other game. This is great for the publisher because they then spread the risk of both games across both games' revenue streams. However, if one game is a bust and the other a hit, the royalty stream from the hit will go to the publisher to defray the costs of the bomb—instead of going to the developer. Of course, if this is taken into account by setting higher royalty percentages for the developer in both games, then fine. However, that rarely (if ever) happens, so avoid these cross-collateralization deals, if possible.

Exercise Your Audit Rights

The developer's audit rights need to be considered both in the contract negotiations and after the game is released. Every developer contract should provide the developer with audit rights over the publisher's financial records regarding the total game sales and a detail of what expenses are used to determine the "net" income that forms the basis for royalty payments.

Although audits are usually limited to one time per year, push to have the audits more often—like every six months. Moreover, be wary of clauses that make audit rights "use them or lose them" propositions, where if the developer does not audit within 30 or 60 days of the end of the accounting period, the rights expire. Use your audit rights and do not allow them to expire

Conclusion

Each developer contract contains similar elements, but a contract is ultimately as unique as the game it covers. Just as the publisher is compelled to protect its economic interests, so should the developer. If the developer does not do everything in its power to protect its interests, no one else will.

Keep in mind that negotiations occur throughout the process, from the first contact through the signature of the formal document. More than one developer has suffered from "negotiation fatigue" and missed opportunities to replace detrimental contract provisions. Don't be afraid to ask for what you want in the contract. No one ever lost a deal for asking. It is just good business sense.

You might think of yourself as a programmer, designer, or artist, but if you want to make a living at this business, when you are working on the deal with the publisher, think of yourself as a businessperson. Apply your attention to the contract negotiations with the same focus and zeal you apply to your game development. Take care and, to the extent possible, surround yourself with competent professionals.

4.6

Pros and Cons of Worldwide and Country-by-Country Deals

Jay Powell

jep@Octagon1.com

A development studio has been working for months on the next greatest game and now it's time to hit the streets and secure a publisher for the game. They're confronted with their first decision: do they want a single publisher, or multiple publishers?

This article gives developers the information they need to decide whether they want one publisher to handle every territory in the world, or whether it would be better for the company to leverage their risk across multiple publishers. Each model has its advantages and pitfalls, but developers need to have a firm grasp on the development status of their game and what their company needs to move forward.

The Alternatives

There are two primary models used for publishing or distributing titles. The worldwide model will place a game with one publisher who will handle everything for the developer and take care of all sales around the world. The country-by-country model will involve selling the game to smaller publishers in each major territory, or having one of these publishers handle a group of smaller territories.

Basic Criteria for Each Model

The first step in deciding which model a developer should go with is to evaluate their game and company. The two primary factors for this evaluation are the state of the development and the amount of cash in the bank. When looking at the state of development, the further in development a company is, the more options they will have.

CASE STUDY 4.6.1: EVALUATING INTELLECTUAL PROPERTY

The following are some of the major points involved in determining whether an intellectual property is marketable as the basis for a game.

Quality of the Property

- How strong are the characters in terms of depth and popularity?
- Is it a well-developed book/television series/film/etc.?
- Is it interesting, could the story add value to a game?
- Is it a very linear story, or is there a broader "world?"

Value of the Property

- Popularity
- Age (has it peaked?)
- Strength of following
- Expected longevity

Target Demographics

- Age
- Sex
- Geographic region(s)

Ability to Translate into Game

- What genres would be appropriate?
- What platforms could it be adapted for?
- Can the story be used in a game, or is it too linear?
- Could it be used on an existing game project or to increase sales to an existing line?

Competing Properties

- What properties are similar?
- Why is this property superior?
- If another developer selects a competing property, how will it affect the market?
- What games would it be similar to?

Worldwide publishers will be able to sign titles on a technology demonstration or design document if your team has a great track record. When developers begin this process, they must realize that as much as three to five months can pass between the initial pitch and the signing of a contract.

When dealing with smaller publishers or country-by-country publishers, this process can take as little as one month. Country-by-country publishers will have to see a working demo of the game, preferably at beta stage. Developers also need a significant base of contacts with these publishers as well as time to contact, follow up, and negotiate contracts with each.

Once a developer understands the position of their company and title, they will be in a position to determine which model is best for them. This article takes a deeper look at each business model and how it will affect their game and company both immediately and in the long run.

Advantages of the Worldwide Model

When most developers begin to think about getting a publisher for their game, the publishers in this category are the ones that come to mind. What most people do not realize is that there are far more publishers that can handle these deals than they think. Around the globe, there are about 30 with the capital and distribution networks to handle a multimillion-dollar game on a worldwide scale. Many developers will only submit their title to the top five or six that they see consistently in the press. Here are the advantages of the worldwide model.

CASE STUDY 4.6.2: WHAT TO INCLUDE IN A PACKAGE TO A WORLDWIDE PUBLISHER

Here is a checklist of the materials you should provide to a worldwide publisher:

- A **10- to 15-page game** overview that includes thought-out and detailed concept, look and feel, details on gameplay including number of hours, types, and depth of gameplay.
- A **sell sheet** that comprises a one-page overview of your game including screenshots, unique selling points, high-level concept, system requirements, and estimated ESRB rating.
- A **technical design review** featuring unique technological aspects, polygon rates, frame rates, and so forth, including how different technological features will affect the budget.
- **Technical requirements** of the final product.
- **Pre-production** time scales and budgets.
- **Estimates of schedules and budgets** for the complete project, including milestones.
- **Video or rendered/interactive demo** that shows core gameplay. With a demo, include a detailed walkthrough.

$\rightarrow$

- **Localization overview** with an estimate of the localization effort, including approximate number of words, files, graphics needing localization, different voices, and so forth, and any unique localization issues, such as a proprietary engine limiting ability to subcontract localization.
- **Competitive analysis,** including similar products in the same category (with sales results for those products) and strengths and weaknesses compared to those products.
- **Copyright information**, including, will specific actors need to be hired? Are there union involvement issues, or specific approvals required?
- **Unique selling points of the game.**

Alleviating the Risk Early

For companies that need to have a source of revenue early in the development cycle, this is the best model to use. Companies in this situation that stand a realistic chance of obtaining a contract with a major worldwide publisher are generally new teams with a wealth of experienced individuals and companies that have been in the industry for some time and want to get a second or third team moving on a project. If a team has a solid track record, these publishers will sign based on design documentation, technology demos, and a solid timetable of milestones. This will allow the team to work on the game without worrying about not being paid, and will save the developers from investing time in a project that will never see the store shelves. Provided all the milestones are met, the contract will cover the expenses of the project as long as it is in development.

Access to Professional Testing Facilities

Few developers have the time or the facilities to fully test a game for gameplay balancing, bugs, and compatibility. Choosing a worldwide publisher will completely eliminate this burden. The publisher will be responsible for this testing and for promptly reporting any problems to the developer. The publisher will also have a wealth of experience with games in the genre to help let you know what features and gameplay elements have worked well with retailers and consumers in the past. Many developers might believe that too much of this input destroys the game that they have envisioned, which is true when this feedback gets out of hand. However, when handled correctly, it can make the difference between a poor selling game and a top 10. Keep in mind that selling to retailers can be as important as selling to gamers. If the buyer for a major chain has a problem with the game, a significant portion of the market can vanish from under your feet—which takes us to our next point…

Better Access to Retailers and End Users

In today's retail market, being excluded from the shelves of one store can put a severe dent in the sell-through of a game. One retailer deciding not to stock a game can cause a ripple effect down the line. Other retailers will see that it is not being stocked and can turn the game down based on this as well. Worldwide publishers not only have great access to all the retail channels, they also have the weight and clout to turn a "no" or "maybe" into a "yes." Through the promise of other titles or promotions, a worldwide publisher can get a title onto some store shelves that a smaller publisher would not have the ability to do.

Worldwide publishers also have the experience with similar titles to know what the end users and press liked and disliked. Developers can use this experience to create a better game and consequently a bigger hit.

Name Recognition

Some worldwide publishers will publish titles that sell great despite bad reviews. How does this happen? Gamers often buy products based on the track record of the publisher; they have faith in that company to consistently deliver a quality product. By signing a contract with one of these publishers, a developer gains an instant fan base and potential customers.

This name recognition will also carry over to the next title from a developer. By having one or more titles published on a worldwide scale by one of the larger publishers, the developer will be able to capitalize on the acquired notoriety when approaching other publishers in the future. This is a valuable tool in the process of selling and negotiating future titles.

Marketing

The larger publishers simply have more money to invest in marketing. More money invested here will generally translate into better sales. The best games in the world will not sell if they are not marketed correctly, and sometimes the extra marketing dollars will save a title that is not receiving the great reviews that everyone had planned. Small publishers will finance a few ads and some Web advertising, but the bigger publishers can produce the TV spots and in-store advertising that really push units out the door.

Worldwide publishers can also afford to pay for more and better shelf space for their products. There is a reason why the games from the worldwide publishers are always up front and in the face of the consumers: the publisher pays a premium for this location.

In addition, the more a publisher markets a game, the more name recognition the developer gets for future products. Again, this is a powerful tool for future negotiations and sales.

Relationships

One of the biggest benefits of working with a worldwide publisher is the relationship that a developer will build. Publishers will generally look to teams with which they have had a positive experience in the past to handle contract deals. These deals, which can range from add-ons to ports to the next title in a franchise series, are difficult to obtain without a prior relationship with the publisher, but can be a huge boost to the team.

A good experience with the publisher will also make things much easier the next time a developer needs to pitch a game to them. They'll remember what went right and what went wrong, and reward good teams accordingly. If a developer created a hit for them, the last thing they want to see is that team working on a project for a competitor.

Drawbacks of Worldwide Publishers

Working with worldwide publishers has a lot to offer if a developer is in a position to move on such a deal. However, these publishers also have their drawbacks.

Time Restraints

When a developer submits a title to one of the worldwide publishers, they should be aware of the time that it will take that publisher to evaluate the title. Most of these companies will have to show the title to multiple offices in North America and Europe to get the approval process rolling. These offices will evaluate the game based on the gameplay, finances, and marketability. If the game passes these steps, a board will generally have to approve the project. The higher the budget of the game, the more processes a developer can expect to go through. This process can take anywhere from one month to three months in some cases.

Contract Negotiations

Once the title is approved, the contract negotiation begins. Again, this is going to take time, as the publisher will have a large and sometimes exacting legal team reviewing the contract at each step. The developer is now looking at another one to three months in negotiation before a single dollar is transferred to them.

The contracts themselves are much more stringent with the larger worldwide publishers. A developer might find that they are not getting the best deal possible with the contract that they have been presented from the publisher, and swinging the points of the contract in their favor will be a long and arduous process.

Overlooked Territories

Very few worldwide publishers have true distribution across the entire planet. In many cases, some smaller territories with a market for the game will be overlooked. True, these territories generate limited revenues, but when added together they can contribute a nice sum of money. If a worldwide publisher has no presence in South America, Portugal, or Eastern Europe, the developer might end up leaving a lot of money on the table. If the publisher has no plans to support the game in a territory, the developer would be better off selling it on their own in those markets.

Sublicensing

Worldwide publishers who do not have their own worldwide distribution will also sublicense to the territories they cannot cover directly. By sublicensing the game to smaller distributors or publishers, the worldwide publisher can generate revenue of their own with little effort. The drawback to the developer is that in most situations they are receiving a percentage of the percentage their worldwide publisher receives. With a little effort, the developer could make these sales directly and earn much more money.

Lower Royalty Rates

The sublicensing factor is not the only downside to the royalties from a worldwide publisher. Depending on the developer's track record and the profile of the project, the overall royalty rate from a worldwide publisher is generally much smaller as well.

This is because the risk associated with completely or nearly completely funding a project is much higher than that involved in acquiring a nearly complete game. Consequently, the royalty rates will generally be much smaller—from 15% to 25% as a general rule. Other deal structures can generate a much higher backend for the developer.

Less Mind Share

Worldwide publishers handle dozens if not hundreds of titles each year. A developer can rarely count on getting the mind share from a worldwide publisher that they can get from a smaller territorial or country-by-country publisher. Less mind share can translate into less time spent with the producer polishing the game, and less marketing attributed to the game. All of this can easily result in fewer sales, which means smaller royalties for the developer.

High Risk for the Developer

One of the biggest concerns with the worldwide model, given the state of the industry over the last few years, is the risk involved in this type of deal for the developer. By signing full rights to a game over to one publisher, that developer has placed all of their eggs in one basket. Without a solid contract and backup plan, this could spell disaster for the developer if the publisher goes bankrupt, is purchased, or loses interest in the title.

Advantages of Country-by-Country Deals

Many developers do not consider this type of deal structure when they are looking to get their game to market. However, if a developer can meet the criteria for doing deals in this manner, they will likely see much larger returns in the long run and sometimes on the advance as well. Starting with the higher royalty rates a developer will see, let's look at the advantages of a country-by-country deal.

CASE STUDY 4.6.3: WHAT TO INCLUDE IN A PACKAGE TO A COUNTRY-BY COUNTRY PUBLISHER

Submitting a project to a national publisher requires very different materials.

Finished Goods

- Copy of product
- Sell sheet
- Localization summary form
- Product walkthrough
- Saved games with descriptions for evaluation aid
- Review and previews
- Cheat keys, keyboard commands
- Installation guide
- Current product competitive analysis

Beta

- Playable demo/beta
- Saved games with descriptions for evaluation aid
- Design overview
- Gold master date
- Completed localization summary form
- Detailed installation guide
- Summary description of all game levels/missions
- Printout of keyboard commands and cheat keys
- Copy of marketing plan
- Trailer of game
- Unique selling points
- Product walkthrough
- Mockup of box design (if available)
- Plan for porting game to other platforms
- Minimum and recommended system requirements
- Timeline for localization
- List of marketing and advertising assets available
- Copy of manual/documentation
- Competitive analysis

Royalty Rates

Royalty rates with these publishers are usually much higher from the beginning. By cutting straight to the source and dealing with a country-specific publisher, a developer can see a royalty rate of 30% to 35%. There are fewer middlemen and lesser margins to factor into the net receipts definition of the contract, so this money is passed on to the developer.

Focused Marketing

Where many worldwide publishers will use one marketing strategy for all markets, a country-by-country publisher will use the strategy that best fits their market. These strategies will vary from country to country, and the companies that specialize in one market will know which channels and strategies work best for promoting a title. The amount of revenue spent will be very close to a worldwide publisher, but the effect will be much greater as the effort is always put in the best place.

Wider Variety of Partners

There are almost 1,000 publishers of videogames around the world. Obviously, some of these publishers operate in territories that generate very small deals, but on the average there are anywhere from 10 to 20 publishers and distributors per territory. With this selection available, it is much easier for a developer to select a partner with whom they are comfortable.

Furthermore, developers will always see a greater response from publishers when they are showing a near complete title, and the options for partners that this model provides makes for a better deal for the developer.

Direct Contact with Decision Makers

When dealing with a worldwide publisher, there is a strong chance that the developer will be dealing with a product manager or producer. When a developer establishes a relationship with a country-by-country publisher, they will most likely be working with one of the principals of the company or someone nearly as powerful. This translates into a better relationship for all parties involved and a much quicker period for evaluations and contract negotiation. In many cases, a title can be evaluated and contract signed within one to two months because of the lesser amount of internal red tape from the publisher.

More Mind Share

The final major advantage a developer will see from this model is the amount of mind share the publisher grants to a project. Some of these companies will release less than one game per month. With fewer games going to the retailers, each is very important to the publisher. This places the interest of the publisher and developer perfectly in line. Both companies have to work well together to ensure a successful launch. The publisher cannot allow one of their games to fail, as it will have a drastic effect on their income for the year. With this type of dedication, the relationship will work out better for both sides.

Disadvantages of Country-by-Country Deals

Signing a contract with a country-by-country publisher has definite advantages to any developer in the industry. Unfortunately, there are several disadvantages to consider and barriers to overcome before someone can adopt this method of publishing or distribution.

Game Should Be Near Completion

One of the major disadvantages to this model is that a game needs to be nearly completed for a country-by-country publisher to invest in the game. In fact, most country-by-country publishers will not evaluate a title unless they can see at least a beta copy. Because they are handling only a handful of titles a year, they are very reluctant to take a risk on a title early in development.

Smaller Advances

As the deals that are being structured in this model only involve one territory at a time, the advances are generally much smaller. Typically, a publisher will guarantee a set amount of units at a fixed royalty rate in dollars, unlike worldwide publishers who set their royalty rates as a percentage. If they don't approach enough country-by-country publishers, a developer might find that their total advance is lower than it would have been with a worldwide publisher. This is usually offset by the royalties on the back-end, as country-by-country deals are much more likely to see a sell-through than worldwide deals. Sell-through occurs when a title sells more units than the publisher guaranteed to the developer. This is the point where royalty checks are issued each month and the revenue from these payments can quickly compensate for a lower advance.

Difficulty Landing U.S. and UK Deals

Due to the small number of publishers in the United States and UK that handle deals for only their market, approaching this model will make it difficult to land a deal in these countries. Most of the publishers based in the United States and the UK only want to acquire titles that they can control on a worldwide basis. These two countries hold smaller numbers of country-by-country publishers than countries such as Germany, France, and Italy, so the deals are harder to find unless the developer truly works hard to acquire them.

Time Investment

This is the biggest disadvantage and hurdle for any developer looking to approach the country-by-country publishing model. Developers will be approaching three to four times as many publishers on average than they would for a worldwide deal. A developer has to take time to build that many more packages, follow up on those packages, and negotiate contracts. In many cases, this is a job for a minimum of two people working only on sales for the company.

Once the deals are secured in all the major markets, the developer then must deal with localization efforts for each of their partners, negotiating each of the individual contracts, handling the press requests, and aiding each publisher with the marketing effort in their country. After the game has been released, the developer must keep in touch with the publishers to continue the press and marketing, and to receive their royalty reports and any money due with each report.

Conclusion

Each model outlined in this article has its advantages and disadvantages. The important thing to remember is that there is no perfect scenario for every deal or developer. Before deciding which route to take, developers should sit down and take an accurate assessment of where they are with their game and finances and where they want to be. Selling a game to publishers is not a secret science by any means; the important things to remember with either model are to always follow up with your leads, never exclude a potential publisher, and be professional with your partners (or potential partners) at all times. In the games industry, one burnt bridge now could easily come back to haunt the company down the road.

4.7

The Whys and Wherefores of Game Agents

Borut Pfeifer

borut@whiteknucklegames.com

Much has been written about developer-publisher contracts ([Rogers02], [Powell02]), and rightly so—for a new game development studio, their first game contract can have a profound effect on the success of their business. However, while agents similar to those employed by writers, musicians, and actors are growing in popularity in the games industry, there is little documentation on contracts between a developer and an agent, and how to go about selecting one. Should a new studio decide to sign with an agent, this might be the first legal contract they will ever enter into. This article describes some of the pros and cons of selecting an agent, to help a studio decide whether an agent is right for them, and some of the clauses in typical agent contracts.

Is an Agent Right for You?

Let's look at the services that an agency provides to a developer, and at the corresponding costs.

Pros

Location and travel. For a team that is not located in California, it can be difficult to work with publishers who want frequent contact with their developers, at least in the initial stages of the relationship. An agent located where the major publishers are located expedites this process for the developer. Even agents who are not located in California can still help the developer in this manner, since they will still save the developer from having to travel as frequently to see the publisher, letting them focus on what drives them: making games.

Knowledge of publisher needs. We would all like to think that exceptionally fun gameplay can sell a demo, but publishers often look for key, hot features, depending on the current state of the market. A good agent will be aware of what features publishers are looking for. They will also know what types of games a publisher is looking for at any particular time, and will therefore be able to tailor the search to the publishers that are looking for your type of game.

Contacts in the industry. A good agent has strong relationships with the right people at the major publishers.

Negotiation. An agent is usually a skilled and practiced negotiator; this will come in handy not just during the initial contract negotiation, but also during the development cycle if some monetary dispute arises between the developer and publisher.

Business knowledge. For an inexperienced team, an agent can bring general business development knowledge to the table.

Cons

Commission. The agent takes a percentage of all income you receive from the publisher, as well as income from sequels or derivative works, and potentially from the purchase of your studio.

Negative publisher image. Publishers might think that a development contract is going to have an artificially inflated price if there is an agent involved, to account for his commission. They still tend to deal with agents, however, since it is a convenient way to find new teams.

Potential loss of control. Typically, an agent does not interfere very much with the studio and its work. However, if the studio wants to control every aspect of development, including publisher relationships, the presence of an agent might prove incompatible with the studio's objectives.

What to Look for in a Particular Agent

The ideal agent is strong in most (if not all) of the service areas listed in the preceding section. In addition, consider these factors:

Attitude. Do you feel the agent is trustworthy? Can you easily get along with him? Remember that you will have to work in close partnership with this person, possibly for a long time.

Experience. Many agents come from other parts of the industry. Some are former publisher or developer employees. The more experience, from as many diverse sources in the industry, the better the agent will be at helping you in general.

Representation. How much time and how many people will the agency use to represent you to the fullest?

Analysis

Now that we've gone through some of the pros and cons, let's consider the situations where it would be most and least desirable to use an agent.

For an inexperienced team, one located far away from industry centers, or one without any significant expertise and/or interest in performing the work required by a sustained sales effort, it's probably worth the cost of going with an agent. Obviously, this is not to say that this team would have no chance to succeed without one, but the benefits of agent representation would likely outweigh the costs.

However, if the team is heavily experienced, it might be able to get a contract based solely on that experience. A good agent could still give this team feedback about the game and thus prevent the negative impressions that might arise from approaching a desirable publisher with an unpolished demo.

It is also worthwhile to study the monetary implications of the agent's presence, and whether he seems reasonable or not. Suppose that an agent secures a $2 million, two-year development contract for you, over the course of a nine-month negotiation process. (It can easily take up to six months to finalize a contract, in addition to the time required to prepare the pitch, visit publishers, and obtain a letter of intent.) If the agent's commission is 10% of the contract's value, you're paying him $200,000 for those nine months of work, but you're also paying for his contacts, the time you didn't have to spend traveling, and for that wonderful benefit, the part about not having to do the sales pitch yourself.

Further, you should consider how many people the agency will assign to your case: is it one person full time, or multiple specialists? Do not make the mistake of simply computing an hourly rate. Keep in mind the qualitative factors mentioned earlier before you use the cost analysis to make your final decision.

Contract Details

If you've decided to go with an agent, it will be useful to know some of the typical clauses you'd see in an agent contract.

Agent's Responsibilities

Agents must try to obtain the best possible offers and contracts for your team. They must be required to keep you informed about all such submissions, rejections, and offers of your game to publishers. The agent might also want to review royalty statements from your publisher to ensure that you (and he) are getting the correct amount of royalties. Most agents will also serve as intermediaries throughout the course of the contract, in the case disputes arise between the developer and the publisher; for example, if the publisher is unduly delaying milestone acceptance.

Developer's Responsibilities

The developer's main responsibility is to send anyone interested in purchasing their titles to the agent, so that the agent can manage all dealings effectively. Providing the agent with past business information (e.g., prior contracts) will also help him to better understand the developer's current business situation.

Commission

The agent is paid by commission. The commission is usually set as a percentage of the developer's gross revenues from various sources of income:

- Any regular game development deal you sign with a publisher.
- Subsidiary rights—sequels, add-ons, ports, etc.
- Derivative works—translations to other media, movies, TV, action figures, etc.
- Purchase of your company by another.

Each of these categories might have a different commission rate attached to it, in general somewhere between 5% and 10%. Note that when considering derivative works, you should keep the commission to a minimum: migration of a game's intellectual property to other media might be a rare occurrence, but if it does happen, you'll probably have to hire another agency to represent you in these other media—and therefore pay another commission.

Terminating the Contract

Termination of the contract is typically allowed by either party, with some period of notice to wrap up any existing business. However, several contractual clauses still apply after termination. Specifically, the agent's right to perceive commissions on the developer's earnings will expire a specific amount of time after the contract is terminated. For example, if, within 24 months of terminating a contract with an agent, the studio develops a sequel to a game for which the agent negotiated a contract, the agent will still receive his commission for that sequel.

Agents will also want you to be prohibited from dealing with publishers they put you in touch with and/or negotiated a deal between the two of you. For a publisher they have closed a contract with you, they will typically want the length of one development cycle, to discourage developers from terminating the contract with the agent and immediately closing a deal with one of these publishers (thereby avoiding the agent's commission). They will also want to prohibit you from dealing with any publisher to whom they have presented your work, but not closed a contract; since the relationship is less advanced, the limit on this is typically shorter.

Indemnification

In most contracts of any type, there is typically a clause or clauses that indemnify each party from a wrongdoing by the other side. Simply, if the other party in the contract breaks the law without you knowing about it, you can't be sued for their wrongdoing. This includes being sued and any financial obligations due to a suit.

Competition

Since agents typically represent multiple developers, you might be worried about an agent working with a client who is a direct competitor of yours (e.g., based on the genre of the game you're working on). You should be able to request the agent's list of clients to ensure to your satisfaction that he is appropriately handling any conflicts of interest. However, don't expect more information on other clients than that, since the agent will typically be bound by confidentiality agreements with regard to clients' projects, technology, and other property.

Payment Procedures

The agent might want to take funds the publisher is to pay to you and have them place it in a trust instead. This way, the agent can deduct his commission before the money gets to you. This practice delays your receipt of payment by a few days. Normally, this isn't an issue, but in tight situations, this delay could mean the difference between paying your team's salaries on time, paying them a week late, or, in the absolute worst case, even going out of business. For this reason, you might want the representation contract to specify that the publisher will send you the money, and that you will then have a short period of time to pay the agent his commission. In this case, you must also give the agent any records of publisher payments upon request, so he can be sure you're paying him the correct amount.

Nongame-Related Work

If you're a small studio, chances are you might occasionally pay the bills with contract work of various sorts. This might include contracting out your art staff to do graphic design for a magazine, or having programmers consult on a networking company's software development projects. If so, it should be clear in the contract that the agent does not receive income from this type of work (unless, of course, he obtains it for you), and that you are not required to fulfill the responsibilities described previously to the agent with regard to this work.

Conclusion

Signing with an agent can help small developers trying to break into the industry to get an edge over the competition. The popularity of game agents has increased to the point where publishers have grown to expect their presence. However, agent representation might not be suited to every team. Study the pros and cons; an agency's services might be what your team needs to increase its odds of success.

References

[Powell02] Powell, J., "Negotiating Contracts That Protect Your Title and Team," Game Developer's Conference 2002 Proceedings.

[Rogers02] Rogers, D. and Summers, M., "Publishers Speak 2002," Game Developer's Conference 2002 Proceedings.

4.8

Public Relations: Making the Most of the Gaming Press

Beverly Cambron

beverly@roccomedia.com

Why do some names consistently appear in the gaming press, while others languish in virtual anonymity? Effective public relations is key to getting your name, product, and reputation out of the shadows. If you're a developer looking for a publishing deal, the publishers need to hear about you. If you're a publisher hawking a game, consumers need to hear about it. Or, perhaps, you're just ready to raise your personal profile in the industry. If any of these scenarios fit you, then it's time you implemented an effective public relations campaign.

What Are Public Relations?

Practically speaking, the first line of relations in public relations, or PR, is with the news and reviews editors at the media outlets who get your news to the public. Editors are the people who decide what news is published, who is interviewed, and which games are reviewed. Effective public relations is really about community relations, from the media to the end user, and includes a host of activities, including press releases and media kits, online interviews, and television and radio appearances. However, to get those interviews and appearances, and to get those games reviewed, you need to begin your PR efforts with the press release.

Ever see an article about one of your competitors in the industry press and wonder why they didn't write about you and your great company? Odds are that you're reading about your competitor because they send out press releases—*effective* press releases.

Writing an Effective Press Release

Press releases are one of the most cost-efficient and effective means of spreading the word about you and your business, if done properly. News articles about your company are premium forms of advertising. Unless you have more business than you can handle, or you're engaged in illegal activities, there really is no reason not to use press releases as an integral part of your public relations strategy.

Further, in the age of e-mail, getting out a press release is pretty simple; you just need a story hook, a flair for concise, effective writing, and a database of relevant press contacts. If you don't have any of those items or abilities, there are plenty of PR professionals who do. Look for more on outsourcing your public relations work at the conclusion of this article.

The Hook

A story's "hook" is what makes your press release newsworthy. It needs to be more than "Hey, we're game developers with a cool new game! Check out our Web site for more cool stuff!" That is not a hook. There are hundreds of game developers who all believe their game is cool and should be checked out. Not only is that not a newsworthy story, it doesn't provide the news editor reading your e-mail with enough information to even care about learning your story.

To find your hook, think about what makes your company unique. If you're a new game developer, what is it about your game or the team behind your game that makes your story newsworthy? Perhaps the team left a particularly well-known company to develop your game? Maybe you're developing a game that has an innovative aspect—or at least an aspect you can make sound innovative.

The hook can also be something as simple as the release of the game's demo, the fact that the game has "gone gold," or that a certain band will be contributing to the game soundtrack. The point is that there is a point to the story, not just a general "check us out."

The Style and Format

Getting your hook is half the battle, but the war is not yet won. Your press release must be professional and well written. You need to stay focused. Pick your hook and stick with it. You can always send out another press release with another hook. Richard Aihoshi, editor-in-chief of IGN Vault Network, finds that simple, straightforward writing that gets to the point and doesn't try to say or do too much makes for a good press release. "The press releases I consider best are short and contain only one central message, which means they don't risk diluting that central message by trying to convey secondary ones at the same time," says Aihoshi.

While your ultimate audience is the person reading the news, your first audience is the gaming press. Who are these people? Well, they're males—mostly. Aihoshi of IGN has worked with staff ranging in age from about 16 to the mid-50s. He also estimates a ratio of "about five males to one female over the course of our existence, although the proportion of women is rising year by year." Gamespot senior editor Andrew Park wants to know a game's developer, publisher, release date, plus a brief summary of what the game is about, including any distinguishing features such as noteworthy licenses or brands, "as well as some sort of brand new or updated information on the product itself." What he doesn't want is "repeated bombardment" of press releases that simply reiterate what has already been revealed in a previous press release. "The best press releases have a good deal of information and don't necessarily have to come out every week," says Park. "Some of the worst ones have barely any new information and come out every week, or even worse, multiple times a week. These should be avoided at all cost."

The Top-Down Approach

So, you have your hook and it's fresh. Now, it's time to put finger to keyboard and start putting it together. As you're doing this, you need to remember to work "top down." That is, place the bulk of your facts in the first couple of paragraphs of the release and then use the remainder of your release to elaborate. Don't make the news editor search for the facts and the story. A press release should be written in such a manner that a publication could remove everything but the first couple of paragraphs and still have a complete story.

The 400-Word Rule

Be clear and concise in your writing. Your press release should be in the 400-word range. You should be able to hit the high points of your story, include a short "bio" on your company, and still be comfortably in that range. The 400-word range certainly isn't a hard-and-fast rule, but it's a good one to follow. If you ultimately distribute your press release via services such as *PRNewswire* or *Businesswire*, you will typically find that their fees increase when the press release exceeds 400 words.

Quotes

As you tell your story, make sure it reads like a story. Take a look at a business article in your morning paper. You'll probably see at least one quote from a relevant party. Put a quote or two in your press release. Who at your company would be appropriate to comment on the subject of your story? Quote that person saying something interesting about the game or the event. At the risk of widespread disillusionment, most quotes in press releases are fabrications of the PR people. Just make certain the person you're quoting approves the quote.

Simplicity

Be sure to simplify the technical language in your press release. Keep in mind that the person reading the press release is most likely not a programmer. Yes, you might have a completely new way of compressing bounding volume data for arbitrary polygon meshes, dramatically reducing memory footprint compared with traditional bounding volume approaches without sacrificing any runtime performance, and enabling you to create worlds of a greater size and scope than was previously possible. However, unless your press release is for hyper-technical journals, you're going to only succeed in putting the news editors to sleep.

There is no need to write in a condescending manner; just keep it smartly simple and always entertaining. Rather than expounding on the technical minutiae, focus on the ultimate point: the technical advances incorporated in your game make its worlds more detailed and robust than any other game on the market. Leave the dramatically reduced memory footprint and compressed bounding volume data for "water cooler" chatter and GDC or E3 sessions.

Finally, as you wrap up your release, be sure to include a short "About Your Company" paragraph. Spend some time creating a two- to three-sentence summary of your company, including who you are and what you do. You can use this brief bio at the end of every press release.

Proofread. Proofread. Proofread.

Now that you've written your release, it's time to proofread. And then proofread again. And then have someone else proofread. Yes, even simple grammatical errors are noticed. While some of these gamer sites are run by kids just trying to get free games, most are run by professionals, and sloppy press releases connote sloppy, unprofessional people. No one wants to follow up with a sloppy, unprofessional person. Although good grammar and proper spelling seem to have become a lost art, and even though you and your buddies communicate just fine, the news editors might have gone to school when proper grammar still meant something. They might be well aware of the difference between "your" and "you're," possessives and plurals, and, whether it makes any sense or not, "tough" is not spelled "tuff."

Make Sure You've Written for Your Audience.

Additionally, as you're proofreading, keep your audience in mind. Does the press release appeal to your audience? Take a glance down the editor photos in a *PC Gamer* and you'll see a row of seven white, male faces, at least at the time this article was written.

So, what does all that mean in terms of your press release? Not to say that these guys aren't in touch with their feminine side, but your best bet will be to focus on the "dude!" elements of your story. How many levels? How many Mechs? How many weapons? Any intense bands on the soundtrack? While the number of female gamers appears to be growing, like it or not, until more women join the ranks of the gaming media, you should probably focus on the guy-appealing aspects of your game.

Accompanying Materials

Gaming news editors also want to see screenshots—lots of them. Make sure you take plenty of screenshots and make them high resolution while you're at it. You can always compress them later for e-mailing purposes. If you're sending out a press release, send out a new round of screenshots as well. They also like demos and trailers. Keep in mind that they need you as much as you need them. They need content that will attract an audience.

Releasing the Release

You've written. You've proofread. And proofread again. You're almost ready to release. However, before doing so, make sure you have a catchy and concise headline that makes clear the point of your story.

Be very certain to include basic information in your release, including a contact name and, at a minimum, contact e-mail. Make sure this is a contact who will actually be available for contact after sending out the press release. Don't send out a press release and then be unable to return e-mail or telephone calls for a week. Hedge your bets and include two different contact people.

As mentioned earlier, e-mail has made sending out press releases a relative breeze. If you are sending the press release out yourself, and have not already compiled a database of contacts, you need to do so. This database is the cornerstone of your PR efforts. With depth and overall quality obviously varying, there are now hundreds of gaming press outlets and they're all relatively easy to find with a quick Google search. Further, many of the online sites pick up news items from other sites, so you should be able to compile a wealth of data fairly quickly. Generally speaking, you're looking for the "news" contact address. While some media outlets are bigger in terms of audience size, you never know who is reading, so include them all. One to definitely include is GamesPress.com, a (currently) free service that is updated daily with submitted press releases and artwork from publishers, developers, distributors, and PR agencies. They then send out an e-mail digest of new material each day to game journalists.

When sending out a press release by e-mail, include the text of your press release in the body of your e-mail, versus as an attached Word document or PDF. Otherwise, you may be complicating the recipient's editing or publishing process; besides, everyone is increasingly virus wary of attachments. In addition, please don't just put a link to your press release posted on your Web site. Again, don't create additional steps to get to your news. In addition, while most people have HTML-friendly e-mail, the best way to go is simple text format. If you absolutely must do HTML, keep your background white and your text black. This is news, not a "prettiest e-mail" contest.

If you use an outsourced PR firm, they will know how to get it out for you. They maintain their own press databases and have established relationships with the media. Using a professional PR firm saves you the time of compiling your own database and allows you the advantage of an already established relationship.

Press release distribution can also be facilitated through the use of "wire" services such as *Businesswire* or *PRNewswire*. If you want to release via one of these services, just be aware that the services are not free, and prices typically range anywhere from a couple of hundred dollars to a thousand, depending on the number of news outlets receiving the release.

If you're also releasing screenshots, a demo, or a trailer in conjunction with your press release, don't e-mail some monster file. Zip files when you can, and if the file is still over 1MB, upload it to your Web site and provide a link where the files can be easily downloaded. While you might have a screaming-fast Internet connection, many e-mail servers reject large files, so play it safe.

Finally, be as specific as possible in the subject line of the e-mail. "Press Release" just doesn't cut it. Journalists and editors are inundated with press releases. Don't make them jump through hoops just to get to the basis of your story.

After the Release

If someone does bite on your press release and asks for more information, answer the questions specifically and in detail. Don't just give them a link to information found on your Web site. It's lazy, unprofessional, and could be the end of the story. Andrew Park of Gamespot finds it particularly irritating to deal with PR representatives who aren't communicative or who ignore repeated e-mails and telephone calls. However, Park says that Gamespot "loves" PR folks who send games and supporting materials out on time, if not early, "and who keep in constant communication about important developments."

And, of course, say "thank you!" If a publication picks up your press release or publishes something nice about your company, show your appreciation. A simple e-mail is all it takes and it will be remembered. The larger publications don't have time to let you know they've written about you, so it's up to you to keep up with the media. There are also companies that provide "clipping services" that do the looking for you for a price. If a news outlet has followed up wanting additional information, say "thank you." And if they let you know they've published something about your company, say "thank you."

Of course, in the event they've written something negative, it might be hard to say "thank you" and not even necessary. However, this is also not the time to lose your temper. Either just bear it and walk away, or have a rational conversation, however irrational you might find their review of your beloved game. Don't burn any bridges.

Beyond the Press Release

Press releases are the first stone on the path to industry fame and glory. Press releases lead to interviews, game previews, and reviews. If you want a media outlet to demo or review your product, you need to make the process as simple as possible. One of the biggest gripes from game reviewers is the lack of support material accompanying review copies of games. Even if your manual hasn't been laid out just yet by the designer, send a plain bound copy of the text. Send a walkthrough, too. With preview CDs, include some game art, screenshots, game logo, and company logo.

For game reviews, have a "press pack" ready to roll, including a box shot (front of the box in a high-resolution format), game logo, company logo, and at least a dozen high-resolution screenshots. In addition, in terms of releasing a game for review, keep in mind that the gaming press typically likes to receive games in advance of their release to the public.

You should also have physical prepared media kits ready to go at a given notice. Have some folders printed with your company logo and, in an organized fashion, put together a nice packet of information about your company, including company history, previous press clippings, game "sell sheets," and archived press releases. You might also include a CD "sampler," which could include product images, demos, contact information, and more.

CASE STUDY 4.8.1: GAME REVIEWER PERKS AND PLAYOLA

In addition to copies of the game, most game reviewers receive accompanying accouterment from game publishers. These typically include t-shirts, caps, backpacks, and other assorted company and game branded items. However, when these perks become over-the-top, such as free trips to Japan and Europe, transportation by limousine, and movie premiers, some critics call this "playola." As noted in an April 2002 article in the *Los Angeles Times* [Cambron 01], while many publications have specific policies forbidding writers from accepting free trips and accommodations, or gifts worth more than $25 to $100, practically speaking, these policies are often unenforceable or inapplicable to freelancers. According to the article, although there is no evidence that the junkets generate more positive reviews, and no writer would admit to being swayed by the extravaganzas, they do, says the author, produce more publicity for some middle-of-the-road games that might otherwise draw little attention.

CASE STUDY 4.8.2: A SAMPLE PRESS RELEASE

The following is a press release sample announcing a publishing deal.

For Immediate Release

GAME PUBLISHER TO PUBLISH GAME DEVELOPER'S MASSIVELY
MULTIPLAYER ONLINE GAME "MOG"

Weston, CT—July 15, 2004—Game Publisher and Game Developer today announced a publishing agreement for "Mog," a massively multiplayer online strategy game that puts the player in command of a massive flying saucer. The retail version will incorporate new levels of gameplay, as well as offer a one-month free trial subscription.

$\rightarrow$

The arrangement between Game Developer and Game Publisher was negotiated by Los Angeles based AndWeHelped, a boutique firm specializing in interactive entertainment consulting.

John Doe, vice president of third-party broker AndWeHelped, was instrumental in putting the deal together. "Joe Smith, president of Game Developer, and his team wanted a publisher who would really get behind and support the game," said Doe. "Game Publisher has exhibited tremendous commitment to all its titles, so we felt this would be a great match."

Mog takes place in a universe splintered by intergalactic war. Humanity has split into two hostile factions, while a new hostile alien race advances into human space. In the midst of turmoil and civil unrest, players start as flying saucer ensigns, piloting smaller saucers, eventually working their way up to saucer fleet admiral, controlling a massive flying saucer and plotting strategic maneuvers in one of the three initial factions.

The Mog universe is alive with many new different subplots. Humans are the dominant species of each beginning scenario, but more advanced scenarios will feature diverse alien races and advanced technologies. Numerous players will focus on their own agendas in this seemingly crowded galaxy, and the player will be forced to deal with circumstances that this creates.

"We are excited to be entering the massively multiplayer world with what we believe to be a particularly well-crafted and well-run game," said Game Publisher president, Peter Leader. "The Game Developer team keeps the game fresh and evolving, which was key to our publishing decision."

About Game Publisher

Game Publisher is a publisher of games for PC and other platforms. Founded by entertainment industry veterans with over 15 years of experience, Game Publisher is committed to bringing to market quality games offering exceptional entertainment. Learn more about Game Publisher at *www.GamePublisher.com*.

PRESS CONTACT: Beverly R. Cambron, Rocco Media, LLC
For Game Publisher: *beverly@roccomedia.com*

Conclusion

One press release does not a PR strategy make. You need to make public relations a consistent and prioritized part of your company's business strategy, whether developer, publisher, or other games industry folk. Recall the question of a tree falling in the woods and no one is around to hear it, does it really make a sound? If you make a game and no one hears about it, have you really made a game? Well, yes, but you've also wasted a considerable amount of time and money. And if you don't have the staff, the time, the writing ability, or the personality to maintain good press relations, then hire someone who does. There are public relations firms, such as Rocco Media, devoted to the games industry. They know the people and they understand the process. Rates vary depending on the expertise of the firm, but whether you're budgeting your own time, or budgeting actual dollars, make public relations an integral part of your business, and you will make the most of the gaming press.

Techniques to Increase Upsell for Online Games

Mason McCuskey

mason@spin-studios.com

If you're selling your game online, as shareware, you live and die by the upsell. Simply put, an upsell is when someone pays you money to get more than what he got for free. Depending on your business model, you might refer to this as an order, a registration, a full version, or an upgrade. Regardless of what you call it, it's how you stay in business.

Since making two dollars is better than making one, here are some techniques for increasing the number of upsells you get. They're presented in roughly chronological order (from your customer's point of view), and are just waiting for you to put them to use in your own games.

Present a Professional Appearance

If you want people to buy your game, you need to look like (and behave like) a professional business. Customers need assurance that they're not getting ripped off, and a professional Web site and a prompt response to their questions will assuage their fears.

Web Site Don'ts

If your Web site doesn't reflect a business mentality, you're going to miss out on some orders. Here are some things you should definitely not have on a business Web site:

Diaries containing personal opinions or rants. Not only is this unprofessional, but also, no one cares, and you run the risk of alienating your customer. "Company News" or development diaries are okay, provided they concentrate on your business.

Meaningless marketing hype about your game. When it comes to explaining why your game rocks, your best bet is to provide an accurate list of the things that make your game fun. Avoid phrases like "the best game on the planet" or "guaranteed to be the only game you'll play for a month," because they make you sound like a piece of spam.

False or misleading statements about what customers are getting for their money. It's illegal and unethical. Stick to listing features that you actually have. In addition, avoid listing nebulous features such as "a totally redesigned gameplay engine," unless those features really do make a difference in the game. Technobabble rarely impresses; the people who can't understand it don't care about it, and the people who do understand it recognize it as meaningless.

Web design gimmicks like mouse trails, animated GIFs, background music, and rainbow text. They make you appear juvenile. The exception to this is Shockwave or Flash-based Web sites, which many game companies use.

Broken links. This is an obvious one. Use software to check your site for dead links or buggy code.

Web Site Dos

Your Web site should definitely include:

Screen shots. A screen shot is worth so much more than a thousand words. Showcase your game's good parts with lots of high-resolution screen shots.

Cohesive, easy-to-navigate design. Use a modern design that works on as many browsers as possible.

Contact information. Consider setting up generic e-mail accounts for sales, orders, Webmaster, and support, even if they all route to your personal e-mail.

A newsletter sign-up. Write newsletters when something happens, and send them out to people who have signed up for them on your site. This not only increases your chances for repeat business, but also keeps your name and products in the forefront of the minds of the people who read the newsletter, which can often result in "word of mouth" sales.

A message board. If you can supply the time to moderate and maintain a message board, it can be boon for your business. However, beware—a dusty ghost town forum can make your company look worse, not better.

There are many other techniques that can prove useful; check out what other software companies are doing, and if something looks like it will work for you, try it!

Make It Easy to Order

This seems like an obvious item, but you'd be surprised how many developers make it difficult for people to order their games.

Start by allowing your player to order the full version directly from within the game. At the start and/or end of the game, you should display a teaser for the full version, and hyperlink that page to the ordering page on your Web site.

In addition, make sure that customers have options regarding how to order. You should accept major credit cards, as well as checks and money orders mailed to a well-publicized address. Setting up a merchant account for credit card processing takes some investment, but if you can't afford it, there are companies out there who will provide this service to you for a percentage of your sales. Do a search or ask around for names of reputable registration companies.

One way to measure how easy it is for people to order your game is to count the number of clicks that must occur before they get their game. You want to keep this click count as low as possible, ideally requiring just one or two clicks.

In addition, spot-check your ordering system, especially if you're using a third-party vendor to handle your credit card validation. Buy software that periodically checks to see if your server is working, and alerts you if it is not. Also check your order pipeline from different systems to make sure that it works equally well in all cases. There's nothing worse than having a whole bunch of people who want to buy your game but can't because they don't have a specific browser or operating system.

Make It Worthwhile

To get the most upsells, you need to achieve a perfect balance between compulsion and boredom. Give your players a large enough demo of your game so that they're compelled to play and get hooked on it—but if you give them too much, they'll get tired of it before they register.

Several different strategies have been employed by games distributed online:

Time-lock. Allow the demo version of your game to be played for a certain length of time, and then force players to register to continue playing. This works well for highly addictive puzzle games.

Date-lock. Give potential customers a certain number of calendar days (usually 30) to play the game without restriction. If they want to play for more than a month, then they must register. This method works better for applications than for games, since it's very possible that a huge fan of your game will complete it within a month.

Tokens. This is a variant on the time-lock method. Allow potential customers to play your game 20, 30, or 40 times before requiring registration.

Episodes. In this scenario, your demo allows unrestricted access to the first few levels of the game, and allows the player to purchase more levels. This is the method id Software got very rich on with their shareware games.

Donations. When it comes to games distributed online, asking for a donation typically does not work; either use a different method, or just release your game as freeware.

Resist pricing your game too high. Games sold online typically cost half of what a game in the store would; $10 or $15 will work well, since games are impulse buys for many people, especially online. Also, remember that most of the people who purchase games online typically would not spend $50 on a videogame, even if it was something they liked.

Follow Through Quickly

One of the easiest ways to irk new customers is to make them wait a long time before they receive what they paid for. For games distributed online, there's no excuse for long order delays—ideally, your customers should receive what they paid for within minutes after paying for it. Of course, to achieve this requires a fully automated order processing system, which makes you vulnerable to bogus registrations and invalid credit card numbers. Work around these problems as much as possible, but not at the expense of your true customers' time.

Be sure to explain your registration process to your customers. Tell them how long it will take, what they should do once their order is processed, and where to send e-mail or call if they feel something is not right.

Use Minimal Copy Protection

For years, developers have debated over how much copy protection a game should have. Today, the standard seems to be to create "light" copy protection—just enough to keep the honest people honest.

Heavy-duty copy protection usually isn't worth it. As you know, no copy protection is unbreakable, and hackers see sophisticated padlocks as challenges. The cracker might not even like your game, but will still crack it just because you've "challenged" him by using sophisticated anti-piracy techniques.

Remember that most of the people who play and buy games online are not technically knowledgeable enough to crack something. They're casual people who enjoy a quick diversion, not hardcore gamers. They don't usually know how to get a crack, much less how to use it.

The most prevalent form of piracy today is called "casual piracy." This is where someone lets a friend copy a game he's bought or got from someone else. Most of the time, if someone copies a CD and the anti-piracy mechanism notices and prevents them from playing the copied game, that person isn't likely to spend time trying to crack the protection. At worst, he might try a few times, enter a few different serial numbers, fail, and either buy the game or move on.

This is great, because it means that you can prevent most of your piracy losses by employing a relatively easy protection scheme. You just need to think about the most common ways a game gets copied, and put a couple of layers of protection on those holes.

For example, Web-validated registration codes work well. The basic idea is that in exchange for a purchase, a customer gets a registration code that he or she types into the game. Then, the game validates the code, either through an internal algorithm (e.g., a checksum), or by "phoning home" to a registration server and querying that server to make sure the code is valid. The game either checks the code each time it is run, or it hides a key/value pair in the system's registry that specifies whether the game is registered.

The main problem with an algorithm-based registration code is that it doesn't prevent someone from writing the code on the CD copy and giving that to a friend. Unless your algorithm is based on something unique to the machine the game was originally registered for, your program has no way of knowing if a code has been used before. If someone posts a registration code on the Internet, your only recourse is to release a new version of your software that disallows that code.

The "phone home" method is slightly better than relying on an algorithm, if you don't mind forcing your customers to connect to the Internet. With phone-home protection, whenever someone uses a code, you know about it. It then becomes easy to prevent the same code from being used on multiple computers, and if you see that a registration code has been leaked out to the Internet, you just add it to your "blacklist" database, so that any game that asks if that code is good gets a "no" answer from your server.

The weak spot for the phone-home algorithm is spoofing. To a cracker, it's pretty easy to write a program that pretends to be your registration server, and tricks the game into believing it's talking to the real registration server. You can mitigate this risk by creating your own communications protocol, but then you're off to the races—you can spend months designing a secure method of communication, but there will always be a way around it.

Another issue to keep in mind if you use the phone-home technique is that users expect to be able to reinstall their games on their own computer if they're forced to reinstall their operating system, if they upgrade to a new hard drive, or otherwise change their system configuration. You need to think about a way they can do this easily, or you'll get a lot of angry e-mails from people who believe their fair-use rights have been trampled.

In summary, you should create some type of copy protection. Most games distributed online use algorithm verification, and/or phone home to a central registration server. Regardless of which method you choose, realize that it's a game of diminishing returns—concede the fact that you'll never stop someone who really wants to crack your game, and concentrate on keeping honest people honest.

Track Where Orders Are Coming From

Companies that distribute games online typically do not have a lot of money to spend on advertising and marketing, so it's important that what you do spend, you spend on the right things. Therefore, it behooves you to track where your page hits and orders are coming from. If 90% of your game's orders come from a shareware download site like download.com, it probably makes sense to spend your advertising money there, perhaps by purchasing an enhanced service plan that makes it easier for your customers to order or download your game from that site. This enhanced service might take the form of a better spot in a search engine, a boldface upgrade, an ad that appears based on user input, and so forth. The possibilities are endless.

In addition, knowing where orders come from helps you design your site better. Make sure that the path most often used to order your game works quickly and reliably.

Keep It Fresh

Games distributed through retail have notoriously short life spans. Consequently, many game companies release expansion packs and add-ons to keep their games fresh. Games distributed online tend to stick around longer than games on the shelf, but there's no reason why you shouldn't also use expansion packs to keep your game fresh and garner repeat business.

Most successful games distributed online have multiple expansions, sometimes called "episodes" or "installments." Usually, these expansions sell for around half the price of the full game, and most companies sell packages that include the original game plus all the expansions, so that newcomers can "catch up."

A big part of keeping a game fresh is fixing bugs. You need to release patches and bug fixes as if you were a large company. Sales for games distributed online usually start slow, and then build up over time as word-of-mouth advertising kicks in, so you shoot yourself in the foot by not maintaining your software.

Conclusion

In this article, we hinted at some of the common strategies for increasing upsell. Don't hesitate to keep looking for other tricks, and don't be afraid to talk about your processes with other shareware authors; it's always valuable to share ideas.

MANAGING GAME PRODUCTION

5.0

Introduction

Securing a contract to have your game published is great. Delivering a game you are proud of, and doing so after a smooth and pleasant production cycle, is even better.

Managing a game development business is hard work—much harder than most outsiders realize. It involves herding an ever-larger group of fiercely independent creative types toward a common goal (seemingly forever), resolving cultural conflicts between artists, designers, and programmers, and constantly adjusting the design to the shifting technological and competitive landscape—all the while dealing with financial constraints that would bring most companies in other fields to their knees.

Much has been written about the games industry's idiosyncratic problems: lack of management acumen, leading to developers signing horrible contracts, then to endless unpaid overtime to ship the games anyway, then to burnouts, then to the hiring of a new crop of bright-eyed youngsters so that the cycle can begin all over again. Less has been said about the companies that have managed to break this vicious cycle. The articles in this section of the book attempt to remedy that situation, by looking at the tricks and techniques elaborated by successful developers to make their jobs easier, smoother, and more predictable:

- In Article 5.1, "The Stages of Game Development," Mike Sellers, veteran designer of Meridian 59 and founder of Online Alchemy, describes the stages of development and how to prepare for each.
- In Article 5.2, "Managing the Development Process," veteran producer Tom Sloper explains how he has managed his 50+ productions over the years.
- In Article 5.3, "Ways to Manage Creative Chaos," producer Heather Maxwell Chandler describes some of the traditional "corporate" management techniques that game developers can apply to their benefit.
- In Article 5.4, "Customer Support in Massively Multiplayer Online Games," Funcom's Terri Perkins explores the delicate topic of customer service in the games industry, specifically in the difficult context of anytime, anywhere massively multiplayer online worlds.
- In Article 5.5, "Offshore Game Development Outsourcing," Javier Otaegui, president of Argentine independent developer Sabarasa Entertainment, looks at the financial and logistical implications of outsourcing parts of the development process to companies in other parts of the world.
- In Article 5.6, "Localizations," Heather Maxwell Chandler discusses ways to make the process of localizing the game for international markets as smooth as possible.

- In Article 5.7, "Leadership: The Making of Effective and Happy Teams," games industry recruiter Melanie Cambron and Heather Maxwell Chandler describe why development companies should strive to keep their teams happy, and how successful leaders have achieved this goal.
- Finally, in Article 5.8, "Quality Assurance: Bug Tracking and Test Cases," Chris Campbell, quality assurance lead on such titles as *Age of Empires*, explains how to implement effective quality control throughout the production process, thus minimizing the need for crunch time at the end of the cycle.

5.1

The Stages of Game Development

Michael Sellers

mike@onlinealchemy.com

Games lead all other forms of software in innovation and interactivity. Unfortunately, games also lag behind other forms of software in their development process. At small studios and large companies, game development today is a chaotic process that differs greatly from team to team and game to game. The process might change during the development of a single game, and is often subject to the passing preferences of individual developers, managers, or publishers. This chaos leads to lost time, money, and opportunity. Games are developed without being designed; they might be killed late in the development process (when it is most expensive); or they are released late—sometimes *years* late—with severe bugs and missing promised features. And sometimes they are completed and released, but simply aren't any fun.

The solution to this is a development process that is practical, realistic, flexible, and takes into account the unique aspects of game creation. Applying the stages of game development discussed here to your projects will clarify your process, and increase your chances of successfully developing a fun game that sells.

Stage 1: Concept

The first stage of game development focuses on figuring out what the game is going to be. Unlike other software development, where the users' set of tasks is already known or can be discovered, in game development the first thing you have to do is create these tasks out of thin air. This is the core of game design, and in far too many projects is left until much later in the process. It's important to resolve this as early as possible, so that at every step you know what kinds of things the player will be thinking about and doing and why the game is fun. Losing sight of this, especially during the long haul of production, is a main reason why so many games fail.

Timing and Participants

The conceptualization process should begin long before the project team is assembled, or even before anyone else knows that the project exists. Typically, one or two or three senior people—a designer, producer, and/or publisher representative—get together to hammer out the game concept. The concept might arrive in a flash in the first hour, but more likely, it's going to take time to emerge. It's important to allow this kind of time; don't try to schedule inspiration. That's one reason why the concept formation should begin before there's a team waiting around for something to do—you need to be able to take the time needed to explore the concept without a project clock ticking loudly in your ears. That said, it's reasonable to assume that this stage will take one to three months to complete, although it might take much longer.

Process and Deliverables

The conceptual design process is critical to successful game development, and has been detailed in [Onder02]. This is necessarily a highly iterative process where the participants look at their ideas from different angles, searching for the most engaging gameplay experience.

When you're finished with the conceptual phase, you should have a clear (if high-level) understanding of what the game is and why it's so incredibly great that you just have to develop it. The primary deliverable from this stage is a clear, concise statement of what the game is. This doesn't mean that you need to create a hefty design bible. On the contrary, you should be able to boil down the essence of the game into two or three sentences. This statement will be the touchstone for you and your team throughout development, so it's important that it's understandable, memorable, and believable. In addition, a brief design document, as described in [Laramée02] and discussed as the Game Overview Document in [Onder02], serves as the basis for pre-production work. This typically includes several paper and electronic mockups depicting key moments in gameplay to give the feel of the game and the player's interactions.

Stage 2: Pre-Production

With a clear, high-level set of ideas in hand, you're ready to expand the team and start putting meat on the conceptual bones for the game. During pre-production, you'll take the overall game concept, iterate on it in more detail to create the design, create an actual playable demo of the game, and prepare for full-scale production in the next stage. The ultimate goal of this stage is twofold: first, to produce a small but playable version of the game that demonstrates the eventual game experience; and second, to provide enough design, art, and technical detail that no huge questions are left hanging at the start of production. Be careful to give this stage the time it deserves. As shown in Figure 5.1.1, you can expect that an effective pre-production stage will take up to 25% to 30% of the overall time allotted for the project, or up to about six or seven months on a two-year project.

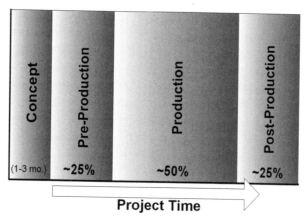

FIGURE 5.1.1 *The stages of game development and the approximate duration of each.*

Participants

This stage of development is led primarily by the game designer and producer. However, during pre-production, you should start adding to the leadership of the team and begin getting contributions from the technical lead, art lead, quality assurance, and in some cases specialized leadership for areas such as sound and music, 3D, database, or server technology. You might also want to add some assistants in areas such as production or design, but be careful to build the team from the top down (or center outward)—you want to encourage bonds between those who will lead the effort for the rest of the development process, and to make sure they understand the game's focus and progress better than anyone else. It's probably going to take time for you to find the right people to add as leaders on the project and for them to come up to speed, but in the meantime, the designer and producer should be working on their pre-production deliverables.

Process

The main point of pre-production is to take the initial concept and build it up. You and your team need to understand what is going to be needed to implement the game, and those outside your team need to understand (and believe in) what you're developing. The first and main part of this is what [Cerny02] calls "macro design." This involves fleshing out the original idea, focusing first on the game systems that will be required, and eventually working down to the details ("micro design") of individual characters, opponents, objects, levels, and player actions. Macro design also includes creating fast, nonfunctional mockups and working prototypes to demonstrate gameplay, camera, and user interface designs, as well as setting the art and sound style direction. These mockups and prototypes are a great way to try out ideas quickly within the team, report progress to management or publisher, and to get early player feedback (looking for comprehension and interest).

Creating the design, mockups, prototypes, and early art begins a process of *convergent iteration* that lasts throughout pre-production and production. Convergent iteration is based on the spiral model of software development [Boehm88] and a number of different rapid development models [McConnell96]. As shown in Figure 5.1.2, you're going to iterate on the main ideas in your game during pre-production—defining them, designing them, implementing prototypes, evaluating them (and having a few players do so), and then starting over, but this time using what you've learned to converge on your goal. The idea in game development is to start with a general concept and home in on an optimal mix of fun and feasibility. By taking the time to do up-front conceptual and pre-production design work, you cover a lot of ground quickly and cheaply, and spend the rest of the project fine-tuning your solution rather than casting about late in development, hoping to find something in it that's fun.

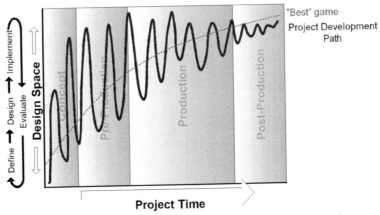

FIGURE 5.1.2   *The process of convergent iteration shown over the stages of game development. Note that the upward strokes are define—design— implement, while the downward strokes are evaluation phases. The number of phases shown will vary by project, and is not meant to be taken literally.*

Convergent iteration also makes it easier to spot design, technology, and process risks. For example, as shown in Figure 5.1.3, without a clear game concept, or with churning external requirements, you can find your project stuck iterating in a cycle, covering the same ground over and over again instead of converging on an optimal gameplay solution. Alternatively, you might rush into production too quickly, and end up exploring the gameplay space later in the process when it is much more expensive and you are already beholden to early ideas that might hobble your game (see Figure 5.1.4).

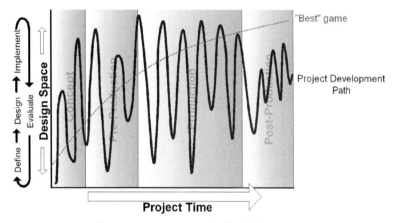

FIGURE 5.1.3   *In some cases you might find that your project is not converging on a single game. This can happen if you did not start with a clear concept, or if external requirements change throughout the life of the project.*

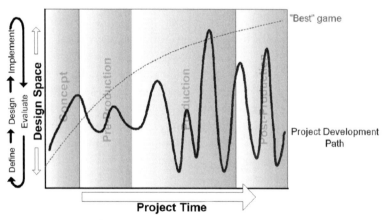

FIGURE 5.1.4   *If you race into production too quickly, you might find your project wandering through the conceptual space in the late (and expensive) stages.*

Many projects never leave the concept or pre-production stages—these are a lot of fun, and moving on requires commitment and making difficult decisions. Alternatively, some projects barely touch on the conceptualization and ramp up fast to production. This inevitably leads to having a lot of assets (art, code, sound) on hand that might get used somehow, and bits and pieces that hopefully will fit together to make a fun game. In either case, it's easy to find yourself late in the schedule with all the ingredients of an actual game, but for some reason it isn't coming together.

The best way to avoid this is to be rigorous about these first two stages of development, and avoid the illusion that being "in production" means you know what you're doing. The gate from pre-production to production should be the most stringent of all. If the game isn't going to be fun, you should know it—and admit it—by the end of pre-production, rather than hoping that your earlier vague idea will somehow turn into something worthwhile.

Deliverables

The output of pre-production is a set of documents, prototypes, and in almost all cases a small but working version of the game. This playable demo, often called a "first playable," might present only a sliver of the eventual game, and yet it contains enough to give nonteam members (i.e., management, publishers) a solid experience of what the game will be. It should also demonstrate the main aspects of the art style and the UI and interactivity style (that is, whether the game is menu-driven, a click-fest, turn-based, etc.). The ability to produce this working game, and to show that there are no major design, technical, or artistic questions remaining open is a clear signal that the team is ready to move into production.

In addition to producing the pre-production documents and playable game, it's also useful to revisit with the team (by now including more programmers, artists, designers, and others who are ready to dive in) the initial overview statement and high-level product goals. It's crucial that before the team enters the "fog of war" known as production that they all understand clearly what the game is and what it isn't. There should be no misunderstandings, no hidden agendas, and no gaps in the design large enough that there is any difference of opinion as to why the game is fun and for whom. Establishing this early on—and reviewing it periodically during production—will prevent many crises on the team and much lost work in the project.

The pre-production documents are more internally than externally focused, although the producer might need to create a marketing-driven document as well. These documents also act in conjunction with the earlier conceptual documents, which might have to be adjusted to reflect changes that have occurred during pre-production. The main documents describe the game from design, art, and technical perspectives in sufficient detail that they can act as a blueprint for assembling the rest of the team and setting production schedules and milestones. They each also outline any significant risks or unresolved issues that remain when going into production.

The pre-production macro design document treats the game design in more depth than the conceptual overview. It includes the main player interactions and the major gameplay systems (NPC AI, level types, combat, magic, inventory, unit types, etc.), but does not yet dive into the details of the systems that are outlined. While it's likely that you'll have actually done some detail design work within each of the main game systems during pre-production (to prove to yourselves that the systems can work, and to add substance to the "first playable" version), keep these separate from the macro design document. The point here is to answer the question, "what is the game?" or "what are we building and why is it fun?" without getting lost in details.

The technical counterpart to the macro/pre-production design document is written by the lead programmer (or engineering manager, technical director, etc.—the titles vary). This document is often called a "technical design" document, as it mirrors the macro design document for the overall game. It outlines the software architecture that will be built during production, highlights any preexisting software that will be used (homegrown or third-party), and references coding standards and source control standards. Any issues regarding these areas should be worked out during pre-production so that the technical team can start to focus on producing robust code and not on which tools will be used. Like the macro design document, the technical design document does not delve into the minutia of the systems to be implemented; it is enough to understand what pieces are going to be needed, how they need to communicate, and where the major unknowns and risks lie. This is necessarily a technical document, and yet the other project team leaders—the producer, designer, art lead, and so forth—should grasp it at least well enough to understand whether it is going to cause significant problems elsewhere on the project.

The lead artist creates an art design document, and often an audio guidebook that parallels the technical pre-production document. This covers the overall art style for the project, presents both inspirational and technical conceptual art, and discusses issues of color usage, camera use, lighting, the look of the user interface, and so forth. While a full art asset list is not typically possible when entering production, an asset creation, naming, and control policy should be included with the document, along with a list that will grow into the full asset list. This list should include the major environments, characters, objects, opponents, and so forth, based on the macro design document. An on-going task during production will be adding items to this list and maintaining it; keeping this up to date and the art integrated with the code all along the way will avoid much heartache later in production.

Finally, during pre-production the lead quality assurance (QA) person should create an overall test and integration plan for the project. This is based on the technical and art plans, and will follow them as their schedules become more detailed. It is not a substitute for unit testing by the programmers, but provides a centralized plan for making sure that all bugs are tracked, systems integrated and project builds confirmed, and all art and sound assets are in place. QA plans like this are often one of the first things that project leaders eliminate in a production time crisis, but their absence can become a major source of trouble later on.

Armed with the first-playable version of the game, a clear statement of what the game is, some early player commentary (from both initial mockups and the playable demo), and the design, technical, and art documents, the team is ready to get the final deliverable to move from pre-production to production: the greenlight from management or the publisher. If any of these items don't stand up, if there are too many issues outstanding, or if the game just doesn't feel fun, then the team should go back and hammer it all out until it does work. Until that happens, sending some part of the team off to start creating art or to start working on the software is more likely to create problems later than anything else—and could just represent expensive, wasted work if the game never quite makes it out of pre-production.

Stage 3: Production

In many game projects, being "in production" is considered to be really working—the game is becoming real. While it's true that it's in this stage of development that code, art, and sound are emerging, if you've handled the concept and pre-production stages appropriately, the game should already be feeling real to the team. Production becomes about implementation that stays true to the concept, macro design, and art direction decided on earlier, and on executing minor course corrections as needed.

The production stage typically takes the lion's share of the project's time—50% or more, or a full year out of a two-year project. Nevertheless, if you've prepared well during the pre-production stage, this stage need not turn into a crisis-filled death march toward an ever-receding goal.

Process

During production, the design, technical, art, and sound teams need to work closely together based on their common vision. There will always be some give and take, problems that must be solved, but as long as this happens within the context of the game concept and design already created, the team and the project will stay on track. During this stage, the focus shifts from design to the technical and artistic implementation. That doesn't mean that design is left with nothing to do—they still have a great deal of detail design work and balancing to take care of as the technical and art teams deliver the software infrastructure and game features.

The technical team's first task, working with the producer, is to lay out a high-level schedule for delivery of program components based on the design document that was delivered as part of pre-production. This schedule typically takes the form of high-level milestones that occur once every four to six weeks—shorter than that and there's not enough time for significant progress, and much longer than that and the team's focus can be lost. During each milestone period, the process of detail design, implementation, integration, and evaluation will take place with one or more major systems or gameplay features. In many cases, these overlap, so that one system is in final integration and evaluation at the end of a milestone, while another is scheduled to be done with its first pass of implementation, and another is scheduled to have its detail design complete.

However, a detailed schedule cannot with any degree of certainty be created in advance for the entire duration of the project. Instead, it's best to plan in complete detail for the current and next milestone, and to make one of the current milestone's deliverables a similar list of the contents of the next two. Further out than that, the milestones should have high-level goals based on the design, art, and software needs.

The order of implementation is different on each project. This is something best left to the technical lead to decide, working in conjunction with the producer and other team leaders. One important factor is to ensure that the software architecture is as robust as possible, but without leaving the rest of the team unable to proceed or play the developing game. After the first playable version, the game should never "go dark" or become unplayable. Making separate prototypes and code branches helps preserve the programming team's flexibility while enabling others to make progress in their areas.

While the technical team is creating the main software systems for the game, the art and design teams are revisiting in detail their earlier macro designs. Now each monster, vehicle, object, animation, environment, and attribute must be examined and reduced to numbers for the designers, and models and pixels for the artists. Communication and integration are key, so that the designers do not, for example, create 10 types of alien troops while the artists create models for only three. Each type of object that will appear in the game is designed in complete detail, including what makes its contribution to the gameplay different from any others, what animations it has and commands it responds to, and its specific attributes (or range of attributes) relevant to the game. This should all be included in a descriptive single-page-per-object type, and the necessary model entries should be added to the art and sound asset lists.

As each asset type is designed, it should also be prototyped and tested in game, evaluated for its appearance and effect on gameplay, and changed (via iterative design/implementation) as needed. This iteration will go much faster if the game objects are data-driven; that is, they receive their attributes from a text-based data file that is easily changed by the designers. If instead the designers have to pass each change to the programmers, progress will be much slower. Note too that "tweaking" game-object attributes is an on-going process, not a one-time activity. To make sure the game is balanced, various object attributes will have to be changed, tried in-game, and changed again. This process lasts throughout the production stage.

Milestones

Most complex game projects live by development milestones as mentioned earlier. These are typically set up by the producer in conjunction with the technical, design, and art team leaders, and often with significant pressure from external management. If the concept and pre-production stages have gone well, the main point of these milestones will be to show that the game is developing as planned, that the necessary game elements are being implemented in a timely fashion, and that the team is not drifting off target. It's easy to indulge in late-stage design, to want to include a new nifty feature someone thought of, or even to take the game in a new direction. Each of these is extremely risky, however, so realistic milestones based on the pre-production plans help the team stay focused and reduce or eliminate these risks.

Each milestone should demonstrate a visible new capability, preferably in the gameplay. Even when the main progress is technical or graphical, this should be expressed in terms of making the game more fun—if a new particle effect doesn't make the game more fun, you should question why your team is spending time on it. However, sometimes at a milestone the game will seem less fun than before. This is important to evaluate carefully: is it less fun because a new system isn't fully implemented, because there's a missing part of the user interface, or because some new objects have thrown off the game balance? All of those are easily evaluated and fixed. However, it might be that the game has become less fun because it's grown too large, tedious, or repetitive. If this seems to be the case, you need to quickly consider where the design or implementation went wrong—you might need to add features or objects, or more likely cut some out.

Stage 4: Post-Production

The end of production is often not as clear as its beginning. The team has worked hard for months, perhaps more than a year, and sometimes it seems the end will never come. But at some point, the project either grinds to a halt under its own weight—not the end you want to see—or it reaches that point when the tasks of producing the necessary software, art, and sound can be called complete—which is not the same as saying the game is finished.

The post-production stage consists of two main milestones that focus on evaluating, fixing, and polishing the game prior to release. This stage can take up to 20% to 30% of the overall project duration, depending on the complexity of the project and on how effective the concept and pre-production stages were. In general, complex multiplayer games need to plan on spending more time in this stage than do more linear single-player games.

Alpha

As development proceeds, the number of unimplemented systems and game features diminishes. There is a milestone, often both loved and feared by the development team, when all the initial features for the game have been created; no art or sounds are missing; and the user interface functionality is complete. This point is sometimes referred to as "feature complete" and is often called the *alpha* milestone. On a well-designed, well-run project, this point is loved because it means the game is *there*—even though significant work remains to be done. At the same time, it's feared because inevitably, cuts have been made to the original concept (primarily during pre-production) and everyone has a pet feature they would love to see put into the game before it is considered complete. On a poorly conceived, crisis-ridden project, the alpha milestone is dreaded because it often represents a point of maximum anxiety and even denial: the game isn't done because the design hasn't been implemented, it's considered complete because there is no more time in the schedule or money in the budget to actually make the game as originally planned.

While the game might be "feature complete," the team's work is far from over. The gameplay is there, but it is hampered by bugs both serious and superficial, and by a variety of balance issues between in-game units or objects. It is important, however, that after the alpha milestone, during all the testing and bug fixing to come, that no new features are implemented without significant oversight from the entire team leadership, and often from management outside the team. The temptation to add a new feature can be strong, but this presents a high risk of delaying the game's eventual release. It can also be tempting to only sketch out the functionality required by a feature or software system earlier in the project, and to call the missing functionality a "bug" to be finished after alpha. This type of dissembling action might save the schedule in the short term, allowing the team to appear to be on schedule at an earlier milestone, but only at the cost of requiring more time and increased risk later in the project, when the costs of failure are higher.

After the alpha milestone, the team should regroup and then begin fixing bugs in order of priority as established by the QA team and their test plans. The design team should focus on gameplay pacing and balance issues, and if necessary on creating additional levels or environments using the existing feature set. This will involve playing the game over and over again, looking for rough spots to be smoothed over via technical, artistic, or design balancing means.

It is during this time that gameplay testing and evaluation using regular players (*not* team members or members of other teams) should begin in earnest. During preproduction, early mockups and prototypes should have been given exposure to players to look at for interest and comprehension—is the game going to be fun and will players understand it? During production, gameplay testing of individual levels, modules, or systems also helps hone the design and keep implementation on track. Now, with the entire game in place, full gameplay testing begins in earnest. This is the best way there is to find surprising bugs, gameplay flaws, obscure in-game goals, misleading art, and so forth. All of the findings from this gameplay testing are fed back into the plan for fixing bugs, art, and design issues.

Once the alpha version of the game has been created, the team will need sufficient time to create and polish any remaining levels or environments out of existing assets, fix up these assets, and fix bugs found during testing. This is typically on the order of half as long as the entire pre-production stage, or about 10% to 15% of the total time needed to complete the project.

Beta

Once all the objects, environments, gameplay systems, and user interface have been completed, evaluated by players, and any problems fixed, the game is finally nearing completion. This is often called "going into beta" or hitting the beta release. During this time, the game is opened up to more players for testing, finding bugs, and gameplay evaluation. The entire team should be hunting down and selectively fixing or documenting any bugs found. As time goes on and the game nears its final release, changing any aspect of the code, art, or sound should require increasing oversight to prevent the last-minute creation of a devastating new bug. The design team should be listening to player evaluations and making final tweaks to the gameplay pacing and balance based on their comments.

In addition, the producer and other staff need to be making final preparations for manufacturing, packaging, distribution, and marketing. These activities are typically outside the scope of the game development process itself, but are nonetheless extremely important and time consuming.

In games with a significant online presence, such as massively multiplayer online games, all the aspects of the service side of the game—in many respects as large and complex as the initial game development process—need to be brought up to speed. Typically, there is a "live" team that will maintain and extend the design and game systems once it is up and running. During the alpha and beta periods, this team should be assembled to provide continuity with those members of the original team who are moving on to other projects. There are also significant activities surrounding billing, customer service, in-game help, and other parts of the on-going online service. Each of these presents new challenges that differ from anything seen thus far in the development process.

The time required for an effective beta period will differ from project to project, but it is typically about as long as the alpha period. At a minimum, the beta period needs to be long enough to have players evaluate the game on their own, report back problems, have the team make the necessary fixes, and have the game evaluated again. This is rarely shorter than six to eight weeks, and might last several months.

Gold Master

Finally, the day arrives when all the aspects of the game have been balanced, all the necessary bugs have been fixed, the animations and sounds are timed perfectly—the game is ready to be frozen in the form of a "gold master" CD-ROM for shipment. Alternatively, this day arrives because of the lead time necessary to get the game to magazines for review and through manufacturing, packaging, and distribution in time for the holiday sales rush. Ready or not, the game goes to gold master.

As you can imagine, this can be both thrilling and frightening, depending on how many and how severe the known bugs are that remain unfixed. In many cases, the team steams right on past the gold master date, with any additional fixes or changes being put into a post-release patch available from the company's Web site. This, however, is an implicit admission that the project got away from the team, and that what is shipped is not as polished and playable as it should be. Your goal should instead be to be able to have a release party (the true end to the development process) without any overshadowing issues or anxieties about whether the game is complete.

Conclusion

Game development is a complex, difficult, risky undertaking. You can best reduce the complexity and risk at any given point in your project by having a solid team, a clear and compelling concept, and by following an effective development process. The stages discussed in this article—concept, pre-production, production, and post-production—should help you understand how a game project progresses and how to allocate your time and activities.

In addition to parceling out your time and focus while developing your game, these stages highlight the reality that in any complex game project, many different areas of expertise are required to bring the game to a strong finish—game design, programming, art, sound, QA, and production among them. Convergent iterative development that makes the best use of each of these domains will result in the best, fastest finish for your project.

Another way of saying this is in this formula I wrote several years ago when trying to explain the different skills needed to complete a game project:

- An idea is not a design.
- A design is not a demo.
- A demo is not a program.
- A program is not a product.
- A product is not a business.
- A business is not profits.
- And profits are not happiness.

It's tempting to jump from the beginning to the end—from an idea to profits and happiness—in one fell swoop. However, the reality is that you have to go through each part of the process, each of the stages of development, to get to the goal at the end.

References

[Boehm88] Boehm, B. W., "A Spiral Model of Software Development and Enhancement," *IEEE Computer* (May 1988): pp. 61–72.

[Cerny02] Cerny, M., and John, M., "Game Development Myth vs. Method," *Game Developer* (June 2002): pp. 32–36.

[Kelley01] Kelley, T., *The Art of Innovation*, DoubleDay, 2001.

[Laramée02] Laramée, F. D., "Writing Effective Design Treatments," *Game Design Perspectives*, Charles River Media, 2002.

[McConnell96] McConnell, S., *Rapid Development*, Microsoft Press, 1996.

[Onder02] Onder, B., "Writing the Adventure Game," *Game Design Perspectives*, Charles River Media, 2002.

[Rodgers01] Rodgers, P., and Mencher, M., "The ABC's of Running a Development Project," available online at *www.gignews.com/abcpart1.htm*, 2001.

[Tomayko95] Tomayko, J. E., "Managing Software Development," available online at *www-2.cs.cmu.edu/~SW_Managemnt*, 1995.

Managing the Development Process

Tom Sloper

tomster@sloperama.com

The more projects you manage and survive, the more you learn about doing the job well. This article outlines the development processes learned from producing 56 unique titles, and numerous localizations, ports, and other projects.

The Secret, Part I: Plan the Unplannable

The real key to finishing on time should be obvious: you have to start with a realistic schedule. Plan for everything that has to be done, determine which things depend on which other things, and adjust the plan to make sure that the schedule is in fact feasible.

Let's go over the planning for a game project in detail by breaking the project down into three phases: pre-production, production, and post-production.

Pre-production is the phase in which the design is written and signed off, and in which the technology decisions are made. This is also when the schedule and budget are determined, and when the producer does the planning for the other two phases.

Production is the phase during which the programmers are busily coding, the artists are creating, the music and audio are created, and you go into a studio to record voice talent or to shoot acting talent.

Post-production is the phase in which you test and fine-tune the game, and get the box, manual, and other paper materials (customarily referred to as "box and docs") made.

The Snowball

Producing a game is like building a giant snowball, rolling it down a long mountain, and trying to hit a target at the bottom of the mountain with it.

The pre-production phase is fairly easy—you're just making a fairly small snowball, so it's easy to push it toward the target and to control its direction. During the production phase, you jog alongside the snowball as it rolls and grows, and it isn't hard to nudge it now and again if it rolls off course. The post-production phase is the one where trouble can really happen. The snowball is really big and heavy. You're tired from all that jogging to keep up with the snowball, and now you're breathing hard, your legs feel like logs, the ball is going faster than ever, and it's really hard to affect the ball's direction. Any missteps or planning errors you made in the earlier phases are harder to correct in the crucial post-production phase.

Pre-Production

Pre-production sets the tone and the pace for the rest of the project. Any shortcuts you take in this phase will haunt you later. It is vital to plan everything now. The process of planning together with the development team becomes a habit, and makes it easier to change the plan when emergencies arise. In pre-production, the producer must plan every aspect of production, post-production, and beyond.

Design

Before you can do anything else, you have to know what it is you're planning to make. In the film industry, producers start with a script and then develop a storyboard. In our industry, we have to start with a detailed design document. (At least, that's the way it's done in the West; as we will see, Japanese companies work differently.) The design has to describe all the game's features in sufficient detail, so that the technical people and the art director can estimate how long it will take to implement.

However, you can't simply set your designer to work on writing a document, then reach over his shoulder, grab it, and ship it to the technical director and art director. Before getting firm estimates on it, you need to make sure that this design will be acceptable to your marketing people, salespeople, and company executives, and, if it's a console game, your console manufacturer. Consensus is vital in the early stages. Especially, plan on making sure that this design is acceptable to your licensor.

Licensor Issues

Many successful games today are licensed games—games based on an existing intellectual property, be it owned by an external party or by your company. If you are developing a game based on an outside party's property, you have to include that party in the process early on.

The final approval is the most important, of course. It should go smoothly if you've been getting approvals in earlier stages. You don't want to spring a previously unseen, now-finished game on your licensor!

We made the mistake of not involving Columbia Pictures early in the development of *Ghostbusters II* for the NES in 1989. We just sent our contact the finished game, expecting an automatic signoff. He was not happy, and although he did approve the game, it could have been a disaster.

Another close call: Activision had created the early *Alien* and *Predator* games under license from Twentieth Century Fox in the late 1980s. When Dark Horse Comics came out with *Aliens vs. Predator,* we got the rights to do games based on the combined license.

Activision went through some dramatic changes during the interim, and we inherited the projects long after the license had been acquired; the producers who had started the ball rolling were no longer with the company. We had sublicensed the rights to Japanese publishers, who funded development on the SNES and Game Boy. Then, we would take the finished Japanese version, localize for the United States, and release domestically. The problem was that the Japanese developer (like most game developers in Japan) was not in the habit of writing detailed design documents to begin a project. After repeated requests, they delivered an outline, which was taken to Fox for approval. That wasn't easy, because the document raised more questions than it answered. Eventually, we got approval to get the Japanese versions released. How-ever, when we wanted the American versions approved, there was a whole new battle to fight because the game had changed significantly since the outline was submitted. The games ended up not being very good, and sold well only because of the license.

After this near disaster, Fox formalized the approval process. They developed a standardized form that would be used for each approval submission. The form indi-cated whether the material being submitted was code, packaging, manual, or advertis-ing materials. The form indicated whether the approval sought was for text, visuals, or functionality. In addition, the form had spaces where the approver could indicate rea-sons for denial, or comments about changes that were needed for approval to be granted. If your own licensor doesn't use such a formal approval process, you should work one out together.

Internal Licenses

Sometimes, the intellectual property belongs to your own company rather than to an external party. In such cases, there might be someone in your company who is the brand assurance person—the keeper of the flame for that intellectual property. Work with this person the same way you would work with an external licensor. Set up an approval process together; plan for the stages at which approvals will be needed, and schedule accordingly.

Technology

You have to trust your technical people and their ability to estimate the time it will take to accomplish the tasks. They have to create a detailed task list, based on your detailed design document, and plan for whatever learning is required to implement the game's features. If you're using acquired technology, have your team look at the documentation and talk to the people providing the technology. Is it well docu-mented? Are their people going to be able to support it adequately for your peoples' needs?

On *Shanghai Second Dynasty*, we knew that we were going to have to implement online play, but our external developer, Quicksilver, wasn't going to do it—we were going to have in-house staff take care of that portion, because then the technology would be compatible with the rest of our online game servers.

One little problem we didn't anticipate was that the programmer who had created the online technology would be leaving the company before getting to this project. In addition, "online gaming" had become a buzzword, and numerous game-related dot-coms were trying to convince us to put our games on their sites. The hesitations and negotiations cost us a week at the end of the production. A week doesn't sound like much, but because of that week, the game was not on the shelves over the Thanksgiving weekend.

Marketing

Marketing will be crucial to the game's success, so you have to work together with your publisher's marketing staff to get them everything they need. Moreover, they have to be sensitive to the fact that once you have planned the project, any changes they introduce to the plan have to be reasonably small, or else the schedule will change. Develop a good line of communication with your marketing people. Patiently educate them on the process.

Demos

One of the most significant marketing needs is the demo disc.

It's usually desirable to release the demo before (not after) releasing the game itself. Therefore, work out a schedule with the marketing department and the technical director. With marketing, figure out when the demo needs to be ready, and what needs to be in it. With your technical director, make sure that the plan is feasible.

A reminder: we're still talking about pre-production planning here. We're talking about the planning stage, many months before the game itself (or the demo) will be ready.

Marketing folks often don't plan and create on the same type of timetable that we do—their lead times are much shorter and they're not engineers, so they just don't see things the same way production teams do. It sometimes happens that, after agreeing on a demo spec and schedule, someone in marketing requests changes to the demo—invariably, changes that can't be implemented without affecting the schedule.

The best you can do in such a case is to patiently reiterate that the demo will contain what was previously specified and agreed, and that it will be delivered when previously specified and agreed. Any major changes to the specs and the timing of the demo might have serious repercussions for the release date of the game itself. Sometimes a producer has to be a teacher as well as a manager and communicator.

The demo will also have to meet requirements set by magazines and/or by the Webmaster of your publisher's Web site. Find out what those requirements are well in advance. Usually, the demo has to be limited to a certain size, because there will be other demos on the disc, or to keep download times to a minimum, or to fit within server limits. Find out in advance what these requirements are so you won't experience delays—and expect those requirements to change if too much time elapses.

Also keep in mind that demos have to go through quality assurance just like everything else. Work with your QA people to plan for the demo, and then see if you can get the same testers to work on the final game.

Material for Magazine Covers and Previews

You might also have to provide material for magazine previews and even cover art to your marketing team. Cover art has to be very detailed, and will have to allow space for the magazine's title and feature blurbs and insets. When marketing asks you for graphics for cover art, ask them to get a guideline sheet from the target magazines; all magazines have this ready at hand. Specifically, you need to know the image size requirements and the appropriate resolution in dots per inch, so that you won't lose any time redoing the artwork.

Not only do you want your image on the cover, you also want screen shots inside the magazine. You will want covers and pages in other magazines too—and no two magazines will use the same image.

You also need to be prepared to have editors visit your team, watch over their shoulders while they create the game, and interview your programmers and/or artists. You might even have to fly to the magazine's office and demo the game yourself. Demands for this type of thing typically happen at the most inconvenient time. Be ready. Plan for it.

Strategy Guides

If there's going to be a strategy guide for your game, it needs to be on the store shelves on the same day as the game itself—which means, again, the issue will come up exactly when the project can least afford it. Your lead designer and/or writer, and your art director will be needed for this effort. Find out in advance about the lead times for making strategy guides, and plan them into the schedule.

Trade Shows

When preparing your schedule, circle the dates of trade shows like E3 and figure out how advanced your game will be on those dates. It sometimes happens that the game will not yet be showable, or that the company will not need it to be displayed at a particular trade show. However, if the game is going to be showable at E3 time, you need to plan ahead for the team to do whatever work is necessary to prepare an E3 demo.

Voice and Acting Scripts

You need completed scripts before you can even schedule studio time. Recording sessions are expensive, so you must make a solid estimate of how many days you need to spend in the studio.

Thus, you can only plan for this once the game is far enough along that you can be sure you didn't miss any crucial scenes or lines. Consequently, timing the studio session into the schedule is a tricky balance. Do it too early, and you might need pickup sessions later. Do it too late, and your ship date might suffer.

Voice or Acting Talent

Add into the schedule when you want to have your studio session. Then, work it backward—before you can have a studio session, you need the talent lined up. Before this can happen, you need auditions. Figure out how long those will take, and plan them in. Before you can have auditions, you need to know who your characters are and what their lines are. You have to be able to describe the characters to the talent agents so they can describe them to the actors.

Studio Sessions

The studio session itself probably won't be very long—a few days, usually. Plan into the schedule when you need to start looking for studios, when you need the studio time, and for your engineers to be there. Your engineers probably won't be doing the actual recording (unless you have your own internal studio facilities), but they need to be there to provide technical guidance on formats and documentation of the recordings made. Then, after the studio session is over, your engineers need to get and process the assets, and deliver them to the production team in the required formats for the main SKU and for any ports you'll be making. Work it all into the schedule.

Executive Greenlight Reviews

Pinpoint the dates in the schedule when the project will hit critical decision points. When the game is at first playable, alpha, and beta, the executives will need to look at it so they can determine if it's on track.

Sometimes, market changes will mandate modifications to the plan. This is what these reviews are for. If you don't plan for them in the schedule, the change requests are likely to come anyway, but at less convenient times. It's better to know in advance.

Console Manufacturer's Approval Cycle

If you're making a game for Xbox, PlayStation 2, Game Cube, or Game Boy Advance, then you have a contact at Microsoft, Sony, or Nintendo. That contact is someone with whom you need to develop a relationship. Discuss your plans and generally keep your contact in the communications loop. Get approval for the game's concept early on, in pre-production. In addition, make sure that your technical folks and your QA department have the console manufacturer's technical requirements.

When your game is looking pretty good and robust, ask your contact if he or she is interested in seeing it. You want the console manufacturer to be enthusiastic about your game.

Don't wait until the last minute to submit your game to the console manufacturer for final approval. Pre-submit if possible. Familiarize yourself with the criteria for approval; check everything you can beforehand.

In final approval, the console manufacturer will nearly always find something for you to change or fix. Figure that you might have to submit three times, and plan accordingly. The manufacturer's representative can probably tell you how long each submission will take—maybe two or three weeks. It's possible that it'll take even longer—talk to your contact, ask about horror stories. You'll hear plenty! Keep your QA lead apprised of your communications in this regard.

The "Box & Docs" Process

Printed materials take longer to manufacture than discs do. It makes a lot of sense to create the box and the manual early in the production phase. However, the creative department usually is under the supervision of someone else, not the producer, and they probably have to get to this at the latest possible date. As for the manual, you might want it written at the last possible minute to incorporate any last-minute changes resulting from QA testing. This, like the studio sessions, is a tricky thing to time. Work with your marketing counterpart to plan this into the project as best you can.

Operations

Work with operations (the folks who get the product manufactured) to make sure that the timing is known. Manufacturing lead times can vary depending on time of year; in September–October, all the game publishers are trying to manufacture at the same time. To make sure that your product gets put on operations' schedule, you'll have to convince them that your schedule is firm.

Shipping lead times have to be taken into account too, if you need the product to hit the shelves by a particular date.

The Quality Assurance Cycle

Don't short shrift the QA cycle. If your QA manager says it'll take eight weeks, then you must allocate eight weeks. Don't forget that QA will also have to approve the box and docs (including the system requirements, for PC games), the demo, the international versions, and the ports. As much as possible, you want the same testers involved on each.

International Versions

Simultaneous shipment worldwide (also known as "sim-ship") is always the goal. It's attainable. Plan it into the pre-production phase. The moment you freeze the script, send it off to be translated—maybe even sooner. Record the localized voices at the same time you do the domestic voices. Prepare the localized title screen graphics or logo as soon as the domestic title screen logo is frozen.

Original Equipment Manufacturer Versions

On *Shanghai Dynasty*, we received late word that we needed to make an OEM version. The business development person who had made the deal told us it had to be 100 MB, with no redbook music, and that it should not require a CD in the drive. He didn't tell us any of the other important details: that it needed to be delivered as a zip file, that the game would be pre-installed on the hard disk, that the zip file would be on a rescue disk, that it had to be done in two weeks or the deal was off. We found out all of that when we contacted the OEM customer. You can't predict everything. The best you can do when a new situation arises is to gather all the information you can and adapt your plans accordingly. As long as you have developed good planning practices and aren't already running behind, you're in a decent position to deal with new situations.

Ports

Asset packs are important for the porting process. When your art staff is finished creating everything, have them make a graphic asset pack—organized and documented so that the port team can easily make any new versions needed. When your tech staff is finished making the game, have them make a complete backup, with all files and path structures, and detailed instructions about how to make a build. Document all compiler switches, and provide information about what compiler to use. Make it easy for someone to pick up the asset pack and make a build of the finished game. After making the asset pack, unpack it onto a fresh computer and test it.

Production Phase

To this point, we've been discussing the pre-production planning for the production and post-production phases. We're past that now, and work has begun on production.

So, during the production phase, what can you do?

Keep performing reality checks. Talk to the technical people and the art staff frequently to make sure that everything is being done on schedule. When work falls behind, spend time together to figure out what you can do to make up for the delay. "We'll make it up in QA" are the last words you want to hear. Nobody makes up for it in QA and succeeds in the eyes of the customer.

Learn to recognize red flags. Anything that impacts your schedule has to be addressed sooner, not later. When anything crops up that looks like a danger to your schedule, you have to take immediate action. Incorporate it into the adapted plan.

Planning doesn't mean "sit down and think about it." Planning always has to be done in conjunction with the team. Discuss the red flag with your technical director, your art director, with QA and marketing. Keep everyone informed about the danger, and what's being done about it. Then, follow up with an update later. Are we back on schedule? Is the red flag becoming paler?

Don't forget marketing and the schedule for your demo; make sure marketing remembers what the schedule and spec are, and that changes are at the expense of the schedule. Stay on top of the release date with QA and operations. Make sure sales is clear on the ship date.

The Secret, Part II: Adapt, Improvise, and Overcome

During production, the ability to adapt, improvise, and overcome will prove to be of tremendous importance to the producer in his quest to keep the project moving forward—to keep the snowball moving toward the target at the bottom of the mountain.

Post-Production Phase

By the time you get to post-production, it's hard to be proactive in making significant improvements to a project that has fallen behind schedule. Remember that rolling snowball? It was small and easy to push around at the top of the hill, but now it's a huge heavy object, it's moving really fast, and you're tired from running alongside it all this time.

If you didn't do your planning right in pre-production, and if you didn't keep on track in production, you're going to have a hard time in post-production.

And After Release?

If you think the producer's job is done when the game ships, think again. Following up after release, to make sure that customers are satisfied, is crucial to the project's ultimate success. For more details on effective management of the after-market phase, see [Sloper02].

Conclusion

This article described how to plan the standard game development process. Of course, nonstandard events will creep into your projects, from marketing rethinks to design team mutinies and morale dips that impact productivity. However, as long as you maintain full command of the standard process and good lines of communication with all your team leaders, you can handle everything else that comes up.

By planning properly, you can increase your chances of finishing on time. In pre-production, anticipate and schedule everything—even subsequent ports and versions. Schedule approvals early. In production, if any red flags go up, work together with the team leaders to revise the plan.

Your particular project might have other requirements that weren't covered here—anticipate those, and plan for them. If your plan covers unplannable events and contingencies, chances are that your project will be a success.

References

[Sloper02] Sloper, Tom, "Following Up after the Game Is Released: It's Not Over When It's Over," *Game Design Perspectives*, Charles River Media, 2002.

5.3

Ways to Manage Creative Chaos

Heather Maxwell Chandler

heather@mediasunshine.com

Although making games is a creative endeavor, several "corporate" techniques are available to manage the development process without stifling creativity. Applying these techniques to a game development team provides effective ways to manage projects, manage people, build teams, communicate information, and conduct meetings. Additionally, these techniques are easily accessible to an inexperienced manager who suddenly finds himself in a leadership position on the team.

Managing Projects

Applying project management techniques to game development can bring some needed organization to the creative process. This article presents some of these techniques; [Lewis01] and [Wysocki03] provide more in-depth information.

Defining a Vision

At the start of the project, define the game's vision. If people don't understand what they are working on, it is hard for them to commit to the project and put forth their best effort. As discussed in [Lewis01], a vision "is what the final result of the team's efforts will look like [...] If everyone doesn't agree on the vision, each person will try to achieve the outcome he or she imagines, with disastrous results."

A unified vision can guide decisions about a game's feature set. For example, if the game's vision is, "create a fun puzzle game for cell phones that is easy to learn and takes 30 seconds to play," using audio cues might be inappropriate—the player may find it necessary to mute the phone while playing, and if the help feature uses audio content, learning to play will become very difficult. Ideally, the team should participate in the vision definition process; they will be more motivated if they have a vested interest in the game.

Outlining a Plan

A plan outlines a way to achieve the vision that has been defined. A series of questions relating to the schedule, budget, and scope need to be answered in order to create this plan; for example:

- Is all the work going to be done internally, externally, or a combination of both?
- Will specialists be needed for any area, or can everything be handled by generalists?
- How much money is needed?
- How many people are needed?
- What is the planned feature set?

Once a plan has been put to paper, the producer or lead has a tangible asset that can be used to track development progress. As [Lewis01] states: "if you have no plan, you have no control." A plan allows you to compare the project's current state with expectations; if they don't match up, corrective action can be taken to get the project back on track, such as cutting features, adding more people, or adding more time to the schedule. Keep in mind that taking corrective action does not guarantee getting the project back on track, especially if there is a large deviation between where the project is and where it is supposed to be.

Creating Schedules

Making a detailed list of the tasks to be completed and estimates of how long each will take is the core of the scheduling process. Even if dates and deliverables are shifting, the schedule's task list can be easily modified with an updated estimate of duration, ownership, and deadline.

For example, the section of the schedule that outlines how to build a level will list a breakdown of each task needed to do so. It may include creating a concept, creating a prototype in 3ds max, building basic geometry, creating textures, polishing the assets, and bug fixing. The important thing to note is that even though dates may change, the actual tasks to be completed usually stay the same, unless the feature is cut.

Tracking Schedules

Once each person has determined his schedule, all the schedules should be merged into a central schedule and tracked by someone on the team. There are several ways to track schedules, and each person will have a preferred method for doing so. One way is to print the schedule and post it in the team rooms. As tasks are completed, they are highlighted on the schedule—when the schedule is colored in, the project is completed. This is a strong visual aid to inform the team of their progress.

One thing is certain: the schedule will not track itself—someone will have to follow up with each team member on a regular basis and keep the schedule updated with everyone's work. Schedule changes must also be added to the schedule right away; otherwise, the person tracking the schedule will not have an accurate picture of where people are expected to be with their tasks.

The person in charge of tracking the schedule can make the job easier by communicating upcoming deadlines to the team. For example, e-mails can be sent to remind the team of critical milestones on the project and what work is expected to be completed. Keep the e-mails short and simple.

If people are not going to be ready for a critical milestone, have them tell you before it is too late. Most people are aware that they are behind schedule, but they always think they can catch up to meet a milestone. While this may be the case in some instances, it is still important to know about any delays ahead of time so contingencies can be prepared. For example, suppose that a milestone is coming up and the game is expected to be feature complete with placeholder content. You find out a week ahead of time that Artist A thinks he may not get his level completed. Since you know ahead of time, you can assign an extra resource to help him get back on track, or alter the testing schedule so that this particular level will be checked last in the testing cycle, buying the few extras days that are needed to complete the level.

CASE STUDY 5.3.1: SCHEDULING AND TRACKING

Wade Tinney, a founding partner of Large Animal Games, thinks that it is critical for the people on the team to create their own schedules. "It is useful for artists and programmers to go through the scheduling process and break things up into specific tasks," he says. "This holds them more accountable to the schedule because they create their own deadline, instead of having the deadline imposed on them by a producer. Additionally, this gets people to think specifically and critically about the things they have to do, before they actually do them."

Because Large Animal Games is a smaller company that works with external clients, scheduling and tracking is critically important. "Hard deadlines must be enforced when we work with a client. They expect us to be finished when we say we will be finished. We detail out every project milestone and deliverable list with the client before we begin work, and track these deliverables carefully. This benefits us as well, because if the client asks for extra work to be completed for a milestone, we have room to negotiate because we are being asked to deliver more than expected for the milestone."

Sam Lewis, a senior designer at Sony Online Entertainment, adds: "A developer is a craftsman first, he should know his trade well enough to say 'I can complete this task in three days.' By doing so, he is applying his knowledge and taking responsibility for the task."

Managing People

Game development is a young industry—both in the amount of time it has been around and in the age of the people involved. This is reflected in the sense of "immaturity" that is prevalent in development teams. There is a misconception by some employees and outsiders that working at a game company is all fun and games. While making games is fun, people are still expected to show up for work on time and be accountable for their work on the project.

Peter F. Drucker is considered one of the foremost experts on management, and has written on the subject of management for several decades. Drucker is a firm believer that people must be managed to their strengths and given opportunities to develop themselves in the workplace. [Drucker01] is a concise reference of his management philosophy and is recommended reading for anyone who wants to become a better manager. Topics discussed in this book include effective decision making, picking good people, knowing your own strengths and weaknesses, and many others that focus on how to be an effective people manager.

Choosing Good Leads

If a game developer has successfully shipped a few games, there is a tendency to assign him to a management position on future projects. The benefit of doing this is that an expert is readily available to offer technical or artistic guidance to team members. However, this person may not have any formal management training, and is suddenly expected to manage other people's tasks and schedules, effectively communicate expectations to the team, and interface with management on high-level issues. These are tasks this person may not even be interested in taking on. He may want to focus on strictly creating assets for the game.

The most effective *managers* should be leads on a project—these are people who are organized, work well with others on the team, have strong communication skills, and are respected by their peers. A lead does not have to be the most artistically talented or technically gifted person on the team. You want to keep these talents doing what they do best—creating high-quality assets for the game. If you move these high-quality content creators to lead positions, they don't have time to create content anymore. Because they are so busy managing instead of creating, the quality of the game content will be less than it can be.

CASE STUDY 5.3.2: TEAM MANAGEMENT

"Companies should have a production track and a management track available for each person," says Sony Online Entertainment's Sam Lewis. "If someone really likes managing and wants to be a lead, they should be provided with the training and opportunities to do so. However, people who are really good at creating con-

→

tent may not be good at managing people. They should be provided with alternative opportunities to progress in the company."

And what are the qualities of a good manager? "Good managers need a willingness to let go and accept change," says Lewis. "They also have to trust their team's judgment and let the team make decisions. The team wants to be treated respectfully and will respond accordingly."

Coray Seifert, a junior producer at Large Animal Games, believes that keeping people focused on the game vision will help them stay motivated. "Having a positive attitude about the game, even when situations are not ideal, is important. A great way to keep the team focused on the positive is to remind them how cool the game is going to be to the fans and consumers. The team gets enthusiastic when they can visualize the bigger picture."

To keep people motivated, Wade Tinney likes to give his staff as much responsibility as possible. "When someone gets involved in the project, I ramp up the amount of responsibility they have quickly, until I see a good mix of challenge and comfort. I have found that people work best when they have some challenge."

[Cambron05] discusses some additional easy ways to motivate and keep people happy on teams.

Training

Making people successful in their positions will likely require ongoing training. After all, people can't be expected to know everything. While there is an implied assumption that people have the ability to perform well on their assigned tasks, this does not mean that they can step into a new role (for example, as a lead) in the middle of a project without any difficulties. While a given person may have the innate ability to lead, he or she may need some coaching or training in basic people management skills, such as conflict negotiation or motivation, before becoming effective in this new role.

Some people are highly motivated self-developers and will find a way to get the training and information they desire. They will tell you what classes and books they need, they will ask questions, and they will ask others for performance feedback. Some people will need more guidance in determining what training and information they need, but it is important to find out what it is and to make sure they get it.

Building Teams

Large Animal Games' Coray Seifert remembers being an inexperienced producer working with an experienced team. "I knew that the best way for me to become part of the team was to establish a personal rapport with them. I went to lunch with them, asked them about their weekends, and played games with them after work. These were very simple things, but I quickly learned about the people I was expected to work with. Also, once the team learned more about me and what I brought to the project, they were able to respect and trust the decisions I made."

Some other simple team-building activities can have a positive effect as well. If there is time, cross-train people. Cross-training is the practice of training people in disciplines they haven't worked in before. For example, have an engineer shadow an artist for the day and learn how to create textures. Or send an artist to work in the QA department for the day and learn how to find bugs and enter them in the database. Once people walk a mile in someone else's shoes, they gain a greater appreciation for that person's contribution to the project.

Also, introduce everyone to each other on the team. Some game projects involve over 100 people; even if two developers have been working side by side for years, they may not know much about each other or their contributions to the project. Have a team meeting in which everyone introduces themselves and briefly states what they are working on. As people put faces to names and see who is responsible for which cool features in the game, they may start talking with people they've never interacted with on a personal level. This is what team building is all about.

Communicating Information

If asked, most people working on a project team are likely to say miscommunication and lack of communication are big issues. There are some simple techniques to improve the situation, but they are not silver bullets; improving communication requires constant effort throughout the development cycle.

Team Web Site

A team Web site is a valuable tool for communicating the game's vision. This Web site can contain the design documents, level mockups, character art, prototypes, and any other assets that explain what the game is and why people will have fun playing it. Keeping all this information in a centralized and accessible place makes it easy for people to get the information they need, when they are available to read it.

Find ways to keep people coming back to the team Web site. For example, note the days people are out of the office, post a weekly newsletter, detail upcoming milestones, and provide meeting schedules along with the minutes from the meetings. Additionally, post pictures of the team members and out-of-office contact information.

Maintaining the team Web site can take time, but is worth the investment. For example, when someone new starts on the team, he or she immediately gets pertinent project information from the Web site. Additionally, whenever marketing or management requests design documents or other project information, they can be directed to the relevant area of the Web site for the information.

Written Communication

During the course of a project, people send and receive a large number of e-mails and must prioritize them. One way to help them do this is to set up mailing lists. For example, create lists for design, art, engineering, the team, and so on. Be selective about who goes on which lists: the point of the lists is to reduce information overflow. Use informative subject headings so people can prioritize them. Keep e-mails short, to the point, and put the most important information at the beginning.

Don't rely on e-mail as your sole form of communication, because it is not particularly trustworthy. An e-mail message may get lost, overlooked, or read incompletely. If the information is critical, communicate it verbally first, and then send a follow-up e-mail.

Verbal Communication

Face-to-face communication is the preferred and most effective form of communication, especially if you are delivering bad news or need to get people motivated to meet deadlines. Face to face is more personal—people can read your body language, you are instantly available for questions, and people are *interacting with* you instead of *reacting to* you.

Additionally, if you communicate with people verbally, you are certain that they heard you and understood what you were asking—especially if you ask them to summarize what you've just communicated to them. It is a good idea to follow up any verbal communication with written communication. This reinforces the message and gives people something they can use to refresh their memory.

Running Meetings

Since meetings are a big part of game development—leads probably spend half their time in meetings—it is important that they be useful. Also, finding ways to make meetings shorter and more effective increases the time people can actually work on the project. This section discusses ways to improve your meetings' effectiveness; [Lewis01] has more.

Agenda

Before the meeting, define the agenda and clearly state the meeting's goals. For example, the goal could be to get more information on how the AI will work in the game, or the goal could be deciding on the game controls. (If you don't know why you are meeting, cancel!) Avoid meetings that combine gathering information and deciding on a course of action. Meetings like this are often frustrating because people will spend a lot of time in discussion mode and very little in decision mode, or vice versa.

Moderator

Appoint a moderator for each meeting. This person is responsible for keeping the meeting on track. The best moderator is someone with a neutral position on the topic discussed. This allows that person to focus on running the meeting smoothly, since he or she will not be involved in the discussion—except to redirect it if the participants get off track.

A good way to get started with moderating meetings is to assign time limits to each topic of discussion. If the meeting is scheduled to last 60 minutes and there are 10 items to be discussed, each topic should get about 5 minutes of discussion. If a topic runs over the allotted time limit, either table the discussion for another meeting, or if the topic is urgent, table the remaining topics for discussion another time. In either case, just remember to keep the meeting focused and on track—and don't forget to set some time aside at the beginning (to state the goals) and at the end (to state the conclusions and action items).

Minutes

Record the minutes of all meetings, no matter the size. How many times have you attended a meeting where decisions were made, and then nobody remembered what the final decision was or mistakenly remembered the wrong decision? Minutes create a record of the meeting and are readily available for future reference.

The minutes should record who was at the meeting, what the goals of the meeting were, what was discussed, what was decided, and what action items resulted from the meeting. A simple template can be put together and used for all meeting minutes. Assign a minute taker for each meeting. Like the moderator, this should be someone who is not involved in the meeting discussion. It is too distracting for participants in the meeting to stop the discussion to take down notes. The moderator and minute taker can usually be the same person. This role is a good learning experience for a junior person on the team and is a good way to train potential team members for leadership roles on future projects.

Action Items

Action items are a critical by-product of meetings. Often, during a meeting, it is discovered that additional tasks need to be performed in order to come to a resolution on the main topic. Record these tasks as action items in the meeting minutes. A table can be created at the end of the minutes that states the date the action item was entered, the resource assigned, the deadline, and the current status. Keep this table up to date and follow up with everyone on their action items.

Conclusion

This article presented a few techniques that can help manage some of the "creative chaos" that is part of game development. Simple things like recording meeting minutes, creating a team Web site, applying some basic project management techniques, or going to lunch with people can have a huge impact on the team morale and efficiency. Most of these techniques are also used in "corporate business" and prove to be effective there as well. This does not mean that creativity has to be stifled: effective management creates an environment where ideas can flow more freely and have a better chance of being heard.

References

[Cambron05] Cambron, M. and Chandler, H. M., "Leadership: The Making of Happy and Effective Teams," *Secrets of the Game Business*, 2nd Edition, Charles River Media, 2005.

[Drucker01] Drucker, P. F., *The Essential Drucker*, Harper Business, 2001.

[Lewis01] Lewis, J. P., *Project Planning Scheduling & Control*, 3rd Edition, McGraw-Hill, 2001.

[Wysocki03] Wysocki, R. K., *Effective Project Management*, 3rd Edition, Wiley Publishing, Inc., 2003.

5.4

Customer Support in Massively Multiplayer Online Games

Terri L. Perkins

terri@funcom.com

Customer service in an online game faces challenges that other service industries do not. Not only is the product always changing and "open" for business 24/7, its customers speak a variety of languages, come from extremely diverse demographic backgrounds and knowledge bases, demand top-of-the-line service for a product they are paying an average of less than 50 cents a day to use, and hold the representatives accountable for many things that are not in the game company's control. If you can imagine a large theme park with only a handful of paid employees and thousands of customers demanding changes to the rides, corrections to the weather, a refund for time they spent waiting in line, demanding the annoying person standing next to them be made to disappear, and complaining that something in the park's pavement is making their shoes slower than everyone else's, then you can imagine the challenges that plague online games.

The challenge then: to provide fair, quick, respectful, and consistent service 24 hours a day, 7 days a week in a dynamic world, to thousands of diverse people scattered around the globe, and to do this for a very nominal fee. Customer support, like your game, is not an end product but a process. Ole Schreiner, customer service manager at Funcom Inc., states:

"One of the most important factors in satisfying customers in an online game is to treat all customers with respect and having a customer service team that can fulfill the customers' needs regardless of the experience level the customer might have with online games."

CASE STUDY 5.4.1: THE IMPORTANCE OF CUSTOMER SERVICE

We asked Craig "Sillirion" Morrison, associate editor of IGN Vault Networks, to comment on the importance of customer service in a massively multiplayer online role-playing game.

"When it comes to reviewing a MMORPG, customer service can be very hard to quantify in the time traditionally given to playing the game before writing the review.

"However, as the genre has developed and more and more reviewers have acquired a firm grasp on the factors that make up a 'good' title, the developers' track record on the customer service front can have a very strong bearing. While the dynamics of online communities are such that a good reviewer will always try and temper the (often polarized) opinions of the gamers that populate message forums, you can't help but pick up on a developer's reputation on the customer service front when doing your research. Indeed, a reviewer can receive a very strong impression of the title before they even step into the game world themselves.

"Paying customers will naturally equate the standard of the customer service they receive to the overall quality of the title, regardless of the fact that the two are not actually related in any technical way. Therefore, if a developer has not invested in their customer support infrastructure, they risk biasing reviews to their detriment. While it is of course unreasonable to expect the developer to satisfy everyone all the time, it is relatively easy to gauge whether or not they have invested sufficiently to provide a reasonable level of customer service to the 'reasonable' majority of the paying audience.

"And since online worlds are subscription-based, ongoing service is an aspect that your average reviewer is not going to be able to separate from their opinion of the graphics, sound or gameplay mechanics when it comes to giving their overall impressions of the game."

Planning to Succeed

If a computer without Internet access is like a car with no fuel, a potential blockbuster online game without well-designed support is like a vehicle that only works in reverse. While no one dares to release a game to the public without painstakingly scrutinizing every artistic shot, line of code, and music score, it is amazing how many will open their doors to the masses completely unprepared to support the players. If one-fifth of the planning that went into the art, design, code, and marketing of online games went toward customer service, the woes that face today's games would be drastically reduced. Early on, during the development planning for the game, plan to implement the coding that will save you time, customers, and countless hours in the long run. Case Study 5.4.2 explains how to do this effectively.

CASE STUDY 5.4.2: PLANNING CUSTOMER SERVICE

While every game will require unique coding for their specific plans, game style, and design, a few elements are common across the board.

Naming: Ability to block offensive names, change names, avoid impostors, and so forth.

Disruption: Ability to silence, temporarily ban, and permanently ban disruptive players. Players need a way to block unwanted communications from each other, but not warnings from the support staff.

Exploits: Ability to check logs of player actions for traces of hacking.

Inventory: Ability to check a player's inventory.

Gameplay: Ability to find players, reach their locations easily, and move them within the game world.

Tracking: Ability to add comments to a player's file for easy viewing from within the game and track for most common causes of support calls. The top problems that are reported are where you need to make modifications in your system.

Reset: Ability to restore a player character's previous state after a problem.

Reward: Ability to grant bonuses to players.

Filtered views: Searchable views by rank, profession, time in game, and other criteria.

Help system: An easily alterable in-game help file system that can be modified as changes occur.

Call: A way for players to request customer service assistance, both in-game and otherwise.

Communication: Secure message boards for player/staff exchanges.

NPC control: A way to create, resurrect, or remove nonplayer characters.

Reporting: Methods for players to report bugs and submit feedback.

Billing and technical assistance: Access to accounting records and a technical problem resolution database.

Make sure you have these functions tested and ready to work on opening day, and extra support staff or plans in place to deal with upgrades, expansions, and new releases.

Policies and Consistency

For each event, create two policies: one for the players and one for the customer service staff. Make sure that both staff and players know the policies; this will save an immeasurable amount of time and manpower. In addition, make sure that the paid staff and volunteers are following the same policies: players will rarely differentiate between the two, and complaints will mount quickly if enforcement is perceived as erratic. This is especially important in multidimensional worlds, as it only takes one person creating his own rules to throw the game off balance and create an uproar. Create and publish policies covering player character names, reimbursement issues, harassment, exploits, player-versus-player violence (so-called "player killing"), and any other issues that are unique to your game.

CASE STUDY 5.4.3: CUSTOMER SERVICE POLICIES

A Sample Player Policy

"Disruptive behavior that might affect others' enjoyment cannot be tolerated. Disruptive behavior might include, but is not limited to, spamming; monopolizing chat lines; use of profane names or language; or interrupting an event organized by another player or a Game Master. Any such behavior might result in your character[s] loss of game privileges for a time, and repeat offenders might be banned from the game permanently."

A Sample Staff Policy

"When you receive a complaint regarding disruption, go invisible, log the incident, and send a private message to the disrupter identifying yourself and asking him to cease the behavior. If the player continues the disruption, silence him for five minutes, warn him verbally and in writing, and note the incident in the player's history file. For extreme cases, notify a senior volunteer or Game Master and ask for a suspension of the player involved."

Choosing Customer Support Staff

When it comes to the heart of the customer service program, you have four basic options: a small paid staff, a large paid staff, outsourcing, and volunteers.

Paid Staff

Hiring only a few paid staff and hoping for the best is generally not a valid option for massive multiplayer games, because of the workload involved.

However, *Ultima Online* and *Asheron's Call* chose this approach after using volunteers for many months, citing legal concerns as the main reason. U.S. Labor law, quite simply, does not recognize such a thing as a volunteer in a for-profit business, and several lawsuits have been filed against companies that use them. See Case Study 5.4.4 for more information on this topic.

CASE STUDY 5.4.4: VOLUNTEERS, GAMES, AND THE LAW

More on volunteers in the legal system can be found at *www.dol.gov/esa/regs/compliance/whd/whdfs13.htm*.

For more information on the lawsuits relating to volunteers and online services, see:

www.salon.com/tech/feature/1999/04/16/aol_community/index1.html
http://dir.salon.com/tech/log/2000/09/21/ultima_volunteers/index.html
www.e3dnews.com/e3d/Issues/200102-Feb/lead.html
www.wired.com/news/print/0,1294,41821,00.html

As of September 2004, none of the lawsuits has resulted in settlements against a gaming company, but the issues are of significant concern and warrant attention.

Unfortunately, the only way to pay for a large staff is to charge considerably more than the average game can reasonably expect from its players.

Simutronics' games have long offered "premium services" where players can opt to pay considerably more for preferential customer service, and this model works extremely well for them. However, the games in question are text-based, with considerably less overhead than their graphical counterparts, and still allow a large number of volunteers to assist. *EverQuest* introduced "Legends" premium service in 2002, but no data is available on its success or lack thereof.

Several companies have tried outsourcing customer service. Most reports are that the customers do not end up happy with this result despite the cost savings over an in-house support group. In addition, to successfully outsource customer service requires a significant investment in communication and time to make sure the teams have up-to-date information. If the company employed does not speak the same language as you or your customers, double the time needed. While it is an option, and a good option for localization teams, it is not one that is recommended for the main bulk of customer service needs.

We have also seen several companies with MMORPGS hire too many initially and have to cut back quite soon thereafter, or in many cases, before the game makes it to launch day.

Volunteers

Despite the threat of litigation, the volunteer approach was chosen by most online games and has worked quite well, although its effectiveness varies due to management issues, willingness to trust the volunteers with commands that have the potential for abuse, and available tools.

As the volunteer service model is the most prominent, it is going to be the focus of the rest of this article.

Why Volunteers?

Cost reductions, although substantial, are not the only reason why game companies create volunteer programs. Often, the players themselves demand it. Most interviews with the developers of future online games feature the question, "Will you have a way for volunteers to work with the game?" [Strand00] states: "I am convinced that online gaming would not be what it is today if it hadn't been for the volunteers."

Volunteers can improve the community aspects of the game world and provide much more game experience and dedication than a temporary agency employee working for near minimum wage. Furthermore, those who excel as volunteers in the industry often hold degrees and lucrative jobs and would not be interested in full-time employment even if the companies could afford them. A large number work with the games for enjoyment and to be a part of the special behind-the-scenes community. Most volunteers are "hardcore" gamers with years of experience as players, and the vast majority are at least part-time students in college.

The downside of volunteer programs is twofold: there is a risk of litigation, and managing volunteers is very time consuming. If your staff is comprised of volunteers who average as little as five hours of work a week, you will need eight times as many volunteers as you would full-time employees to offer the same coverage. Worse: in reality, you might end up needing *30 times* more volunteers than you would paid staff, because you must account for the fact that you cannot force a volunteer to adhere to a specific, regular schedule.

Asheron's Call, Ultima Online, EverQuest, DragonRealms, and *Anarchy Online* all began life with the devotion and caring of hundreds of volunteers. *Asheron's Call* later disbanded their volunteer customer support staff, and *Ultima Online* removed their volunteers in the North American and European game worlds due to concerns of legality.

CASE STUDY 5.4.5: THE FUTURE OF CUSTOMER SUPPORT

Nick Duros, volunteer staffing coordinator on Anarchy Online, describes the future of massively multiplayer customer support in these terms:

"I feel the future of customer service in MMORPGs is in the hands of automated help and, if a company plays their cards right, volunteers. Both are dynamic, help cut costs by requiring fewer employees, and the presence of volunteers lowers response times for players who actually need to talk to a real human being about a problem.

"Many customer service requests are performed many times in one day, for many players. Automated help would reduce the workload for customer service personnel and lower response times to nearly zero. Right now, if your *Anarchy Online* character gets stuck in the environment, all you have to do is type /stuck and your character is moved to a safe spot on the playfield. Additionally, *Anarchy*

→

Online has a dynamic FAQ system that learns from the petitions the players send in. A lot more will become possible in the future.

"Volunteers can take over for the automated system when a real person's judgment is required. Volunteers are a largely untapped resource in MMORPG customer service; they often have the enthusiasm and the will to put forth as much effort as regular employees, while requiring little more than the chance to meet and work with some of the people behind the scenes of the game they love as compensation. Just like automated help, volunteers free the employees from the mundane so that they can concentrate on critical issues.

"However, the problem with using volunteers is that there is a very fine line between not using the untapped resource and abusing it. As a volunteer, I don't like it when my skills are underused because I can't gain access to the tools I need to perform to the best of my ability, and I dislike it when employees who lack the will to perform certain tasks use the volunteer program as a crutch. There is no easy way to navigate past these issues, but doing so may be the key to the future of customer service in online games."

CASE STUDY 5.4.6: COMPARISON OF GAMES AND SUPPORT MODELS

Game	Producer	Player Base	Type of Game	Customer Service
EverQuest	Sony/Verant	Very large	MMORPG	Paid staff/volunteer mix.
DragonRealms	Simutronics	Large	Pay to Play Mud	Paid/volunteer mix. Primary help in game, with secondary assistance via e-mail.
*Asheron's Call	Microsoft	Very large	MMOG	Paid staff only.
*Ultima Online	Origin	Very large	MMOG	Paid staff only.
Anarchy Online	Funcom Inc.	Large	MMOG	Paid/volunteer mix. Primary support in game, secondary via Web and e-mail.
City of Heroes	NCSoft	Very Large	MMOG	Paid staff.
Eve Online	CCP	Large	MMOG	Paid staff with volunteer mix.

*Both games started with large volunteer staff groups and discontinued for fear of legal complications.

How Many Customer Support People Do I Need?

A good rule of thumb is to take your player base and multiply by 1% to arrive at a minimum number of support personnel needed. Note that this can greatly vary depending on whether your game has one "dimension" (i.e., copy of the game world) or many, how advanced your customer service tools are, how complex the game is, how much support you want to provide, whether you plan on an all-paid staff or the use of volunteers, and how much power you are willing to place in the hands of your volunteers. The 1% rule is followed primarily by medium to large games with more than one dimension that use a combination of paid staff and volunteers.

For example, a game with 50,000 players providing 24/7 support might be able to survive adequately with four paid staff on at all times, but will most likely be better off planning to have one paid staff on at all times and 10 volunteers on at any given time. However, what many games fail to plan for is the number of staff needed to administer the volunteer program itself. As of 2004, the most successful volunteer programs required one to three paid staff managing the volunteers. However, it is vital to note that these programs empower several of the volunteers with extended abilities and allow for approximately 10% of their volunteers to work in supervisory and administrative capacities.

CASE STUDY 5.4.7: STAFFING A VOLUNTEER PROGRAM

Demographics for Funcom's program ARK (Advisors of Rubi-Ka) show the average volunteer to be a college student with one to five years of gaming experience. Polls of their volunteers showed over 60% to be in the 21 to 30 age group, approximately 15% in the 18 to 21 range, and 15% in the 30 to 40 range. The majority of volunteers are male, which is also reflective of the player base for the game. Three years after the program began, 10% of the volunteers had been in the program for over one year, and another 10% had remained with the program for over two years. Fully a third of the volunteers had been involved with the program for six consecutive months.

Types of Volunteers

Typically, you can expect to get three types of volunteers:

Desirable: Those who have the time, energy, and knowledge to effectively improve the customer service program for the company. Many volunteers in this category have college degrees and lucrative careers, but simply enjoy the challenges and friendships that come with such a venture. A large number in this category are also college students seeking a "foot in the door" of the games industry.

Temps: Those who just want to see what they can learn or get by being a volunteer, or who genuinely want to try it out and find that it's too much like work. Temps drain time and energy, and usually give up within 45 days.

Problems waiting to happen: Volunteers who join to find information to abuse game mechanics, share with other companies, or to get an inside edge to assist friends.

Proper recruiting, training, and monitoring will keep the latter two categories to a minimum.

Turnover

Turnover in volunteer programs is normally very high, and is directly affected by the ability of the volunteers to receive satisfaction from helping players, the manner in which the company treats the help, and the "family" feel to the program. Programs that do poorly in these areas can expect a 25% turnover ratio *per week*. Even the best-managed programs will still see a turnover of 3 to 7% depending on the season. One measure of a volunteer program is how long the volunteers remain active, as well as their level of activity. As in any business, happy people stay longer and produce better results.

In short, the secrets to a successful volunteer program are responsible empowerment, good management, correct tools, and the right people:

- Ensure that volunteers sign a well-written nondisclosure agreement (NDA), that rules for volunteers are clearly posted, and that you pursue violations.
- Verify that the volunteer is of legal age. This extra step can save you in child labor laws and NDA violations.
- When recruiting representatives, ensure that they can write proficiently if they will be dealing with customers online and that they have a friendly "online presence."
- Provide training. Some programs give a help file to volunteers and let them go. Some programs train, mentor, and teach tools and customer service basics. The latter cannot be stressed enough. Customer service does not come naturally to all. Training your representatives in diffusing difficult situations, how to escalate problems, and how to use positive statements along with the game mechanics will pay for itself when your staff is on the front line.
- Make the volunteers feel respected by the company. Developer chats, meetings with paid staff, informal discussions, and occasional telephone calls can go a long way toward building relationships.
- Empower volunteers to do what needs to be done. The number-one complaint of volunteers is invariably, "I don't have the tools or permissions to help the players when they have a legitimate need." If your volunteers can only answer players with "I'm sorry I can't help you," or "Let me refer you to (fill in the blank)," no one is benefiting. If your company cannot excel at internal customer service, there is no hope of it excelling with the external customers.
- Have the tools to monitor and deal with staff problems immediately. Make sure you can catch abuse of power or poor customer service and that you deal with these issues appropriately when they arise.
- Get good management and treat them well. Consider money spent on customer service an investment for the future rather than an expense. Strong leadership and personable people in both the paid and volunteer programs of customer service will save you time, money, and customers.

- Provide rewards and recognition for the volunteers. Thank people, publicly recognize them, and provide tangible benefits when possible.

CASE STUDY 5.4.8: REWARDING CUSTOMER SERVICE STAFF

Here is a handful of ways in which effective service representatives can be rewarded for their work, and therefore retained longer:

- Unique items for their characters
- Renaming items in the game after employees/volunteers
- Letters of recommendation, awards, and parties
- Increased responsibility, ranks, and titles based on longevity
- Recognition on public Web sites, boards, and in the game itself
- Rewards of game points that can be used to purchase items or skills
- Preferential employment opportunities
- Invitations to participate in developer chats
- Beta testing of other company games
- Trips to gaming conventions

Monitoring the Progress of a Customer Support Program

To make sure that your support program is performing appropriately, follow these simple steps:

- From time to time, perform a simple Web search on "customer service" and "your game." See where people are discussing your support program, and what their concerns are.
- Monitor the fan sites and message boards daily. Take this information to heart and plan to have staff respond on these forums.
- Periodically review a sample of the feedback. Make sure you know what the top issues are and what's being done about them.
- Consider surveys or a customer service audit by an independent firm. While most businesses employ some method to follow up on customer satisfaction, this is an area the gaming industry as a whole has not given a great deal of attention. Very few games today seem confident enough to employ this technique.
- Track statistics on wait times. Set goals and plan for emergency situations to keep your customers from spending an undue amount of time waiting for assistance.
- Create a quality control team to check on customer service. Test your staff. Take a walk in the customers' shoes and see what the view is.

Customer service surveys for *Anarchy Online* taught the company three important lessons:

- The quicker customers received assistance, the higher they rated the overall customer service of the game.
- When customer service staff were given survey results that pertained to them, the same staff rated a full point higher on the next round in over 90% of the cases.
- Customers, even when given an answer they are less than thrilled with, are much more responsive and likely to remain loyal if given a timely answer.

Conclusion

Customer service is an ongoing commitment to provide quality assistance and build customer loyalty. The best game can lose money by failing to focus on quality service. As a study done by the Rockefeller Foundation and quoted in [Griffin97] shows, almost 7 out of 10 customers who leave a regular service provider go to the competition because of poor customer service. Quality customer service requires good planning, effective policies, smart management, effective tools, relevant training, and dedicated people. By taking control of these measures in your game, you are taking control of your customers' satisfaction.

Using volunteers in a massive multiplayer game can be a very effective tool, but it is not without costs in time, energy, resources, and management. While many game companies have recently shied away from the volunteer customer service model due to legal concerns, no legal action has been successful yet. The top MMOGs in terms of customer service are continuing to recruit volunteers and do so not only for monetary reasons, but because it's what the customers have asked for and the quality can be superb. Word of mouth is still the best advertising for any MMOG, and customer support plays a very important role in determining what words are being spread about your game and your company.

References

[Griffin97] Griffin, K., *Customer Loyalty: How to Earn It, How to Keep It*, Lexington Books, 1997.

[Strand00] Strand, T., "Anarchy Online Developer Journal," available online at *http://aovault.ign.com/features/journal/100500.shtml*, October 5, 2000.

5.5

Offshore Game Development Outsourcing

Javier F. Otaegui

javier@sabarasa.com

The classical definition of outsourcing applies when a company transfers one or more recurring processes to another organization under a contractual agreement. Outsourcing is different from subcontracting and other similar business practices in that it focuses on recurring processes instead of one-time projects [Kelly01].

In the game development community, outsourcing is used as a synonym for subcontracting: a game company hiring another to handle a task such as programming, 2D art, modeling, texturing, audio design, music, scripting, levels, research, testing, porting, or even a complete game development project.

Offshore outsourcing occurs when a company located in another country (usually outside of North America and Western Europe) is hired. The main justification for this growing phenomenon is monetary: offshore game development professionals can be hired for a fractional part of what U.S. or European game developers earn [Yourdon96]. This can imply savings of 50% and up to 70% for the entire project budget, a significant and important figure to take into account for your new game development projects.

Why Should You Outsource?

Experts believe that outsourcing is essential to prosper in the twenty-first century. According to [Berger02], companies that outsource will be able to focus on their core competencies, rather than handling a lot of time- and effort-consuming tasks that would better be done elsewhere. For example, some game development companies could focus on game design and production (their core competency) and outsource the noncore activities of programming, artwork, testing, and so forth.

Beyond this reason, perhaps the most important and decisive factor for many companies is the significant cost reduction that offshore outsourcing implies. Outsourcing to Asian and Eastern European countries for this reason has been a common

357

practice for several years, and recently, new countries (e.g., Argentina and Brazil) have entered this worldwide market, due to devaluation processes, with interesting advantages that we will examine.

Additional Benefits of Offshore Outsourcing

Additional benefits of offshore outsourcing can be summarized as follows:

On-budget delivery. Contracts for outsourcing are commonly milestone driven, with set payments for specific work, so you can rest assured that the project will be tied to the original budget.

Reduced operating costs. You can hire outsourcing solutions on an as-needed basis, instead of paying full-time staff during downtimes, reducing your operating costs significantly.

Access to specialized skills. You don't need to train your team with a specific technology or methodology; you can simply hire a specialized team that will be able to do the work without need of training.

Access to preexisting code, tools, and libraries. Your development time will be shorter because you will gain access to the contracted developer's in-house tools and libraries, with the additional benefit that the programmers will already be familiar with them.

CASE STUDY 5.5.1: THE PROVIDER'S SIDE

We asked Sergei Herashenko, from Frogwares (*www.frogwares.com*), a Ukrainian company specializing in game development outsourcing services, to describe their experience in offshore outsourcing.

Q. Can you tell us what makes your company successful?

"We have many clients who are very satisfied with our quality and terms of work, and they are much more than happy when they realize that they pay half of the market price for the work we are doing for them! Key factors of success include quality of work, being serious in every detail (terms, deadlines, etc.), and a personal approach to every client."

Q. How do you manage to make it work despite distance and language issues?

"Most of our clients come to Ukraine to see our development branch, to meet project managers and other people they are working with distantly. The company was set up to be able to work for clients who speak different languages and with considerable time differences.

"All of our developers and designers speak at least English, and some speak other foreign languages. It is very easy to work with European clients because the time difference is only a few hours. With America, it is more difficult, but we can always find a solution, such as adjusting our work schedule to the client's needs."

Myths about Offshore Outsourcing

Deciding to outsource is rarely easy, and it is almost certain that the transition will create uncertainty, controversy, and even active resistance [Kelly01].

The fear of losing control is the most typical objection to outsourcing, commonly reflected in thoughts like, "if I want it done right, I'd better do it myself." [Kelly01] points out that in fact, outsourcing increases the ability to manage and control vital business processes. Outsourcing is based on contracts, schedules, and milestones that specify key objectives and guarantee performance.

Another common myth about outsourcing is that people usually think of it as being financially uncertain. Concerns about upfront costs and ongoing service fees are commonly present; however, with an appropriately written contract, the financial benefits become clear. Structure the contract by milestones and periodical reviews, issuing payments on an approval basis. This eliminates all uncertainty about hidden costs.

How to Outsource

There are three well-defined stages in the game development outsourcing process. The first stage involves the request for proposal and the proposal, with schedule, work planning, and budget. The second stage is concerned with preparing and signing the contract. The third stage involves the development of the game, and the tracking of milestones and bugs.

The Proposal

The outsourcing process starts when the customer sends the *Request For Proposal* (RFP), which usually includes the *Game Design Document*, to the provider for evaluation. The RFP should be as complete and accurate as possible, as it will dictate both the estimated schedule and budget. The customer should also indicate if there are strict deadlines, so the provider can assign more people (if possible) to the project. The RFP should also specify the tasks that the provider will assume, whom they will report to, and how the approval process will be structured.

The provider then prepares a proposal for the customer. This proposal must include all the functional requisites of the game, as well as a detailed time schedule for project management. Although this is not required, the provider could also inform the client of how many people will be involved in the game's development, and each individual's specific skills and résumé.

The proposal must also include logical divisions of the project in order to specify the milestones. A good rule of thumb is to include a milestone per month. This implies constant supervision and satisfaction from the customer, as well as monthly payments for the provider. Financial stability is expected from the provider, so that they (and the project) can keep going in case of late delivery of milestones.

Milestone definitions contain lists of features and content required for approval. Specifying a process by which specific requirements can be exchanged between milestones during development can also help deal with unforeseen events. This interchangeability will allow the development process to grow more naturally than with imposed artificial schedules.

Finally, the proposal should include a description of how the work will be done: a context diagram of the most important parts of the program, any tools that also need to be developed, and so forth, and a payment structure for the milestones. The final milestone usually has a bigger payment associated with it (approximately 30% of the project).

The Contract

Contracts can be signed for a single project or for a set of related projects. [Paul01] recommends not to become entangled in a long-term contract to maintain the flexibility necessary to deal with changing market conditions. This also allows for more dynamic process allocation to different outsourcing groups.

Contracts must clearly depict each party's responsibility. If you are working with separate groups for programming and artwork, you should clearly specify whose responsibility it is, for example, to convert artwork to final game data files; who is accountable for each component; and how performance will be evaluated. Although programming and artwork might depend on each other, separate milestone threads should be used for each, especially if they are subcontracted to different companies.

One important issue is code ownership. The customer will demand ownership of the final product, as he is the one who is paying for the work, but the framework and generic game libraries should be of shared ownership for both the developer and the customer.

Finally, the contract should include the proposal as an appendix, to fully describe the job to be done.

The Development Process

Once the contract is signed, the hard work begins. The developer and the customer now enter into a close working relationship that will last until the project is delivered. Thus, contracting an outsourcing studio that shares your corporate culture and vision is crucial to successfully develop the product [Jenkins01].

Communications between the provider and the customer are extremely important to the project's success. E-mails, instant messenger, bug trackers, conference calls, periodical releases, and reviews form the communication tools spectrum the game designer must implement when hiring an offshore outsourcing development studio. Constant feedback is a must, especially when artwork is being outsourced.

The bug tracker is an important communications channel. The best solution is to use a Web-based system where you and your testers can post details about every issue requiring attention. The customer should be the one who definitively closes the bugs (i.e., officially declares them fixed).

The instant messenger is an effective tool, but only when both parties are located in countries with compatible time zones. A South American team working for a U.S. company will have little trouble coordinating; not so for a team in Russia or Taiwan.

CASE STUDY 5.5.2: PLATICO GAMES

We asked Nicolás Massi, from Platico Games (*www.platico.com*), an Argentine company specializing in Web-based game development outsourcing services, to describe their experience in outsourcing.

Q. How would you qualify your company as an outsourcing provider?

"We are set up to take on small and medium projects in which time is of the essence. Given the size of such projects, we can take on several at the same time."

Q. Why is outsourcing beneficial? Who should outsource?

"We would especially emphasize our ability to leverage specialized teams and the low costs associated with our services. We have specific experience with advertising games, often sought after by clients who have neither the time nor the capabilities to develop them internally. These agencies do well to outsource."

Q. What are the key factors to look at when choosing an outsourcing provider?

"It is very important that the provider offer ample human resources and an organized work methodology. It is critical to secure a guarantee of time and quality for development, and to reduce cost and risk for your project."

Q. How should the client prepare its own team to work with an outsourcing provider?

"It is absolutely necessary that the company assigns a project leader who understands the details necessary to complete the project. It is also critical that the client promptly provide materials requested by the provider, once the requirements are agreed upon. In general, problems occur when the requirements documentation is incomplete, incorrect, or ambiguous."

Q. What is the work cycle like? Do you use reviews? Milestones?

"Usually, it is based on delivery dates with rounds of revision agreed upon at the beginning of development. Then it is possible to make constant updates based on the client's evolving needs."

Choosing the Appropriate Outsourcing Provider

There really are no sure-fire recipes for successful game development outsourcing, but there are several minimum guidelines that should help you when hiring an outsourcing company to develop your games.

The most basic issue is language. Both you and the development team should be able to write and speak the same language. (It is not necessary that they both share the same mother tongue, as most communication will be written.) In addition, make sure that the language used in documentation will also be used in the code and in the comments. The usual option is to adopt English.

As the outsourcing relationship is long term, it is very wise to find a team that matches your own culture. It must understand your business and goals, and it must share the same values and information [Jenkins01].

It is highly recommended that you hire a team with experience in both game development and outsourcing, with at least one contract project completed. Although hiring an inexperienced team might be tempting because of lower prices, it pays to choose a stable and trustworthy partner [Paul01].

Timing

Some Asian companies depict as positive the 12-hour time shift between the client offices and them, because they can work on the requirements and bugs found while the client sleeps. If real-time communication is a crucial factor in your case, you should hire an offshore team that shares time zones with your home country. This makes nations such as Argentina and Brazil excellent candidates for clients in the United States and Europe; their recently devalued economies can lead to savings of 50% to 70% in development costs.

CASE STUDY 5.5.3: THE CLIENT'S SIDE _____

We asked Tenzing Kernan, game designer and producer at Cardoza Entertainment (*www.cardozaent.com*), for his comments about the outsourcing economy.

"It is not difficult to find a good developer (and lots of not so good ones) by searching on the Internet. However, working with a foreign development team does pose some additional problems, mainly the language barrier, time zone differences, and communications delays. If the language barrier is too great, you must find a new developer. Daily exchange of ideas and feedback is essential. To make sure that the hurdles can be cleared, you should exchange a few practice e-mails with the key people on the project, before committing to the developer.

"You will almost certainly communicate with the developer (especially an overseas one) mostly via the Internet, using both e-mail and chat. Feedback can be slow with e-mail, and even slower if the time zones are incompatible. You should set a time period during the day when an online chat session can happen. While chatting, many issues can be talked about and resolved in a short period of time. When sending e-mails, include lots of details, and spell everything out clearly—or a simple 10-minute fix might take two days.

"Finally, while it is tempting to go with the developer with the lowest price, it is absolutely essential to choose a developer who will complete the job. Many things can derail a project before completion. The experience of the team's members is more important than their formal education. The key members of the team

→

must have completed a project of a similar size and complexity, or you are taking a big risk."

CASE STUDY 5.5.4: MANAGING OUTSOURCING

Max Meltzer, director of development at Tea-N-Turtles GmbH in Germany, has consulted with several developers and publishers on the proper management of outsourcing projects.

"Choosing the right outsourcing studio can have fantastic creative results for the developer," says Meltzer. "In addition to lower costs and quick turnarounds, a quality outsourcing provider can offer a settled and synergized team with experience in a particular area a developer might otherwise not have. A good example is how UbiSoft outsourced the multiplayer mode of *XIII* on Xbox to Southend Interactive because they had vast experience of Xbox multiplayer technology that UbiSoft lacked. The result was a good multiplayer mode, delivered on schedule and inexpensively."

When searching for an outsourcing provider, Meltzer considers many factors. "The most important one is to analyze how working with an outsourcing studio would affect the current internal team. Once I've done this, I have a good idea of what I want (and don't want) the outsourcing partner to do. An outsourcer also needs to demonstrate a high proficiency in developing assets of a similar style (and identical or better quality) to that of the in-house team. Of course, they must have the appropriate level of experience to communicate maturely; typically, the relationship between the in-house team and outsourcer is more efficient if both work in similar time zones, and if the team isn't full of bilinguals, a foreign outsourcer may not be a practical choice either."

Meltzer also feels that it is vitally important to visit the outsourcer's studio to evaluate their actual operating status and ability. "If I feel that there is any risk that working with an outsourcer could have a negative effect on the in-house team, I disqualify this provider and look for a more suitable one."

Conclusion

Offshore game development outsourcing is an excellent way to reduce the development costs of your game project, sometimes to half the original budget, or to drastically increase your product's quality by hiring more quality people for the same price.

Recent national economy devaluation in both Argentina and Brazil provide an excellent scenario for game development outsourcing in Latin America: lower costs, overlapping time zones with the United States and Europe, and companies with proven track records.

References

[Berger02] Berger, J., "The Value of Outsourcing," *DecisionOne*, January 2002, available online at *www.decisionone.com/d1m/news/white_papers/white_paper_08.shtml*.

[Jenkins01] Jenkins, D., "The New Standard for IT Outsourcing: Delivering on Accountability Will Drive the Future of All Relationships," *The Outsourcing Institute*, 2001, available online at *http://verizonit.com/pdf/oi_brief.pdf*.

[Kelly01] Kelly, T., "Is Application Outsourcing Right for Your Business?" *BlueStar Solutions*, December 2001, available online at *www.bluestarsolutions.com/industry/Is_Outsourcing_Right_For_You.pdf*.

[Paul01] Paul, L., "Classic Outsourcing Blunders," *Darwin Magazine*, August 2001, available online at *www.darwinmag.com/read/080101/blunders.html*.

[Yourdon96] Yourdon, E., et al, "Offshore Outsourcing: The Benefits and Risks," *Cutter Consortium Research Reports*, November 1996.

5.6

Localizations

Heather Maxwell Chandler
heather@mediasunshine.com

Creating International Content

Localization is often the last thing on people's minds and the last thing that is completed in the game development cycle. If localizations are planned for in advance, they can be completed in a timely fashion and get the game more exposure in international markets. These days, most publishers localize their games into French, German, Spanish, and Italian. This article mainly concentrates on these languages, but this information can also be applied to localizations for other languages such as Korean, Japanese, and Polish. Determining which languages your game will be localized into at the beginning of the project will save time in the long run, since you can prepare for any problems you are sure to encounter.

Get International Input Early

Think about how the name and content will sell in other countries. Will you be able to sell very many copies of a "Route 66" adventure game in Japan if no one there has any idea of what "Route 66" is? How about trying to market a real-time strategy game called "Third World" in Mexico—where connotations of this phrase are completely different from the United States? Will a baseball game sell very well in Europe?

Create special hooks or exclusive content to appeal to an international market. If making a car-racing game, include a special French car that is available exclusively in the French version. If designing a skateboarding game, include a skate park from the UK or Italy. The same goes for music. If licensing music from well-known American bands, on the German version, replace one of the tracks with the hottest band in Germany.

Avoid making specific references to American culture and slang, unless it is necessary for game design. For example, avoid references to the *Survivor* TV show like "The tribe has spoken." And don't use slang like "Keep it on the D.L." and "That is whack!" This will also prevent the setting of your game from appearing too dated.

Usually, the U.S. version is completed and then the localized versions follow. In some cases, the localized versions will need to change or remove some of the assets that were originally intended for the U.S. market. For example:

Electronic registration. You don't want to include U.S. electronic registration on international builds, but you might want to include country-specific registration. This might require you to get different registration software for each national version of the game.

Subtitles. In lieu of fully localizing the product, you can subtitle the voice-over. If this is the case, subtitling functionality needs to be built into the game engine.

Blood. Germany has strict censorship guidelines, particularly concerning blood and violence. Adhering to Germany's censorship guidelines might require you to make a separate German master, especially if you are not going to alter the violence for release in other countries.

European Ratings Boards

Europe has recently set up a centralized rating system for entertainment software called Pan Europe Game Information (PEGI). All games released in Europe need to be submitted to PEGI for a rating. Germany is the exception, as they have their own national ratings process to which all games released in Germany must adhere. If you are planning to release a game in another country such as Australia or Japan, inquire about their software rating system and submission requirements. You might need to modify your game before it can be released in a particular country. Some of the international software rating boards are:

United States: Entertainment Software Rating Board (ESRB) *www.esrb.org*
Europe: Pan European Game Information (PEGI) *www.pegi.info*
Germany: Unterhaltungssoftware SelbstKontrolle (USK) *www.usk.de*
Australia: Office of Film & Literature Classification (OFLC) *www.oflc.gov.au*
Japan: Computer Entertainment Rating Organization (CERO) *www.cero.gr.jp*

Determining Costs to Localize

Before you localize, make sure it is financially viable to do so, in terms of time and money. Start by figuring out how many assets need to be localized, how much the translations will cost, and how much development time will be needed. Once you have this information, you can work with sales and marketing to determine if the sales numbers point to a financially viable localization. Traditionally, French, German, Spanish, and Italian are the main European localizations that U.S. game companies create.

Licensing deals are sometimes made to create localizations for other countries such as Brazil, Japan, and Korea. In the case of a licensing deal, a localization kit is delivered to the licensees and they handle all the translation, integration, and testing.

Staggered Release versus Simultaneous Release

Of course, each localized project will have a different schedule, but if localizations are planned for in advance and run according to schedule, you can expect to spend no more than two to three months localizing a game. Some developers prefer to wait until the U.S. version is completely finished before beginning work on localized builds. The advantages to this include:

Code is final. If you have already planned for the technical necessities needed for localizations, the code base probably will not change. Therefore, most of the team can be offloaded to work on other projects. You will only need two to three core people to integrate the assets and create builds. The other advantage is that the QA department will not find as many code-related bugs.

U.S. assets are final. If the U.S. assets are final, tracking localized assets will be much easier. You will not need to constantly update the translators with any text or voice-over changes, greatly simplifying the asset tracking, translation, and integration process.

The disadvantage to working on localized versions after the U.S. version is finished is not having a simultaneous worldwide release of the game. Therefore, people who don't live in the United States will have to wait two to three months to play the game. In addition, this lag time for international releases gives software pirates more time to get illegal copies of the game into international channels.

Ideally, you want localized versions of the game released simultaneously with the U.S. version, or as close to that as you can get. This is very difficult to do, especially if no advanced planning has been done. The main obstacles to achieving simultaneous code release are not being able to work with final assets and not starting the asset integration process soon enough. You will need to work very closely with designers, artists, and engineers to finalize batches of assets that can be sent off for localization. Once assets have been sent off for translation, restrict access to the U.S. versions so that changes cannot be made without first notifying the person managing the localizations. Often, there are last-minute asset changes before the game code releases, and these changes need to be carried over into the localized assets.

The disadvantage of not working with final code means that the QA department will take longer to test since they will be finding many more bugs, and these bugs will be duplicated across all the versions. One last deterrent for trying to localize simultaneously with the U.S. version is the increase in manpower and workload. It is very difficult just getting the U.S. version completed on time; if you add localized versions on top of the U.S. version, your team will need to split their already limited time between the U.S. and localized versions.

Scheduling

Create a rough schedule of all the tasks needed to complete the localization. The duration of the tasks depends on how many assets need to be localized and tested. Table

5.6.1 illustrates an asset overview form that you can use to estimate the number of assets to be translated. Additionally, this form provides valuable information so the translators can determine the translation costs and know the format in which the assets need to be delivered.

Table 5.6.1 Asset Overview Form

Title	Platform	US Code Release Date	Foreign Languages	Localization Contact
TEXT ASSETS IN-GAME	**quantity**	**delivered format**	**final received format**	**Comments**
Number of words as in-game text strings				
Number of text files to be modified				
ART ASSETS	**quantity**	**delivered format**	**final received format**	**Comments**
Number of words in images				
Number of art files to be modified				
ASSETS IN-GAME	**quantity**	**delivered format**	**final received format**	**Comments**
Number of words in script				
Number of audio files to be modified				
Number of main speakers				
Number of supporting speakers				
Total time of voice-overs (min:sec)				
CINEMATICS ASSETS	**quantity**	**delivered format**	**final received format**	**Comments**
Number of words in script				
Number of movies to be modified				
Number of main speakers				
Number of supporting speakers				
Seconds performed as lip-synch				
Total time of cut-scenes (min:sec)				$\rightarrow$

PRINTED MATERIALS	quantity	delivered format	final received format	Comments
Manual—number of words				
Manual—number of graphics to be modified				
Box—number of words				
Box—number of graphics to modify				
Keyboard ref. card—number of words				
Any other printed materials?				

When planning your schedule, make sure to include time estimates for these major areas:

Organizing assets for translations. Make sure that all of the assets are organized so that the text and context are very clear for all the translations you need. This includes such things as creating a glossary, adding time codes to the VO script, and creating a master sheet with all the in-game text.

Translations. Get estimates from the translator for how long it will take to have everything translated. If doing voice-over, you need to include time for translating the script, casting actors, recording the voice-over, adding special effects, and converting to the necessary audio format.

Integrating translated assets. Schedule time for things such as integrating text files, modifying art files, adding localized VO, and compiling the build.

Testing localized builds. This can be one of the most time-consuming aspects of localizations. You have to check all the translations in the game and make sure no bugs were introduced when the localized assets were added. You need to allow for several rounds of testing and bug fixing. The amount of testing time will depend on the size of the game and how much translated text needs to be checked.

Budgeting

Once you have a schedule, and an overview of the assets to be localized, you can get an idea of how much all of this is going to cost. The translator needs to provide translation costs, and you need to figure out development and testing costs. Table 5.6.2 is a form to help you determine development and testing costs. You fill in the daily rate of the person doing the work and then multiply it by the amount of time he or she spends on the project. This is just an estimate, and you should track the actual time spent on the project to see how close your original estimate was. You can use this information to estimate future localizations.

Table 5.6.2 Estimate for Development Costs

Translating	Resource Name	Task	Daily Rate	Est. Days	Cost
	Engineer	Extract text for localization	$0.00	0	$0.00
	Associate Producer	Organize assets for translation	$0.00	0	$0.00

Integrating	Resource Name	Task	Daily Rate	Est. Days	Cost
	Engineer	Asset integration, making builds for 4 languages	$0.00	0	$0.00
	2D Artist	Update 2D art (if necessary)	$0.00	0	$0.00
	3D Artist	Localize cinematics	$0.00	0	$0.00
	Associate Producer	Assist with asset integration for 4 languages	$0.00	0	$0.00

Testing	Resource Name	Task	Daily Rate	Est. Days	Cost
	QA Manager	Copyprotect GMs (4 languages)	$0.00	0	$0.00
	Asst. System Admin	Set up localized machines (4 languages)	$0.00	0	$0.00
	QA Analyst	Test game (2 rounds of testing, GM certification)	$0.00	0	$0.00
	Tester (German)	Test game (2 rounds of testing, GM certification)	$0.00	0	$0.00
	Tester (French)	Test game (2 rounds of testing, GM certification)	$0.00	0	$0.00
	Tester (Italian)	Test game (2 rounds of testing, GM certification)	$0.00	0	$0.00
	Tester (Spanish)	Test game (2 rounds of testing, GM certification)	$0.00	0	$0.00
	Engineer	Fix bugs, make builds	$0.00	0	$0.00
	Associate Producer	Fix bugs	$0.00	0	$0.00

Localization Friendly Development

Sit down with the development team during pre-production to discuss ways they can make the game more localization friendly. This means creating assets that are easy to pull out for localization and easy to integrate after they have been translated. For example, keep the text in a separate layer for art assets. This way, you can easily modify the text without having to use an artist to recreate a localized version of the asset from scratch. The more streamlined you can make the localization process, the less time and resources you need to use.

Staffing

One person, usually the producer or associate producer, should be in charge of managing all aspects of the localization. This person is the main point of contact for all localization issues. If you have too many people involved, it is easy to lose track of things, which can add time and cost to the schedule. In addition, you need at least one engineer to help with integrating assets, creating builds, and debugging code. If there are many art assets to be localized, you need an artist part-time on the project as well. For testing, you will need testers to check both the linguistic and functional aspects of the game. Discuss your testing needs with the QA department and make sure there are enough testers available to get the project done on time.

Determining Which Files to Localize

Avoid hard-coding text into the game code. Instead, all text should be easily accessible in a separate file that can be modified with a text editor. Make sure the development team is keeping all the assets that need to be localized in an accessible place in the game. Opening and searching dozens of source files for text strings to be replaced is very time consuming and error prone. One method of organizing assets to be localized is to create an English-specific directory that contains all the text and voice-over used in the game. Examples of files that contain language assets include:

Text and tool-tip files. For example, text that pops up when you mouse-over a button.
Images containing embedded text. For example, billboard signs.
Voice-over files. Text spoken by actors, as well as audio help files.
Embedded commands. For example, "Do you want to quit?"
Control messages. For example, "Please wait" or "Press any key."
Fonts. Make sure fonts support special characters and accents.

Technical Considerations

The engine needs to be able to handle both uppercase and lowercase versions of special linguistic characters, such as ä, Ó, and Ç. If you are localizing a title that uses an Asian font, the engine must be double-byte enabled and capable of using bidirectional and right-to-left text.

If allowing players to use the keyboard for input, for example in typing in a multiplayer name, they need the use of accentuated characters. Double-check this functionality in the test process to make sure that using special characters will not crash the game.

In addition, determine how the keyboard commands will be mapped to the keyboard. If the keyboard commands are mapped by location (e.g., the far left key on the bottom row will reload a weapon), make sure this key functions the same way on all international keyboards. Moreover, the manual writer for each language will want to make a note of the exact key when writing the manual, since the name of the key will be different in each country. If the keyboard commands are mapped directly to the keys (e.g., ~ will switch the weapon the player is using), make sure that all versions of the keyboards have this key available. If not, you will have to pick a different key to map the command to for that language.

If you are working on a console game, you might need to make a PAL version of the game for release in Europe. Contact the console manufacturers to find out what requirements they have.

Game Layout on the Disc

Plan for an increase in file size when working with localized assets, since most of them are at least 10 to 15% larger than their U.S. counterparts. Make sure there is enough room on the game CD to accommodate this size increase.

If there is enough room, you might decide to include several languages on one disc. If this is the case, you need to determine how users will get the appropriate language installed—will they have an on-screen option to select a language, or will language be auto-selected by the users' language settings or operating system?

Screen Real Estate and User Interfaces

Keep the text size increase in mind when designing user interfaces. Implement scrolling text boxes or scalable buttons to accommodate these increases. This will decrease the amount of overlapping and truncated text you have to fix in the testing phase. In addition, don't have too many buttons crowded onto the screen. When possible, use icons instead of words. For example, use an open door with an arrow pointing through as an exit symbol instead of the word "EXIT." If you did not plan ahead for these increases, you might find that you have to redesign the UI and screen layout for the localized versions. Activision's Jeff Matsushita offers these examples:

"For instance, Japanese text cannot be displayed in as small a font as European text. As such, if a very small font is used for the U.S. version, the Japanese version might require a layout change to accommodate the larger text size. Another consideration is the width of German text. German has some very long words that can easily overrun a text box and might require either a new screen layout or a retranslation— neither of which is cheap. At the design phase, the developer should avoid having screens that jam tons of text into small spaces, since the localized text might not fit into those spaces. "

Other UI considerations need to be taken into account for console games, since television screens have a lower video resolution than computer monitors do. You want to avoid having a cluttered UI screen that will be hard to read when displayed on a TV. Regarding PAL conversions, Jeff states, "Since PAL formats have more lines vertically than NTSC, the screens might have to be laid out again in order to match the larger screen."

Organizing Assets for Translation

You can create a complete localization kit and send it to the translator, or you can send assets as they are finalized. In either case, you need to make sure everything is clear and well organized so the translator can work efficiently. If things are disorganized or the assets aren't finalized, you will spend a lot of time sending different versions of the assets back and forth to the translator. Doing this is a sure way to lose track of the current assets and create additional bugs in the game. Establish a naming convention early on so that you can quickly determine what each file contains and if it has been localized.

If you are going to send a localization kit, it should include:

Documentation. This includes a table of contents of what is included in the localization kit, design documents, technical guidelines, instructions on how to use the tools, voice-over casting notes, and any documents that will help the localization house reproduce the look and feel of your game.

Tools. If a special text editor is needed to open the text files or a special plug-in is required to open the graphics files, these tools must be included in the kit, along with instructions on how to use them.

Assets. Include all the text, audio, art, and cinematics that need to be localized. In some cases, like cinematics, you need to provide raw data that can be translated, since the files will need to be compiled before adding them to the game.

Source code. This is all the code and assets the localization house will need to create and compile a completely translated version of the game.

Organizing Documentation

Send game-specific documents to make the context of the game clear to the translators. Having these resources makes it much easier for the translator to translate within the correct context. You should send:

Copy of game. Provide an up-to-date version of the game. It is helpful to send a game even before you send assets to be localized. The translator can become familiar with the game and be better prepared to provide exact translations.

Design documents. Provide all the design documents so the translator knows exactly what features are included in the game and which areas need special attention from a localization standpoint. These documents can also clarify any questions the translator might have while playing through the game.

Cheats/walkthroughs. To check the translations quickly in the game, cheats and walkthroughs need to be provided so the translator can quickly jump to different levels, screens, characters, and so forth. They need access to all areas of the game that are going to be localized.

Voice-over casting notes. To maintain audio quality standards, provide detailed casting notes of the major and minor voice-overs in the game. The translators need information such as gender, voice pitch, character description, and how this character fits into the game. This makes is easier to direct the VO session so that the localized VO files maintain the same overall emotion and context as the English VO files.

Glossary. This is useful for describing common and technical terms specific to your game, such as mission names, character names, and slang phrases that appear in the game.

Technical overview. This includes detailed information on file delivery formats, video editing requirements, and any post-production or integration work required to create the localized assets. If integrating cinematics, the technical overview should also include information on any compression tools used.

Organizing Text Assets

Organizing the text assets for translation can be very easy or very hard, depending on how the text assets are laid out in the game. If all the text is located in a single text file, you can just drop the text to be translated into a spreadsheet, add notes about context, and send it to be translated. If the text is located in various files throughout the game, you need to track down all text that needs to be localized and organize it into a table that is easy for the translator to work with. Ideally, as seen in Table 5.6.3, this table should list the filename, context, and text to be translated. This can be modified based on your translator's needs.

Table 5.6.3 Spreadsheet for Text Translation

Filename	Context	Text to Be Translated
Prision.rsf	This appears in game when a player tries to access a locked door.	You cannot use this door; find a different path.
Prision.rsf	Appears in game when your team is in control of the enemy base.	You have captured the enemy base!

Organizing Art Assets

When creating art for your game, do not embed text in the images. Instead, layer the artwork so that the text is on a separate layer. If you cannot layer the text separately and have to embed it, save a version of the file without the text embedded to include in your localization kit. This will make is easier for the translators to modify the art assets.

When the art assets are ready to be translated, put the text to be translated in a spreadsheet similar to Table 5.6.3. The developer can then import the translated text into the text layer of the image, or the translator can do this if he or she has the technical expertise. If the translator does it, make sure he or she has the necessary software to modify the files, like Adobe Photoshop and any necessary or proprietary plug-ins. Additionally, a full font, with special linguistic characters, should be provided for any text that needs to be altered in an art asset.

Organizing Audio and Cinematic Assets

Organizing audio files is more involved since you have to cast actors and record in a studio. Additionally, you must be very clear about the format you need the localized files delivered in, since there are many technical variations of audio files. The delivery format should be included in the original asset overview (Table 5.6.1) and the technical overview that you gave to the translator.

Include casting notes so parts can be properly cast. Sometimes, the tone of the selected voice actor does not go with the game and can pull the player out of the game. As seen in Table 5.6.4, you need to include the filename, name of the character, the context of the line, and the timing of the file if you want lip-syncing.

Table 5.6.4 Spreadsheet for Audio Translation

Audio Filename	Length	Character	Context	Text to Be Translated	Comments
Medic.wav	1.2 sec	Sammy	A teammate has been wounded and Sammy is calling for medical help.	We need a medic here, stat!	Time sync. Max length= 2 secs

Provide the original English audio files to the translator. This will ensure that the translators, director, and actors have a good reference for the voice-overs and that the localized files correspond to their English equivalents.

If voice-over files are overlaid with sound effects or music, keep these as separate files. Be sure to specify where the music and sound effects are needed. You will also need to maintain uncompressed versions of your cinematics so you can easily integrate the localized voice-over. This information should be detailed in the technical overview.

If the game has lip-syncing, you need to provide additional information such as the length of the voice-over in minutes and seconds. You might also need to provide a time-coded PAL Betacam tape (for live video action), or sections of AVI video playback to ensure accuracy with lip-syncing in the localized versions.

Additional Assets That Need to Be Localized

In addition to the actual in-game assets, there might also be other game-specific content that needs to be localized. Be sure to include these items in your budget and schedule. Examples include:

- Manuals and box text
- Screen shots for manual and box
- Keyboard reference card
- Customer support information
- Readme file
- End user licensing agreement
- Installer

Integrating Translated Assets

Integrating localized assets is time-consuming work because it involves a lot of file modification and file replacement. Basically, there are two major ways developers can handle this process. One way is for the developers to do the asset integration themselves and rely only on translators to provide the translated text. The benefits of this are that technical difficulties can easily be addressed, the integrity of the assets is maintained so they can easily be placed in the build without introducing any additional crash bugs, and the developer has more control over the time and resources. The drawbacks are that the developer has to spend additional development time and has to rely on translators to provide corrected text to fix some linguistic bugs. Furthermore, the developer often has to rely on a third party (usually international marketing) to approve the final versions. This can be very time consuming, as the third party might go back and forth on minor bugs and hold up the release of the game.

The other way to integrate localized assets is to contract a localization house to do the translations, asset integration, and testing. The benefit to this is that the developer does not have to spend any additional time creating localized software. The developer just needs to provide a localization kit. The drawback is that the quality of the game can be compromised because no one is maintaining the same standards of quality for the voice-over actors, translations, and so forth. Moreover, some localization houses might not have the technical expertise to independently localize a game, resulting in the developer getting involved to fix a problem created by a translator's error. If you are going to use external vendors to completely localize your game, make sure they have experience localizing game software and the technical expertise to work with the assets.

After creating the initial set of translated assets, check them into a version control system so you can easily track them during the bug-fixing phase. Version control is especially important if you have several people fixing bugs. Additionally, if you are working on multiple languages at one time, you can track each language more closely and avoid having German assets appear in a French version.

Testing Localized Builds

This can be the most time-consuming part of localizations since you have to do both linguistic testing and functionality testing. You can save some testing time by using two teams to do concurrent linguistic and functionality testing. Additionally, many of the QA strategies discussed in [Campbell03] would also apply to testing localized builds.

Linguistic Testing

Linguistic testing is where you check all the assets in the game to make sure that text is not overlapping, truncated, misspelled, or grammatically incorrect, and that all the voice-over files play correctly. Linguistic testing should be done by a native speaker of the language being tested. Translation houses often provide this service. Be sure to include time in your testing schedule for sending CDs to the testers, especially if they are in another country.

For linguistic testers, make sure they are familiar with how to play the game and know where all the translations need to be checked. One way is to have them check the text in the game against the text translation spreadsheet they already completed—just add a column for where to look for the text in the game. You can also send them a test plan for the U.S. version of the game. Make sure to provide cheats and walk-throughs.

Determine how you want linguistic bugs reported. If you do not provide a bug report form, you might not get enough information about how to fix the bug. This is especially true in cases where fixes are being made by people who don't speak the language for which they are fixing bugs. In cases where you need to get additional text translated, organize it all and send it back to the translator in the same spreadsheet format you used previously. Table 5.6.5 is a sample bug report template for linguistic bugs. It includes information on where to find the bug, what the current (incorrect) translation is, and what the correct translation should be.

Table 5.6.5 Linguistic Bug Report Template

Bug #	Language	Location in Game	Description/ Comment	Original Localized Text	Corrected Text	Status
3	Italian	Mission 4 – Briefing	Please use lower-case letter.	…Come forse sapere, il colpo di Statoad Addis Abeba…	…Come forse sapere, il colpo di stato ad Addis Abeba…	FIXED
9	Italian	After Action Screen (single player)	Text not translated.	Originals Only	Solo originali	CLOSED

Functionality Testing

Functionality testing is testing the general functionality of the localized build. You are checking for any bugs that the localized assets created that require a code change to fix. Normally, you should not get any functionality bugs since you are only swapping assets. However, if you did not plan for special characters or have text field length restrictions, you might find that you need to make code changes to accommodate the localized assets. Functionality testing can be done by the same QA team that did the U.S. version, since they are basically just running through the U.S. test plan. Bugs can be reported the same way they were for the U.S. version. Take special care to check keyboard input of all the special characters and the keyboard commands.

In addition to equipment used for testing the U.S. versions, you will also need to have multiple copies of each language's operating system and the appropriate keyboard for each language. You should include time in the testing schedule to have these machines set up for testing, especially if you are testing multiple languages at one time.

Conclusion

High-quality localizations can give your game a lot of positive exposure in international markets. While localizations can be time consuming, they can go very smoothly and efficiently if they are well thought out beforehand. When planning for localizations, keep the following in mind:

- Create international content.
- Determine costs and schedules before you start the localization process.
- Keep game development "localization friendly."
- Organize all final assets before sending them to be translated.
- Carefully plan and execute the asset integration process.
- Allow enough testing time to find and fix all linguistic and functionality bugs.

Each localization will have different pitfalls, but if you plan the known variables, you will have more time to deal with problems as they arise.

References

[Campbell03] Campbell, C., "Quality Control: Testing Plans and Bug Tracking," *Secrets of the Game Business*, Charles River Media, 2003.

[Chandler04] Chandler, H. M., *The Game Localization Handbook*, Charles River Media, 2004.

[Dowling98] Dowling, P., "Localizing for Lands Beyond the Wild Frontier," available online at *www.gamasutra.com/features/production/19980828/localization_01.htm*, August 28, 1998.

[Kano95] Kano, N., *Developing International Software for Windows® 95 and Windows NT™*, Microsoft Press, 1995.

[Puha01] Puha, T., "Eurospeak: Localizing Games for the European Market," available online at *www.gamasutra.com/features/20010403/puha.htm*, April 3, 2001.

5.7

Leadership: The Making of Effective and Happy Teams

Melanie Cambron

melanie@melaniecambron.com

with Heather Maxwell Chandler
heather@mediasunshine.com

Rather than spending loads of cash on relocation fees, recruiter fees, immigration fees, and to save valuable production time, companies should focus on keeping their teams happy and productive. European game companies have been particularly successful in this area. Why? They make the effort. There are simple yet effective steps you can take as a leader to create a legendary and legendarily happy team.

Why Is Team Happiness So Important?

The benefits of hiring, managing, and keeping happy team members can be limitless: higher quality of work, milestones met, bonuses paid, projects shipped, additional projects from pleased publishers, good reputation earned. However, if no effort is made to keep developers content, the results can be devastating to the happiness of the individual, the morale of the team, the timeliness of the project, and, in some cases, the future of the entire studio. Companies are quick to throw money around to land the perfect game developer, but often do not bother to expend any time, money, thought, or effort to keep this necessary link in the development chain.

There Once Was a Programmer from Scotland: A True Story

- Airfare from Scotland to Texas: $1,700
- Hotel stay during interview: $200
- Immigration attorney: $2,000
- Second immigration attorney: $2,000
- Relocation allowance: $7,500

- Recruiter's fee: $14,000

A well-known game developer and publisher spent nearly $28,000 just to hire this one programmer. Given that sort of cash outlay, you would think the company would make an effort to keep the employee happy and on board.

Strike One: His second Monday on the job is the Fourth of July. No one told him it was a holiday and that he did not need to be at the office, and no one invited him to the informal company barbecue. While the programmer would not have celebrated the holiday back home, leaving him out of a company event is questionable—and sending him to work alone, inexcusable.

Strike Two: A couple of months later, he is told he needs to work on Sunday. Canceling personal plans, he dutifully works *alone* from dawn to dusk in a completely empty studio because, apparently, there really was not that much urgency in the project. After this incident, he finally spoke up and asked that he not be asked to work on holidays or weekends unless it was expected of the entire team.

Strike Three: After six months of flawless performance, and having been described by the vice president of production as the *best* hire the company had ever made, he is asked to repay the majority of his relocation allowance, because he had not actually moved much furniture or other personal property. However, there were no stipulations, guidelines, regulations, or rules covered in his offer letter stating how the relocation money was to be used. Therefore, when the programmer pointed out that the cost to actually move the contents of his two-bedroom flat and his car to the United States would have been significantly more than what he had spent, the company relented and dropped the issue.

Nevertheless, the programmer never forgot the rather financially stressful episode. While he was committed to completing his project, his heart was no longer with the company. He had worked hard, delivered above and beyond expectations on a million-dollar game, and, yet, the employer chose to create a problem that simply should not have existed. This type of behavior on the part of management affected many members of the team. Moreover, after seeing so many of the talented individuals he truly enjoyed working with walk out the door, he soon followed suit.

Why would a company spend approximately $28,000 to hire someone and then treat him as a disposable commodity, especially an employee who had exceeded all expectations? It's difficult to explain or understand, but it happens regularly.

Warning Signs of the Unhappy Team

Employees might give numerous signals to indicate their discontent with the work environment. If you notice any of them in your workplace, you could easily amend the negative situation before losing a valuable team member.

Absence

Do they come to work on time? Do they leave early? Do they frequently miss work? While excessive absences could be related to personal issues at home and might not necessarily mean they are unhappy, they could also be an indication that your employees are actively searching for employment elsewhere. It could also be an indication that they don't feel their contributions to the projects are valued and, therefore, are bitter about coming to work.

For example, suppose a production tester is constantly late by one to two hours a few times a week. He might no longer feel challenged on the project and might be resentful that his ideas are not more favorably received.

In some cases, there is little you can do to make the position on the project more challenging, especially one involving testing different configurations of the same product repeatedly. However, simply ignoring the problems is also not the answer. To deal with this issue, you need to discuss the employees' expectations of their positions, and provide solutions.

Lack of Effort

Are they productive when they are at work? Do they miss deadlines or not care if they do? If they have assigned tasks and deadlines, do they use their time productively completing the tasks, or do they waste a lot of time away from their desks, chatting with other employees, surfing the Web, or playing games and calling it "research?"

Note that this could also indicate that employees are overwhelmed by their tasks, and are afraid to discuss this with management. Rather than tackling the issue head-on, they just waste time hoping the problem will go away. The mere idea of talking to management can be intimidating for many employees.

Complaints

Do they frequently complain about management? Do they complain about other team members, specifically those in leadership roles? For example, "I could do his job better. Why did they hire this guy? He doesn't know anything about..." People who are disgruntled with management tend to think the grass is greener on the other side. The more proactive complainers will look for other jobs. The less proactive complainers will stay on, but their complaining will create an unpleasant work environment for other employees. This environment could potentially lead to more dissenters.

Commitment

Are they reluctant to commit to long-term assignments? Anyone who is thinking about leaving a job will be reluctant to commit to a long-term assignment. They will invent some excuse, but if they are unwilling to commit to long-term tasks, you need to find out why.

Apathy

Have they asked other people about their own job satisfaction? If they are dissatisfied, they will start talking to other employees to see if they can find other people to whom they can relate. Particularly if they are unhappy with management, they will talk to other people to spread their unhappiness. Again, this could create an environment of snowballing discontent.

Unfulfilled Requests

If an employee has requested something, like a new computer, and has yet to have his or her needs addressed without a good explanation, the perceived lack of caring can have long-lasting consequences.

How to Address the Signs

The first thing to do when spotting a potentially unhappy employee is to talk with him. If you see any of the aforementioned signs, it is your job as a manager to find out what is going on. Obviously, you would deal with someone who has personal issues differently than someone who has work-related issues, but you must uncover the issues first. Use questions such as, "What do you think about this project? Is there anything you would like to have done differently? How would you handle this situation?" (A good question to ask in instances when there are known problems with the project.) The answers to these questions can reveal a considerable amount of information about why the person is unhappy and what can be done to improve the situation.

Open communication is the key to spotting and addressing these signs. Is someone coming to you repeatedly about the same problem, even if you have addressed the problem? This probably means that you have not provided an acceptable solution for this person. You need to be open with this person and find out why he is dissatisfied. You cannot be all things to all people, and some people will never be happy with what you do; however, some might have specific, fixable, reasonable requests. If you can discuss these reasons with them, you come closer to having happier employees and creating a better environment.

As a manager, you need to be able to deal with all personality types effectively. Some team members respond well to blunt criticism, while others need more guidance and nurturing. Some people might be motivated by tight deadlines and will do their best and most productive work while they are in crunch mode. You need to deal with your team as both individuals and a team. You need to create the best working environment you can for the individual, while still doing what is best for the team.

CASE STUDY 5.7.1: REAL-LIFE TEAM LEADER TALES OF AND TIPS FOR SUCCESS

The industry staying power of Billy Cain, vice president of development, and Matt Scibillia, president and CEO, of Critical Mass Interactive in Austin is testimony to the importance of forming and keeping a happy team. Their story is comparable to that of the phoenix rising from the ashes and truly displays what a group can overcome and accomplish when working together as a big happy family.

After their first studio grew from 4 to almost 40 employees, they were purchased by a large international publisher that then suffered a bankruptcy. Undaunted, the team kept going, generating self-sustaining cash flow from contracts, and formed a new company of their own. And they didn't lose a single team member in the process.

When Cain and Scibillia tell their story, they do so in such a matter-of-fact fashion that it is easy to forget the fact that the company that owned them filed for bankruptcy. How were they able to keep every single employee during such incredible upheaval when other companies lose scores of employees for reasons that pale by comparison?

They credit their ability to conquer what could have been a devastating situation to not only having the finest development team in the industry, but also some extremely talented senior managers who kept cool heads through the many chaotic transitions. The team worked diligently to keep everyone together and focused on the future of their newly formed company. In the role as producer, Cain kept the team on track and healthy and acted as liaison with the publisher. Having a skilled support staff that stayed focused on getting the group up and running enabled the development team to stay focused on making games and make the transition from studio owned by a bankrupt publisher to independent studio as seamless as possible.

Cain and Scibillia put forth the necessary effort to maintain the talented folks they had. Although saddened by the news of the parent company's bankruptcy, they knew it was their obligation to complete their contracts in good faith for their clients. Scibillia emphasizes that taking this responsibility seriously, weathering the resultant difficulties, and seeing these projects through were conscious decisions on the part of every team member.

So, what is the magic formula for assembling that kind of team and keeping it together? These industry survivors, and thrivers, say that you must start with a core of experience in establishing a studio that encourages the inclusion of ideas and abilities from all team members. To this core, add a management team whose purpose is to create an environment conducive to creativity and problem solving, and, finally, if not most importantly, always be as honest as possible and provide as much information to your team as you can.

How to Avoid the Problems in the Future

It is important for management to be in touch with what goes on from day to day. Encourage an open door policy and be open to hearing complaints and suggestions.

Several successful studios have used some of the following benefits to create a work environment in which the employees feel welcomed and appreciated. You should consider trying some of these or your own creative ideas.

Good benefits (full medical, dental, paternity leave). Start with the basics and add benefits as your company grows. One game studio negotiated discounted automobile insurance, day care, and homeowner's/renter's insurance. Their human resources director seeks out every money-saving, net income benefit she can for the employees.

Flexible working hours. The games industry thrives on its wealth of creative geniuses. Not everyone has his or her creative juices flowing by 9 A.M. Countless studies on business psychology have shown that flexible work schedules improve productivity, increase retention, and reduce absenteeism and tardiness.

Up-to-date, functional hardware. Employees quickly grow frustrated when dealing with equipment that is inadequate for the task assigned.

Downtime to play competitor's games. There is no greater bonding experience than tearing apart the competition's product.

Free sodas and snacks. These can be purchased very inexpensively by the case at wholesale clubs.

Dinner provided during crunch time. The team appreciates the free meal, and less downtime occurs by having dinner at the office.

Working with others who are passionate about the project. The quickest way to sabotage a project and ultimately a company is to hire a bunch of burned-out, indifferent sourpusses. Game development has enough obstacles; you don't need any on your payroll.

Health club membership. Not only does it keep you fit, exercise is a known mood elevator. Mentally and physically healthy employees result in less absenteeism and increased alertness.

Ice Cream Day to celebrate monthly birthdays. Or cake or whatever. It's the thought that counts.

Monthly pizza for lunch. An inexpensive gesture that is greatly appreciated by a hungry team of developers.

Creative and appealing work environment. This doesn't mean designer copper-topped conference tables. Paint is cheap. Appealing colors inspire creativity, increase productivity, and relieve stress.

Launch/ship parties. A development studio in Austin does Mexican food and margaritas. They rent a margarita machine and order loads of the spicy cuisine. Reward the group for a job well done. It's much cheaper than replacing them for the next project.

The Power of Veto

There are certain hiring strategies that companies can also use to better their chances of creating a well-adjusted team. For years, Ensemble Studios in Dallas, Texas has incorporated the veto into the interview and hiring process. Anyone in the company has the right to veto a candidate. Members of a game development team work too closely and rely too heavily on each other's work to not get along. It is imperative that the additions to the team be cohesive with current members for things to run relatively smoothly. Be mindful of the fact that you are asking team members to spend a horrific amount of time working, communicating, eating, and playing with this newest member of your game development family. The only way to determine if the chemistry will work is to allow the individual developers to have a voice in the matter. Without that, you risk creating an environment that could cause project delays, missed bonuses, employee resignations, and ultimately project cancellation. This veto strategy has been successful for Ensemble for years, so successful that other companies such as Big Huge and Iron Lore are now following suit. The psychological benefits of the power of veto are also numerous. By allowing team members to have a voice in the hiring process, you give them a sense of ownership in the company that translates to increased sense of pride and responsibility. With this augmented feeling of commitment to the company and the products created, the team is sure to benefit in quality of work produced, as well as loyalty to the team and company.

Corporate Culture and "Quality of Life": Not Just a Slogan

Everyone has heard the adage "the family that plays together stays together." Well, the same is true for game development teams and companies. If you are able to create an environment that encourages respect and even friendship between the members of the team, retention is certain to increase. If individuals enjoy working with and feel obligated to their counterparts, it makes the decision for them to leave the company a great deal harder. Often, the reason employees resist leaving their current company is because they fear disappointing their teammates. Pretty powerful. Many companies such as Turbine Entertainment put a great deal of thought and effort into creating a pleasant work environment that often extends into social events. For example, Debbie Waggenheim, human resources director for Turbine, includes planning movie screenings, company parties, and more as a crucial part of her job, ensuring that the employees feel not only appreciated by the company but also committed to it.

It's Not about the Money

Studies have repeatedly shown that money usually is not the reason why employees develop wandering eyes. Faced with losing a talented game developer, companies often counter offer in an effort at retention. Remember that it's rarely just about the money. Survey after survey has shown that only a small percentage who accept the counter offer remain with the company longer than six months. It's the intangibles that really create that sense of belonging to a studio.

Communication

Management needs to be forthright with the game developers. Learn how to talk and listen to the plethora of personality types involved in the creative and technological world of game development. Encourage communication from the team members; listen to them when they voice their opinions on everything from hiring to game design. When a potential problem begins to arise, address it immediately by talking with, not at, the individual.

Unity

 Be mindful of what you are asking your team members to do. Although it sounds like something your Aunt Edna might have embroidered on a pillow, the golden rule still works, and works well. If you are going to require your team members to cancel their plans to come in on a Sunday, you, too, had better be present. No faster way to breed feelings of malcontent than to require game developers to be in a fluorescent-lit office while management is out riding jet skis on a sunny afternoon. In addition, creating opportunities for the group to play in a social setting increases the bond they have to the team, the project, and the company.

Appreciation

You don't have to shell out the big bucks to let your game developers know you value their efforts, but you do have to actually take the time to say or show it. A simple verbal or written acknowledgment of a job well done still means something. Pick up breakfast on Fridays—a dozen doughnuts are only a few bucks. When milestones are met, send folks home early.

Conclusion

The sweatshop style of studio management should be long gone, but it is still very popular—and still very expensive in the long run. If you squeeze employees until they have nothing left to give, they'll leave at the first available opportunity. Recruiters have actually had programmers call in tears begging to get them out of these sweatshop studio scenarios. Initially, it might seem as if you are getting your money's worth out of that overworked and underappreciated game developer, but remember that you will later be hit with downtime to search for a replacement, downtime while the replacement acclimates to the new environment, a recruiter's fee, a relocation allowance, and several other unforeseen costs. As in so many other areas of game development, when forming and managing a game development team, it is imperative to see the big picture. And when looking at that big picture, you should see one happy, smiling team.

5.8

Quality Assurance: Bug Tracking and Test Cases

Chris Campbell

torgo@videogamestumpers.com

Months of planning and years of long nights go into the typical game development project, but those efforts will be in vain if the resulting product is shipped to the public with crippling bugs. The quality of the title is a direct reflection of the care put into the game and determines the developer's future reputation

Quality assurance (QA) is based in common sense. Everyone uses a QA process without even knowing it. Let's say that you want to prepare an extravagant dinner for a special occasion. Before you go to the grocery store, it makes sense for you to prepare a list of the things you need so you won't forget anything. While making the list you will check the pantry for items you already have. You will double-check the prices of your key ingredients to make sure the dinner won't bust your rent budget. Once at the store, you will check the ingredients for texture, color, and ripeness. While cooking, you will monitor temperature and taste—and above all, make sure nothing gets burned.

Creating and using a quality assurance system in game development is no different. The manager in charge of the QA process needs to know the "recipe" for the game's design, what "ingredients" or tools are already available, and how many bugs already exist in the "pantry." He needs to make a list of the bugs still to be found, and prepare a strategy to find them. Even before programming or "cooking" begins, the manager will be checking the quality of the tools and planning for the events to come. It's not an easy job, but every game's survival in the marketplace depends on the final quality of the product, so it is essential to do it right.

This article is designed to provide you with ideas on how to start a bug-tracking system and how to formulate ways to find the bugs using test plans and statistical analysis. You will be surprised to learn how easy a system can be to set up, but be ready for the never-ending task of finding bugs.

The First Step Isn't Finding, It's Tracking

Most people mistakenly believe that the primary job of the quality assurance manager is to find software bugs. However, before a manager can find the bugs, he must also have a system in place to trace the bugs when found and track them until they are fixed. Unless you have a tracking system in place, a development team will spin its wheels trying to fix errors while missing new ones.

Why is tracking so important? Obviously, bug tracking allows you to log bugs as you find them so they are not forgotten and can be fixed. The real power in tracking comes when you use the data collected to form patterns and make some simple assumptions on where they might occur in the future. You can also identify programmers who are prone to making coding mistakes and those who ignore fixing requests.

Charts and graphs can be made showing combinations of data to your advantage. Unless you have a way to collect and store data, you will be missing out on many time-saving clues. For example, what if you wanted to know how many bugs were being found each month in a given area (see Figure 5.8.1)?

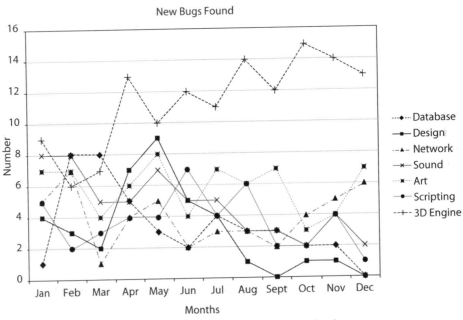

FIGURE 5.8.1 *New bugs found each month in each game development area.*

By using time as your x-axis, you can rapidly see areas that might raise alarms. In this example, the number of bugs found in the 3D engine keeps growing. The manager needs to determine why and whether more resources are needed. However, there are few bugs found in the Design area at the end of the chart. Maybe the team has solved nearly all of the design issues, but perhaps more attention needs to be focused in that area so it does not become neglected.

Without using a report of some type, this data is hard to see. You can also track your personnel to make sure they are fulfilling their responsibilities to correct errors as they are found (see Figure 5.8.2).

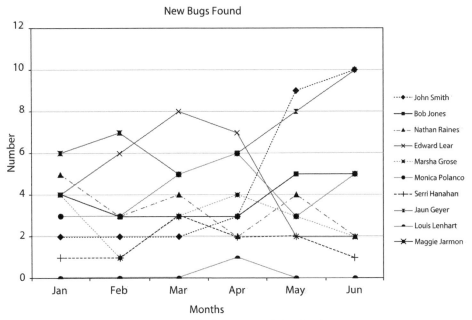

FIGURE 5.8.2 *Open bugs at the end of each month by developer.*

In June, Monica and Louis are having trouble correcting their bugs at the end of the month. The manager needs to know if this is because of lack of motivation on the developer's part or some other reason. We can also see that Louis consistently closes out his bugs each month. Charts and reports make information like this readily available. Other reports can be generated to show average length of time a bug stays open, developer productivity, and success and failure rates of test cases. All this requires is a bug-tracking database.

Creating a Bug Tracker

What do you need to start a bug-tracking database? You can talk to several vendors who sell software packages that can do the job. If you have the money and are short on time, this can be a good way to get started. In most cases, however, you can save money by doing it yourself with a simple database using SQL or Access as the front end. It's even possible to build a simple tracking system using a spreadsheet or e-mail based system, although this type of system would not be as flexible. Always keep in mind your budget and time constraints. It takes time to create and adjust a custom tracking system. In some cases, the time savings associated with buying a ready-made system will outweigh the costs.

In most cases, some level of customization of off-the-shelf systems will be necessary. Begin the database creation by outlining on paper what you want your bug entry form to look like. From there, you can determine what is required in the database fields. You would want to include areas for the date and time the bug was found, and the version of the program in which the bug was found. Include areas for a description of the bug, the steps to reproduce the error, and any other special notations about the specific bug. It is highly recommended that you include an area for saving metadata such as log files or screenshots. Anything that would help the programmer replicate and understand how the bug was created should be included on this form. In fact, try to get feedback from the programmer about what is needed on the form during the creation process.

Case Study 5.8.1 contains a sample bug report form.

CASE STUDY 5.8.1: HOW TO REPORT BUGS

Your Company Name: _____   Bug Number: _____

Reported by: _____   Assigned to: _____

Status: (Open/Closed/Hold)   Priority to fix: (High/Low)

Program: _____   Version: _____

Error Type: _____   Severity: _____

Programming error1. Fatal

Design issue2. Serious

Art3. Minor

Database

Hardware

DirectX

AI/Scripting

Documentation

Attachments? (Y/N)   →

Description of problem:

_____

_____

_____

_____

_____

Steps to reproduce:

_____

_____

_____

_____

Resolution: _____Fixed in Version: _____

Fixed

Hold

Not able to reproduce

Not fixed due to design

Not fixed due to other restraint

Withdrawn by tester

Need more info

Comments:

_____

_____

_____

_____

Resolved by: _____   Fix Tested by: _____

Once you have a rough draft on paper, you can quickly identify the database fields needed to store the information. Just by using the Wizard interface in Access, you can easily turn this form into a powerful tracking tool. It's also easy to convert the form for Web use using an HTML interface and an SQL-compatible backend. However, remember that a tracking tool is only beneficial if it used consistently. Unless your team members use the tool daily, it will quickly become worthless. It is the quality assurance manager's job to ensure that no one treats bug tracking lackadaisically.

Test Case Planning: The Headhunter Method

Quality assurance can be tiring, tedious work. Do what you can to make it fun, but also ensure that the job is getting done. One way to remove the tedium from tracking bugs down is to treat it as a challenge. The following four-step method can help you in this regard.

Step One: Focus on the Target

Test case design starts at the earliest design phases of a game. If the game design calls for lots of role-playing action, you can start gearing your test cases toward heavy database test cases. If it calls for a first-person shooter, then in the initial phases of game testing you can expect to work with more API and game engine testing.

You also want to orient your testing toward the current milestone's requirements and to quantify your results. By using metrics, you can quickly establish baselines for each milestone and see where the project stands from a quality standpoint at any time.

For example, if the milestone requirement states that the game engine needs to be in a "playable state," you quickly need to define "playable." It could mean that the game runs at 20 frames per second or more. It could also mean that 30 out of 40 planned features are functional. Work with the designers and programmers to quantify the expected results of your test.

In addition, be aware of intangibles. The player's level of fun or frustration cannot be easily measured. One example: the design document for a space-simulation required that a reflection of the pilot appear on the glass canopy and that his emotions be indicated by that reflection. When the feature was implemented, it passed all the functional requirements, but the reflection impeded the gameplay. To handle situations like these, focus on the requirements and find the best possible way to implement them. Removal of a requirement at the QA stage should only occur after careful consideration by senior management.

Step Two: Lay Out the Bait

Now that you have selected a goal, plan the test's execution accordingly. The basic rule is, if something can be measured, it can be tested. Thus, it is often best to work backward when preparing a test case. Ask yourself, "If the game were to fail in this area, how would I catch it?"

In addition, don't be afraid to combine multiple test cases, but be careful not to make your test scenarios so long or complicated that you can't analyze the results.

For example, consider boundary testing. Here you are testing the input and output limits of the program. How many commands can you queue up before the interface breaks? Exactly how many items can you carry? What if your text input box contains more than 255 characters?

Focus on visible state transitions. Every time you perform an action that changes the range of choices available to the player or modifies the display, you have made a state transition. The category includes menu systems, chat windows, display screens, and GUI changes. Test each option in every menu.

Testing the input/output interfaces can also reveal bugs. When the game is accessing the hard drive or CD-ROM, send a heavy load of commands. Can the I/O interface handle the load? What about networking? If too many packets are dropped or a connection is lost, how does it affect the game? Check for malformed data instructions or packets. Seeing how your game can handle extreme cases can quickly show areas of weakness in your programming.

Step Three: Set the Trap

You've planned your test case and now you are ready to execute. The first consideration is your test environment. The machine you are testing on should be as generic and pristine as possible to avoid any potential contamination problems from previous tests and exotic hardware. Therefore, in a test lab, it is advisable to set up a "ghost hard drive" image to copy to other machines when needed to start a new test case.

Make sure you have the tools necessary to perform the test and properly record a log of the test. There are plenty of tools freely available on the Internet that can capture screens, network packets, and chart running API threads.

Set your test run's objectives ahead of time. If testing in a multiplayer environment, make sure everyone involved is trained in proper testing procedures and has received precise instructions concerning their roles. Nothing is more frustrating than one person forgetting what to do at a critical moment in the test.

Step Four: Capture the Bug

When a bug is found, make sure that you have enough information to document it. Were screen captures made? Are the logs complete? The more information you have, the better. If time permits, try to replicate the bug as many times as possible. Vary the conditions to see if you can narrow the variables that cause the bug.

If no bug was found, the game might be working, or your plan might be flawed. Remember, you test to find bugs, not to see if everything in the game is working correctly. Go back to the drawing board. Alter the conditions somewhat in the area you are testing. Throw everything you have at that area of the game. If your tests continue to reveal no bugs, save your test cases for another day for regression testing.

Retracing Your Steps

The fact that a bug wasn't found one day doesn't mean that it can't be found the next—or in the next version of the game. This is where regression testing comes into play.

Regression testing means retracing your steps and rerunning all your test cases. Perform it at successive milestones, and especially when code is locked down, at which point you should be able to run all of your test cases without a single failure. If one does occur, a bug has been inserted since the last round of regression testing. Fix the code and try again until you are able to achieve a perfect success rate.

Don't Forget to Test the Installation Routine

Once you have built your gold master, don't forget to design a few test cases for the installation and removal routines. With console design, the installation routine isn't important, but it can cause major headaches on personal computers. More than one software recall has been caused by an uninstaller that erased the entire hard drive!

If you have any extra material being placed on the master, make sure that it conforms to company standards and formats. While the inclusion of static art assets for the enjoyment of the user wouldn't require a lot of formalized testing, don't forget to test other dynamic content such as screensavers, videos, and even music to ensure that they work with most platforms and players.

Other Resources and Methods to Consider

Once the method is in place, it becomes a matter of finding resources to execute the preceding plan. A common question is, how many quality assurance staff should a company hire? Microsoft is often cited as having a 1:1 tester-to-developer ratio. Gaming companies rarely have the financial resources to achieve more than 1:3 or 1:7; the key lies in finding the balance for your company. Hire too many testers, and they won't have enough work to do; hire too few and there will be gaps in your testing strategy.

Many tools exist to help you make a better product, but none is more effective than a well-trained workforce. Most bugs and defects can be prevented when everyone has the skills necessary to do their job. You should also use quantitative methods to monitor the progress of your testing. *Defect seeding* consists of purposefully inserting bugs into the code to see how many of them are found and to estimate how many actual bugs remain in the program. The formula [McConnell01] that applies in this context is:

$$Defects_{total} = \frac{SeededDefects_{planted}}{SeededDefects_{found}} \times NormalDefect_{found}$$

For example, if 30 defects are planted throughout the code and your testers find 14 of those along with 40 new ones, it is likely that the code contains about (30 / 14) × 40 = 85 defects, of which 45 remain to be found.

Conclusion

At some point, you need to release your product to the public. When does testing stop? For practical reasons, the criterion is usually a specific amount of time during which bugs of a certain priority level have not been found, or a mathematical equation like that previously mentioned estimating the number of bugs remaining in the code. Other companies stop testing when they feel adequate test coverage has been given to the game design. And sadly, some companies stop when they run up against the final milestone deadline. Plan ahead and choose a criterion—and do so when you design your test cases, not when the deadline catches up with you.

Careful planning and accurate testing will help you avoid the stigma of a post-release patch. By testing often and testing early with a tracking system in place, a quality assurance manager can avoid many pitfalls that can delay a game's path to the marketplace.

References

[McConnell01] McConnell, S., "Gauging Software Readiness with Defect Tracking," available online at *www.computer.org/software/so1997/html/s3135.htm*.
[Rice02] Rice, R., "The Elusive Tester to Developer Ratio," available online at *www.riceconsulting.com/tester_to_developer_ratio.htm*.

Additional Resources

Software Assurance Technology Center, NASA, available online at *http://satc.gsfc.nasa.gov*.
International Organization for Standardization, "ISO 9000," available online at *www.iso.ch/iso/en/iso9000-14000/iso9000/iso9000index.html*.

INDEX

2by3 games, 63
3D programming, 20
3D Realms, 97
3D Studio, 20
9-on-9 real-time game, 120

A

Absolute Quality, 101
Access (Microsoft), 389, 391
Acclaim, 6, 247–249
Acquaria, 11
acquiring game companies
    adapting valuation, 204–205
    advisors, 206–207
    business plan for, 202–205
    completing picture of parties
        involved, 205
    contracts and due diligence, 206
    emotion factor, 201
    evaluating companies, 204–205
    financial data, 203–204
    loans for, 205–207
    putting plan to work, 205
    target company, 201
acting talent and scripts, 330
Activision, 36, 327, 372
add-ons, 132, 306
Advanced Cardiac Life Support, 67
advances
    advance plus royalty deals, 28
    country-by-country publishing/
        distributing, 282
    earning back, 28
    game pricing, 32–33
    negotiating, 252–253
advergaming, 55
advertising
    agencies, 102–103
    for job candidates, 193
    in marketing campaigns, 130
    white space, 110
advisors, financial, 206–207
Age of Empires, 7
agents, see game agents
Aggressive Inline, 248
Aihoshi, Richard, 292
Aitken, Neil, 12
Alien, 327
Aliens vs. Predator, 327
alpha milestone, 320–321

Amazon.com, 47
America's 10 Most Wanted, 170
America's Army, 64, 69, 121
Amusement and Music Operators
    Association Expo, 121–122
Anarchy Online, 350–351, 355
Andersen, Jason, 117
Anhembi-Morumbi University
    (UAM), 11
animation service providers, 98–99
application programming interfaces
    (APIs), 21
approvals, 330–331. *See also* schedules
arcade games, 120–122
Arcane, 33
ARK (Advisors of Rubi-Ka), 352
art and animation service providers,
    98–99
art design document, 317
Artifact, 50–51
artificial intelligence (AI), 231
Asheron's Call, 7, 55, 348, 350, 351
assets, company, 204–205
Atari, 10, 31, 36, 127, 131, 170
Atomic Games, 66
audience identification and psycho-
    logical profiling, 219–227
audits, 270

B

Baggaley, Sean Timarco, xv, 159
balance sheet, 185
bank funding, 213
Barnett, Scott, 63
Barrett, Mark, 78–79
Bartlett, Ed, xv, 217, 235
Barzilay, Ohad, 9
BATNA (Best Alternative to Nego-
    tiated Agreement), 91
Battlefield 1942, 175
Battlefront, 63
BattleZone, 121
Beijo do Vampiro, 11
Ben's Game, 8
Best Buy, 109
best-selling games, 30, 38–40
Beta Breakers, 101
beta milestone, 321–322
Bethke, Erik, 14, 15
Bibby, Brett, 9

Big Brother Brazil, 11
Big Huge, 385
Bioware, 97
Black Box, 139
Blockbuster Video, 108
Blue Fang Games, 114–116, 144
BMX 2, 248
Bocska, Steve, xv, 85, 135, 217, 219
bonuses, 268
brainstorming, 224–225
brands, 166–167
Brazil, game development in, 10–11
breaches, contract, 269
BreakAway Games case study,
    122–123
bridge loans, 184
budget games, 126, 170–171
budgets
    for localizations, 231, 369–370
    for pitching games, 241
    in submission package, 230–231
    typical AAA, 169
Bullfrog, 166–167
bundles, 133
Burnout 2: Point of Impact, 248
Buscaglia, Thomas, xvi, 217, 261
business plans
    for acquiring companies, 202–205
    balance sheet, 185
    capital structure, 187
    cash flow statements, 185, 186
    company description, 181–182
    contents, 178–179
    creative risk management, case
        study, 184
    current market conditions, 180
    development plans, 182–183
    earnings statements, 185, 187
    financial planning, 184–187
    financing deals, types of, 184–185
    financing proposition, 185, 187
    growth targets, 183
    length of, 179
    market analysis, 179–181
    marketing strategy, 180–181
    minimizing cost of money, case
        study, 187–188
    modular business plans, case
        study, 179
    pro forma financial statements,